School-Centered Interventions

SCHOOL PSYCHOLOGY BOOK SERIES

School-Centered Interventions

EVIDENCE-BASED STRATEGIES FOR SOCIAL, EMOTIONAL, AND ACADEMIC SUCCESS

DENNIS J. SIMON

AMERICAN PSYCHOLOGICAL ASSOCIATION
WASHINGTON, DC

Published by
American Psychological Association
750 First Street, NE
Washington, DC 20002
www.apa.org

To order
APA Order Department
P.O. Box 92984
Washington, DC 20090-2984
Tel: (800) 374-2721; Direct: (202) 336-5510
Fax: (202) 336-5502; TDD/TTY: (202) 336-6123
Online: www.apa.org/pubs/books
E-mail: order@apa.org

In the U.K., Europe, Africa, and the Middle East, copies may be ordered from
American Psychological Association
3 Henrietta Street
Covent Garden, London
WC2E 8LU England

Typeset in Goudy by Circle Graphics, Inc., Columbia, MD

Printer: Bang Printing, Brainerd, MN
Cover Designer: Mercury Publishing Services, Inc., Rockville, MD

The opinions and statements published are the responsibility of the authors, and such opinions and statements do not necessarily represent the policies of the American Psychological Association.

Library of Congress Cataloging-in-Publication Data
Simon, Dennis J.
  School-centered interventions : evidence-based strategies for social, emotional, and academic success / Dennis J. Simon.
    pages cm. — (School psychology book series)
  Includes bibliographical references and index.
  ISBN 978-1-4338-2085-4 — ISBN 1-4338-2085-4 1. School mental health services.
2. Learning disabilities—Treatment. I. Title.

  LB3430.S452 2016
  371.7'13—dc23
                                        2015015856

British Library Cataloguing-in-Publication Data
A CIP record is available from the British Library.

Printed in the United States of America
First Edition

http://dx.doi.org/10.1037/14779-000

To Kathy, Kristie, Cheryl, and Jeffrey.

CONTENTS

SERIES FOREWORD

Outside of their homes, children spend more time in schools than any other setting. From tragedies such as Sandy Hook and Columbine to more hopeful developments such as the movement toward improved mental and physical health and academic achievement, there is an ongoing need for high-quality writing that speaks to ways in which children, families, and communities associated with schools worldwide can be supported through the application of sound psychological research, theory, and practice.

For the past several years the American Psychological Association (APA) Books Program and APA Division 16 (School Psychology) have partnered to produce the School Psychology Book Series. The mission of this series is to increase the visibility of the science, practice, and policy for children and adolescents in schools and communities. The result has been a strong collection of scholarly work that appeals not only to psychologists but also to individuals from all fields who have reason to seek and use what psychology has to offer in schools.

This book continues the strong tradition of the series. Schools are the most common location for providing mental health services to youth. Blending pertinent research with his extensive clinical experiences in schools,

Dr. Dennis Simon explains the state of the art in school-based therapeutic interventions. Readers will leave with an enriched understanding of how the school context interfaces with evidence-based interventions as well as effective strategies for implementation.

Many individuals have made significant contributions to this book series. I thank previous series editors Sandra L. Christensen, Catherine Christo, Jan Hughes, R. Steve McCallum, David McIntosh, LeAdelle Phelps, Linda A. Reddy, Susan Sheridan, and Christopher H. Skinner for their wonderful service. I also thank Linda Malnasi McCarter, Beth Hatch, and Ann Butler of APA Books for their editorial work and support as well as all of the people at APA Books who have worked behind the scenes to bring this book to fruition. Finally, I thank Dr. Simon for providing the vision, dedication, and knowledge that is on display in this work. We are all the beneficiaries of his effort and talent.

The leadership of Division 16 welcomes your comments about this volume, as well as your ideas for other topics that you would like to see explored in this series. To share your thoughts, please visit the Division 16 website at http://www.apa.org/about/division/div16.aspx.

—David Shriberg, PhD
Series Editor

ACKNOWLEDGMENTS

This text is rooted in over 3 decades of clinical and school experience supported by many mentors and colleagues. Their passion and commitment to find what works to help children is embedded in these pages. Our efforts were sustained by the youth and families who were our clients and collaborators.

I am indebted to David Shriberg, School Psychology Book Series Editor, for his support for this project, his encouragement throughout the process, and his commitment to ensuring that all students have access to quality psychological and educational services. Thanks to Beth Hatch, APA Books Development Editor, and the peer reviewers for their helpful reviews and editorial support. My appreciation also goes to Karen Burger, Wes Clevenger, Jane Haeger, and Stuart Rabins for their valuable assistance with case examples. I am thankful for Mark Swerdlik, a frequent collaborator, and my colleagues at Loyola University, who have encouraged my teaching activities and value the importance of field experience for training the next generation of psychologists for evidence-based practice.

My deepest gratitude goes to my wife, Kathy Kapp-Simon, whose support has sustained me personally and professionally in every venture. An accomplished psychologist and researcher, she was the first editor of this text and not only encouraged me throughout the process but also made this book better, chapter by chapter. I am grateful for the support, encouragement, and inspiration I receive from my children and their families: Kristie and Nick, Cheryl and Dan, and Jeffrey.

School-Centered Interventions

INTRODUCTION

After family, schools function as the center of children's lives. Family and community identities and activities emanate from local elementary and secondary schools. These educational institutions are the center of service delivery to children and adolescents not only for academic instruction but also for extracurricular activities and a large range of community services. Community organizations and special events often convene within the school setting. Public schools remain one of the few mandated service providers for youth. Within the context of special education requirements, schools provide mental health services to children and adolescents even when other agencies or private practitioners may deflect or limit services.

As a focal point in the lives of children, adolescents, and their families, schools can be the optimal setting for the provision of psychotherapy for youth. School psychologists, social workers, and counselors observe, assess, interact, and intervene with students within their natural work and social

http://dx.doi.org/10.1037/14779-001
School-Centered Interventions: Evidence-Based Strategies for Social, Emotional, and Academic Success,
by D. J. Simon

environments where issues and problems commonly emerge. They may follow students and work with families periodically over the course of many years. Mental health service providers in community supported clinics and private service delivery settings must work closely with schools to understand the character and manifestation of the child or adolescent's psychological symptoms. Then, they must collaborate closely with school staff for problem solving and intervention planning, integrating aspects of treatment into the school context.

A central assumption of this text is that school-centered therapy is the most effective format for addressing social, emotional, and behavioral issues for children and adolescents. Therapeutic interventions are more likely to benefit students when strategies are integrated across individual, family, and school contexts.

But there are challenges to integrating such programs in schools. Although there is a growing recognition of the link between academic success and mental health, schools struggle to develop effective strategies to integrate services. There has been limited guidance provided for the adaptation of empirically supported clinical strategies to the school context. Too often, therapy is conceived as an isolated task with minimal attention paid to educational interventions or influencing the social contexts in which problems occur. Insufficient frameworks exist for therapists outside the school setting to collaborate with educators and implement interventions to address functioning at school. This text will provide strategies to address these issues.

As a former director of a zero-reject public therapeutic day school in a large metropolitan area, I have been privileged to work with diverse students who have experienced the most severe impairments from psychological disorders. Our staff collaborated with multiple partners working both within and outside of the school setting—chief among them teachers, other educators, parents, and youth—to design and implement therapeutic interventions for children experiencing internalizing and externalizing disorders. The same integrated approach proved effective in work in standard school settings.

Drawing on this extensive personal experience designing and providing therapeutic services within elementary and secondary schools, I present in this book a practical framework for delivering evidence-based interventions (EBIs) in schools. I suggest how to both select interventions and make appropriate adaptations for the school context. The text covers interventions in both standard and special education programs, and it advocates for a comprehensive multitiered approach.

In this book, I cover the major symptom patterns affecting youth, provide practical examples of intervention strategies, and point the reader to specific empirically supported protocols. It is beyond the scope of this text to describe each intervention component in complete detail; rather, I provide broad descriptions, focusing on how these interventions interface with the school context and what this means for implementation. My overall goal is to help bridge the gap between research and applied settings. This book is appropriate for school psychologists, social workers, and counselors and for clinical psychologists and other community mental health practitioners who work closely with schools to treat the psychological issues faced by the children and families they serve. Classroom teachers will benefit from each section's description of instructional supports.

I use case examples to illustrate case conceptualization and intervention protocols, drawn from my own direct clinical experience as well as that of my colleagues. To protect client confidentiality, cases have been blended or modified.

I address interventions for both children and adolescents. When there are developmental differences that must be addressed regarding assessment and intervention, I have made distinctions between the two groups. When a concept applies across developmental levels, I refer to *children and adolescents*. At times, however, for economy of expression, I use the terms *children* and *youth* to refer to students at all age levels.

The remainder of this chapter provides essential background conceptual information about evidence-based interventions in schools, followed by an explanation of the book's organization.

MOVEMENT TOWARD THE DELINEATION OF EVIDENCE-BASED PSYCHOTHERAPY

Psychological treatment research is focused on defining reliably effective treatment protocols for addressing the full range of child and adolescent psychological disorders (Weisz & Kazdin, 2010). The search for EBI strategies has emerged as the central research mission in child and adolescent psychology (Silverman & Hinshaw, 2008). Significant progress has been made in defining what intervention strategies work to address specific psychological disorders and symptom patterns. The goal is to define and implement empirically supported treatment protocols that can effectively treat children across all settings in which children are served.

The "efficacy" of treatment strategies is generally determined on the basis of randomized controlled studies using standardized intervention protocols that clearly attribute client change to treatment applications. Many of these findings have been noted in controlled research settings, and the subsequent challenge is to demonstrate the "effectiveness" of the intervention protocol in inherently more complex and less controlled clinical practice settings. The research community is concerned that EBIs are not finding their way into community and school settings. On the other hand, field practitioners note that research subjects are often dissimilar to community and school clients in terms of complexity of symptom manifestation, number of comorbidities, initiation and sustenance of treatment, and expressed motivation for change. The challenge for clinicians is to persist with the application of EBIs but to refine and modify protocols to establish effectiveness in field settings. The challenge for child intervention researchers is to measure the transportability of treatments, assessing their effectiveness beyond research settings to deployment in a range of clinical settings (Ollendick & King, 2012). A related effort is the study of implementation practice, which examines the strategies and supports required to successfully transport methods to field settings (Forman et al., 2013). Recognizing the promise and the limitations of current treatment research, school-centered therapists apply EBIs in practice, modify strategies as necessary for client and setting, and continue to monitor the effectiveness of their interventions.

BRIDGING THE GAP: APPLYING EBIs IN SCHOOLS

Mental health practitioners have a responsibility to apply empirically supported assessment and intervention strategies to benefit their clients. School-centered therapy efforts hold promise for bridging the practice gap that is often perceived to exist between controlled studies conducted in university settings and the complexity of field practice. The introduction of the response to intervention (RtI) paradigm to academic curriculums in schools presents an interesting parallel to the needs for mental health services delivery (Sugai & Horner, 2009). Regarding academic instruction, RtI emphasizes the need for using both core and remedial instruction based on scientifically supported practices while continually evaluating curriculum effectiveness through routine progress monitoring. Outcome measurement informs the need to modify intervention strategies. Education's emphasis on data-based decision making is a natural fit for the implementation of EBIs in mental health services.

Assessment

Research sets the foundation for understanding the variables that contribute to the etiology, manifestation, and sustenance of social, emotional, or behavioral symptoms. EBI research clearly defines its target population and uses evidence-based assessment strategies to accurately define treatment subjects' symptoms and needs. Care is taken to isolate which intervention protocols work for which populations. This approach recognizes that one size does not fit all. The empirical literature delineates specific strategies for children exhibiting different diagnostic patterns. This assessment-to-treatment link is critically important. Assessment leads to selective application of EBIs to youth displaying different symptom patterns. Analogous to differentiated academic instruction, individualized approaches to psychological intervention are used based on what is known from EBI research.

School systems are reasonably reluctant to attach diagnostic labels to students. The identification of an emotional disability qualifying for special education services requires substantial interference with academic progress. However, the designation of an Emotional Disability remains a broad description covering a wide diversity of psychological orders. Attention-deficit/hyperactivity disorder (ADHD), a relatively high-incidence disorder with clear educational impact, may fall under the Other Health Impaired eligibility category, whereas other psychological disorders with clear neurological or biological characteristics may not. What this means for the application of EBIs to school-centered therapy is that practitioners must be careful to also use specific symptom profile assessment strategies to ensure appropriate selection and application of EBIs. At times, there are subtle differences in presentation that can prompt selection of substantially different intervention strategies. For example, for their empirically supported school-centered anger management programs, J. Larson and Lochman (2010) differentiated the intervention paths required for students displaying proactive versus reactive aggression.

The establishment and transmission of EBIs rely on data collection. Schools routinely collect and track a large amount of data. Therapists associated with schools have access to significant quantitative and qualitative data beyond formal psychological assessments. School psychologists, social workers, and counselors are involved in the same setting as the child and his or her peers for up to 7 hours per day, permitting multiple opportunities for observational data and helpful access to environmental conditions.

Applying EBI Protocols

To ascertain which intervention strategies are effective, research programs often initially limit the number of treatment variables or factors that are targeted. The challenge for school-centered practice is to define, account for, and target interventions to address a wider range of contributing factors. However, the very complexity of the field context also presents some advantages as well. Therapists working within and closely with schools possess superior knowledge of contextual variables such as family, school culture, peer networks, and community influences. Their expert understanding of the local context, systemic variables, and setting demands provides a distinct advantage for effective modification of EBI protocols. Their awareness of key systemic and environmental factors improves their capacity for tailoring interventions to the student's context and selecting treatment modules that are best fits for this student in this setting. Association with schools provides enhanced access to key contextual participants. Parents, teachers, and representatives of community resources can readily convene for problem solving.

Because they work within the school, these practitioners also may have long-term opportunities for access, support, and treatment booster sessions. Interventions do not have to be completed in one continuous series, and these therapists can track progress and initiate follow-up contacts on their own. Community mental health service providers who integrate their intervention work with schools can create many of these same advantages.

Intervention Manuals

EBIs are typically developed with detailed procedural manuals outlining the therapeutic elements that were validated in efficacy studies. Fidelity to implementation of the core features of the intervention manual are required to ensure that empirically supported strategies are actually used. Some have objected that this approach is mechanistic and attempts to merely turn therapy into a technical exercise while undervaluing unique therapist variables and individual creativity. However, the alternative of reliance on instinctual "seat of the pants" strategies to guide interventions risks limiting the reliability and validity of treatments and negates the potential for development of core strategies that can consistently address similar issues across children. See Ollendick and King (2012) for a more extended review of this controversy.

Effective therapists recognize the need for conducting therapy within the framework of empirically supported practices. Experienced therapists are aware of the self-correcting elements of therapeutic interactions where clients either communicate the limitations of our case conceptualization or demonstrate the need for intervention modifications through inadequate or stalled progress on treatment goals. Expert therapists responsively and responsibly adapt core methods to individual circumstances while continuing to operate within the general framework of defined EBI strategies, assessing progress through repeated collection of outcome data. When faced with the most difficult cases within school settings, it is important to avoid premature abandonment of EBI protocols. These challenging cases tend to present with more severe symptoms, complicating contextual factors, and additional barriers to treatment. Persisting in the application of EBIs and patiently "staying the course" are essential in these treatment-resistant cases. These clients typically face both extraordinary stressors and more frequent damaging environmental events. Although flexibility and adaptation are necessary, the child, parents, and teachers all require enhanced support and focus from the therapist on sticking to the plan and proven methods to achieve goals. Progress may be slower and more incremental, but past attempts at solutions have generally been fleeting and prematurely terminated.

Flexibility Within Fidelity

Kendall and Beidas (2007) coined the catchphrase "flexibility within fidelity" to frame the application of manualized treatments in a balanced and practical manner. Kendall is the lead author of the widely applied manualized EBIs for child anxiety management, *The Coping Cat* (Kendall & Hedtke, 2006). He argued that manual-based treatments cannot be applied as inflexible cookbooks. Instead, manuals are designed to provide a structure, focus, and outline for intervention strategies. Manuals outline the essential elements of a protocol, the sequence of intervention application, and operationalized strategies for therapeutic activities. When firmly grounded in an understanding of an empirically derived protocol, practitioners can then flexibly adapt techniques to the needs and challenges of working with an individual client within a specific family and school context.

In a similar fashion, Ollendick and King (2012) asserted that manuals should be perceived as providing guidelines and structures that specify the principles and strategies that were supported in efficacy studies. Information in manuals goes beyond a reference to a broad approach or school of psychotherapy such as cognitive behavioral therapy (CBT) or psychodynamic by specifying the elements of the umbrella approach that require implementation for success with this client in these circumstances. For example, family therapy strategies have proven efficacy to address a variety of issues, but different procedures and strategies are used to address different clinical problems and divergent family systems. Even though they possess many common underlying features, a family therapy manual for treating eating disorders differs in essential elements from one targeting juvenile addictions. Chorpita, Daleiden, and Weisz (2005) suggested that manuals emphasize the principles rather than the procedures of change. However, therapists need to be careful that the scope of their modifications of manual strategies does not render their efforts as merely random and devoid of any empirical foundation.

School-centered therapists are typically generalists required to respond to the full range of presenting child and adolescent psychological disorders. Intervention manuals provide them with the necessary structure and guidelines to address diverse treatment targets with proven methods. Their broad experience qualifies them to thoughtfully and flexibly adapt protocols to address the needs of children in their school and community settings. School-centered therapists frequently face cases with multiple comorbidities. In most cases, they need to target the most life-interfering problem first. Fortunately, a reduction in primary symptoms can reduce general stress and contribute to either a corollary lessening of other symptoms or an improved readiness to respond to interventions specific to a secondary condition. Because within CBT approaches, coping and problem-solving skills treatments contain many common elements, acquisition of adaptive skills to address one disorder can contribute toward improvement in other areas.

Modular Approaches

Chorpita (2007) proposed an additional strategy for implementing EBI strategies. He suggested dividing empirically validated treatment protocols into modules containing clinical strategies for targeting specific subgoals. The therapist assesses the needs of an individual client and selectively chooses the strategies necessary for this symptom presentation. Although the sequence of application of techniques might make a difference in some circumstances, it is likely that affected children with the same diagnosis will still demonstrate variable skills deficits. For example, some children with social anxiety may have sufficient foundational social skills but be constrained by cognitive distortions that block social involvements, whereas others may require treatment modules that focus strongly on both elements. Whether a certain treatment module is used and how much time is devoted to its implementation will depend on the profile and responsiveness to intervention of the particular client. This approach remains rooted in the EBI movement but provides a rational alternative to the rigid application of manualized programs.

DEFINITIONS AND SELECTION OF EBIs

The term *evidence based* is used across many different disciplines. Many attempts have been made to categorize levels of empirical support within psychology; however, an attempt to specifically define EBI remains challenging (Ollendick & King, 2012). Kazdin and Weisz (2010) suggested that *evidence based* should be viewed as a spectrum rather than a clear definitive categorization. They noted that there is no single cutoff criteria yet established. Interventions that are labeled as *evidence based* require controlled efficacy research that clearly specifies characteristics of the target population, uses operationally defined intervention procedures, and reports multiple outcome measures. Replicated random control designs provide clearest data. Programs that are also supported by effectiveness research in field-based settings stake the strongest claim for empirical support. Chorpita et al. (2005) suggested that when several variations of treatments demonstrate evidential support, it is possible to identify common elements across protocols that may be defined as central contributors to positive treatment outcomes. For example, exposure strategies have been found to be a core element of various empirically supported protocols for anxiety management.

It is beyond the scope of this text to provide a full discussion of issues surrounding the definition of evidence-based research. For the purposes of this text, I integrate EBIs from the spectrum of evidence-based findings as described by Kazdin and Weisz (2010). I will particularly present protocols represented in respected major compendiums of EBI clinical practice for children and adolescents (see Kendall, 2012b; Mash & Barkley, 2006; Reinecke, Dattilio, & Freeman, 2003; Silverman & Hinshaw, 2008; Weisz & Kazdin, 2010). Preferences are given to interventions that have empirical support for their effectiveness in clinical settings or contain elements that can be readily used in practical school-centered applications. There is an emerging body of EBI research involving protocols designed for and validated within schools (J. Larson, 2005; J. Larson & Lochman, 2010; Stark et al., 2007). These works are of particular relevance to this effort and justify extended treatment.

MULTITIERED SYSTEMS OF SUPPORT

Contemporary educational practice organizes assessment and intervention practices within multitiered systems of support (MTSS; Stoiber, 2014). This framework is designed to serve the needs of all students. It emphasizes prevention, early intervention, universal screening, social-emotional learning for all students, routine progress monitoring, the application of evidence-based assessment and intervention strategies to address problems, and matching the intensity of intervention to level of need. Usually conceptualized within three tiers, the first tier addresses the needs of the general student population. The second tier provides early intervention services to those identified at-risk for problems or demonstrating early or moderate symptoms. The third tier provides intense services for students exhibiting significant difficulties.

School-centered therapy contributes substantially to MTSS. Its multiple evidence-based methods and formats respond to students at all levels but are particularly responsive to the challenges experienced in second and third tiers. The text's concluding chapter presents a comprehensive model for psychological service delivery within MTSS that incorporates school-centered therapy.

ORGANIZATION OF THIS BOOK

This book consists of three parts. Part I addresses central foundation issues in the provision of mental health services in schools. Chapter 1 explores the advantages of mental health work in schools, highlighting the critical needs for therapeutic services for children and adolescents and the potential for schools to provide increased access to these essential services. It delineates the substantial benefits of intervening with youth in the natural environment where they are required to exhibit adaptive social, coping, and problem-solving skills on a daily basis. Chapter 2 provides an overview of the current state-of-the-art psychological interventions for children and adolescents. It summarizes how these strategies are extended to universal psychological education, prevention, and early intervention programs. Chapter 3 presents a comprehensive case conceptualization model that provides an overarching framework for intervention planning across all symptom profiles. Built on a foundation of cognitive behavioral and systemic approaches, it sets the stage for the selection and implementation of EBI protocols. Its goal is to link assessment to intervention to outcome.

Part II presents therapeutic interventions for specific child and adolescent psychological disorders and considers how these interventions relate to the school context. The chapters in Part II cover ADHD (Chapter 4), disruptive behavior disorders (Chapter 5), pediatric bipolar disorder (Chapter 6), depression (Chapter 7), anxiety and trauma (Chapter 8), and autism spectrum disorder (Chapter 9). Each of these chapters examines and integrates the following six domains:

- diagnostic characteristics and assessment frameworks;
- developmental considerations for assessment and intervention;
- child- and adolescent-specific therapeutic intervention strategies;
- instructional supports, educational accommodations, and coordination with school-centered intervention protocols;
- crisis intervention protocols; and
- family and systemic supports and interventions.

Finally, the book's Afterword places school-centered therapy in the context of comprehensive multitiered service delivery in the schools. Psychological education is being recognized as an essential educational task. Schools recognize that learning adaptive social, coping, and problem-solving skills is core curriculum alongside reading, mathematics, science, and history. With the introduction of response to intervention strategies, mental health prevention and intervention efforts are being organized into multitiered intervention models that not only strive for early intervention but also recognize that some students require therapeutic interventions to succeed academically and socially in school. Therapists working closely with schools must understand the possibilities and supports within this multitier schema; therapists in schools must ensure that EBIs are practiced to benefit students at every level of service need.

School-centered therapy provides an opportunity for integrating therapeutic services into the center of the daily lives of children and adolescents. The critical need for increasing access to mental health services and integrating multidimensional service delivery has emerged as a theme not only within the psychological and educational communities but also within policy-making centers. Although the call for full-service schools is not new, national funding for school health centers, which include mental health services may provide unprecedented opportunities for helping children. Both challenges and opportunities abound. Program development will require vision and creative resource management. Innovative practices must continue to be informed by the growing empirical understanding of what best serves the needs of children and families.

I

FOUNDATIONS OF MENTAL HEALTH SERVICES IN SCHOOLS

1

ADVANTAGES OF MENTAL HEALTH WORK IN SCHOOLS

In this chapter, I set the stage for examining therapeutic interventions within the school setting. I define the need in terms of the incidence of psychological disorders and their direct impact on children's educational progress. I briefly summarize the shift that is occurring within schools toward inclusion of psychoeducational curricula and early intervention practices to promote social–emotional health for all students. Promising complementary developments in research and practice within the clinical and school professional communities are laying the foundation for new paradigms of service delivery that are school centered. Herein, I outline a framework for integrating therapeutic strategies into the full multitiered continuum of psychological services within schools. This approach is designed to increase children's and families' access to services, enhance effectiveness, and counter the stigmatization that too often interferes with their participation in therapeutic interventions. Access to mental health care services for children is being severely

http://dx.doi.org/10.1037/14779-002
School-Centered Interventions: Evidence-Based Strategies for Social, Emotional, and Academic Success,
by D. J. Simon

compromised with the increased limitations on funding for community mental health centers and minimal insurance coverage for psychological treatments. Schools must take an increasingly central role in the provision of psychological services.

HIGH INCIDENCE BUT LIMITED ACCESS

The U.S. Surgeon General's report on mental health estimated that 20% of children experience mental disorders that impair their daily functioning, with 5% to 9% of the youth population experiencing "serious emotional disturbance" (U.S. Public Health Service, 2010). National Institute of Mental Health (NIMH) surveys have estimated 16% to 22% of children experience child mental health disorders (NIMH, 2009). NIMH estimated that merely half of these affected children receive professional services, and as low as 7% receive appropriate services from mental health professionals. Even if children are enrolled in psychotherapy, persistence with treatment is alarmingly insufficient, with estimates of three to four sessions as the average length of child psychotherapy treatment in community settings (McKay & Bannon, 2004). To make matters worse, studies suggest that severity of problem is a predictive factor for premature withdrawal from treatment (Kazdin & Mazurick, 1994). In my own experience in a therapeutic day school setting, I have seen an inverse relationship between the severity of a problem and the likelihood of accepting a referral for treatment beyond the school setting. Families of youths with the most severe psychological symptoms are often the least likely to accept or persist with outpatient clinical services.

Unfortunately, in the face of this great need for treatment are crises in funding for mental health services and widespread cutbacks in community mental health services. Urban budget crises have prompted some cities to close as many as half of their community mental health centers, and many states have implemented parallel cuts in services. Despite the federal Mental Health Parity and Addiction Equity Act (2008), there are continued challenges in accessing insurance reimbursements for psychotherapeutic interventions. Threatened funding cuts to Medicaid services are not only impeding poor families' access to services but are also resulting in staffing and service cuts at the clinics that have continued to try and provide services to these especially needy children. Despite a mandate to provide services when psychological disabilities impair academic learning, special education funding resources are ill prepared to take up the slack in the delivery of mental health services to children.

IMPACT ON LEARNING

The negative impact of psychological disorders on learning and academic achievement has been well documented (Doll & Cummings, 2008). Social, emotional, and behavioral problems directly interfere with learning, compromise work production and academic participation, and are frequently comorbid with learning disabilities. Unresolved psychological problems can contribute to increased risk for school dropout and delinquency, stress-related health issues, and poorer postschool outcomes. Even the most capable students will struggle in their professional careers if they experience social, emotional, or behavioral impairments that interfere with collaboration and social problem solving.

EDUCATING THE WHOLE CHILD

Given this understanding of the importance of psychological health and skills, there is a growing recognition that the educational mission of schools must involve teaching the whole child. This recognition has been partially evident for many years with the introduction of physical education and health curricula and the central role that extracurricular activities play in an individual school's identity. Now it must include psychological education to promote mental health. Core curriculum no longer merely involves the traditional three "Rs" of *reading, 'riting, and 'rithmetic* but adds the fourth "R" of *relating*. Instruction in social, coping, and problem-solving skills is as important for preparation for a productive and healthy life as are the traditional core academic skills. The brilliant student who is unable to adaptively manage stress or engage in healthy interpersonal interactions is not truly prepared for a successful transition to adulthood.

To address the importance of psychological education, some states have begun to mandate the implementation of a social–emotional learning (SEL) curriculum for all students. These initiatives are taking many forms. They may involve school-wide positive behavior support programs that promote specific adaptive behaviors; direct instruction in social, coping, and problem-solving skills; and targeted programs for specific behavioral issues such as bullying or substance abuse. The psychoeducational nature of cognitive behavior therapy (CBT) provides a natural framework for both the design and support of SEL programming. Therapists working with schools play a key role in coaching educators in the implementation of SEL programs. In the classroom, therapists and teachers partner to present weekly lessons to the entire class, and then the teacher reinforces that learning throughout the school week. As mental health experts, therapists are also directly involved in assessment and intervention for students seen as at risk for serious academic and life-interfering psychological disorders.

DESTIGMATIZATION OF PSYCHOLOGICAL INTERVENTIONS

Concerns for the psychological welfare of children and adolescents intensify when they exhibit social, emotional, and behavioral problems at school. It is in this context that learning and social progress are routinely monitored with ready comparisons to the developmental status of peers. Concerns escalate when a student's behaviors begin to negatively affect the learning environment of classmates.

School discipline officials frequently meet with parents to report student misbehaviors and urge families to seek outside assistance for underlying stressors or psychological disorders. Because few families sustain external treatment relationships, school staff frequently find themselves repetitively reviewing cyclical patterns of misbehavior. Parents become increasingly overwhelmed and come to dread the "phone call" from the school office. In some cases, school staff can become frustrated that unresolved family issues may be impairing their attempts to address deteriorating school concerns. For too many families, going to a therapist outside of school carries an uncomfortable mental illness stigma that either delays or rules out a willingness to seek psychological support services. In the absence of treatment alternatives, the school intervention strategy often becomes increasingly reactionary and exclusionary: detentions, suspensions, expulsion.

It is necessary to shift the character of these parent–school interactions from a "report and refer" process that merely informs parents and sends them to seek assistance elsewhere or a punishment focus to change-oriented collaborative problem-solving interventions. The latter approach engages parents in the search for solutions while minimizing their fears of stigmatization. School therapists can participate in these sessions to guide problem-solving efforts. Taking advantage of the pressure for change inherent in these difficult moments, the school conferences can become brief therapeutic interventions. A simple entry point into therapeutic work is the utilization of family–school contingency contracts. This intervention tool can address needs for change within the school and family systems simultaneously with a balanced emphasis on support, limit setting, and positive reinforcement (Murphy & Duncan, 2007; Simon, 1984). Planned follow-up sessions keep parents engaged without waiting for the next behavioral incident. These sessions demystify the therapeutic process and can build an alliance that supports the transition to more intense therapeutic programming at school or a more receptive attitude toward referral to community services. Community mental health specialists who work closely with the school may be able to serve as active consultants at the very beginning of this process.

School personnel work daily with students and have ready access to parents. The schools' educational mission requires support for academic, social, and emotional functioning. Schools provide the most advantageous and least stigmatizing access point to therapeutic services.

PROMISING DEVELOPMENTS IN CLINICAL AND SCHOOL SERVICE DELIVERY

As the professional community struggles to increase access to and participation in mental health services, several promising developments are providing encouragement for these efforts. Within the clinical community, the movement to design and test child therapy intervention models to ensure that they are empirically sound and up to the challenge of differentiating treatments for children with different symptom displays is making great strides. Evidence-based intervention (EBI) protocols are being developed, tested, and disseminated at an accelerated pace. More important to note, significant attention is now focused on effective transfer, adaptation, and implementation of EBI protocols designed in controlled research settings to the challenging community-based settings where barriers to treatment success frequently multiply.

EBIs for youth are increasingly being designed to be delivered within school contexts. These successful intervention programs address a broad range of childhood issues. Systematic social, coping, and problem-solving training programs have been designed for and employed in schools for many years and have demonstrated clear, empirically supported impact (A. P. Goldstein, 1999). In addition, there are now EBI clinical programs such as ACTION (Stark et al., 2007) and the Adolescent Coping with Depression Course (Clarke, Lewinsohn, & Hops, 1990) targeting depression. EBIs for aggression issues and anger management designed for implementation in schools include the Anger Coping Program (J. Larson & Lochman, 2010), Think First (J. Larson, 2005), Aggression Replacement Training (Glick & Gibbs, 2010), and Keeping Your Cool (W. M. Nelson & Finch, 2008). The Incredible Years Program, targeting externalizing behaviors in children 2 to 12 years of age, has over 2 decades of research support (Webster-Stratton, Hollinsworth, & Kolpacoff, 1989; Webster-Stratton, Reid, & Hammond, 2004). These are just a few examples of empirically supported programs specifically designed for delivery within the school setting. In Part II, I examine many of these programs in detail.

These programs all share a psychoeducational component rooted in cognitive and behavioral intervention approaches that are a natural fit for educational settings. All use group formats capable of serving larger numbers of children while placing skills training within the social context of groups of peers. Embedding treatments within the daily center of children's lives not only increases access but also destigmatizes participation and provides an opportunity to reinforce treatment goals beyond the therapy hour through collaboration with teachers and other school staff. Goal setting and monitoring for behavioral and coping skills taught in treatment and critically relevant to adaptive school functioning can be reinforced throughout the school day. These programs involve consultation with teachers, use checklist monitoring tools, and implement contingency contracts to both enhance treatment outcomes and support adaptive school functioning. There is a growing awareness that clinical treatment programs must be implemented at the "point of performance" in the student's natural environment if they are to produce effective outcomes (Barkley, 2006). Although initial instruction in social and coping skills can occur in the therapy room, relevant progress, authentic skill acquisition, and problem resolution must occur in the contexts where children spend their day, specifically the school and familial contexts.

Within the school arena, significant shifts are occurring in the design of psychological support systems (Doll & Cummings, 2008). Increasing emphasis is being placed on prevention and early intervention programs. Proactive school-wide programs like SEL and others referenced above hope to promote mental health and thus reduce the need to treat advanced psychological disorders. Emerging universal screening protocols for mental health concerns are striving for early identification of and intervention with children facing social, emotional, and behavioral distress in hopes of limiting the course and severity of problems. There is an emerging awareness of the futility and harmful effects that suspensions and expulsions have on students demonstrating serious psychological concerns (Fenning et al., 2012). Excluding students from school removes access to school-centered intervention services and seldom serves to protect the remaining students. The tragedy of recent school shootings has heightened public awareness of the need for interventions for troubled students. These traumas have also accelerated the development of comprehensive crisis preparedness and response protocols aligning the efforts of school and community responders.

The contemporary foci within both clinical and school psychology service delivery are converging in an emphasis on data-based decision making. The investigation and deployment of evidence-based strategies, the link between assessment and intervention contributing to differentiated interventions, and the importance of progress and outcome monitoring are in the forefront of clinical and educational practices. Clinical practice is recognizing the importance of collecting school data on child functioning to drive assessment and intervention decisions. Particularly in disorders like attention-deficit/hyperactivity disorder (ADHD) and autism spectrum disorder, adapting classroom management practices is as important as applying interventions within therapy sessions. In addition to academic curriculum scores, schools are implementing data systems to track student behaviors on a routine basis with the goal of early intervention for at-risk students.

Another phenomenon in emerging practice is the realization that the most challenging and complex cases require coordinated multiagency support. Clinical multisystemic family therapy (Swenson, Henggeler, Taylor, & Addison, 2009) and school initiated wraparound service delivery (Eber, Sugai, Smith, & Scott, 2002) each strive to coordinate community-wide resources to support youth facing the most significant challenges. They not only bring service delivery into school and family but also extend it into the community as well. Not only do these complementary initiatives in psychology and education promise to redefine service delivery, with proper collaboration they also have the potential to increase access to psychological treatment services.

FULL-SERVICE SCHOOLS AND SCHOOL HEALTH CLINICS

Intensive and broad-based efforts are occurring to ensure that therapeutic services for children and adolescents are evidence based and relevant to the context of their daily lives. These movements provide opportunities to initiate significant system changes in mental health service delivery models for youth and families. The concept of full-service schools that collaborate with community agencies to address medical and mental health, social service, and recreational needs of children is not new, although it remains largely unrealized (Bucy, Swerdlik, & Meyers, 2002; Dryfoos, 1998). An extension of this concept is required to meet the current crisis in access to child mental health services. Increasing the scope and intensity of early intervention for at-risk students and using multidimensional therapeutic interventions within schools for students with significant emotional and behavioral challenges would not only increase access to services but would also boost their effectiveness because the interventions would occur within the natural environment of children served.

A significant opportunity to advance integrated service delivery is proposed in the Affordable Care Act (ACA; Patient Protection and Affordable Care Act, 2010). This legislation proposes funding school health centers that include mental health service delivery. Its purposes are to increase access to health care and accelerate early intervention. To achieve its goals, it will require unparalleled cooperation among school and community resources and significant expansions of the roles that school psychologists, social workers, and counselors play in addressing the mental health needs of their students.

Building from the initiatives just described, the ideal mental health delivery system for youth would be centered in the school context. Schools are community centers that can provide ready access to all children in a nonstigmatizing context. Delivering psychological interventions within this setting would enhance the effectiveness of treatments by deploying them directly within the child's daily environment. The access to critical contextual factors that affect children's functioning can accelerate the effect of therapeutic interventions and in some cases shorten treatment. Family–school partnerships can increase generalization of treatment gains across settings. Data collection through routine progress monitoring in schools can readily assess maintenance of treatment gains and quickly flag the need for therapeutic booster sessions to prevent relapse. The effect of these advantages is that school-centered therapies carry the potential for reducing the costs of services (Kutash, Duchnowski, & Lynn, 2006). At the same time, the proximity of service delivery to the target population would contribute to case finding and facilitate access to treatment for children whose problems may have remained unidentified. This might particularly support students with internalizing issues like anxiety and depression, who often receive less attention in schools than those exhibiting disruptive externalizing disorders.

CHANGING PERSPECTIVES ON MENTAL ILLNESS

As the science of human behavior better defines the associations among biological, psychological, and sociocultural factors, new perspectives on the nature, etiology, acquisition, and maintenance of psychological disorders are emerging. For a large number of psychological disorders, the realistic goal is not to cure mental illness but to manage its symptoms and build the social, coping, and problem-solving skills necessary to support adaptive and healthy functioning (Kendall, 2012c). Given the present limitations of medical science, physicians treat children with chronic illnesses such as diabetes and asthma to manage symptoms so that they will become less life interfering. In the same way, conditions like ADHD, bipolar disorder, and autism spectrum disorder present lifelong intervention and monitoring challenges. Effective intervention protocols are being developed, but the character of these disorders is chronic. When a child's life is impaired by debilitating anxiety, the treatment goal is not to end anxiety but to return it to normal limits. Indeed, some level of anxiety is protective, adaptive, and enhances performance.

This chronic illness perspective is similar to the disability perspective found in special education services in schools. Students with learning disabilities receive instruction to remediate their learning issues to the extent possible, but they also learn how to use their strengths and accommodate for their weaknesses to lessen the impact of their disability. Instructional supports and environmental modifications support their individual efforts and promote academic success.

This changing perspective on the nature of mental illness points to the need for regular checkups for students at risk for or in recovery from the symptoms of a psychological disorder. Treatment maintenance reviews and booster sessions support the management of chronic conditions throughout the elementary and secondary school years. Therapists working within or closely with schools are in the best position to support students with focused intervention and periodic maintenance support. Similar to primary care physicians, therapists intensify their involvement when problems significantly interfere with adaptive functioning, withdraw when symptoms subside, but remain available to intervene when either old problems begin to resurface or new issues emerge. The advantage school-centered therapists have is their ability to directly recommend and support proactive prevention programs to support students through key developmental transitions like the onset of adolescence and graduation into high school.

TIME FOR SYSTEM CHANGE

Increasing Youth Access to Mental Health Services

Crisis points often create opportunities for positive systemic change. As I have detailed, there is a crisis of limited access to mental health services for children and adolescents. At the same time, research on effective treatments is suggesting new protocols that are more integrative and prompt new formats for service delivery. School-centered therapy attempts to deliver EBIs in an integrative fashion addressing both individual and contextual factors, coordinating intervention efforts across individual, family, and school domains. With service delivery within or closely aligned with schools, this approach can increase access to treatment.

The current crisis in access to service is in part rooted in financial constraints. An increasing number of EBI programs are designed to provide treatments in the school setting during the school day. These efforts simultaneously increase access and reduce treatment costs. Centering intervention work within the school context also provides an opportunity to coordinate the clinical work of school staff with community practitioners in a way that strengthens both access to treatment and its effectiveness. Family and individual treatment can be offered in the school setting before and after the school day. School buildings are typically underutilized (except for gym space) in the evenings and on weekends and would be available centers for clinical work, requiring only a solid spirit of collaboration and shared use of space. Reducing the costly overhead from external community child mental health programs by relocating them within school campuses would free up funding for additional service delivery. Multisystemic interventions that bring together probation officers, child welfare workers, clinical therapists, and school staff could be delivered in the school context, once again increasing access and destigmatizing the required multiagency involvements. Interventions occur and resources unite close to the child's home. Some school therapists could shift part of their work hours from the school day to evenings and weekends to bridge service delivery, enhance access, and ensure that collaborating professionals do not work in isolation. These changes in the system of service delivery would be consistent with efforts to develop full-service schools to reach more children in need and would be consistent with the goals of ACA.

Changes in access and service delivery models might not occur easily. However, efforts would be advantaged by new school and clinical infrastructures. Recent developments in school psychoeducational programming and early identification and intervention systems are innovative and expansive and create a foundation for further system change. Significant organizational changes almost always require changes in roles and autonomy. To integrate efforts of external and internal mental health practitioners within schools, a diverse group of professionals would need to learn how to cohabitate within the same facility and share resources. The challenges to autonomy and comfortable routines would be outweighed by the supports inherent in professional collaboration and the clear benefits for children.

This is not a time for limited vision. Who in 1975 could have envisioned the extent that PL94-142 would impact the education of children with disabilities? Few would have bet that response to intervention (RtI) and multitiered support services (MTSS) would be defined as preferred practice and implemented across so many schools. When behavioral psychologists first called for "giving away" psychology in the 1960s, the conceptual foundation was laid not only for focusing therapy on equipping clients with adaptive psychological skills but also for educational efforts to promote psychological health for the general population (G. A. Miller, 1969). Few would have anticipated the numbers of empirically supported parent training and child-focused social, coping, and problem-solving training programs; the systemic therapies that are delivered in homes, schools, and courthouses; or even the prevalence of sports psychology in our culture (see Weisz & Kazdin, 2010). For the sake of children, it would be heartwarming to be able to reflect 20 years from now on the vision and work that occurred in this decade to provide critical access to empirically supported mental health services in more integrated and effective ways.

Practical Initiatives

System change generally requires collaborative initiatives among a variety of stakeholders and the design and implementation of joint pilot projects. Several such ventures readily come to mind. University training programs can pilot partnerships with special education cooperatives and school districts to design, research, and implement EBI child therapy in school-centered programs. This would extend personnel, enhance graduate training, and align research efforts with the point of service delivery.

Private and public community practitioners could be invited to participate in school-centered prevention, early intervention, student support groups, and parent training programs. In exchange, they would benefit from positive exposure within the community and increased access to teacher observations and reports of student behavioral and emotional performance. Community-supported mental health centers could be afforded the opportunity of using some school office space before and after the school day to enhance their access to and compliance with treatment appointments. These family friendly time frames and the locations destigmatize services.

Parents and school staff have long been concerned about managing the regression risks inherent in the gap in school-based services between the end of summer session and the start of fall programming. Similar to Pelham's summer treatment camps for children with ADHD, summer recreational programs that integrate social and coping skills training models into naturalized environments could be designed to occur after summer school is complete (Pelham et al., 2010; Pelham, Greiner, & Gnagy, 1997). These programs could be piloted as joint ventures through collaboration among community and school practitioners and local community recreational agencies. Multiagency initiatives are generally more successful in acquiring funding support, and these kinds of local ventures would appeal to many families of children with needs in this area.

TIME FOR ACTION

The above suggestions provide a starting point for responding to the crisis in children's access to mental health care by relocating EBI child therapy services into school centers. The damaging effects of the compartmentalization and underfunding of our mental health services to children are readily apparent. Our children deserve bold initiatives to provide true access to psychological services by destigmatizing these services. Schools provide the local community center that can best respond to this crisis of care. Mental health work in schools provides access to service within students' daily environment, where social, emotional, behavioral, and problem-solving skills are required.

2

OVERVIEW OF PSYCHOLOGICAL INTERVENTIONS FOR CHILDREN AND ADOLESCENTS

In Chapter 2, I discuss the general history and focus of psychological interventions for children and adolescents. I highlight the field's evolution toward evidence-based treatments that emphasize therapeutic techniques and processes, while acknowledging the importance of therapist variables as well. Unique considerations for child therapy include the importance of maintaining a developmental perspective, understanding the implications when youth are involuntary or assigned clients, and responding to the challenge of frequent comorbidity in child and adolescent disorders. The integration of cognitive, behavioral, and systemic intervention approaches is prominently represented within the EBI literature (Kendall, 2012c; Weisz & Kazdin, 2010).

This chapter summarizes the implications of this integrative approach and what it means for intervention assumptions, goals, settings, and strategies for child therapy. Multicultural and diversity perspectives are addressed. This chapter sets the stage for the later delineation of a school-centered

http://dx.doi.org/10.1037/14779-003
School-Centered Interventions: Evidence-Based Strategies for Social, Emotional, and Academic Success,
by D. J. Simon

therapeutic intervention framework and notes the extension of these strate-gies to universal psychological education, prevention, and early intervention programs emerging in multitiered intervention systems in schools.

DEFINING EVIDENCE-BASED INTERVENTIONS FOR CHILDREN AND ADOLESCENTS

The last 2 decades have seen an exponential growth in studies of child psychotherapy. Before this surge, research on interventions for youth signifi-cantly lagged behind adult studies. Many approaches to child treatment ini-tially evolved as adaptations of empirically supported adult methods. Landmark shifts in therapeutic strategies, such as Beck's (Beck, Rush, Shaw, & Emery, 1979) cognitive approach to treating depression and Meichenbaum's (1977) cognitive behavior therapy (CBT), focused on work with adults; the principles, guiding theories, and strategies of these approaches were later adapted to work with children.

The challenge inherent in these adaptations centered on the need to account for significant developmental differences not only between adults and children but also between younger and older children. For example, the focus on rational analysis techniques in cognitive therapies for depression and anxiety could be easily modified for teens but require extensive adaptation for younger elementary age children. On the other hand, the present-oriented, problem-solving, and coping-skills focus of these adult models proved to be a good fit for work with children.

A significant amount of early work on interventions for children involved behavioral therapy. Its principles were rooted in experimental analysis and required operationalization of therapeutic strategies and outcomes consis-tent with the evolving focus on empirically supported treatments. Patterson and his colleagues' (Forgatch & Patterson, 2010; Patterson, Reid, Jones, & Conger, 1975) pioneer work on youth aggression was a significant foun-dation stone in the search for evidence-based treatments and can serve as an example of key trends in child therapy research. Their initial approach centered on operant conditioning principles examining the reinforcement contingencies that promote antisocial behavior. Patterson and his colleagues developed a social learning perspective to explain the influences of parent-ing practices and peer interactions on the development of deviant behav-iors. Their intervention protocol focused on parent management training, that is, teaching parents to alter their familial interaction patterns to modify their children's behaviors: A specific focus was replacing counterproductive coercive parenting with positive parenting. Parents were trained in skills for teaching through encouragement and positive reinforcement, developmentally appropriate monitoring and limit setting, emotional regulation, and problem solving.

Patterson's work illustrates significant trends in the search for EBIs for youth. He integrated behavioral and social learning theories. He was sensitive to the developmental factors both in terms of the development and the treatment of psychological disorders. He investigated and addressed ecological factors and thus the need to address both the individual and the environment. Patterson's focus on parent management training rather than direct individual work with children differed from typical therapy with adult clients.

The complexity of designing and studying interventions for child and adolescent disorders is readily apparent. The range of internal and external variables that need to be addressed is extensive. In his review of trends in child therapy research, Mash (2006) proposed a cognitive behavioral systems perspective as a principal organizing framework for investigating EBI. This approach takes into account internal cognitive and affective, external behavioral, family, peer, and other contextual factors and the interaction among these variables. Most contemporary EBI strategies attempt to target some or all of these domains. The complexity of these intervention targets reveals the challenge inherent in the task of constructing intervention manuals that can be reliably implemented for youth with diverse symptoms at varying developmental levels by different therapists.

In the Introduction to this volume, I outlined the challenges and controversies surrounding the search for EBIs. The goals to bring science to practice, increase the use of empirically supported treatments, and investigate intervention effects at the field level remain central to contemporary research and practice regarding therapeutic interventions for children and adolescents. Significant progress has been made in identifying intervention protocols that positively address a wide range of psychological disorders affecting youth.

Given the nature of these problems, treatments typically require multidimensional intervention strategies. Research has focused primarily on the total effect of interventions with multiple components. As a consequence, treatment packages that work have been identified, but not necessarily their mechanisms for change. A gap exists between the understanding of the efficacy or beneficial effects of intervention protocols and the processes within which change occurs. Focused on omnibus intervention packages, research on effective treatments often falls short of identifying specific mediating variables that identify the critical elements that are essential for the positive impact of treatment. As mental health practitioners in applied settings strive to meet the challenge of adapting EBIs from research settings, it is particularly important to know which treatment strategies influence change the most and must remain included in any field-based modifications. Analysis of the impact of individual components of intervention protocols remains a priority for future child therapy research.

Some moderating factors affecting treatment effects are well understood. These conditions influence the likelihood that an intervention will succeed. Cognitive developmental status affects selection of strategies and child participation in goal setting and direct intervention. When parents and their children share the same goals and commitments to change, treatment outcomes are generally enhanced. Family therapists take this a step further and specifically analyze moderating influences within the family system and target those variables that are deemed changeable. Although the field's understanding of moderating factors is growing, there is an ongoing need to better understand the effects of setting and client differences and how these factors may require variations in intervention strategies to achieve effective outcomes. More study is required to understand the circumstances under which interventions are more likely to be effective or, alternatively, rendered less effective. Child treatment research is necessarily complicated by the reality that complex problems embedded within multiple systems require complex multidimensional intervention strategies.

Despite limitations, significant progress has been made in defining EBIs for children and adolescents. Differentiated protocols for varying presenting problems have been delineated and evaluated. These therapeutic strategies form the core of contemporary intervention approaches. Although there has been a recognition of the need for further innovation to build on this developing foundation, it is also understood that adaptations and new experimental practices that are introduced must be monitored to assess their contribution to therapeutic outcomes. This process ensures that an emphasis on the application of empirically supported practices will continue as the standard in the field of child therapy.

THERAPIST VARIABLES

EBI research has focused on theories of change and intervention practices. However, therapy remains an interpersonal process. It is universally understood that therapist factors such as the therapeutic alliance and empathic presentation are essential contributors to the effectiveness of therapy. Interpersonal factors contributing to positive engagement may even be more important when working with children than with adults. Youth are not likely to have referred themselves to treatment and in some cases may directly resist intervention. At younger ages, children may not be able to fully comprehend the purpose and process of therapy. The ability to relate effectively to children at various age levels and to understand and connect with troubled adolescents requires both clinical skills and the capacity to build a trusting and motivating relationship. Intervention manuals often underline the need to take time to establish rapport with youth clients but seldom prescribe specific strategies for doing this.

The core facilitative conditions of empathy, unconditional positive regard, and genuineness initially delineated by Rogers (1957) and person-centered therapists continue to be seen as essential therapist characteristics. The American Psychological Association Division 29 Task Force (Ackerman et al., 2001) study of empirically supported therapeutic relationships highlighted these attributes plus collaboration and consensus between therapist and client in goal setting. Shirk and Karver (2003) examined the impact of therapist relationship variables in work with children. Their meta-analysis of 23 studies supported the principle that the quality of the therapeutic relationship was moderately associated with therapeutic outcomes across diverse kinds of presenting problems, different treatment modalities, and various developmental levels. They noted that children with internalizing disorders were more likely to form positive therapeutic alliances than those with externalizing disorders. It would be natural to expect that youth who might display oppositional or antisocial behaviors could prove more difficult to engage in a collaborative intervention process; however, this underscores the importance of rapport building and a working alliance with these children.

In a study of adolescent depression, Jungbluth and Shirk (2009) noted that therapist behaviors that managed resistance and fostered an alliance included taking the time to explore the teen's motivation, attending to the teen's perspective on his or her experience, and providing limited structuring. They suggested that effective therapists helped adolescents discover their own paths toward solutions using techniques like Socratic questioning or guided discovery to help youth examine the implications of their thoughts and actions. Less didactic approaches built stronger engagement with clients. This did not equate to a nondirective approach or therapist inactivity but rather focused on responding to the youth's subjective experience of pressures. This practice speaks to the necessity of being patient with the pace of therapy with reticent clients and establishing a strong enough relationship bond to set the stage for more directive and structured therapeutic activities.

Kendall (2012c) advocated for maintaining fidelity to treatment protocols while still using flexible clinical judgment. He suggested that therapists have to be sufficiently expert in core aspects of EBI strategies so that they can flexibly individualize protocol components to respond to unique client presentations. Within this framework, adhering to the principles of treatment tasks and maintaining a resolute focus on treatment goals and methods are essential, but rigid application of manualized steps without gaining an alliance with the child is counterproductive to securing involvement in the change process. As therapists accumulate experience, they learn to approach the same intervention task in a variety ways to engage the child.

Ormhaug, Jensen, Wentzel-Larsen, and Shirk (2014) examined the impact of the therapeutic alliance in the treatment of children who were victims of trauma, presumably a challenging target population for establishing a trusting and effective therapeutic relationship. In their randomized clinical trial, Ormhaug et al. compared the contribution of therapeutic alliance across two treatment conditions, trauma-focused cognitive behavioral therapy (TF-CBT) and nonspecific treatment as usual. Their findings shed significant light on the questions regarding the relative importance of relationship and strategic factors. Although alliance ratings were comparable across conditions, alliance was associated with positive outcomes for the TF-CBT group but not the treatment-as-usual group. Ormhaug et al. suggested that a positive working relationship enhanced client participation in structured CBT tasks and that a manualized intervention protocol did not limit the ability to establish a collaborative therapeutic relationship.

Consensus on therapy goals and collaboration between therapist and client are beneficial for successful intervention. But achieving this cohesion can be challenging when working with youth and their parents. Children are generally sent to therapy by the adults in their lives. They may not grasp the need for therapy or understand the processes of therapy and hence at times may be reluctant or actively resistant. Parents and teachers may or may not have congruent goals for the child. When parents are integrated into treatment activities, the therapist needs to establish an effective alliance with each member of the family even though members may at times be in conflict with one other. This requires an ability to communicate an empathic understanding of the individual perspectives of each participant, negotiation skills to develop common goals, and coaching skills to engage family members in collaborative intervention activities. Although these can be challenging tasks, the application of structural family therapy strategies that work toward clearly defining roles, establishing proper parent to child hierarchies, and protecting age-appropriate individuation can support a broad-based therapeutic alliance (Minuchin, 1974).

Therapeutic alliance also requires clear rules and expectations relative to confidentiality. Specific, transparent rules regarding confidentiality of family members and the child identified as the client should be articulated at the start of therapy. Although regulations may vary from state to state, children do have rights to confidentiality, but it is reasonable for parents to expect to understand the treatment methods and progress for their children. Also, developmental status can affect confidentiality considerations. In particular, establishing engagement with adolescents requires respecting their privacy and clear communication in advance of what will be shared with whom and under what circumstances.

When a difficult youth self-disclosure needs to be discussed with parents, it is often helpful to take the time to prepare the child to make that disclosure him- or herself with the presence and support of the therapist. Therapists working in and with schools need to clearly delineate what will be shared with teachers and school referral sources. Clearly articulated guidelines, procedures, and structure support transparency, build trust, and contribute to collaborative relationships. Collaboration with parents and teachers can greatly enhance the power of therapeutic interventions. Altering individual and contextual dimensions affecting problem behaviors increases the likelihood of sustained change. However, this team effort requires significant work by the therapist in communicating empathy, positive regard, and a sense of common purpose to diverse interested parties.

Although gaining rapport is essential, novice therapists working within schools must be careful to avoid being overly concerned about being liked by child clients. Their role is that of helpful professional adult and not friend. At times, limit setting is important for establishing respect and trust and ensuring that the therapeutic setting is safe. It is necessary to establish rapport to achieve therapeutic goals, but the focus must always remain on outcome and positive change. Similar to Baumrind's (1967) concept of authoritative parenting, therapists need to communicate empathy, concern, commitment, hope, and positive regard and yet establish clear boundaries, appropriate limits, and behavioral expectations.

Shirk and Karver (2011) summarized therapeutic practices that foster effective therapeutic alliances with children and adolescents. They recognized that establishing a therapeutic bond with youth can entail interpersonal skills such as humor and other informal exchanges that promote engagement but are challenging to measure. They suggested that therapists must pay attention to developing alliances with parents, children, and all relevant participants in the change process. Although a positive alliance is predictive of successful intervention outcomes, it must be monitored and maintained throughout treatment to ensure continued participation and achievement of goals. Intervention plans must attend to the potentially diverse perspectives of children and the significant adults in their lives and craft goals and activities that can be supported by common perspectives. A successful therapeutic alliance has been shown to enhance outcomes more strongly when paired with empirically supported programs, with data suggesting particular additive benefits in behaviorally oriented therapies. It is likely that the performance-based and activity-focused methods involved in CBT require collaborative relationships to secure sufficient client participation. Rather than viewing relational and technical factors separately, it is apparent that both therapeutic alliance and specific empirically supported treatment components are required to attain positive intervention outcomes. Weisz and Kazdin (2010) summarized the complexity of this essential task:

> Effective use of such treatments may require agile, multitasking therapists who can maintain attention to a structured treatment plan, remain responsive to what youths and parents bring to the session, find ways to connect the treatment agenda to the youngsters' real life concerns, nurture a warm relationship, and make sessions lively and engaging. (p. 563)

This eloquent summary underlines the challenges of the therapeutic task and the complex dynamic integration required of social and technical elements.

DEVELOPMENTAL CONSIDERATIONS

Although developmental status is an important variable in all psychotherapy, it is particularly important in intervention work with children and adolescents. Assessment and intervention strategies may vary according to developmental level. In some cases, the manifestation of symptoms may differ substantially depending on age of onset. For example, in bipolar disorder early onset mood cycling may be rapid and frequent, whereas late adolescent onset may mirror adult characteristics of lengthy manic and depressive episodes with normal functioning between episodes. Addressing conduct and anger management problems in a 5-year-old may require different strategies than for similar issues in a teenager who is already encountering legal problems and may be substantively influenced by a delinquent peer group. Holmbeck, Devine, and Bruno (2010) noted that treatment effects can vary by age, developmental status can moderate or mediate treatment effects, and the influence of developmental factors should be addressed in all assessment and intervention protocols.

Knowledge of the differences between expected normal and uncommon problematic development is essential to the assessment process that determines potential need for intervention. Important considerations for developmentally competent assessment and intervention include an understanding of (a) developmental tasks at varying ages; (b) the requirements for successful transitions at key developmental stages; (c) the impact of practical transitions, ranging from geographical moves to progression to middle or secondary schools; and (d) the opportunities and vulnerabilities to environmental inputs during sensitive periods of development.

Work with children, in particular, is always implemented against the backdrop of a progression toward mastery and autonomy. Developmental status is evaluated along multiple continua: dependence to independence, external to internal locus of control, environmental dependence to self-efficacy, family centered to community supports and engagement, and parental to personal motivation and goal setting. The degree to which a child or adolescent is successfully advancing along these dimensions within general age expectancies helps to define both the need for treatment and potential intervention methods. Capacities for certain kinds of interventions may particularly be moderated by cognitive development. For example, it can be challenging to teach perspective taking to young children. Although metaphors and analogies may be used at varying developmental levels, the capacity for understanding symbolism and social complexity becomes more prominent in adolescence.

Language development influences intervention techniques as well. A teenager may be able to grasp the subtlety of reframing and problem-solving metaphors directly through language, whereas a younger child may require dolls or other manipulatives to understand relationships and procedures. Experiential learning and intervention practice activities can be powerful therapeutic tools but require differing strategies for children at various developmental levels. The nature of the presenting symptoms and the influence of systemic factors are essential factors to integrate into therapeutic decision making as well. For example, adolescents may present with strong verbal skills and a drive for autonomy; however, if family conflict is a central contributing element to symptom manifestation, focused conjoint work with parents and teenager together might be required.

Developmental expectations and exposure to activities and environmental influences vary from culture to culture. It is important to understand differing cultural definitions of healthy behavior and emotional expression. Empathic understanding by the therapist includes the ability to strive to view development through the cultural lens of the family while at the same time being attuned to the potential conflicts that may arise when children are more rapidly and eagerly integrating into the new culture than their parents. Cultural perspectives on gender, disability, and diversity vary greatly. Although the therapist must understand these factors, it is not necessary to accept unhealthy or unnecessarily limiting role definitions, such as those that too often burden or constrain female individuals. Assisting families in navigating the cultural differences between minority and majority cultural expectations is often an important but challenging task that can particularly affect the developmental progression of immigrant families.

Holmbeck et al. (2010) stressed that developmental tasks may be appropriate treatment targets themselves. Learning the skills to master a developmental task or achieving an appropriate developmental milestone promotes healthy psychological development in children experiencing developmental delays. For example, addressing debilitating separation anxiety may require the acquisition of autonomy and interpersonal skills that not only reduce the distress over separation from parents but also propel the child to a more appropriate level of social development and new opportunities for personal growth. In other situations, symptoms can be exacerbated by lagging development in specific areas, and thus therapeutic intervention is directed toward both symptom management and developmental task acquisition. Sometimes the symptoms of a disorder interfere with the development of age-appropriate skills. For example, attention-deficit/hyperactivity disorder (ADHD) impairs emotional and behavioral regulation, which in turn compromises peer relationships. Interventions need to stabilize regulation issues and then teach developmentally appropriate interpersonal skills.

Skill development can vary from child to child and within the same child. Not all children develop at the same pace, and not all age-level skills are equally developed within the same child. Therapists cannot assume that because a child is a certain age he or she is capable of a certain task or amenable to a specific treatment intervention. It is important to ascertain developmental strengths in children to use as foundational supports for acquiring new skills.

Relevant to assessment and intervention, the field of developmental psychopathology is attempting to ascertain the influence of developmental factors on the emergence of psychological disorders. In their review of this literature, Cichetti and Rogosch (2002) used principles from general systems theories to explain research on developmental pathways. They noted that different developmental pathways or environmental influences exist for a single disorder consistent with the concept of *equifinality*. Pathways are also characterized by *multifinality*, meaning that the same developmental event may lead to different adjustment outcomes. Psychology has long been fascinated by the phenomenon that two children can experience the same traumatic event at the same age, but one will be significantly scarred and the other will cope sufficiently to adapt and move on. Reactions to early traumatic events such as abuse or loss may also sometimes appear to have been adaptively managed but reemerge as issues at later developmental stages.

At first glance these concepts may appear discouraging in terms of trying to ascertain and then respond to the influence of developmental factors. Although they underline the complexity of engaging in child and adolescent therapy, these concepts also further highlight the importance of incorporating developmental considerations into all aspects of assessment and intervention planning. Assessment requires evaluating the influence of key historical events impacting development and the current status of mastery of key developmental tasks. Informed by this background, interventions may need to help the child resolve the constraints of early negative experiences and also directly teach developmentally appropriate adaptive skills. Therapy must use developmentally sensitive strategies and take developmental status into account to inform decisions about incorporating parents and teachers into sessions and intervention plans. Booster sessions and other follow-up work can anticipate developmental transitions and proactively prepare children and families for successful adaptation. Just as pediatricians perform routine physical checkups on their patients to monitor healthy development, school-centered therapists need to monitor the progress of at-risk youth at critical educational transitions and developmental milestones.

BEYOND THE OFFICE DOOR: SETTINGS FOR YOUTH TREATMENT

Although all psychotherapy must achieve change that generalizes to natural settings, elements of youth intervention work often occur directly in those settings and may involve a range of collateral participants such as parents, teachers, siblings, extended family, community, or legal officials. Family change plans and classroom management initiatives closely structure adult involvement and support for treatment implementation. A social and coping skill learned in the office may be prompted, monitored, and reinforced at home, in the classroom, or on the playground. A variety of milieu approaches are specifically designed to program coordinated group and individual interventions (e.g., Hensley, Powell, Lamke, & Hartman, 2007; Pelham et al., 2010). Therapists directly engage significant collaborators within those settings and monitor third-party reports of intervention effectiveness and client progress.

COGNITIVE BEHAVIORAL SYSTEMIC INTERVENTION MODELS

The contemporary literature summarizing evidence-based treatments for youth largely centers on applications of individual and group CBT and systemic interventions that may include parent training, family therapy, classroom management, or peer-group-centered protocols (see Kendall, 2012b; Mash & Barkley, 2006; Silverman & Hinshaw, 2008; Weisz & Kazdin, 2010). Although this suggests a broad common ground, significant variation remains in regard to strategy selection, procedural focus, combinations of techniques, and intervention sequence. Contemporary research focuses on differentiating what strategies work for which targeted symptom patterns. Although some core CBT principles may be present in protocols addressing internalizing disorders such as anxiety or depression and externalizing disorders such as conduct or anger management, specific applications are differentiated. For example, rehearsed self-instructions may help a child with obsessive–compulsive disorder tolerate an exposure task to resist compulsive behaviors, whereas a child with bipolar disorder sensing an agitated mood and fearing loss of control may be coached to use self-talk to "talk back" to or ward off a pending affective storm (*externalizing the symptom*). Systemic interventions are not limited to direct family therapy targeting changes in family structures, communications, and interaction patterns. Variations of parent support and training programs attempt to address child problems by altering parental practices. Classroom management protocols and instructional accommodation plans are not only central elements in treatments for ADHD but also essential components of comprehensive intervention plans for a large range of problems.

Treatment Assumptions

Several core treatment assumptions underpin this integration of CBT and systemic approaches. Cognitive therapy contributions assume that how youth process information, appraise threat or opportunity in events, attribute meaning to experiences, define their roles and self-concept, and what they say to themselves because of these thoughts and conceptualizations have a direct impact on feelings and behavior. For example, if two children experience the same event, one might see threat, feel anxious, and withdraw, whereas the other might see fun and opportunity and become excited and engaged.

CBT places a strong emphasis on the development of self-awareness to promote self-control and self-efficacy. In addition to cognitive processes, understanding emotional experience and providing empathy for feelings are essential parts of therapy. Overwhelming emotional arousal can hinder cognitive and behavioral resources. It is more difficult to think clearly or effectively problem solve when experiencing acute emotional stress. Within a CBT framework, emotional management comes from calming physical arousal, restructuring thoughts and self-talk, and developing new response patterns.

Systemic treatment assumptions note that problem manifestation is often influenced and maintained by contextual factors such as constraining family interaction patterns or problem-solving routines. Peer influences may also be a target for intervention, such as antisocial peer pressure or victimization from bullying. The systemic treatment assumption requires that the context or environment be changed to support individual growth and maintain symptom reduction. In the absence of contextual change, unhealthy, unsupportive, or invalidating environments can block or reverse individual gains. Many neurobehavioral disorders (e.g., bipolar disorder) are not caused by environmental factors, but debilitating episodes can be triggered by external familial, peer, or even academic stressors.

The behavioral components of CBT are compatible with the systemic perspective. Operant conditioning principles require a functional analysis of behavior and a clear understanding of the antecedents that prompt behavior and the consequences that maintain it. Functional and behavioral family therapies and many parent training programs teach healthy parental contingency management to establish developmentally appropriate limits and teach adaptive behaviors (Alexander, Waldron, Robbins, & Neeb, 2013; Robin & Foster, 2002). Although behavioral chains are typically viewed in a linear fashion, the systemic paradigm expands this view to include multiple dynamic interactions and contingencies that create reciprocal influences. Multisystemic therapies venture beyond a focus on the family unit to include interventions and collaborations with other systems that affect the child's symptoms (Henggeler, Schoenwald, Borduin, Rowland, & Cunningham 2009). The treatment assumption here is that the most severe externalizing disorders (e.g., those involving delinquency and substance abuse) require changes and positive supports from multiple layers of systems that have a potential stake in the youth's treatment goals. In a way, it adopts an "it takes a village" approach to intervention in severe cases. Specific attention is given to coping with antisocial peer groups and toward collaboration with schools, courts, and community organizations.

Therapy as a Psychoeducational Process

Contemporary approaches to youth psychotherapy view key elements of intervention as a psychoeducational process. Sometimes this process provides direct information on the characteristics of specific disorders—for example, teaching the child and parents about ADHD, its effects, and ways to manage its impact. Similarly, therapy may provide information on typical developmental processes, including strategies to support a child's transition to a new developmental stage such as adolescence.

Additionally, direct instruction in social, coping, and problem-solving training has evolved into a core treatment strategy. Built on principles of social learning theory, psychological skills are broken into component parts and application sequences, operationalized for instruction, modeled, practiced through behavioral rehearsal, and then prompted and reinforced in the natural environment. Systematic instruction for interpersonal skill development for adults dates back to the 1960s and 1970s with the work of Carkhuff (1971), Egan (1975), and others. Part of its focus was on helping skills training for counselors. Skills training was subsequently introduced into work with children both to remediate interpersonal deficits and to promote healthy social development. Shure and Spivack (1982) introduced social problem-solving skills training programs to young children. A. P. Goldstein (1999) introduced his Skillstreaming series and *The Prepare Curriculum* curricula to teach pro-social competencies. Glick and Gibbs (2010) extended A. P. Goldstein's skills-training work into revised editions of *Aggression Replacement Training*. A host of other programs incorporated psychoeducational skills training into treatment programs for specific psychological problems, such as Kendall and Hedtke's (2006) Coping Cat program to treat anxiety and J. Larson and Lochman's (2010) anger management program. Many of these programs were specifically designed for implementation within school settings.

These training programs are consistent with the CBT premise that skill deficits account for key dimensions of psychological problems, and direct training can remediate maladaptive behaviors by teaching adaptive alternatives. Different skill sets are necessary at varying developmental levels and transitions. As children mature and master key developmental tasks, they become capable of applying more complex and effective problem-solving strategies. For instance, as teenagers develop enhanced perspective-taking skills, they gradually become capable of displaying increased levels of empathy and of applying social problem-solving strategies that incorporate an understanding of others' points of view. As systematic skills-training programs evolved, increasing attention was paid to cognitive processes involved in coping strategies. Contemporary psychoeducational programs integrate the strategies derived from learning theory, interpersonal skills training, and cognitive restructuring.

Group Work

Psychoeducational curricula and skills-training programs are readily integrated into group formats. Direct instruction, role playing, and game-like activities benefit from a group context. The relevance of a peer group format to work with adolescents is readily apparent. Similarly, the peer context of a counseling group is appropriate for teaching and practicing a variety of interpersonal and problem-solving skills for younger children. When organized around skills-training protocols, group work with children has become much more structured than open-ended groups dependent on participant self-disclosure and initiation of an agenda. Relevant issues of the moment are addressed but in the context of a structured curriculum. Psychoeducational skills-training groups are a natural fit for school-centered interventions. Individual and group methods can be integrated to practice generalization of skills learned in one-on-one sessions and to focus participation in groups (Simon, 2013). For example, a child with social anxiety can rehearse introducing a topic with his or her individual therapist and then practice the skill in the group session with guidance and prompting from the group leader.

ESSENTIAL PRINCIPLES OF CHILD AND ADOLESCENT THERAPY

Goals

The goals of CBT-systemic approaches center on the development of self-understanding and self-control, effective and reciprocal participation in families and social groups, and adaptive stress management and problem solving. Although attention is paid to the influence of past events, therapy is present oriented, active and experiential, performance focused, and skills based. Intervention outcomes target differences in performance across all natural environments.

Core Therapist Skills

The focus on integrative therapies defines a broad set of core therapy skills. Active listening or accurate empathy and the ability to model and teach direct communication of feelings, needs, and experiences remain essential entry points for establishing a therapeutic alliance. Engaging and collaborative questioning and probing skills assist clients in articulating and examining all aspects of their experiences to enhance self-awareness and case conceptualization. Behavioral analysis and intervention skills that include applications of operant and respondent conditioning support behavior change. Exposure strategies are essential to anxiety management. Cognitive restructuring and rational analysis strategies are central techniques for addressing issues with stress management, depression, anxiety, and anger. Competency with systematic and integrated social, coping, and problem-solving skills training supports skills acquisition and performance goals. Systemic analysis and intervention skills enable therapists to intervene with families, teachers, and classrooms. Altering interaction patterns, modifying contingencies that support maladaptive behaviors, and structuring multisystemic supports promote treatment gains across natural environments.

Multicultural and Diversity Competency

Cultural and diversity competency are essential therapist skills, but they are challenging to define. It is important to understand cultural influences, perspectives, traditional roles, parenting practices, and attitudes toward emotional expression. At the same time, it is necessary to recognize that there is significant diversity within cultures, and avoidance of stereotyping is critical. Attention must be paid to the effect of immigrant experiences and the degree and interest in acculturation. Generational differences in cultural identification can create stresses within families. Diversity is not merely cultural. Gender, sexual orientation, blended families, and other factors influence children's needs and intervention approaches.

Family therapy approaches have a long history of attending to cultural and socioeconomic factors. Minuchin's (1974) innovations in structural family therapy grew out of his work with minority and poverty-stricken families. Breunlin, Schwartz, and Mac Kune-Karrer (1997) described various *metaframeworks*, including culture and gender, that needed to be integrated into assessment and intervention in family work. Falicov's (2013) work on therapeutic interventions with Latino families addressed the effects of migration, complications for families who are geographically separate, and common challenges for second-generation families. Employing a brief strategic family therapy model adapted from structural family therapy, Robbins, Horigian, Szapocznik, and Ucha (2010) targeted substance abuse and delinquency issues in Hispanic adolescents and reported promising outcome data.

Huey and Polo's (2010) review of the status of EBIs for ethnic minority youths is cautiously optimistic. They noted that emerging outcome data from studies focused primarily on African American and Latino youth show promise that general EBI approaches can be efficacious for these populations as well. It is not yet clear whether treatments with enhancements specifically identified as "culture-responsive" present advantages. The concept is difficult to define and operationalize and requires better research methodologies to truly assess impact. Huey and Polo noted three critical challenges in work with minorities: minority youth less frequently access treatment; more often terminate treatment prematurely; and when they access treatment, they are less likely to receive an EBI. From a social justice perspective, these issues point to the problematic disparities in access to mental health services and inadequate training and funding responses to address these concerns.

PREVALENCE OF COMORBIDITIES

The presence of comorbid conditions complicates intervention with children. For example, 87% of children with ADHD experience another disorder, and 67% have two or more disorders (Kadesjö & Gillberg, 2001). For pediatric bipolar disorder, estimates of comorbidity have ranged as high as 90%, with most studies indicating a strong likelihood of comorbidity (Frias, Palma, & Farriols, 2015). The comorbid presentation of anxiety and depression is common in both youth and adults (Hirschfeld, 2001; Merrell, 2008). It is possible that these data reflect our underdeveloped understanding of childhood psychopathology, but nonetheless comorbidities dramatically impact intervention planning.

Several therapeutic considerations arise from these data. Therapists must carefully assess whether what appear to be primary symptoms merely mask an underlying central problem or diagnosis; for example, acting out behaviors may be the result of undisclosed trauma. It can be necessary to address primary symptoms first no matter what the etiology or underlying factors might be, for example, addressing suicide risk. Consideration must be given to whether the treatment for one disorder will compromise the treatment for another or exacerbate symptoms. For instance, in some cases stimulant medication prescribed for ADHD symptoms has increased aggression in youth with untreated bipolar disorders. In other cases, efficacious intervention strategies may require riding out the storm of symptoms getting worse before they get better sometimes described as "bursts before extinction" or meltdowns during response prevention in exposure treatments. Addressing dual diagnosis in conditions like comorbid substance abuse and depression generally requires simultaneous strategies for addressing both issues.

Often a multistage approach to intervention is advised. For example, in some teens with emerging borderline issues, it may be necessary to initially focus on the reduction of self-harm risk or devise a program to stop "cutting," then address chronic depression issues that may require cognitive restructuring strategies (A. L. Miller, Rathus, & Linehan, 2007). Subsequent intervention stages might systematically teach stress management and problem-solving skills and then eventually apply new skills to family and peer interactions.

Kendall (2012c) noted that successful intervention can have "spillover effects" that positively impact the functioning of collaterals and thus circle back for further benefit to the child client. Remission of symptoms that contribute to family stress may result in more positive parent–child interactions, which create the opportunity for other social benefits. Also, CBT coping strategies applied to remediate anxiety symptoms have much in common with some techniques for management of depression or impulsive behaviors. Progress in depression management may alter social withdrawal tendencies; the resulting increase in positive social activities might improve other aspects of psychological functioning. A family therapy intervention that increases an underinvolved parent's participation in family life may enhance overall structure and appropriate limit setting, having wide-ranging effects on the multidimensional problems associated with youth conduct disorders.

REALISTIC EXPECTATIONS AND TIMELINES

In Chapter 1, I noted the growing perspective within the field that many psychological disorders present as chronic illnesses that may require symptom management over extended periods of time, specific progress monitoring, and possible additional intervention needs arising at the onset of key developmental transitions. Healthy psychological development is a lifelong process. Those who experience serious psychological issues may require occasional booster sessions or a series of brief therapies extended over time. The service delivery framework for child and adolescent therapists might be best conceptualized as similar to that of primary care physicians. They must intervene when symptoms occur, monitor sustenance of progress, be available for follow-up as needed, and schedule periodic checkups. Rather than viewing therapeutic intervention as a singular all-or-nothing process, relapses and regressions are anticipated and addressed as predictable bumps in the road that can be successfully managed.

An increase in the systemic components of intervention is designed to hasten and sustain generalization of skills learned through therapeutic interventions. Hopefully, as schools develop multitiered intervention programs, psychological health and timely intervention for social, emotional, or behavioral symptoms will become destigmatized and more readily available. Therapists working within or closely with schools are positioned to provide early responses to relapses and regression. They can build in follow-up procedures and problem prevention programs to assist with challenging developmental transitions or unanticipated stressful events. This practice is consistent with the reconceptualization of many psychological interventions as a psychoeducational process that requires ongoing support for continuing personal development and healthy psychological adaptation.

3

CASE CONCEPTUALIZATION IN THE CONTEXT OF EVIDENCE-BASED INTERVENTIONS: LINKING ASSESSMENT TO INTERVENTION TO OUTCOME

Case conceptualization is the essential skill for all problem-solving and therapeutic intervention planning. Comprehensive and accurate case conceptualization sets the foundation for clinical decision making. It requires a systematic model that links assessment to intervention selection, selectively applies evidence-based intervention (EBI) strategies, coordinates interventions for individual and systemic change, and maintains a focus on observable outcomes.

The individual elements of a comprehensive case conceptualization model must address the complexity of human experience. The case conceptualization model delineated in this chapter integrates intervention strategies that address experiential, physical, cognitive, emotional, behavioral, and contextual factors. The model demonstrates the interaction among these key dimensions of psychological functioning and how their interplay contributes to either adaptive or maladaptive coping. Assessment and intervention

http://dx.doi.org/10.1037/14779-004
School-Centered Interventions: Evidence-Based Strategies for Social, Emotional, and Academic Success,
by D. J. Simon

strategies articulated for each domain emerge from empirically supported psychological treatment literature. The integration of these strategies into a case conceptualization framework organizes intervention planning to address the full range of psychological disorders. It sets the foundation for therapeutic planning that incorporates EBI treatment protocols specific to individual disorders and symptom profiles. Empirically supported cognitive behavioral and systemic protocols can then be applied to complex individual, family, and classroom problem-solving challenges. Individual case conceptualization and intervention planning are monitored and modified by routine progress monitoring and outcome measurement. Feedback from data collection on treatment effects establishes a feedback loop that enables case conceptualization to remain a flexible and dynamic process.

AN INTEGRATED APPROACH TO UNDERSTANDING HUMAN EXPERIENCE

The field of psychology strives to understand the complexity of human experience, the development of personality characteristics and behavioral patterns, and our capacity and strategies for stress management. Schools of psychotherapy emerged to treat psychological disorders that overwhelmed coping abilities and interfered with life functioning. Historically, treatment approaches tended to develop with emphases on singular aspects of human experience.

Individual Schools of Psychotherapy

Psychoanalysis focused on the development of cognitive insight into how past experiences have influenced current functioning. Exploration of unconscious factors influencing behavior and the role of defense mechanisms for coping with stress became central features of psychodynamic assessment and intervention. Behaviorism shifted the focus from internal factors to an examination and management of overt behaviors. Originating in experimental learning theory, operant conditioning viewed the influence of external environmental factors as central to understanding and treating psychological problems. Respondent conditioning studied physiological responses to stress and developed treatment strategies that included physical relaxation training. Client-centered treatment took a less deterministic view of human development. The empathic communications of the therapist were meant to enhance clients' understanding of their emotions. Fostering self-awareness would eventually contribute to healthy self-determination. Cognitive therapies emphasized the role of cognitive appraisal and attribution in influencing our feelings and behaviors. Changing thinking patterns and improving ratio-nal perspectives regarding problems would increase adaptive coping. Group therapy formats focused on the interpersonal dimensions of psychological functioning. Family therapy addressed the systemic context of symptom development and maintenance. From this perspective it was necessary to alter family interaction patterns to support change in individual behaviors.

Integrative and Multidimensional Approaches

Each of these seminal schools of therapy made significant contributions; but each placed primary emphasis on differing dimensions of human experi-ence. Adding to this diversity has been an increased understanding of the influence of biological, neurological, and genetic factors on the etiology of psychological disorders. In contrast, the emerging contemporary perspective is increasingly integrative and holistic. It is clear that there is an inseparable link among biological, neurological, cognitive, social, emotional, behavioral, and contextual domains of human functioning. Not only does each domain influence the development of healthy and unhealthy adaptations but also each factor moderates the impact of the other dimensions. As this perspec-tive has emerged, contemporary psychology has moved toward more integra-tive therapeutic models and increased awareness of contextual variables such as family, school, and peer group. Arnold Lazarus (1997, 2008) developed his multimodal approach to therapy applying "technical eclecticism" to select treatment interventions from the full array of schools of therapy depending on the needs of the individual client and the character of the presenting prob-lem. Stricker (2010) summarized the psychotherapy integration literature.

Cognitive behavioral therapy (CBT) and family therapy have played a central role in the development of integrative and multidimensional thera-pies for children and adolescents. In an attempt to capture the current state of evidence-based interventions for youth, Kendall (2012c) created a complex hybrid to incorporate the essential components of contemporary child therapy: "cognitive-behavioral-emotional-developmental-familial therapy." In the end, he settled on CBT as a less cumbersome title but with a clear assertion that effective treatment required attention to more than just cognitive and behavioral factors. Mash (2006) used the term *cognitive-behavioral systems* to emphasize that EBI for children and adolescents integrated individual and systemic dimensions. Summary compendiums of child and adolescent treat-ment research (e.g., Kendall, 2012b; Mash & Barkley, 2006; Weisz & Kazdin, 2010) support this perspective.

CBT interventions are central resources for effective psychotherapy for youth. Emanating from this framework, systematic instruction in social and coping skills is an essential component not only for treatment interventions for children experiencing problems but also for social–emotional learning curriculum promoting healthy life-skills development for all students in schools. CBT's psychoeducational framework provides an excellent fit for working within the school environment. A similar skills training framework can be used for prevention and intervention efforts. Dialectical behavior therapy (DBT) builds on CBT principles to provide empirically supported interventions for suicidal adolescents (A. L. Miller, Rathus, & Linehan, 2007).

Systemic interventions can take many forms and target various social contexts. The individual student may be aided by changes in the family, classroom, school, or community environments. A depressed, anxious, and vulnerable student who is the victim of bullying requires individual supports to help him manage his overwhelming feelings. He also might need assertion and problem-solving skills training to assist him in standing up for himself and reducing the likelihood that he would be targeted by bullies. At the same time, systemic interventions are required to alter the school climate that permits bullying and to ensure that there is adequate adult supervision. Thus, intervention strategies target individual and contextual change.

Contemporary EBIs rooted in family therapy protocols target the individual and multiple systems simultaneously (Alexander, Waldron, Robbins, & Neeb, 2013; Henggeler, Schoenwald, Borduin, Rowland, & Cunningham, 2009; Liddle, 2009, 2010). Cognitive and behavioral techniques may be used with the child and family members to build social and coping skills, but treatment focuses on altering the structure and character of family interactions and peer networks. Networking with the larger system of essential community resources is frequently included in treatment planning. Parent skills training programs present another systemic approach to changing problematic behavior in children and adolescents (Barkley, 2013b; Forgatch & Patterson, 2010; Webster-Stratton & Reid, 2010). The introduction of universal positive behavioral support programs is a systems-wide strategy to improve school climates, promote healthy social-skill development, and prevent behavior problems (Sugai & Horner, 2010).

Cultural and Diversity Factors

To fully understand the impact of context on an individual child's experience, it is necessary to incorporate the influences of cultural factors. Cultural differences affect child-rearing practices, attitudes toward emotional expression and regulation, the pace of development toward individuation, gender roles and expectations, nonverbal communication patterns, perspectives on psychological disabilities, and family structures and expectations. Competent therapists carry the responsibility to understand the cultural backgrounds of their clients and the potential impact of their own cultural experiences. Care must be taken to avoid stereotyping since significant individual differences abound within all cultures. This sensitivity does not require acceptance of unhealthy or limiting cultural norms in terms of disability and gender.

The increasing diversity in the make-up and definition of family has had implications for child-rearing contexts. School conferences and therapy sessions may include biological parents from an intact marriage, two sets of parents from blended families, or a single parent primarily responsible for child rearing. In some cases, there will be significant extended family and multigeneration participation. Children may live with adoptive parents. Foster parents may be temporary caretakers and require caseworker support for engagement in counseling interventions. Growing acceptance of diversity has increased the number of children adopted by gay and lesbian partners. The iterations on diversity are extensive. To understand and intervene in the context of the child's life requires attention to the full range of cultural and diversity factors.

Genetic and Familial Predispositions

The family context adds an additional dimension affecting intervention planning when one of the child's biological parents has been diagnosed with the same psychological condition. Some conditions are more likely to be influenced by genetic factors. We have conducted family sessions with parents of a child with pediatric bipolar disorder where a parent has struggled with similar mood disorder symptoms. The parent's psychological health and available personal resources may affect intervention planning. It can make a positively significant difference if the parent was accepting of his or her diagnosis, received treatment, believed in the use of psychotropic medications, and presented with a positive outlook on symptom management. On the other hand, denial, prior negative treatment experiences, and pessimistic expectations can severely compromise intervention planning and outcomes.

Schools as Pivotal Context

Additional contextual factors include peer group, school, community, and socioeconomic status. The power of school-centered therapy lies in its ability to assist the child within the two primary life contexts of school and family. Schools provide a unique access to the intersection of these two critical systems. As outlined in Chapter 3, child and adolescent therapy research demonstrates that maintenance and generalization of therapeutic gains requires intervention at the "point of performance" or the natural environment of the youth. Social, coping, and problem-solving skills learned in therapy must transfer to school, peer, and family settings to truly remediate problems and produce enduring results. The school setting with its potential for close collaboration with parents provides unique access to the point of performance for children and adolescents. It is the natural setting in which they immerse their lives.

TREATMENT ASSUMPTIONS

Case conceptualization must be anchored in current research and best practice in child, adolescent, and family treatment. As noted above, the model described in this chapter begins with the assumption that an integrated approach to understanding experience, assessing needs, and devising intervention strategies is necessary and that interventions must address both individual and contextual factors. Treatment assumptions are multidimensional. Understanding emotional experience and providing empathy for feelings are essential characteristics of therapy. Empathy helps to build a therapeutic alliance and promotes increased self-awareness for the client. Heightened emotional awareness enables the child to become less overwhelmed by experiences and permits exploration of the necessary connections to thoughts, actions, and other dimensions of personality and patterns of response to life's events.

How we process information and attribute meaning to our experiences, thoughts, and cognitions directly affects our feelings and thus our behaviors. In a reciprocal manner, changing behaviors can alter thoughts and feelings. Effective interventions build toward an integrated understanding of the connections among thoughts, feelings, and actions. Changes in one domain will impact the others. Thus, treatment delineates strategies for each dimension of human experience. It is often necessary to modify the systems or contexts that influence problem manifestation to effect change and sustain improvements.

Contemporary child therapy centers on practical problem solving and focuses on measureable outcomes. It includes direct instruction in social, coping, and problem-solving skills. Its goal is to teach essential daily living skills that enable youth to manage daily stressors, cope with extraordinary events, establish positive reciprocal peer relationships, and independently apply these skills to future challenges. Enhanced coping skills foster self-management.

Therapy addresses the cultural and systemic factors that emerge from family, peer, and school contexts. More so than in adult treatments, child and adolescent therapy not only strives to help the client adjust to challenging contexts and environments but also attempts to change the actions and influences of the context. Coaching parents and teachers to change routines, procedures, and response patterns can have a direct effect on achieving therapeutic goals. Facilitating participation in supervised prosocial youth activities might counterbalance the risks for involvement in antisocial peer groups.

Unlike historical insight-oriented approaches to treatment, there is no assumption that improved insight will automatically, by itself, lead to behavioral change. This does not mean that insight is unimportant. Enhanced understanding of the links among experiences, bodily reactions, thoughts, feelings, and actions is a core intervention task. As these connections are facilitated, it becomes equally important to gain insight into how social and coping responses influence the outcomes of problem-solving attempts and impact personal satisfaction. Improving self-awareness enables children to exert increased self-control over their behaviors, but specific therapeutic action plans must facilitate observable change.

A comprehensive case conceptualization model can organize assessment and intervention planning. However, no single treatment approach has been proven to be effective for all children and adolescents across all symptom patterns. The current state of both the art and science of youth therapy requires differential therapeutic intervention responses to treat each psychological disorder or symptom presentation. One-size-fits-all protocols are insufficient to address the nuances of childhood psychological disorders. For example, a crisis intervention response to a student having a meltdown influenced by sensory overload may require a different clinical response than an aggressive student with oppositional defiant disorder who is prone to power struggles with adults; and in each case the response protocol is different from the response necessary to calm an explosive outburst from a student experiencing a manic episode.

Some common factors must be systematically addressed across all symptom patterns. Developmental status, current life stressors, physical health, comorbidity, and other relevant factors are analyzed in each case. There are some overriding principles of therapy (e.g., the need for empathy) and some common clinical frameworks (e.g., the assessment of reinforcers that maintain behavior) that are incorporated into all case conceptualization and intervention planning.

Efforts are being made to define transdiagnostic mechanisms for the treatment of youth disorders (Ehrereich-May & Chu, 2014). This approach is attempting to define overarching theoretical frameworks to explain what are considered diverse psychological disorders. In part, this is a reaction to the categorical approach toward identification of psychopathology and a promotion of dimensional schemas for defining clinical problems. Transdiagnostic approaches hope to define broad underlying clinical dimensions across psychological conditions and corresponding common treatment mechanisms that can successfully address diverse symptom presentations. If this were possible, it would facilitate therapeutic treatment for many children who display significant comorbidity. To some degree, the history of psychotherapy has continually searched for a common paradigm, and when a treatment approach demonstrated success addressing one condition, it was applied to other conditions until it proved insufficient or ineffective. Ehrereich-May and Chu (2014) highlighted their view of the importance of this quest while underlining its complexity and the necessity for significant research development in this area.

Practitioners working in and with schools need to conceptualize and organize therapeutic interventions in light of what we currently know through outcome studies. The case conceptualization framework proposed here presents an overarching protocol for organizing assessment and intervention across conditions, but then it is necessary to also implement specific strategies empirically supported for addressing specific psychological disorders.

A FRAMEWORK FOR CASE CONCEPTUALIZATION: THE SELF-UNDERSTANDING MODEL

Intervention planning requires an assessment process that addresses the multifaceted dimensions of children's experiences. Stressful events impact us physically, cognitively, and emotionally. Our responses in each of these domains influence our behavioral patterns. The repetition of inadequate or unhealthy coping strategies contributes to the development and maintenance of psychological symptoms. Effective case conceptualization requires the development of an integrative and multidimensional intervention scheme that addresses the same critical domains of experience examined during the assessment process. The self-understanding model (SUM) provides an organizational framework for case conceptualization that is practical, comprehensive, and readily links assessment to intervention (Kapp-Simon & Simon, 1991; Simon, 2012). As its name implies, the goal of the SUM is to foster self-awareness in the child or adolescent in a manner that can contribute to understanding therapeutic goals and strategies and eventually enhance self-management of symptoms.

Case conceptualization strives to assess symptom manifestation and maintenance by understanding the connections among a student's experiences, physical reactions, thoughts, feelings, and behaviors. Because all human experience is contextual, it is also necessary to understand the influence of family, peer, school, and other relevant systems that influence responses within each of these domains. Assessment questions examine how the student is affected within each domain and how the domains affect one other. Does an anxiety-provoking experience lead to stomachaches, racing negative thoughts, feelings of panic and hopelessness, or result in withdrawal or avoidant actions? Is the physical tension and panic so pronounced that the child immediately leaves the situation to seek relief? Are the child's immediate thoughts so dominated by fears of failure or risks of harm that he is blocked from a more realistic evaluation of possible actions or outcomes? Do those catastrophizing thoughts intensify feelings of panic? What is this child's self-awareness about his personal experience in each of these domains? Is one domain primary, for example, physical tension drawing all of his focus and driving his withdrawal response?

Any experience that carries an emotional impact, positive or negative, is immediately accompanied by an instinctual physical sensation. Individual visceral reactions may vary but can include tightening in the stomach, tense neck muscles, or a rush of adrenalin. Sometimes these bodily reactions interfere with the ability to remain calm, focus on the moment, and make sound decisions. An overstimulated child may act carelessly. An overly anxious child may quickly withdraw from a situation to secure immediate relief from overwhelming physical tension. An angry child may release physical tension by lashing out aggressively. Physical stress can interfere with our judgment in interpersonal encounters or even contribute to actual physical illness. We've all experienced the difference between a healthy level of physical tension that reminds us to focus in an anxiety-provoking situation and debilitating tension that keeps us from performing at a competent level. For example, if a student is teased and embarrassed in front of his peers, he may experience a rush of bodily tension sensing tightening muscles twitching to explode. The student's heightened alertness may create the sensation of blood racing and heart pounding. Angry thoughts might flood his immediate awareness, distorting the importance of the situation at hand (e.g., "If I don't lash out at him, everybody will think I'm weak; and I'll just be picked on all the time"). Uninterrupted, this physical tension and flood of negative thoughts can increase the intensity of his feeling. His initial embarrassment can escalate into an overwhelming anger and may result in an explosive behavioral incident. His loss of control and mismanagement of his physical tension, self-defeating thoughts, and rising emotions may lead to significant negative consequences. If he were to impulsively strike the provoking peer, he might risk harmful retaliation. The encounter could result in school disciplinary action. His relations with peers would be further compromised.

A summary review of this problematic scenario underlines the interactions among the physical, cognitive, emotional, and behavioral components of this boy's experience. Each component influences the others, and their interplay contributes to the resulting maladaptive social outcome. An initial assessment of this child's functioning delineates current patterns within each domain and highlights their influence on other areas of his experience. An analysis of the sequence of their interactions reveals patterns that result in either adaptive or maladaptive coping responses. Ingrained problematic patterns contribute to negative personal and social outcomes that can turn into reflexive unhealthy psychological functioning.

The assessment of functioning patterns in these domains can directly link to initial intervention considerations. Let's review this same scenario with the student displaying a more adaptive set of coping strategies across these same domains. If he had learned through experience or been trained to recognize his tightening muscles as a signal that he was tense and in danger of losing control, he could have taken immediate steps to begin stress management. Taking a deep breath to calm his bodily tension and pause his fight-or-flight instincts could also buy time for interrupting automatic distorted and combative thoughts that might unnecessarily exaggerate his appraisal of the social threat posed by his peers' taunts. Uninterrupted, escalating physical tension and a flood of catastrophic images of social humiliation could combine to transform his feelings of embarrassment into uncontrollable anger and contribute to an impulsive counterattack and an explosive incident. Instead his rapid recognition of his emerging bodily reactions permits him to execute a calming strategy to gain control over his sensory arousal. The tension becomes a signal not only of heightened alertness but also a cue to prepare to cope. Physical calming enables him to initiate a less distorted cognitive appraisal and increased rational thinking (e.g., "Easy, don't explode and go after them and get into trouble and make matters worse . . . don't let them get to you"). Then he can tell himself to begin a rehearsed coping strategy (e.g., "Take another deep breath, tell them to back off without losing your cool . . . keep it short . . . don't show them that it gets to you, just walk away"). Managing his physical tension and altering his thought process controls the intensity of his initial angry affect and enables him to execute a different and more adaptive behavioral response to the stressor. Interventions in each domain assessed enable an integrated and adaptive coping response that maintains self-control and avoids a damaging outcome.

A wide range of personal and social challenges and the full continuum of overwhelming emotional reactions can be adaptively resolved through the targeted application of coping and social strategies that arise from changes in our response to physical cues, thoughts, and feelings.

The scenario just described involved a social dilemma and required anger management, addressing externalizing behaviors. The same approach can be applied to internalizing behaviors as well. A common intrapersonal challenge involves the management of performance anxiety. The following example illustrates the application of SUM analysis to a case involving the rise of potentially debilitating anxiety at the onset of taking a high-stakes test like a college entrance exam.

Students prone to performance anxiety may feel particularly stressed and vulnerable during high-stakes testing such as college aptitude examinations like the ACT or SAT. In this case, Sally has settled into her seat at the testing center, and the examination materials are being distributed. As Sally begins to take the tests, she experiences a range of physical reactions. Her stomach tightens. She begins to perspire. She feels the early onset of a headache. As she notes the physical signs of her anxiety, her thoughts cloud with negativity and predictions of impending failure (i.e., "I never do well on these tests. I'm afraid I'm going to freeze up and forget what I know. I'm never going to get into college"). These self-defeating thoughts exacerbate her initial feelings of performance anxiety, and she begins to feel overwhelmed, teetering on the verge of panic. As she begins to attempt to answer the first items, she quickly encounters one she does not know how to correctly answer. Preoccupied with her nervous tension and fears of failure, she begins to lose focus. Sometimes she spends too long on one problem, begins to fear that she won't finish the exam, and moves too quickly through the next series of items. With the recognition that her test-taking approach is not working, her anxiety increases, her attention and effort dissipate, and Sally begins to resign herself to failure.

Sally's bodily reactions and self-defeating thoughts escalate the intensity of her anxiety and contribute to the breakdown of her test-taking approach. These counterproductive behaviors only serve to increase her disappointment in her performance and heighten her physical tension and racing self-defeating thoughts. Each domain of her experience is affected and affects the others. If we apply the SUM case conceptualization framework to this scenario, it is possible to devise coordinated interventions for each critical component of her experience to lesson her performance anxiety, increase her coping capacity, and improve the outcome of the test.

Because our sensory experience is the first indicator that we are encountering significant stress, it is the starting point for teaching coping strategies. In the past, Sally has viewed her initial awareness of her uncomfortable physical symptoms of anxiety as the dreadful signal that she was about to be overwhelmed by stress. The physical sensations triggered automatic self-defeating thoughts, and her panic cycle took off beyond her control. To alter this sequence, she was taught a variety of self-calming strategies such as deep breaths and alternating tightening and relaxing of muscles attempting to find a strategy that she found comforting and realistic to use. Armed with a strategy to counter the instinctual rise of physical tension, she could now turn her awareness of the first physical signs of stress into a signal to immediately initiate self-calming strategies to assert control over her approach to managing the stressor.

After taking a few calming deep breaths, Sally monitors her immediate automatic self-defeating thoughts and replaces them with rehearsed self-instructions to direct her coping strategies (i.e., "Take a deep breath . . . if you don't know the answer skip it for now and come back, concentrate on the ones you know you can get correct"). As Sally calms her bodily tension, interrupts negative racing thoughts, and focuses on implementation of her practiced coping strategies, her feelings shift from debilitating to focusing anxiety. Now she is able to execute adaptive test-taking strategies and coping strategies. She has exerted self-control over her performance anxiety and successfully executed the test-taking strategies that can increase the opportunity for success. Her covert self-talk now includes reinforcement that she has gained self-control and maintained focus.

In the second example of Sally's encounter with performance anxiety, interventions were planned for each domain of her experience as outlined in the SUM. Just as her debilitating anxiety escalated with the negative interactions among the physical, cognitive, emotional, and behavioral dimensions of her experience, she successfully coped in the second instance by addressing each domain and altering how they affected each other. In the first scene, the breakdown of her test-taking approach intensified the negative experiences in each domain, whereas in the second scene, her successful application of effective test-taking strategies diminished bodily tension, countered self-defeating thought patterns, and reduced the intensity of harmful affect.

CBT Sequence for SUM Domains

These two examples demonstrate how case conceptualization with the SUM can be used to link assessment to intervention, addressing both externalizing and internalizing variables. This framework readily incorporates elements of empirically supported CBT strategies into treatment planning and execution and can appropriately be applied to interventions for a wide range of psychological challenges.

The effective entry point for change for each individual may vary. Just as there are learners who tune into visual inputs more readily than auditory ones, individuals may differ in awareness of and attention to physical, cognitive, emotional, and behavioral aspects of their experiences. However, even if it is not always recognized, the earliest cue or recognition of distress is always physical. Clients can be taught greater awareness of their sensory experiences. Understanding bodily reactions is crucial for teaching adaptive coping particularly for anxiety and impulse disorders.

Although individual applications may vary, a coordinated sequence of CBT strategies is typically effective within SUM for the management of stress and problem behaviors.

- Recognize the earliest physical cue (e.g., tension in the back of the neck) that could be attributed to feeling anxious, threatened, depressed, angry, and so forth.
- Perform physical calming action (e.g., take a deep breath and shrug my shoulders to release tightness).

- Assess my current thoughts and appraisal of the situation (e.g., "What am I telling myself?" "Am I exaggerating threats?" "Are my thoughts reflexively negative and self-defeating?").
- Tell myself to stop self-defeating thoughts and not to assume that only negative outcomes can happen.
- Give myself specific instructions that direct me to engage in coping actions, rehearsed covert self-instructions that push out reflexive and counterproductive self-defeating thoughts.
- Execute my coping plan as I talk myself through each step, giving myself covert positive reinforcement for successful coping.
- Seek out appropriate social supports if necessary such as a trustworthy adult or peer who can help keep me coping and problem solving.

This coping sequence addresses the physical, cognitive, emotional, and behavioral components of the SUM in an integrated fashion. Its successful implementation relies on extensive preparation and practice. Before application, therapeutic work addresses individual challenges within each domain. It is necessary to practice strategies individually and in tandem. Role plays of troublesome scenarios can enhance skill acquisition. Within the school setting, students may benefit from reminders and prompts to use coping and problem-solving skills. Classroom teachers can be prepared to offer this support. Parents can provide similar guidance at home.

Within the SUM framework, treatment goals include enhanced self-awareness, self-control, and self-efficacy. Interventions are designed to equip the child or adolescent with the social, coping, and problem-solving skills essential for self-management and healthy independent psychological functioning. This approach is a particularly good fit for adolescents striving for increased self-determination and independence, but it also provides positive growth toward independence at all stages of development.

Addressing Contextual Factors

Interventions must also account for the contexts of the family, the school, peers, and the community. Environmental and systemic factors have a significant effect on the emergence and maintenance of symptoms. A long-time lament of therapists focused on individual work with children is that although the child has improved and learned new adaptive skills, the benefits of treatment keep getting unraveled by family, school, or peer actions. Not only must case conceptualization within the SUM framework understand individual patterns of bodily reactions, thoughts, feelings, and behaviors in response to stressful problem cycles but schema must also analyze the impact of these other influences. Contextual analysis must take into account the full range of environmental factors that can affect the child's symptom manifestation and attempts at problem solving. These factors include parenting practices, social modeling, structures for support and supervision, family stressors, peer pressures, classroom environment, instructional approaches, social-economic status, and medical issues. Because many psychological disorders can be influenced by genetic factors, it is important to conduct a full family history. All of these contextual factors can present resources or barriers for change. Just as individual assessments must identify strengths and underused potential, contextual exploration should delineate positive resources and supports. Reviewing contextual influences on prior adaptive problem solving can point to potential supports and ensure that the assessment process provides a hopeful and well-rounded picture of functioning.

Parent training programs and family therapy strategies are well represented within the EBI literature (e.g., Alexander et al., 2013; Barkley, 2013b; Forgatch & Patterson, 2010; Webster-Stratton & Reid, 2010). EBI family therapies address multidimensional factors and multiple systems beyond the individual family including peer networks, school programing, legal systems, and community agencies (Henggeler et al., 2009; Liddle, 2009, 2010). These treatment approaches have addressed complex and change-resistant symptoms like advanced delinquency and substance abuse. Although it is challenging to manualize intervention protocols to address this complex web of environmental influences, core intervention strategies and targets have been successfully delineated.

School systems are also beginning to focus programming on contextual factors. Multitiered intervention models are designing prevention and early intervention programs that include goals for creating supportive educational environments and equipping teachers with skills for teaching students' social problem-solving skills (Osher, Dwyer, & Jackson, 2004). For example, anti-bullying initiatives not only intervene with and address the needs of bullies and victims but also focus on changes in faculty supervision practices and school culture (Olweus, Limber, & Mihalic, 1999).

Integrative Clinical Case Example

The following clinical case example illustrates the integration of individual, interpersonal, and contextual dimensions into a comprehensive intervention plan organized within the SUM framework. It outlines a school-centered intervention protocol for a student with social anxiety and school avoidance.

Sam is a second grader whose family moved into the community last spring. In the brief time he was in attendance at his new school after the move, he presented as shy and withdrawn, requiring significant encouragement to participate in classroom activities. Over the summer, he played with his younger brother but had minimal contact with other children. Family planning for summer activities was compromised when Sam's grandmother became seriously ill and moved in with the family. Sam has been more prone to illness than most children his age. Particularly on Monday mornings, he often complains of stomach pains, nausea, or a headache. Sam resists his parents' attempts at reassurance and soothing. When they insist he go to school, his physical complaints escalate, and at times he cries and deteriorates into an emotional meltdown. When he is at school, he frequently requests to see the school nurse and asks whether he can be sent home. Sam's parents report that he has always presented with excessive anxiety. The case illustration focuses on the multidimensional intervention responses organized within the full SUM schema.

Bodily Reactions

Sam is already very sensitive to his body's physical reactions to stress. Intervention strategies in this domain focus on early recognition of the physical cues that indicate escalating anxiety. Signs such as nausea and headaches might need to be redefined from warnings that he is getting sick into cues that he is getting nervous. He can then be taught self-soothing strategies that calm some of his bodily tension, for example, pairing deep relaxing breaths with gently massaging his temples and forehead. Because Sam tends to be hypersensitive to physical distress, it is necessary to avoid belaboring the focus on sensory awareness. Instead, these relaxation strategies need to be paired with a distracting activity like engaging in a structured routine of activities at home before leaving for school to focus his attention and limit down time. Self-calming actions can eventually be paired with a self-instruction protocol to guide Sam's execution of a coping plan.

Feelings

It is important to provide Sam empathy for the impact of his panic, but it must be paired with persistent reassurance that he can successfully cope. It is particularly important that his parents are coached in providing empathy and support in a way that comforts but does not feed into his social withdrawal and anxious flight from his school attendance. Their expressions of support must be accompanied by repetitive, firm communication of the expectation that he needs to go to school and will be able to manage the challenge. In this process, Sam learns to understand and label his anxiety. This enhanced self-awareness is a critical step toward eventual stress management.

Thoughts

Sam's thoughts are filled with imagery of social failure and isolation at school. Even in the absence of negative experiences at school, he anticipates and presumes social rejection. He worries about academic failure and fears embarrassment in front of classmates and his teacher. Interventions within this domain include "cognitive restructuring" and "rational analysis" techniques appropriate for his age level (see Friedberg, McClure, & Garcia, 2009). Although some of this occurs in conversation with the therapist, given his developmental status, Sam's negative imagery is more likely to be abated through supported experiences. A therapy session including his classroom teacher permits a calm exploration of support needs, delineation of routines, and more realistic and reassuring understanding of teacher expectations. In addition to the therapist, the teacher can serve as a surrogate for parental support. Some transitional dependency on the teacher may be necessary to wean Sam from his sole dependence on parental support.

It is challenging for Sam to stop his self-defeating negative thoughts. He will require active replacement of his overlearned anxious script. The therapist works with him to design a covert self-instruction protocol that guides him in actively coping through his anxiety-provoking stimuli. This protocol links to his sensory awareness of mounting anxiety, includes a prompt for physical self-calming, and includes specific reminders and directives that he and his therapist have created to address each step of his morning routine leading to arrival at school. It may go on to include self-instructions for managing anxiety within the classroom and seeking appropriate teacher support. Role plays of anxiety-provoking scenarios are necessary to rehearse the application of these adaptive self-talk scripts, if necessary including trial after school or weekend visits to school. Even with practice, it will be necessary that parents and appropriate school personnel are prepared to prompt the use of these cognitive strategies.

Behaviors–Actions

Various practice runs targeting each step of school attendance can prove helpful. These runs begin with routines at home, transportation to school, any waiting period outside the building, entrance into the school, accessing the classroom, starting work, and asking the teacher for assistance. Physical and cognitive coping strategies would be used and, if necessary, modified throughout the practice activities.

Like many students with anxiety-based school avoidance behaviors, Sam has had his panicky withdrawal behaviors reinforced through escape conditioning. When overwhelmed with anxiety at school, his wish to be taken home will intensify and likely include physical symptoms that may even include vomiting and a slight fever as he becomes increasingly overwrought. The nurse in the school health office can be involved in a plan to design a safe haven within the school that replaces home as his temporary sanctuary. The nurse can attend to any physical complaints that occur, provide a location within the school for him to pull himself back together from his overwhelming anxiety, while refusing to let him go home or talk to his parents on the phone for reassurance. This time-out sanctuary should be safe and reassuring but also boring and time limited. It is critical to block his insistent attempts to return home or contact his parents even if it requires weathering some emotional meltdowns. This strategy provides temporary support, counters his avoidance conditioning, and shields any emotional meltdown from peer observation. His intervention plan can include permission near the end of the school day to call home to "brag about" making it through his school day or to share some positive classroom anecdote. Thus, parental reinforcement is paired with successful coping rather than harmful escape behaviors.

Interpersonal–Peers

Sam's relative social isolation has hampered his acquisition of confident social skills for engaging with peers and compromises his capacity for reciprocal peer relationships. A component of his therapeutic protocol is instruction in interpersonal skills to remediate his skill deficits that interfere with social initiation, participation, and friendships. To support social comfort and create relatively safe occasions for peer interactions, Sam can be assigned a peer buddy for some class activities. His classroom teacher can also take care to assign him to socially safe instructional groupings. If Sam were the victim of teasing or bullying by peers, interventions to prevent reoccurrence and equip him with a response plan would be appropriate.

Family System

When social anxiety and separation and individuation issues occur, it is necessary to assist parents in finding a balance between providing supports and sustaining insistence on age-appropriate independence. In Sam's case, two critical factors have interfered with his transition to school. First, his family's recent relocation to a new community necessitating his engagement in a different school and peer group has created significant transitional anxiety. Second, his grandmother's illness and move into his family's home has created significant family stress, changed routines, and diminished parental capacity for providing Sam support for engaging in youth activities beyond the home. Therapeutic consultations with parents can assist them in rediscovering a balance in family energy and time and assist them in their own stress management. Together the therapist and parents can brainstorm ways to involve Sam in structured extracurricular peer activities. Because it is possible that a component of Sam's anxiety is worry about his grandmother's health or his parents' quite evident stress, he may require periodic reassurances from his parents that although they are greatly affected by grandma's illness and the changes it has entailed in their lives, they are managing these challenges. Further, they can communicate to him that his success at school would go a long way toward lessening their stress and that his grandmother will be well-taken care of while he is at school.

The therapist will explore other developmental areas in which anxious escape behaviors are subtly maintained through avoidance of task demands. Given the range of family stressors, the parents may feel some unnecessary responsibility for Sam's school avoidance and inadvertently predisposed to respond to his anxiety with overprotection. As the child therapy proceeds, the therapist can teach parents to substitute prompts for initiating coping strategies for any reflexive counterproductive rescuing actions. It might also be effective to reframe Sam's school refusal as "disobedience" to diminish parental overprotective instincts in response to his intense anxiety. To this end, it can be helpful to ask parents about other situations in which Sam refuses to follow their directions. The goal here is to support the firmer, more executive stances of the parents so that they can insistently nudge him toward school participation and replace the current subtle reinforcement of his avoidance with clear and specific reinforcers for his successful participation. It is better for a special activity time with a parent to be earned through school participation than increased home time engineered by school avoidance. The therapist reviews the essentials of behavior management with parents and guides them in the design of collaborative home-school contingency contracts to reinforce all of his subgoals for management of anxiety and school attendance.

Although anxiety-based school avoidance may develop through accidental learning, it is important to explore the possibility that the child's anxiety serves an unrealistic "protective" function in the family. In this case, without directly realizing it, does Sam stay home to support his mother's depression over grandmother's serious illness; or, because of his special relationship with grandma, does he feel he needs to spend time with her to help out or even ensure her survival? If either of these confounding factors were the case, treatment interventions would need to be designed to address these systemic issues and support a healthy role for Sam within family dynamics.

Classroom Instruction and Supports

The critical roles of Sam's teacher and the school nurse have already been noted. Sam's comfort level and ability to overcome his anxiety will be enhanced by his ability to trust key adults beyond his family. School staff may need to provide some extraordinary supports in the early stages of the intervention plan as Sam struggles to leave home and stay in school. Any learning issues and deficits must be addressed through modifying instructional strategies and designing programming to limit performance anxiety. It is not uncommon for school-avoidant students to exhibit debilitating performance anxiety, which gets exacerbated by missed lessons. Sam requires a classroom-specific behavior management protocol with defined reinforcers for time in class, work completed, and appropriate teamwork within student instructional groups.

If necessary, essential school staff should be prepared for a crisis intervention routine that is individualized to meet the target student's profile. In this case, responding staff should be prepared to calmly respond to any anxiety-laden meltdowns, prompt coping strategies, communicate reassurance and expectation that he will be able to rebound, understand the role of the nurse in providing a temporary safe haven, and avoid inadvertent reinforcement of escape-maintained behaviors.

This case example illustrates an integrated multidimensional intervention protocol organized within the SUM framework. If not already addressed by strategies targeting specific domains, the final case-planning step would explore symptom- or disorder-specific evidence-based strategies. In this case, treatments for anxiety and school refusal would be examined to see if they would point to incorporating additional intervention strategies.

APPLICATION OF DIFFERENTIATED EVIDENCE-BASED INTERVENTIONS

One of the final steps within the SUM case conceptualization framework is investigation of the empirically supported intervention strategies specific to the symptom profile or diagnosed psychological disorder that has been assessed through this process. The SUM involves a synthesis of core CBT and systemic strategies that are appropriate for the full range of child and adolescent problems. However, therapy research is emerging that delineates specific strategies to address different clinical presentations. It is necessary to incorporate these differentiated protocols into the intervention plan. For example, there are some research-supported strategies specific to the treatment of mood disorders that might be different in focus and implementation from those proven to be beneficial for a child presenting on the autism spectrum. Part II of this book summarizes these differentiated intervention regimens in detail.

Therapy with children and adolescents involves both art and science. Using empirically supported intervention approaches in the school setting requires essential fidelity to proven techniques while recognizing the need for individualization and creative adaptations. Assessment data are used to define the need for therapy, record baseline functioning, set treatment goals, and arrive at exit criteria. This same data-driven approach is involved in progress monitoring and outcome evaluation. The delineation of goals and needs defines the parameters for investigation and selection of the appropriate EBI strategies. As EBI strategies are incorporated into therapy, it is necessary to monitor the integrity of treatment implementation to ensure that it is consistent with case conceptualization and empirically supported protocols. Research into effective child and adolescent therapies remains a work in progress. Even within successful controlled studies with detailed treatment manuals, not all children benefit. Adding in the complexity of the school and community setting adds additional challenges.

Kendall (2012c) suggested that EBIs should be implemented with "fidelity and flexibility." From this perspective, empirically supported protocols for specific disorders are structured guides for organizing the focus, sequence, and application of treatments. Clinical sensitivity to the personalization of therapeutic activity to the individual child, adolescent, family, or school setting remains essential. However, adaptations remain guided by general empirically supported frameworks such as those incorporated into the SUM. Routine progress monitoring informs the need for individualization and modification of treatment approaches. Ongoing data collection evaluates the impact of modifications to the protocol. In some cases, treatment is individualized by selecting relevant modules from overarching comprehensive treatment protocols. Chorpita (2007) delineated the necessity of evaluating individual skill sets and intervention needs for children even if their symptoms as a whole fall into a clear diagnostic profile. He divided his treatment protocol for children with anxiety into modules targeting various clinical needs. For example, although almost all children with anxiety will require some form of exposure treatment, not everyone will require training in social initiation skills. So core principles of empirically supported protocols are maintained, but there can be individual differences in intervention selection and application. Careful initial assessment and continuous progress monitoring informs treatment targets, progression, and any required midcourse modifications.

PUTTING IT ALL TOGETHER

Figure 3.1 provides a visual presentation of the dynamic interactions of the components of the SUM case conceptualization model delineated in this example. Each element is addressed in assessment and intervention planning

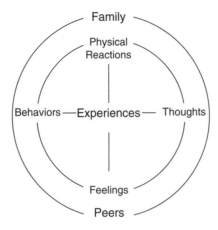

Figure 3.1. Case conceptualization.

both individually and in relation to other dimensions. The Appendix presents a case conceptualization flow chart that therapists can use as a guide to systematically address all domains highlighted within the SUM. It provides a sequential approach that moves from assessment to intervention to progress monitoring and outcome assessment. The resulting intervention protocol integrates empirically supported CBT and systemic strategies into a comprehensive intervention plan.

Throughout the case conceptualization process it is important to address individual and contextual resources and barriers to change. Therapists must identify strengths within the student, the family, and in school relationships. It is essential to support key caregivers at home and school and promote development of their interpersonal and problem-solving skill sets. Individual symptom patterns are often cemented through repetition and overlearning. Negative interaction cycles within families and classrooms can become entrenched and resistant to change. Motivational interviewing strategies can be helpful in responding to resistance to change (W. R. Miller & Rollnick, 2012; Naar-King & Suarez, 2011). Rather than fighting oppositional behaviors, this therapeutic stance focuses on empathic responding, recognizes the power of constraints to change, emphasizes choices, and juxtaposes the consequences of inaction versus the risks of change.

Although the goal is to make therapeutic interventions as brief and parsimonious as possible, it is important to remain patient and maintain realistic time frames. Distinct advantages of school-centered treatments include the opportunity for phased treatments, periodic booster sessions, on-site crisis intervention, adjustments at key developmental transitions, and readily available consultation with teachers.

The SUM case conceptualization model provides a comprehensive framework for linking assessment to intervention to outcome. Its foundation is an integrated approach toward understanding human experience. The model guides assessment and treatment planning in the construction of an integrative multidimensional intervention protocol that addresses the individual student and relevant contextual influences. It provides a structure for the application of empirically supported interventions within school-centered therapy.

II

THERAPEUTIC INTERVENTIONS FOR SPECIFIC CHILD AND ADOLESCENT PSYCHOLOGICAL DISORDERS

4

ATTENTION-DEFICIT/ HYPERACTIVITY DISORDER

Attention-deficit/hyperactivity disorder (ADHD) is a relatively high-incidence disorder that can result in significant academic, behavioral, and social difficulties in the school setting. ADHD is one of the more thoroughly researched childhood disorders, yet our understanding of its core features continues to evolve. Substantial research exists to guide intervention strategies, but new targets, such as executive functioning skills, continue to emerge. Treatments for ADHD are multidimensional, involve collaterals such as parents and teachers as central intervention participants, require specific supports for academic progress, and use behavioral strategies to manage the interaction between environmental and individual factors. Defined as a developmental disorder, ADHD is one of the few disorders in which treatments first emerged for children and then were later extended to adults. Particular attention in this chapter is given to instructional supports, classroom management, and parent

http://dx.doi.org/10.1037/14779-005
School-Centered Interventions: Evidence-Based Strategies for Social, Emotional, and Academic Success,
by D. J. Simon

training strategies. Home–school collaboration and coordinated intervention plans are central to evidence-based interventions (EBIs) for ADHD.

DIAGNOSTIC CHARACTERISTICS AND ASSESSMENT FRAMEWORKS

The classic triad of ADHD symptoms described in the *Diagnostic and Statistical Manual of Mental Disorders* (fourth ed., text rev.; *DSM–IV–TR*; American Psychiatric Association, 2000) and *DSM–5* (fifth ed.; American Psychiatric Association, 2013) are inattention, hyperactivity, and impulsivity. As Barkley (2006) summarized, factor analytic studies of behavior ratings have demonstrated a strong association between impulsivity and hyperactivity. The *DSM–5* delineates symptoms under two clusters: inattention and hyperactivity/impulsivity. The *International Classification of Diseases, Tenth Revision, Clinical Modification* (ICD–10–CM) diagnostic codes parallel the *DSM*: ADHD, predominantly inattentive type (F90.0); ADHD predominantly hyperactive type (F90.1); and ADHD, combined type (F90.2; Goodheart, 2014).

Inattention

Inattention has come to be viewed as a multidimensional construct. In the neuropsychological literature *attention* refers to alertness and arousal, the ability to focus on a task, sustain attention, and not be easily distracted by competing stimuli (Smith, Barkley, & Shapiro, 2007). Children struggling to maintain attention often display trouble with *vigilance*, the ability to persist with sufficient focus for extended periods of time. Vigilance is evident not only in academic work but also during many play activities in which inattentive children tend to make more rapid shifts in activities. Sustained attention is particularly compromised during low-interest tasks or those that present limited immediate positive consequences for completion. Thus, if a student finishes an assignment that merely permits him or her to move on to the next academic task, sustaining attention may be more difficult than when successful assignment completion results in permission to go to recess. The *DSM–5* presents a lengthy list of nine inattention symptoms with specific examples that in many cases directly apply to schoolwork such as the following: misses details, has difficulty with focus during lectures, is disorganized, struggles with sustained effort in schoolwork, loses school materials, or is easily distracted.

Hyperactivity–Impulsivity

Hyperactivity refers to excessive activity levels and a general motoric restlessness. Excessive fidgeting, a high need for stimulation, and even sensation seeking are common. The *DSM–5* symptom list describes this characteristic as always being "on the go" as if "driven by a motor" and often struggling to sit still and remain seated even when required, as is generally expected within a classroom. Although the external physical signs of hyperactivity may subside somewhat as the child moves into adolescence, teens with ADHD continue to report restless feelings and thoughts (Barkley, 2013b; Smith et al., 2007).

Impulsivity symptoms manifest in multiple ways. They involve the tendency to act quickly without planning ahead or processing the potential consequences of actions. Children who struggle with impulse control display a limited capacity to inhibit behavioral responses. Struggling to delay gratification, they respond to immediate rewards but have difficulty engaging in behaviors or tasks that require waiting for more temporally distant reinforcers. Following multiple-step directions and adhering to rules and prescribed procedures are challenging. Barkley (2006, 2013b) described this characteristic as difficulty with *rule-governed behavior*. Quickly drawn to other appealing stimuli, these children exhibit significant off-task behavior in school and struggle to follow instructions and directions. Once an impulsive action is initiated, they have a difficult time interrupting the behavior. Difficulty inhibiting responses can lead to interrupting others' activities, blurting out answers, or being socially intrusive. The need for immediate gratification coupled with limited recognition of the impact of personal actions on others can compromise friendships and result in social difficulties.

Contemporary Focus on Behavioral Disinhibition and Executive Functioning

Barkley (2006) labeled the central dimension of impulsivity as *behavioral disinhibition*. He defined the core feature of ADHD as difficulty in self-regulation. Youth with ADHD struggle to regulate their behavioral and emotional responses. They tend to emit their first powerful response to an event demonstrating reduced ability to delay initial actions or to interrupt and pull back from an impulsive response. Attention and response patterns react to the strongest stimulus and the most immediate reinforcers. Barkley (2013b) suggested that a key contributing factor to disinhibition is insufficient internalization of self-directed-behavior. Children with ADHD demonstrate a limited capacity to use self-talk or imagery to delay, guide, or manage behavioral responses (Barkley, 2006). Although generally covert, self-directed speech serves a function of guiding and regulating behavior. In early stages of development spoken self-talk may guide behavioral planning and task management, eventually transitioning to subvocal self-directing language. Children with ADHD have been shown to demonstrate less mature self-talk and delayed progression from aloud to covert (Barkley, 2006). Impulsive acting before planning or thinking through a response creates many of the difficulties that students with ADHD experience.

Inattention commonly occurs across a wide range of disorders (Barkley, 2006). Despite being a core symptom of ADHD, it may not be the best discriminating symptom for differential diagnosis. Barkley (2006) reviewed discriminant-function analysis studies to support his assertion that impulsivity, specifically behavioral disinhibition, is the hallmark characteristic that differentiates ADHD from other disorders that present with inattention as a significant symptom. There is a parallel here to the role the symptom of irritability plays in pediatric bipolar disorder. It is a dominant feature of the illness, but because it is also present in several other externalizing disorders, it alone is not sufficient for differential diagnosis.

A significant amount of contemporary research regarding ADHD has focused on the role of executive functioning deficits. As the term implies, executive functioning skills serve regulatory and control functions for behavior. Children with ADHD display deficits in organization, planning, and follow-through skills. Both verbal and nonverbal working memory deficits are evident. This can result in difficulties with some multistep problems. Affected students may struggle to hold information in their heads and then use it for another step in a problem later. These difficulties have a direct impact on academic performance. Students with ADHD may struggle with following directions, applying necessary sequencing strategies when problem solving, seeing how the parts relate to the whole, and following through to task completion. Keeping track of assignment responsibilities and organizing approaches to schoolwork completion are frequent challenges. Difficulties with regulation of emotions and arousal are also evident. The executive self-regulation skills that recognize and manage emotions and support sustained motivation and goal-directed behavior are often insufficient to manage emotional stress. As a consequence, inhibiting impulsive behavioral responses and sustaining motivation and attention to task when faced with stress or appealing alternative activities can be compromised.

Barkley (2006) proposed that four central areas of executive functioning can directly impact behavioral disinhibition and motor control: nonverbal working memory, internalization of speech or verbal working memory, self-regulation of affect and arousal, and reconstitution (i.e., the analysis and synthesis of behavior that supports planning and generation of creative and flexible responses to new challenges). These components interact to impair executive control of behavior. Limitations in using hindsight and foresight, engaging in self-directed rule-governed responses, regulating affect and motivation, and analyzing new strategies converge to impair the capacity to inhibit impulsive behavioral responses and to sustain motivation and goal-directed behavior.

Predominantly Inattentive Presentation

The *DSM-5* continues to specify distinctions among combined, predominantly hyperactive–impulsive, and predominantly inattentive presentations of ADHD. Lacking the disruptive hyperactive–impulsive characteristics, the inattentive presentation still has direct negative consequences for academic learning. However, students with this profile may be slower to be identified because they are less likely to demonstrate acting out behaviors that can complicate instruction for an entire classroom. Milich, Balentine, and Lynam (2001) argued that the inattentive type should be considered a distinct disorder. Their extensive literature review highlighted characteristics for the inattentive type that have often been termed *sluggish cognitive tempo* (SCT). In contrast to the hyperactive profile, these children exhibit hypoactivity, passivity, sluggish or slow-moving response styles, excessive daydreaming, or an "in-a-fog" inattentiveness. The character of their inattention may be less impacted by external distractions. There is some indication that they may be more prone to internalizing rather than the externalizing comorbidities. Smith et al. (2007) suggested that ADHD predominantly inattentive type as currently conceived is a heterogeneous disorder, with some children merely falling slightly below *DSM* diagnostic threshold levels for the combined type with hyperactivity–impulsivity and others falling into the SCT category with a distinct profile. Barkley (2013b) noted that students with an SCT profile are likely to be quiet while working but neither fully focused on the task at hand nor productively attentive. Students displaying combined hyperactive–impulsive and inattentive symptoms are the ones commonly referred for therapeutic intervention. Although noting the significant needs of students with primarily inattentive characteristics, our treatment of ADHD focuses on the combined symptom profile most likely to exhibit externalizing behaviors.

Assessment

An accurate and comprehensive assessment of ADHD requires a multidimensional approach that obtains data from multiple sources using a range of methods.

Family–Social-Developmental History

A family–social-developmental history is important to assess potential heredity factors, relevant medical history, the course of symptom manifestation, environmental moderators, developmental events that might explain or influence symptoms, prior attempts at addressing problems, and resources for implementing intervention strategies. Substantial evidence exists for the impact of heredity on ADHD (Biederman, Faraone, Keenan, Knee, &

Tsuang, 1990; Faraone, 2000). Estimates of occurrence in children with parents with ADHD range from 40% to 57% (Smith et al., 2007).

Classroom Observations

ADHD can significantly impair educational functioning. Systematic classroom observations contribute critical information to the assessment process. Observations should occur at varying times of the day, across academic subjects, and across teachers. Targeted data collection can be guided by teacher referral concerns and a focus on key discriminating ADHD symptoms. Collecting comparison data on classmates sheds light on potential behavioral disparities and provides some adjustment for classroom structure and instructional variables. Although the focus is on the at-risk student's functioning, it is important to note any changes in symptom manifestation across learning environments.

Functional Behavioral Assessment

A *functional behavioral assessment* (FBA; Steege & Watson, 2009) assists in defining the functions of behaviors, analyzing setting factors, and delineating antecedents and consequences that influence and maintain behaviors. Because contingency management is a central intervention strategy for ADHD, FBA data serve a major pillar for the foundation for intervention planning. It is important to conduct an FBA for both home and school settings. Behavioral and attentional requirements may vary across settings and influence symptom display and intensity.

Behavior Rating Scales and Assessment of Comorbidities

Behavior rating scales completed by teachers and parents are a staple of ADHD assessment. Broadband rating scales like the Achenbach System of Empirically Based Assessment (ASEBA) scales (Achenbach & Rescorla, 2001) and the Behavior Assessment System for Children—Second Edition (BASC–2; C. R. Reynolds & Kamphaus, 2004) collect data specifically relevant to ADHD but also assess a wide range of externalizing and internalizing disorders and symptom patterns. These instruments provide an overview of psychological functioning and identify possible confounding or comorbid factors. Because other disorders may result in significant attentional difficulties, it is important to initially assess with a broad lens rather than merely zeroing in on ADHD symptoms. This step also contributes to ruling in or out potential comorbid conditions. Youth self-report measures have generally not been shown to add sufficient incremental data for the assessment of ADHD, but self-report data related to broad areas of behavioral functioning can prove useful (Smith et al., 2007).

Although estimates vary, comorbidity is more the norm than the exception (Kadesjö & Gillberg, 2001). Smith et al. (2007) asserted that 80% of children with ADHD have a secondary disorder and 60% have more than two or more comorbid disorders. On the basis of parent-reported data from the National Survey of Children's Health, 67% of children with ADHD experienced other disorders, and 46% of children with ADHD also were diagnosed with learning disabilities (K. Larson, Russ, Kahn, & Halfon, 2011). Co-occurring externalizing disorders, particularly conduct disorder and oppositional defiant disorder, have been reported as most common (Barkley, 2006; Pelham, Fabiano, & Massetti, 2005; Pliszka, 2015). However, anxiety disorders are also frequently comorbid, so it is necessary to explore the full range of possible comorbidities (March et al., 2000). Treatment planning needs to focus on the functional impairments emanating from the full assessment profile and may need to address a broad range of symptoms (Barkley, 2006; Pelham & Fabiano, 2001).

As symptom patterns suggestive of ADHD emerge from broadband assessment data, ADHD-specific rating scales are administered. Frequently used instruments include the Conners-3 (Conners, 2008) and the AD/HD Rating Scale–IV (DuPaul, Power, Anastopoulos, & Reid, 1998). These instruments have both parent and teacher rating scales. Although *DSM–5* requires symptoms to be present across at least two settings, it is necessary to assess the differences in setting demands. In some cases, the academic and behavioral demands within the school setting may exacerbate symptoms. When reviewing rating scale results, it is important to assist parents in understanding the environmental demands that are likely to worsen or lessen ADHD symptoms.

Semistructured Interviews

Semistructured clinical interviews provide an opportunity to collect a broad range of data about behavioral functioning, patterns of strengths and weaknesses, antecedents and consequences for behavioral difficulties, potential motivators for change, and occurrence and presentation of ADHD symptoms. The Semistructured Clinical Interview for Children and Adolescents (McConaughy & Achenbach, 2001) is specifically related to the ASEBA rating scales (Achenbach & Rescorla, 2001) and provides an excellent framework for interviewing children and adolescents. McConaughy (2013) developed companion semistructured parent and teacher interviews, which not only cover overall functioning but also can include a specific section targeting assessment of *DSM* ADHD symptoms. The data from these interviews directly contribute to the development of a hypothesis of the function of behavior (i.e., FBA) and subsequent intervention planning. Smith et al. (2007) developed the ADHD Checkup based on the structure and principles of Dishion and

Kavanaugh's (2003) Family Checkup. Its unique contribution is its direct incorporation of W. R. Miller and Rollnick's (2012) motivational interviewing strategies to enhance parental commitment to an intervention program. Although it might not be necessary at this point because of the robust data already collected, the National Institute of Mental Health (NIMH) Diagnostic Interview Schedule for Children Version IV (Shaffer, Fisher, Lucas, Dulcan, & Schwab-Stone, 2000) is an empirically supported structured interview that can directly assess *DSM* symptoms of ADHD.

Executive Functioning Measures

The emerging focus on the role of executive function deficits in ADHD has led to the inclusion of measures targeting this area in ADHD assessment. Some measures focus on observable impairments that result from these deficits (i.e., difficulties in planning, organization, follow-through, etc.). Commonly used instruments include the Behavioral Rating Inventory of Executive Functioning (BRIEF; Gioia, Isquith, Guy, & Kenworthy, 2000) and the recently published Barkley Deficits in Executive Functioning Scale—Children and Adolescents (BDEFS–CA; Barkley, 2012). The BRIEF has rating forms for parents and teachers, whereas the BDEFS–CA only surveys parents. Because they collect data regarding the daily interference of executive functioning deficits, these measures have ecological validity and directly relate to intervention targets.

In contrast, neuropsychological instruments directly assess the child's functions on tasks related to executive functions. The Delis-Kaplan Executive Function System (Delis, Kaplan, & Kramer, 2001) measures factors such as cognitive flexibility, planning, and impulse control. One domain of the broader NEPSY–II (Korkman, Kirk, & Kemp, 2007) contains a series of subtests that assess attention and executive function skills. Subtests targeting executive functioning are designed to measure factors such as inhibition of learned and automatic responses, self-regulation, vigilance, the capacity to establish and maintain response sets, and cognitive flexibility. Neuropsychological measures may enhance diagnostic clarity in the area of executive functioning. However, Pelham et al. (2005) and Barkley (2006) asserted that impairment measures based on observation of daily life tasks present "real-life" advantages and a more direct link between assessment and intervention.

Computer-administered continuous performance tests (CPT), such as the Conners CPT–3 (Conners, 2014), have been widely used measures of sustained attention, vigilance, and impulsivity. Summary reviews suggest that CPT instruments can assess ADHD characteristics but have been found more reliable at determining group rather than individual differences, may produce too many false negatives, and do not necessarily add enough to discriminant validity to be standard elements in an ADHD assessment protocol

(DuPaul & Stoner, 2014; Smith et al., 2007; Tobin, Schneider, Reck, & Landau, 2008).

Eligibility for Specialized School Services

A diagnosis of ADHD indicates interference with learning, a major life function noted in Section 504 of the Rehabilitation Act of 1973. Thus, students with a disability, in this case ADHD, qualify for supports to ensure that they receive reasonable accommodations to fully participate in public education similar to their peers. Families and schools work together to develop a 504 Plan to outline what supports are required based on the student's individual needs. For students with ADHD, sample supports may include organizational aides, alterations to assignments, and changes in evaluation and test-taking formats and schedules. Students do not need to be designated as eligible for special education services to receive the supports inherent in a 504 Plan.

If there is substantial interference with learning because of the psychological disability of ADHD, a student may qualify for formal special education services and an individualized education plan (IEP) governed by the Individuals With Disabilities in Education Act. Special education services provide more detailed and expansive interventions and services and may include supports or instructional placements in some special education classes with specially trained teachers and therapeutic supports incorporated. Students with ADHD often receive services through the eligibility characteristic of Other Health Impaired (OHI), which contains descriptors specific to some common ADHD symptoms. However, since these students commonly experience significant comorbid conditions, they may be served under an Emotional Disability (ED). The most common circumstance for ED eligibility would be if there are substantial externalizing behaviors consistent with a Conduct Disorder or Oppositional Defiant Disorder occurring along with ADHD symptoms. Within special education, a student can be designated as eligible under more than one category. It has been my experience that preferred patterns for designating eligibility under Individuals With Disabilities in Education Act for students with ADHD vary significantly from one district to the next. The assessment process outlined earlier in this chapter provides a comprehensive and sufficient framework for providing an ADHD diagnosis and for determining eligibility, needs, and goals for both 504 Plans and IEPs. The FBA process recommended above is a key component in preparation of behavior intervention plans (BIP) built into IEPs. As the assessment of ADHD characteristics defines needs and impairments, a direct link from assessment to intervention is established. IEP goals can then focus on impairments in behavior and learning in ways that can be operationalized and measured.

DEVELOPMENTAL CONSIDERATIONS FOR ASSESSMENT AND INTERVENTION

Estimates of the prevalence of ADHD generally fall in the range of 5% to 7% of the population (Roberts, Milich, & Barkley, 2015). The *DSM–5* projects an incidence at 5%. Gender differences are significant, with boys outnumbering girls at a ratio of 6:1 in clinic samples and 3:1 in community-based samples (DuPaul & Stoner, 2014). It is likely that the higher incidence of disruptive behaviors in males would contribute to the higher level of treatment referrals. Less data are available on females with ADHD. A summary of the extant literature suggests that females with ADHD exhibit similar symptom presentations but with lower levels of aggression and less likelihood of comorbid conduct disorder or oppositional defiant disorder (Barkley, 2006). However, their levels of physical and relational aggression tend to be higher than those of their female peers and impair development of positive peer relationships (Zalecki & Hinshaw, 2004).

As a neurobehavioral disorder, ADHD symptoms can be evident in early childhood. Their emergence may be moderated by setting demands, familial structures, and other environmental factors. Because a great deal of variability exists in the pace of development across all domains—particularly in very young children—it can be challenging to identify symptoms in preschool-age children. Many young children display high activity levels, difficulties with sustaining attention, and disinhibited behaviors. Reasonable caution should be applied to ruling out immaturity or the impact of interfering developmental events such as medical concerns or stressful familial events when determining whether ADHD symptoms are emerging. However, for the majority of children later identified, caregivers report deviations from typical functioning beginning as early as ages 3 to 4 (Smith, Barkley, & Shapiro, 2006). Managing excessively active and impulsive behaviors is typically identified very early as a concern.

For other children, identifying symptoms are not clearly evident until students are required to respond to the attentional and behavioral demands required in school activities where expectations to delay responses and gratification, remain seated, and persist with tasks dramatically accelerate. The *DSM–5* changed the criteria for age of onset from before age 7 to before age 12. Excessive difficulties may emerge when there is less structure, such as during transitions from one class or activity to the next; during group interactions, particularly when required to engage in turn taking; when frustrated; or when sitting still for lengthy periods. Difficulties in these areas further complicate the acquisition of emotional and behavioral self-regulation skills. If these behaviors persist and exacerbate during early elementary school years, these children will begin to require increasingly extensive external controls for managing behavior and frustrations. Opposition may emerge as well as aggressive responses when thwarted or frustrated. Sensation- and stimulus-seeking actions may increase.

As children move toward adolescence, motoric restlessness and overt hyperactivity may decline (Hart, Lahey, Loeber, Applegate, & Frick, 1995; Smith et al., 2006), but difficulties with behavioral disinhibition, sustaining attention, organization, and planning persist. In some cases, risk taking may escalate to more dangerous situations. Particularly if ADHD symptoms remain untreated, behaviors associated with conduct disorder and oppositional defiant disorder, including heightened aggression, may emerge. Delinquency and substance abuse risks escalate. As a group, adolescents with ADHD experience more accidental injuries (M. Miller & Hinshaw, 2012). Family conflicts can intensify in adolescence when troubles with rule-governed behavior, failure to responsibly meet school and home responsibilities, and inadequate problem-solving skills converge with developmentally expected wishes for increased independence and individuation (Barkley, Anastopoulos, Guevremont, & Fletcher, 1992; Robin, 1998). The number of observed symptoms required to qualify for a *DSM–5* ADHD diagnosis is reduced for adolescents; however, evaluations of impairments because of ADHD symptoms and assessment of the presence of complicating comorbidities take on even heightened importance.

Although a diagnosis of ADHD requires childhood onset, in most cases the impact of ADHD persists into adulthood. Even if social and emotional regulation concerns lessen, executive functioning deficits can compromise employment and career activities. (See Barkley, Murphy, & Fischer, 2008, for a summary of the current literature on adult manifestation.)

This brief review of the developmental progression underlines the importance of early assessment and intervention. Even if the etiology of ADHD is biological, the course of its symptoms and the severity of their presentation are affected by environmental factors. Although sometimes a patient "wait-and-see" approach may be warranted to avoid false-positive identifications of very young children and premature medical interventions, in most cases immediate behavioral interventions are warranted to address emerging symptoms. Evaluating response to interventions may assist diagnostic clarity, and this proactive approach may serve to modify the potentially negative impact of ADHD as school demands for skills in affected areas are magnified.

CHILD- AND ADOLESCENT-SPECIFIC THERAPEUTIC INTERVENTION STRATEGIES

Multimodal Treatment: Evidence-Based Intervention Framework for ADHD

Although still evolving, an extensive research base has developed regarding the treatment of ADHD. A combination of medication and behavioral treatments has emerged as a core intervention strategy (Barkley, 2006; M. Miller & Hinshaw, 2012; Pelham & Fabiano, 2008). The National Institute of Mental Health Multimodal Treatment of Attention-Deficit Hyperactivity Disorder Study (MTA) was one of the largest multisite treatment studies of a childhood disorder ever attempted, and its various findings remain historically important (MTA Cooperative Group, 1999a, 1999b). Over time, the data have been subject to extensive additional analysis and follow-up study (Conners et al., 2001; Jensen et al., 2001, 2007; MTA Cooperative Group, 2004; Swanson et al., 2001). These studies clarified the positive effects of medication and behavioral interventions. There is no question that for many children medication can have a significant positive impact on ADHD symptoms. Combined medication and behavioral treatments have demonstrated the strongest positive impact on ADHD symptoms (Barkley, 2006; Conners et al., 2001; Swanson et al., 2001). With relatively conservative definitions of successful outcome, Swanson et al. (2001) found that 68% of those receiving combined medication and behavioral treatments demonstrated significant improvement. It is important to note that parental satisfaction with treatment was stronger for the combined intervention and behavioral treatment-only groups than for the medication-only group (MTA Cooperative Group, 1999a). Given the chronic course of ADHD and the importance of sustaining a long-term treatment regimen, parental support and commitment are essential to long-term improvement.

Behavioral Interventions

Behavioral interventions for ADHD have focused on parent and teacher training in behavior management, particularly the application of environmental structuring and contingency management; behavioral and instructional supports in the classroom; and social, coping, and problem-solving skills training in the natural setting requiring these skills (Barkley, 2006, 2013b; M. Miller & Hinshaw, 2012; Pelham & Fabiano, 2008; Smith et al., 2006). Unlike therapeutic treatments for many other conditions, interventions for ADHD focus primarily on systemic–ecological interventions with only limited individual therapy with the child. Challenged by behavioral disinhibition and limited self-regulation skills, the child with ADHD requires extensive external supports and structure to set the foundation for acquiring improved self-management skills. The focus of behavioral interventions is not merely on ADHD symptom reduction but on observable improvement in performance in areas of impairment delineated during the assessment process that impact behavior at home and school and academic progress within the classroom.

Interventions at Point of Performance

Intervention strategies are effective and more likely to be maintained and generalize across settings when they occur at the point of performance, as close as possible to the natural setting. Orientation to interventions, communication of strategies and expectations, and behavioral rehearsal may occur in individual sessions, but intervention implementation, monitoring, support, and direct coaching are designed to occur at home, in the classroom, in extracurricular settings, and in community activities. To be effective, interventions need to be linked to contingency management based on principles of operant conditioning (M. Miller & Hinshaw, 2012). Isolated pull-out groups in clinics and schools for teaching social skills have not proven effective with this population (Pelham & Fabiano, 2008). However, programs that integrate social, coping, and problem-solving skills instruction and actively reinforce adaptive behaviors have proven successful (M. Miller & Hinshaw, 2012; Pelham et al., 2010). Students with ADHD require extra scaffolding and support to apply skills within natural environments.

Behavior Management Principles

Children with ADHD require intensified structure, predictability, and external supports across all critical life domains. Because these children lack the internal management skills necessary to adequately process information and regulate behavioral and emotional responses, parents and teachers must externally engineer environmental conditions and externalize relevant information regarding rules, procedures, and expectations (Barkley, 2006). These children are more successful in environments that are highly structured and well supervised, with more frequent prompts and feedback for appropriate performance. Because they struggle with rule-governed behavior, they benefit when (a) expectations are reviewed before activities begin, (b) behavioral prompts are provided while performing tasks, (c) rules and directions are posted, (d) reminders are presented for potential earned reinforcers, and (e) differential positive or negative reinforcement for behaviors is administered.

Pfiffner, Barkley, and DuPaul (2006) and Barkley (2013a, 2013b) have provided excellent summaries of behavior management principles for both school and home settings. The behavior management focus for teachers and parents must be proactive in anticipation of potentially challenging circumstances. Contingency management methods that manipulate antecedents and use both positive reinforcement and response cost consequences are required. Limit setting is important for students who struggle to exert internal controls. However, response cost is not designed to be overly punitive but to use loss of points or tokens within contingency contracts, brief time-outs that remove social reinforcers, or loss of privileges. Within behavior management point systems, the opportunity to earn back lost points by accepting correction and redirection and then readily demonstrating appropriate alternative behaviors can turn disciplinary moments into learning opportunities (Hensley, Powell, Lamke, & Hartman, 2005).

Powerful reinforcers easily linked to emitted behaviors are necessary to focus attention and motivate efforts for children with ADHD. This population can quickly become satiated with specific reinforcers; thus, frequent changes in reinforcers are often necessary. Conducting a preference assessment with the child can create a menu of potential reinforcers. Shaping and contingency management programs are initiated with continuous reinforcement schedules. Contingency contracts may present long-term incentives but must begin with short-term reinforcers. The application of reinforcers needs to be immediate and strong. Aversive reinforcers need to be timely and salient as well. Positive reinforcers should be emphasized over punishers, but limit setting and establishing healthy boundaries are essential. Goal setting for earning rewards and privileges provides a framework for applying point or token systems that can facilitate immediate reinforcement in any environment, monitor progress, and motivate with powerful incentives. Either failure to earn points or loss of points (response cost) can serve as a consequence and influence reduction of behavior.

Home–School Contingency Contracts

Coordinated home and school contingency contracts are effective mechanisms for behavioral improvement for children with ADHD. These instruments provide many benefits to support treatment goals. Teachers and parents share clearly defined goals and similar instructional and behavioral management strategies. This collaboration not only enhances intervention consistency for the child but also provides mutual adult support necessary for persistence in sustaining the extensive external supports required for these students. Parents have a larger repertoire of motivators and incentives that they can offer to encourage behavioral improvement and thus to support school efforts. Contingency contracts also serve to shape adult behaviors. They provide a structure and set of procedures based on sound behavioral change principles. When exasperated or fatigued by behavioral management challenges, teachers and parents can stick to a positive plan and avoid counterproductive overreaction to misbehaviors.

Externalization of information, rules, and feedback is necessary. Points or tokens used in monitoring contingency contracts can serve this purpose. For younger children, physical tokens may prove helpful. Point systems can be effective through adolescence as well. In this case, point out similarities to grades, performance monitoring during employment, and statistical monitoring of athletic performance can support teen motivation. Maintaining visual charts or point sheets that explicitly include personal goals and incentives that can be earned documents progress and motivates students. The use of points or tokens enables teachers to provide immediate reinforcers while continuing to teach class and helps parents to provide immediate reinforcers in the context of multiple family and other child-rearing responsibilities. In this way, reinforcers are delivered at the point of performance in the setting when and where adaptive behaviors are required. A common methodology creates ease in coordinating home and school plans. Daily report cards are a mechanism commonly used to summarize and communicate behavior progress at school (Volpe & Fabiano, 2013). To underscore mutual support, in daily report cards teachers can summarize progress in home and school settings, enhancing two-way communication and full-day plan implementation.

Points or tokens are only useful if connected to meaningful salient reinforcers. Involving children in selecting and negotiating reinforcers increases the likelihood that they will be sufficient for enhancing motivation. Because satiation with singular reinforcers is common, working with students to develop a menu of reinforcers can provide variety essential to sustain effort. Younger children may prefer smaller immediately accessible rewards over larger delayed rewards. For all ages, a menu of immediate, intermediate, and long-term incentives contributes to sustained motivation and behavioral improvement.

The FBA developed for both home and school settings delineates secondary gains that support and maintain problematic behaviors. When the function of problematic behaviors appears to be attention seeking or social recognition, it is important to turn the tables so that the desired alternative behavior serves the same function. For example, attention-seeking behavior can be redirected by a plan that enables a student to earn special time with a favored teacher by resisting disruptive behavior. Similarly, designing rewards that result in special activities with parents requires the child to demonstrate appropriate behaviors to earn parental attention. It is necessary to reduce the attention given to inappropriate attention seeking while reinforcing appropriate behaviors. Verbal redirections and prompts should be brief, and points should be given or removed swiftly and in a matter-of-fact way without continued warnings or engaging in lengthy negotiations. Lectures are counterproductive and may be subtly reinforcing of negative behaviors. As soon as possible, defocusing from the interaction with the child and instead returning later to provide brief verbal recognition when the child is behaving appropriately works to extinguish inappropriate attention seeking and is more effective. Initial implementation of practices designed to switch the outcome of attention-seeking behaviors may at first lead to an exacerbation of inappropriate behaviors, what has often been termed an *extinction burst* (Steege & Watson, 2009). Persistently waiting out this storm, using brief time-out procedures if necessary, is a critical step in engaging the child in pursuit of appropriate social activities and contingency contract goals.

The focus of intervention plans is not merely to stop problematic behaviors but also to teach and reinforce adaptive replacement behaviors. For example, efforts to reduce inappropriate talking out during class instruction should be coupled with teaching and reinforcing appropriately raising one's hand and waiting to be recognized before asking questions or contributing on task comments. Targets for replacement behaviors should be carefully chosen and aim to reduce impairments. It is better to reinforce accurate completion of work products than merely time on task in school or time working on homework. The goal is not to just quietly put in time but also to learn to appropriately focus on academic tasks and increase production and skills. Similarly, children who attempt to get their way through temper outbursts need to be taught not merely to hold in frustration but also to appropriately communicate needs and wants and use specific problem-solving skills as alternative adaptive behaviors.

Clear contingency reinforcement systems also serve to promote the acquisition of consequential thinking skills. Children with ADHD often act impulsively, without thinking about the impact of their behavior on others or personal consequences. Delineating choices in advance or processing them afterward can be framed in an "if ____, then ____" format. Then, when coupled with differential reinforcement, they can be coached toward learning to anticipate the consequences of their actions.

The eventual goal of contingency management procedures is to shift from external to self-monitoring of behavior. When behavior reinforcement plans are effective, earning both verbal and tangible reinforcers builds self-efficacy. To support self-regulation, it is important that parent and teacher language specifically state that the child is earning either positive or negative consequences because of her or his behaviors. Communication must be clear that points or rewards are neither gained nor lost by arbitrary adult decisions but instead straightforwardly reflect the actions of the child who earns consequences. Contingency contracts must clearly describe behavior and consequence connections to ensure that this approach is not merely a play on words. Although the goal of operant conditioning programs always entails eventual fading of adult-monitored external reinforcers, children with ADHD may be dependent on external supports longer than youth with other externalizing disorders.

ADHD is a chronic condition that requires long-term management. Children with ADHD do not tend to respond well to intermittent reinforcement plans. Therapists need to continuously evaluate the youth's growth in capacity to self-regulate. Demonstration of task-specific progress in self-monitoring, self-instruction, and self-reinforcement can be built directly into intervention plans. Children who grow tired of contingency plans and are exhibiting significant progress may be motivated to demonstrate more self-monitored behavior. Independent self-regulation should be increased gradually. As adolescents increase their self-awareness of what is required to manage their ADHD symptoms, specific planning and practice should prepare them for postsecondary education or employment where increasingly independent functioning is required.

Reinforcing the Reinforcers

After the therapist has assisted parents and teachers in designing and implementing contingency management plans, therapeutic intervention work centers on monitoring progress, adjusting intervention plans as necessary, and directly supporting not only the student but also the parents and teachers, who are the primary behavior plan implementers. Sustaining fidelity to plan implementation in the face of occasional setbacks can be tiring and at times discouraging for parents and teachers serving as contingency managers. Achieving consistency in supporting behavior change requires persistent effort, repetitive instruction, and confidence that in the end goals will be successfully achieved. Progress seldom occurs in a straight upward line. When adults have seen a child with ADHD successfully demonstrate some behavior improvement and then temporarily backslide, the temptation emerges to judge the misbehavior as more willful and more easily controlled by the child than is realistic. Point-system fatigue can emerge as adults long for the child to accelerate growth toward improved self-regulation. Patience is required to avoid withdrawing contingent supports prematurely. Unrealistic timetables for improvement and premature fading of supports can thwart success. ADHD is a chronic condition without quick fixes. A critical role for the therapist is to persistently reinforce the primary reinforcers, parents and teachers, to ensure integrity and sustenance of plan implementation.

Cognitive Behavior Therapy Linked to Point of Performance

Children with ADHD demonstrate significant difficulties in social, coping, and problem-solving skills. Difficulties with behavioral disinhibition and self-regulation often compromise development of healthy peer relationships (Barkley, 2006). Given these skills deficits, structured training in both individual and group formats seems warranted. However, skills training that is isolated from school and home environments has not proven effective (M. Miller & Hinshaw, 2012; Pelham & Fabiano, 2008). Generalization of social, coping, and problem-solving skills instruction can fail when training is neither directly linked nor actively reinforced at the point of performance in the child's natural environment. Effectiveness is also compromised when the length and intensity of training does not match the need children with ADHD possess for extensive repetition, scaffolding, and behavioral rehearsal. Successful CBT programs are characterized by lengthened treatment, extensive scaffolding consistent with the needs for external organizers, repetitive behavioral rehearsal that is engaging and directly mirrors daily challenges, and explicit linkage between skills trained in sessions and coaching and monitoring in home and school environments (M. Miller & Hinshaw, 2012; Pelham et al., 2010). In vivo training, active adult prompts and coaching, and realistic simulations of target environments are essential for skill acquisition and generalization.

Because schools are a primary point of performance, skills training with a focus on generalization and consistent with the principles just noted can be an important component of a comprehensive intervention program. Although their learning needs may be unique, students with ADHD can benefit from involvement in skills-training groups with diverse membership. Whereas the other members may have their own skill deficits, they can provide skill modeling in their areas of strength, which can be beneficial for students with ADHD. Diverse membership avoids the behavior management challenges that a group leader would face with a group solely populated by students with significant hyperactivity and impulsivity. However, the child with ADHD may need to participate in a series of groups over the long term to demonstrate improvement in social, coping, and problem-solving skills within the targeted natural environments.

Target behaviors for CBT skills training must be explicit, monitored, coached, and supported in the classroom and home settings. Skills introduced in sessions are rehearsed through role plays in session with immediate attempts to transfer application to the classroom, playground, and home settings using prompts, active coaching, and contingent reinforcers. The skill of the week or month can be directly included in coordinated home–school contingency contracts. Externalization of prompts in the classroom may include visual reminders of sequence steps for demonstrating a skill or engaging in problem-solving strategies. If the school uses a social-emotional learning curriculum for all students, the externalization of prompts can be integrated into classroom posters, personalized by being taped to the student's desk, and integrated into general teacher prompts for healthy social behaviors that would occur throughout the school day. Preteaching is particularly important before transitions and during less structured activities, which can be especially challenging for students with ADHD.

A school-centered therapist should take time to observe, coach, and intervene directly within the classroom. During the assessment phase, classroom observations help establish the need and agenda for intervention. Periodic follow-up observation and consultation presence within the classroom supports school staff, connects skills training to classroom behaviors, and ensures generalization of training. Within this approach, similar to athletic coaches, therapists help the student to learn and practice new skills outside of the classroom in simulated exercises and then provide game-time support at the point of performance.

Special attention needs to be given to recess and lunch free-play supervision for students with ADHD. For some affected students, these too often undersupervised settings, with their limited structure, are especially challenging, lead to behavioral episodes, and compromise peer relationships. In these cases specific plans for supervision and support of appropriate social behaviors should be designed. If supervision is provided primarily by volunteers, consultation regarding interventions for behavioral difficulties may be especially important. With proper supports, these play situations can become profitable social and problem-solving skills learning opportunities. At our therapeutic day school, therapists always accompanied students on field trips and provided support during special activities. Sometimes reward activities delivered by therapists involved short bonus recess periods that included select classmates.

Summer Treatment Program Intervention Model

The prototype for comprehensive multidimensional CBT interventions for ADHD is the summer treatment program (Pelham et al., 2010). This empirically supported therapeutic recreation model for ADHD integrates a comprehensive protocol for social-skills training into a summer camp program incorporating interventions directly into recreational and academic activities. CBT skills training occurs in vivo throughout a full day of academic and recreational activities. Because of behavior management issues, many children with ADHD struggle to succeed in ordinary camp programs and may either wind up excluded or socially disconnected. Pelham, Greiner, and Gnagy (1997) developed a comprehensive manualized summer treatment program designed to teach social and problem-solving skills for peer relationships, positive interactions with adults, academic productivity, and self-efficacy in the context of a highly structured summer camp with low staff-to-student ratios. Key elements of the program include a point system with rewards and response cost for appropriate behaviors; extensive social reinforcement; systematic instruction in social skills that are then modeled, coached, and reinforced throughout the day's activities; classroom instruction that focuses on work completion and accuracy; and sports skills training focused on following rules, sportsmanship, and improved motor skills. Extensive parent involvement includes a brief daily report card session, weekly parent-skills training during camp, and monthly booster sessions during the school year.

The summer treatment program was originally designed to be a full-day program spanning up to 8 weeks. Extensive staff training, resource allocation, and time commitment undoubtedly contribute to its efficacy but raise questions about its capacity for widespread dissemination. Pelham et al. (2010) documented successful attempts to transport these methods into other community settings such as youth activity centers, schools, and clinics that partner with these agencies. The intervention components of the program can be readily adapted to the school setting, an important point of performance for most youth. To be replicated within schools requires particular attention to teacher and parent training and collaboration, the implementation of coordinated home and school behavior management plans, and consistent behavioral prompts and contingent reinforcement within the flow of classroom and home activities. Daily report cards that reflect both home and school behaviors enhance parent–teacher alliances and increase the power of contingency management plans.

Structured CBT Developmental Play Groups

Reddy et al. (2005) developed a structured group curriculum using developmentally appropriate games to teach social skills, self-control, and anger and stress management strategies to very young (8.5 years and younger) children with ADHD. The skills are operationalized and taught at a developmentally appropriate level. The training sequence involves modeling, role playing, and performance feedback. To foster generalization of skills, children engage in typical play scenarios with adults mediating the application and generalization of skills through coaching and feedback. Developmentally appropriate games are structured to be enjoyable, thematic, without winners and losers but with opportunities to use skills such as speaking "nice talk," using self-control, coping with anger, not interrupting others, and other adaptive social and coping skills.

Reddy et al. (2005) reported positive gains on teacher and parent report measures related to ADHD symptoms at 4-month follow-up. Those gains were enhanced when this structured play intervention was incorporated into the Child ADHD Multimodal Program, a broader multidimensional treatment program that included parent training and behavioral consultation at the school (Reddy et al., 2005). The Developmentally Appropriate Games program could be implemented in school settings for children in the primary grades as one element of a multimodal intervention program. (See Reddy, 2012; Reddy, Spencer, Hall, & Rubel, 2001, for a more detailed description of the curriculum.)

Cognitive Strategies

Children with ADHD struggle to use verbal mediation skills to direct behavior. Barkley (2006) suggested that delays in internalization of language and thus in the capacity for self-instruction to guide and regulate behavior contribute to behavioral disinhibition in ADHD. However, simply providing training in self-instruction strategies has not proven effective in reducing ADHD symptoms (M. Miller & Hinshaw, 2012; Pelham & Fabiano, 2008). Cognitive strategies alone or as primary intervention strategies have not consistently received empirical support. Behavioral approaches emphasizing external supports for management of behavior are the evidence-based starting point for ADHD interventions. However, as evidenced in the Summer Treatment Program and in the Child ADHD Multimodal Program, cognitive problem-solving approaches have been successfully integrated into multidimensional behavioral intervention protocols for ADHD.

M. Miller and Hinshaw (2012) noted that significant cognitive elements are present in contingency management and other behavioral treatments. They argued that the long-term goal of any intervention protocol must be to move beyond external management toward self-management and development of a larger array of interpersonal and problem-solving skills. This movement becomes increasingly important in secondary education where contingency management programs are more difficult to execute. Self-management is essential in college and employment settings. Programs that have shown some promise in teaching self-monitoring and self-reinforcement skills have all treated those tasks as behaviors to be learned through direct instruction, coaching, and contingent reinforcement that is eventually faded (DuPaul & Stoner, 2014; M. Miller & Hinshaw, 2012). In his family treatment and problem-solving training protocol for adolescents with ADHD, Robin (2006) integrated cognitive restructuring, monitoring and compensatory strategies, and negotiation skills training interventions.

As Pelham et al. (2010) noted, because of its biological etiology and chronic course, ADHD requires multifaceted treatments administered with intensity and extended duration. Because deficits in cognitive self-regulation are central to ADHD, continued efforts to support skill development and discover new intervention strategies in this area are essential. Cognitive mediation and self-instruction strategies cannot be taught in isolation but rather need to be integrated into other aspects of training with extensive modeling and repetition over significant time periods. Cognitive actions can be treated as behaviors to be shaped by rewards and consequences. Modeling and behavioral rehearsal strategies are appropriate for self-instruction training. Applying overt self-instruction strategies to academic problem solving such as math problems broadens the use and student acceptance of self-guidance scripts. The technique can then be applied to social and stress management situations. Self-management techniques are framed in the context of gaining self-control with less dependence on adult monitoring.

Instruction in self-monitoring requires extensive scaffolding and persistence. Students are taught how to observe and record their own behavior and may need an extended period of collaborative monitoring with the teacher or therapist. As the student learns the routine, he or she is reinforced for accurate completion of self-monitoring tasks. This transition can be facilitated if, when using point or token systems, students complete their own point sheets with teacher review.

Teaching scripted frameworks for specific social and problem-solving skills requires repeated rehearsal and coaching at or near the point of performance. Although this may seem artificial at first, it is similar to the awkwardness of learning any new skills from athletics to academics to the arts, and direct analogies to these other tasks can support student effort. When possible, corrective replays of difficult behavioral incidents with demonstration of alternative positive behaviors guided by verbalization of typically covert self-talk can be beneficial. Throughout all of these procedures, appropriate reinforcers are used for compliance with skills training and evidence of successively approximate applications to problematic situations.

Disability Perspective

As a chronic disability, ADHD requires long-term intervention and support across the life span. In this regard, it is similar to asthma, diabetes, and other health conditions. Unfortunately, similar to other chronic conditions, sustained compliance with treatment interventions can be a complicating issue. Successfully managing symptoms requires knowledge about ADHD, acceptance of its implications, and persistence with intervention and support strategies. Gains from treatment may not persist when withdrawn. Medication interventions do not cure ADHD, and improvements are not sustained when medication is discontinued. Although a student may tire of applying time-consuming organizational strategies to support academic progress, abandonment of these supports is likely to result in regression. Compliance issues can become increasingly problematic in adolescence (Blotnicky-Gallant, Costain, & Corkum, 2013).

Training in developmentally appropriate skills for self-advocacy and self-efficacy is important for long-term management of ADHD symptoms. This involves teaching the child to understand the nature and implications of ADHD and accept his or her disability. Training in skills for eventual self-management of symptoms should be coupled with coaching for personally requesting appropriate accommodations and supports. Extensive bibliotherapy supports are available to assist this training. Unfortunately, many myths circulate about the nature of ADHD. Psychoeducational programs for youth and parents counter misinformation and appear promising for promoting sustained compliance with treatment regimens (Blotnicky-Gallant et al., 2013; Monastra, 2005). APA's Magination Press presents resources specific to ADHD (see, e.g., Quinn & Stern, 2001).

Medications

All practitioners working with ADHD need to understand the role of medication in treating the disorder and common protocols for its administration. The efficacy of medication supports for ADHD has been clearly documented (MTA Cooperative Group, 1999a). Stimulants such as Ritalin remain the most common prescriptions. Additional common brand names include Concerta, Focalin, Adderall, and Vyvanse. When possible, extended-release formulas of stimulants are now commonly prescribed to avoid the *behavioral rebound effect*, wherein some children's symptoms dramatically increase as medication effects wear off. Atomoxetine (Strattera), a norepinephrine reuptake inhibitor, has become a common alternative prescription, particularly for those patients who experience significant side effects from stimulants. The antihypertensive guanfacine XR (Intuniv) has also been FDA approved as an alternative to stimulants.

School-centered therapists do not prescribe medication, but they often play a significant role in encouraging families to accept a referral for a medication evaluation. If medication is prescribed, it is important for therapists to maintain communication with the prescribing physician to provide routine feedback regarding behavioral treatments and progress-monitoring data regarding home and school functioning to support appropriate monitoring of medication effects and dosage.

Parents may require significant support when considering a medical referral for ADHD. With so much misinformation circulating in portions of the media, the following information is particularly important for parents and youth (appropriate to their developmental level) to understand. Medications for ADHD have proven effective in reducing symptoms for many children. The benefits of medication often include increased capacity to benefit from academic instruction and behavioral treatments. Medications support management of ADHD, but they do not cure the disorder, and benefits generally disappear when medications are discontinued. However, the bettered capacity to benefit from nonmedical interventions may contribute to long-term improvements. Research has shown that combining medication and behavioral interventions produces the most benefit. Participation in behavioral interventions may reduce the dosage needs of medications, enlarge behavioral and psychosocial repertoires in ways that persist, and contribute to remediation of comorbid conditions. Schools have a responsibility to provide academic and therapeutic services as appropriate to students identified with ADHD regardless of whether they are participating in medical treatments. Barkley's (2013b) revised and updated parent guide for ADHD has an excellent concise summary regarding medications that can be a useful resource for parents and teachers.

Addressing Comorbid Conditions

Treatments for comorbidities are often complicated by ADHD symptoms, particularly impulsivity. The general recommendation is to use a comprehensive protocol of EBI for ADHD and then integrate elements of EBI for other conditions prioritized by impact on impairment. It is important to take the influence of other disorders into account when designing intervention plans. For example, when ADHD and anxiety are comorbid, the impulsivity and behavioral disinhibition characteristics of ADHD might be exacerbated by the physiological tensions and fearful thoughts associated with anxiety. The physical and affective characteristics of anxiety and environmental stressors that influence its intensity may need to be addressed in an ADHD intervention protocol. On the other hand, the cognitive therapy elements of CBT interventions for anxiety might well be more challenging for a child with ADHD. The initial interventions for anxiety may require greater reliance on behavioral rehearsal and scripted self-instruction strategies, whereas other cognitive strategies may need to wait until ADHD symptoms are better managed.

INSTRUCTIONAL SUPPORTS, EDUCATIONAL ACCOMMODATIONS, AND CLASSROOM PROTOCOLS

Academic and behavioral difficulties in school are a central concern for children with ADHD. They demonstrate problems with initiating, focusing, and sustaining attention on academic tasks. They exhibit difficulty with independent seatwork, struggle to organize materials, and struggle in particular with academic work that requires more complex problem solving and more sustained organizational strategies (i.e., multistep long-term assignments). Prone to impulsive disruptive behaviors, children with ADHD appear overactive, fidgety, may have a hard time remaining in their seats and keeping their hands to themselves, and struggle to wait their turn. Easily frustrated, they may display frequent escalations to poor temper control, excessive attention seeking, or oppositional behaviors. Furthermore, the incidence of comorbid learning disabilities is 30% to 40% (Barkley, 2013b; DuPaul & Stoner, 2014; Forness & Kavale, 2001). When indicated, evaluations and subsequent interventions for learning disabilities should be incorporated into school support plans. Classroom management and instructional accommodations are central elements in comprehensive intervention plans for ADHD. Direct supports to compensate for executive functioning deficits are required. Given the incidence of ADHD and its significant impact on academic progress, all educators must be prepared to assist these students. Although isolated overview presentations about teaching students with ADHD are helpful, it remains necessary for therapists to actively consult with teachers around specific children to ensure the appropriate application of intervention strategies.

Instructional Strategies

Given their impulsive response styles, it is important that students with ADHD be properly oriented to assignments. They require repetition of instructions or visual step-by-step guides and frequent check-in supervision to ensure they are proceeding appropriately. Calling on them frequently during class discussion and activities supports attention and engagement. Strong instructional stimuli are necessary to focus attention on academic tasks and to block out external distractors. Multimethod instruction using a variety of inputs, including frequent use of hands-on activities addresses the full range of learning channels and fosters attention. The addition of physical and kinesthetic dimensions to analyzing and problem-solving tasks strengthens learning. The use of manipulatives, concept maps, index cards for presentations, and physical models for academic outputs can be beneficial.

Frequent task shifts, variations in inputs and outputs, and shorter individual assignments enhance focus and work production. Over time the same amount of material can be covered but with frequent shifts in methods and the nature of tasks. Focus should center on production and accurate completion of assigned work rather than merely time on task. Long-term assignments are more likely to be completed when they are broken into smaller sections with specific due dates. Just as they may struggle with individual seatwork in the classroom, students with ADHD often find homework completion difficult. Homework assignments need to be tailored to their strengths, and parents must be enlisted to provide external supports that might be required for some assignments. Home–school contingency systems are often necessary to support accurate homework completion.

Computer-based instruction can be a productive addition to curriculum methodology. Educational software programs build in immediate feedback and reinforcement and permit the student to proceed at his or her own pace. Many electronic programs mimic the captivating features of video games presenting strong stimuli that engage focus with clear visual prompts to guide participation. Students with ADHD who have developed oppositional behaviors are less likely to engage in power struggles or manipulation with a machine. Programs can track academic skill development.

Organizational Supports

Executive functioning deficits compromise organization and planning skills. Consequently, these students require anticipatory sets to focus attention, frequent cuing, and detailed outlines of tasks requiring multiple steps. Easily followed overt organizational systems support work completion. If the student has trouble remembering materials, it might be helpful to have a duplicate set of textbooks available at home, making it no longer possible to miss doing work because "the text was left in school." Personalized and verified assignment notebook systems support assignment completion. Alternatively materials and requirements can be entered into a computer or phone app file or simply e-mailed to the student's account and then can be retrieved from anywhere. These organizational supports have applicability to postsecondary schooling or employment. Contingency contracts can include rewards for appropriate independent implementation of assignment responsibilities.

Organizational schemas are required to support behavior management as well. Visual representations of rules and procedures, preteaching before transitions, rehearsed behavioral and problem-solving scripts, and motivating reminders of potential earned contingencies support self-regulation. Practiced structured routines for managing stress and behavior escalation including establishing prearranged locations for time-outs can limit the length of acting-out episodes.

Behavior Supports

Classroom management approaches must be consistent with the comprehensive therapeutic intervention plan that bridges home and school environments.

Individualized operant conditioning reinforcement strategies are designed to support positive behaviors and respond to negative incidents. Design of the behavior intervention plan is guided by data from the school setting functional behavior assessment and must include sufficient supportive resources for both the teacher and the student to permit effective intervention implementation. Coordinated home–school contingency contracts are a particularly powerful and effective tool, ensuring full day consistency and critical support for both parents and teachers.

The classroom setting is a critical point of performance for supporting instruction in social, coping, and problem-solving skills. In collaboration with the student's therapist, teachers can create protocols to prompt, monitor, and reinforce psychosocial skill development. The therapist, teacher, and parents can coordinate efforts by using common language for prompts for both overt behavior and covert self-instructions. Psychological education is appropriate for all students. When skills training includes the whole classroom, skill components and problem-solving steps can be posted in the classroom and reinforced and referred to throughout the school day. Individualized visual cues will still be required for the student with ADHD, but as an extension of classroom protocols these supports are likely to be more acceptable.

Some students benefit from periodic staff-directed physical movement. These motor breaks can be useful but must be individualized. Some students calm down after energy-releasing physical activity, but others may get over-stimulated and struggle to reintegrate into classroom routine and instructional expectations. A routine for cooling down and reviewing classroom reentry expectations is essential.

Time-outs from positive reinforcement and social engagement have proven helpful for many children in response to serious disruptive or severe attention-seeking behaviors (Barkley, 2013a, 2013b; DuPaul & Stoner, 2014; Pelham et al., 2010). This mild form of punishment can be framed as a temporary logical consequence for interfering with classroom learning. It involves removing the student from the disruptive context into another part of the classroom, a study carrel if available, or to a designated time-out room or location outside the classroom if staff supervision is available. Time-outs are designed to remove the student from the social reinforcers obtained through inappropriate attention-seeking behaviors. Consequently, it is critical that the supervising adult does not inadvertently turn the time-out into a socially reinforcing experience. Time-outs are not designed to be used as routine interventions and should never be used in the absence of a positive behavior support program promoting adaptive behaviors. This strategy should be short term, usually 1 to 5 minutes, and individualized with scripted expectations and activities. An assigned coping task such as deep breathing or another physical calming activity may be useful. Preteaching behavioral expectations for the return to class is important, and some children may benefit from repeating these expectations immediately before reentry into the normal flow of instruction.

Care must be taken that directives to initiate time-out interventions do not unintentionally communicate rejection or exclusion, with particular care given to tone of voice. Work contingencies need to be monitored to ensure that the student is not using time-outs to avoid academic tasks. When this appears to be the case, it is important that the avoided academic task be completed later in the day before returning from time-out or, if necessary, after school. Time-out procedures are temporary measures and should not be viewed as core intervention strategies. The long-term goal is to assist the student in gaining the self-monitoring skills necessary to avoid disruptive behaviors. The core effective intervention measures involve contingency management, psychosocial skills training, and instructional adaptation measures already outlined.

Maintaining an Educational Disability Perspective

Students with severe ADHD symptoms, particularly if coupled with oppositional behaviors, can be challenging for teachers. Therapists and faculty colleagues provide support for maintaining a disability perspective similar to children with learning disabilities and other disorders that hinder learning. The student's strengths need to be emphasized and tapped. This helps to separate the child's persona from the symptoms. In the face of disruptive, oppositional, or defiant behaviors, it is important to avoid personalizing attacks and engaging in power struggles. In this regard, teachers find that seeking opportunities to interact with the student when there are minimal task expectations can build rapport that in turn provides benefits for managing challenging behavioral episodes. Yet, working with students with ADHD can be as rewarding as it is challenging. With proper behavioral and instructional supports, they can flourish academically and socially.

CRISIS INTERVENTION PROTOCOLS

Planned crisis intervention protocols provide an automatic response to serious acting-out episodes. Serious incidents are more likely to occur when fueled by comorbid conduct disorder or oppositional defiant disorder symptoms. Existing plans for behavior and instructional supports serve a preventative function, and their approaches provide the framework for crisis de-escalation.

Crisis intervention protocols are consistent with behavior management plans specific to ADHD. When internal self-regulation capacities have been overwhelmed, external supports presenting firm boundaries and limits are essential. The responding adult engages in concise persistent verbal redirection in an assertive but matter-of-fact tone of voice. Directions are kept brief, clear, and achievable. To avoid secondary gain from the attention of others, the student should be removed from any potentially reinforcing audience to a less stimulating atmosphere, and although the adult provides essential support, care must be taken to avoid making outside-of-classroom social interaction so rewarding that it inadvertently reinforces the crisis cycle.

When it is necessary to use a time-out strategy, the guidelines outlined above apply. Students with ADHD may appear increasingly hyperactive when emotionally escalated. When possible, channel that energy into performance of a physically active coping task that lowers arousal, such as deep breathing or tightening and relaxing large muscles. Immediate and salient reinforcement for any observable calming behaviors and engagement in adaptive activity contributes to de-escalation. Avoiding long time-outs, lectures or arguments, and power struggles is important.

Verbal processing and debriefing occur when the student is calm and more available for reflection on the impact of his or her behavior on others. Maintaining a positive relationship with the teacher is important for the student—if in anger the student vents complaints about the teacher, the crisis responder can provide empathy for the frustration but must be careful to not side with the student against the teacher. If possible, it is helpful to process the crisis-interaction sequence with the teacher before the student returns to class. Tracking the time of day, the type of academic task, and the subject matter may reveal whether an academic challenge was a trigger to the episode. If so, practicing with the student how to appropriately voice frustration and seek assistance must occur. As soon as possible after an out-of-control episode, reengagement in schoolwork is initiated with short-term reinforcement contingencies clearly identified and readily administered. Maintaining sensitivity to the impact of ADHD as a disability is important, but students must be coached to take responsibility for managing their behavior and using the supports and training offered through the primary intervention plan.

FAMILY AND SYSTEMIC SUPPORTS AND INTERVENTIONS

Parent training is a core empirically supported treatment component for ADHD (Barkley, 2006, 2013a, 2013b; Barkley & Robin, 2014; M. Miller & Hinshaw, 2012; Pelham & Fabiano, 2008). Parent training focuses on orienting parents to the neurobehavioral nature of ADHD and the current research-supported medical and behavioral treatments, teaching behavior management principles with a focus on contingency management, providing planning and organizational supports to address executive functioning deficits, and working closely with schools regarding the impact of ADHD on learning. The focus and scope of training parallels teacher training.

ADHD as Chronic Disability

Parent training begins with an overview of the nature of ADHD and underscores that the condition is neither the parent nor the child's fault. Presenting analogies to other conditions that require long-term management, such as diabetes and asthma, can be helpful so that parents can understand that long-term interventions and supports will be required. Parents are oriented to the nature of executive functioning deficits and how they present unique challenges, particularly for school functioning. Countering the sobering information regarding chronicity, psychoeducation for parents highlights the hopefulness that has emerged with empirically supported multidimensional interventions and the clear benefits of coordinated action planning with school personnel. At the same time, parents learn that ADHD is not something that a child is likely to outgrow and that if not addressed, risk increases for problematic comorbidities, in particular, externalizing conduct problems and school failure. The lack of evidence for interventions focused on diet, sugar intake, and food additives is described.

Educational Implications

Parents learn the educational implications of ADHD and an array of instructional approaches and educational accommodations that may provide assistance. The parental role in assisting with organizational supports and homework completion is specifically addressed. P. Dawson and Guare (2009) presented a comprehensive program for teaching executive functioning skills designed for parents to implement. They provided a wide range of practical organizational, planning, and behavioral support strategies that address everything from completing daily routines, teaching task initiation, and fostering time management and organizational skills to address both school and home responsibilities. In each case, training in organizational skills is supported by contingency management. Emphasizing the importance of maintaining realistic developmentally appropriate expectations, Guare, Dawson, and Guare (2012) outlined a program specific to teens. Their core methods for teaching executive skills center on developing simple external organizational and planning strategies that are modeled, taught, and contingently reinforced with specific strategies for fading adult supervision.

Behavior Management

Instruction in core behavior management principles to be deployed at home mirrors school intervention protocols. Behavior management training protocols emanate from social learning and operant conditioning principles. Training centers on contingency management principles, understanding the role of antecedents and consequences in supporting and responding to behaviors. The emphasis is placed on positive reinforcement and the employment of tangible or activity-based incentives before using punishment procedures. The need for more frequent, immediate, and supportive and corrective feedback and consequences is emphasized. Parents are taught how to design token or point systems for home to foster contingent reinforcement at the point of performance and provide a practical framework for managing behaviors in the midst of the full array of parenting responsibilities.

Parents learn the importance and the application of external structure to support positive behaviors. Parents are taught strategies for planning ahead, preteaching expectations while noting contingent rewards and negative consequences, providing clear step-by-step directions, using natural consequences and external motivators, maintaining consistency, and avoiding lectures and counterproductive second chances but following through consistently with actions that enforce expectations.

Just as time-outs might be used in the school setting to support self-control, parents are trained in the effective use of this strategy in both home and public settings. Parents learn to anticipate what settings increase the risk of acting out behavior. Barkley (2013b) emphasized the importance of advance planning for managing disruptive behaviors in public settings. He recommended articulating rules and expectations before an event, specifically reminding the child of external incentives for compliance and punishments for noncompliance. Because boredom and the resulting stimulation-seeking behaviors can trigger behavioral episodes, prevention includes providing the child with manageable solitary physical activities to engage in (e.g., drawing materials, electronic games) while in stores, restaurants, or other public environments. Parents are encouraged to take a problem-solving approach to episodes when they do occur, when necessary removing the child to a more private space within or immediately outside the setting. Tone of voice should be controlled but assertive. Discipline responses must be delivered as promised but not in a coercive manner fueled by parental embarrassment or frustration. The importance of avoiding personalizing misbehavior is emphasized. This requires a commitment to the disability perspective and the often tedious process of supporting skill development and behavior change.

Generalizing Social Skills Lessons

Similar to teachers, parents are frequently present at the point of performance requiring social, coping, and problem-solving skills. Thus, they possess many opportunities to model, prompt, and reinforce skills taught to their children in therapy sessions and training programs. To be effective, parents must be equipped with information regarding skill definitions and how to support them in the moment they are required. Optimally, school staff, the therapist, and the parents are using a similar language to define and operationalize skills and prompt their adaptive use. Parent training programs should specifically address strategies for psychosocial skill development for their children. Empirically supported multimodal programs for children with ADHD have included parent training groups that parallel and reinforce youth skills training (Pelham et al., 2010; Pfiffner & McBurnett, 1997; Reddy et al., 2005).

Individual Family Therapy Interventions

Family-specific therapeutic supports apply the focus and principles of parent training to unique individual family interaction patterns and circumstances. Rooted in structural and behavioral family systems approaches, families are counseled to provide sufficient structure, supervision, and support to match risk factors associated with ADHD (Robin, 2006). If ADHD symptoms have not been sufficiently or successfully addressed before adolescence, risks for delinquency and substance abuse can increase to potentially serious levels. If behavior escalates in adolescence, the clinical reality is that external supports and training in psychosocial and self-management skills are required before healthy self-monitoring can be achieved. Particularly in cases with comorbid conduct or oppositional disorders, family therapy may be necessary to develop healthy crisis intervention response patterns. Family therapy guides parents through the balancing act of increasing external structure and accountability while responding to the teen's developmentally appropriate strivings for increased independence.

Case Example

Greg was a fifth grader who struggled to stay on task; completed limited amounts of work; engaged in impulsive behaviors like talking out, leaving his seat, and horseplay with classmates; and argued with teachers when reprimanded. Although his behaviors could be exasperating, his personality was engaging, and if removed from class for disruption, he would enjoy his time in the office. The school's FBA hypothesized that his externalizing behaviors were sustained by escape from academic demands, intermittent reinforcement through getting his way, and continuous reinforcement through attention and sensation-seeking behaviors. His time out of the classroom was viewed as reinforcing misbehavior because it removed him from work and eventually resulted in positive one-on-one social attention.

The intervention plan for classroom management and academic instruction was multifaceted. A behavior point system was instituted so that reinforcers for work completion and appropriate demonstration of targeted prosocial behaviors could be immediately earned to count toward school and home incentives. An individualized instructional program was devised involving frequent task changes and many short lesson activities. To provide him adult attention and organizational support, a classroom aide helped Greg get started on his work, making sure he understood and followed directions. After successful completion of a short assignment, he transitioned to a study carrel with a laptop to work on basic skills with visually engaging educational software. Successful completion of the lesson's skill test earned Greg

5 extra minutes of computer time with an enticing graphic design game that could be continued over an extended number of sessions. If he successfully completed the first two academic tasks, he could rejoin the class for the last segment of the period. The aide helped him transition back to his regular seat and intermittently checked in with him to support on-task behaviors. Remaining in his seat and raising his hand before speaking were reinforced with points. Points earned were entered on a chart at the end of each class period and totaled during last period. At school, points could earn immediate rewards such as sport cards or 10-minute game time before dismissal and longer term rewards such as helping the physical education teacher in a class with younger children and a snack time with the assistant principal.

If he began to engage in disruptive behavior, every attempt was made to keep Greg in the classroom. Staff would calmly redirect him and remind him of his motivators, but persistent disruption (clearly defined for him and staff) resulted in a loss of points earned (response cost). If behavior escalation necessitated class removal because of impact on others, he would be taken to an isolated area of the building rather than the office. The accompanying staff member minimized verbal interactions. When he was able to complete a short assignment, he was returned to class. Successful reentry into class resulted in partial earning back of lost points.

Greg brought home a daily report card that summarized his school day, points earned, and homework. A similar multifaceted contingency plan was instituted at home, targeting homework completion and specified positive home behaviors. Home incentives could be earned through a combination of positive school and home behaviors. A home portion of the daily report card was completed and returned to school symbolizing the integration of the plans and parents and teachers mutual support. The therapist's primary role was to work with the adults to devise effective instructional and behavioral plans and support their adherence to the protocol. The plan addressed both academics and behaviors in both home and school settings. Although addressing many complex contingencies, it was easily understood and enforceable. To prepare for fading these supports, the therapist's individual work with Greg focused on problem-solving, organizational, and self-monitoring strategies. This example illustrates an integrated multifaceted intervention plan for ADHD.

5

DISRUPTIVE BEHAVIOR DISORDERS

Disruptive behavior disorders (DBDs) involve acting-out behaviors, such as conduct problems and aggression, that generally impact not only the individual child but also those in his or her important social environments. These externalizing disorders involve disruptive misbehaviors in the home and classroom—repetitive rule breaking, temper tantrums, verbal and physical aggression, antisocial and delinquent behaviors. Unlike internalizing disorders such as anxiety and depression, DBDs draw attention to themselves and result in the largest number of school discipline and clinical treatment referrals. When conduct problems are unresolved in childhood, they can increase risks for depression and substance abuse and may result in serious legal problems as well (Barkley, 2013a).

For the purposes of this chapter, I use *DBD* as the broad term to include the formal clinical diagnoses of oppositional defiant disorder (ODD) and conduct disorder (CD), for which many of the empirically supported

http://dx.doi.org/10.1037/14779-006
School-Centered Interventions: Evidence-Based Strategies for Social, Emotional, and Academic Success,
by D. J. Simon

interventions are similar. Attention-deficit/hyperactivity disorder (ADHD) is a common comorbid condition, which I addressed in Chapter 4. Some of the most severe forms of DBD occur in adolescence in youth who display complex comorbidities and multiple clinical problems that may simultaneously include severe acting-out behaviors, delinquency, substance abuse, and significant impairments in family, school, and community functioning. A growing body of evidence-based intervention (EBI) strategies is emerging to intervene with these dangerous combinations of problems.

DIAGNOSTIC CHARACTERISTICS AND ASSESSMENT FRAMEWORKS

Because of the visible disruptive behavioral displays that accompany DBDs, case finding does not tend to be an issue. However, because many conditions and circumstances can lead to acting-out behaviors, it is important to accurately assess DBDs and to account for any environmental circumstances or underlying psychological conditions that may contribute to externalizing behaviors. ADHD is characterized by behavioral disinhibition and impulse-control difficulties that can lead to highly disruptive behaviors. Although core interventions for DBDs may apply to ADHD, there are additional ADHD-specific characteristics and treatments that must be accounted for in intervention planning (see Chapter 4). Autism spectrum disorder (ASD) can also include disruptive behaviors that challenge parenting and classroom behavior management. However, repetitive or restrictive behaviors, sensory issues, and communication challenges may be central contributing factors not present in CD or ODD. Depression and anxiety can also prompt acting-out behaviors. In some cases, particularly after a significant personal loss, such as death of a parent, or negatively perceived changes in life circumstances, such as a divorce or geographical move, disruptive behaviors may emerge. In these cases, it is critical to address the feelings associated with these contributing factors. For example, interventions to address depressive symptoms prompted by a significant loss may prove sufficient to diminish disruptive behaviors. Thus, the assessment process for DBDs must rule out or rule in other conditions to ensure that intervention protocols are properly prioritized and administered.

DSM–5 and ICD–10–CM

Under its section Disruptive, Impulse-Control, and Conduct Disorders, the *Diagnostic and Statistical Manual of Mental Disorders* (fifth ed.; *DSM–5*; American Psychiatric Association, 2013) provides diagnostic criteria for the two most common DBDs, ODD and CD. Although many psychological conditions center on difficulty in behavioral and emotional control, these categories focus on symptoms that negatively affect others through behaviors such as overt and covert aggression; challenge authority relationships in unhealthy ways; involve repetitive rule-breaking, including illegal activities; and compromise healthy interpersonal relationships (American Psychiatric Association, 2013). ODD is characterized by angry or irritable mood; short temper; a negative, hostile, and defiant stance toward authority figures resulting in frequent power struggles; an argumentative and annoying interpersonal style; vindictive or spiteful actions; a tendency to blame others; and overriding control needs. CD is characterized by significant behaviors that impact the rights of others in any of the following areas: repetitive rules violations, excessive limit testing, aggression to people or animals, destruction of property, theft, deceit, and/or delinquency. A third related disorder is intermittent explosive disorder (IED), which is marked by recurrent impulsive aggression that is grossly disproportionate to any provocation. It is differentiated from CD, in which aggression may at times be premeditated and other antisocial patterns are generally evident. In this chapter, I focus on the more prevalent ODD and CD. Anger management interventions described here generally apply to IED as well.

The *International Classification of Diseases, Tenth Revision, Clinical Modification* (ICD–10–CM) distinguishes between childhood (F91.1) and adolescent (F91.2) onset CD and includes a category for symptoms confined to the family context (F91.0; Goodheart, 2014). ODD (F91.3) descriptors are similar. IED (F63.81) is categorized under impulse disorders.

Assessment Activities

DBDs are characterized by heterogeneity of symptoms. Assessment activity focuses on delineating the number, types, and severity of symptomatic behaviors; the resulting impairments in family, school, and peer settings; and the environmental factors that contribute to the initiation and maintenance of disruptive behaviors. In most cases, behaviors are exhibited across multiple settings; however, because of the difference in setting demands, behaviors may be more severe in some rather than in other settings. The school setting places particular demands on following rules, cooperation with authority, task completion on demand, and positive social interactions. School misbehaviors can also be triggered or compounded by frustration because of learning problems. Although the same issues may be observed at home, there may be times in the context of a permissive household with limited expectations for performance and minimal rules that disruptive behaviors would be less evident. Thus, assessment must seek to understand the relationship between behavior displays, setting demands, and environmental influences.

Multiple factors can contribute to the etiology of a DBD. McMahon and Frick (2007) highlighted the importance of attempting to understand the developmental pathways that may have contributed to the occurrence of problematic behaviors in anticipation that these data might influence intervention planning. This is clearly beneficial when there have been historical events that significantly altered parental structure, such as the loss of a parent, or where parenting practices, such as coercive or overly permissive parenting styles, have influenced the emergence and maintenance of disruptive behaviors. Age of onset, degree of emotional reactivity, character of aggression and misconduct, and temperamental dispositions all appear to influence the nature and course of a DBD and the selection of intervention strategies. Significant developmental considerations are explored in more detail below; however, it is necessary to caution that research has not yet reliably linked the full range of developmental pathways influencing symptoms to effective treatments.

Parental reports regarding disruptive behaviors at home and school generally initiate referrals for assessment and intervention. School data on discipline referrals and recordkeeping within school-wide positive behavior support programs, which collect data on targeted behaviors and office referrals for misconduct, include significant information relevant to the assessment of a DBD. It is important to note differences in behavioral performance across settings and in relation to differing authority figures; mothers and fathers, for example, sometimes report different observations and concerns. School office referrals may reflect variations in teacher tolerance, classroom management skills, or a student's difficulties with a particular subject.

Assessment activities for DBDs determine types and severity of problem behaviors; compare symptom profiles with developmental status and normative population; analyze parenting and school behavior management practices; delineate repetitive sequences of antecedent and consequence chains that trigger and maintain disruptive behaviors; hypothesize function of behaviors; investigate developmental and environmental factors that influence symptom development; collect information regarding any antisocial peer-group participation or involvement in delinquency; and explore the presence and influence of any comorbid psychological conditions, such as ADHD, depression, or anxiety. Assessment methods include parent and child interviews, a social-developmental history, behavior rating scales, tabulation and profiling of critical behavioral incidents, behavioral observations, functional analyses of behaviors, delineation of strengths and resources for change, social and coping skill capacities and deficits, and barriers toward improvement.

Behavior Rating Scales

Broadband behavior rating scales such as the Achenbach System of Empirically Based Assessment (ASEBA; Achenbach & Rescorla, 2001) and the Behavior Assessment System for Children—Second Edition (BASC–2; C. R. Reynolds & Kamphaus, 2004) have parent, teacher, and child versions that can be integrated into a comprehensive report. These instruments have been extensively used in research on DBDs, assess potential externalizing and internalizing comorbidities, provide substantive normative comparisons, and are sensitive to monitoring intervention effects. The ASEBA syndrome scales include Rule-Breaking Behavior, Aggressive Behavior, and Attention Problems. This instrument's DSM-oriented scales include ADHD, ODD, and CD Problem Scales. The BASC–2 has scales on Aggression, Hyperactivity, and Conduct Problems. These broadband scales serve to screen for comorbid disorders, which require additional symptom-specific assessment. Of particular concern related to DBDs are ADHD, depression, and anxiety. It is important to note that youth self-report is generally considered more reliable for internalizing rather than externalizing behaviors, particularly before age 9, and may be subject to positive response biases (Barkley, 2013a; McMahon & Frick, 2007). Given other confirming data, broadband rating scales are generally sufficient for problem identification and normative comparison. Barkley's (2013a) Home Situations Questionnaire and School Situations Questionnaire are brief surveys that strive to identify environmental variables associated with disruptive behaviors.

If more specific information on an extended range of disruptive behaviors is necessary, McMahon and Frick's (2005, 2007) reviews of evidence-based assessment recommend the following behavior rating scales: the Eyberg Child Behavior Inventory for parents and the Sutter-Eyberg Student Behavior Inventory—Revised for teachers (Eyberg & Pincus, 1999) to identify both a larger number of behaviors and their intensity; the Self-Report Delinquency Scale (Elliott, Huizinga, & Ageton, 1985) to target adolescent delinquency; the Reactive–Proactive Aggression Questionnaire to distinguish different types of aggression (Raine et al., 2006); and the Ratings of Children's Social Behavior (Crick, 1996) to assess relational aggression.

Parent, Teacher, and Child Interviews

Parent interviews generally provide the most critical assessment data directly linking assessment and intervention. Parental descriptions of problematic family interaction patterns directly contribute to the development of a functional behavior assessment (FBA), which sets the stage for behavior intervention planning (Steege & Watson, 2009). DBDs may negatively affect the lives of parents in significant ways. Clinical interviews begin by soliciting parental concerns; they next identify the child's and family's strengths and personal resources; collect relevant social developmental history data; systematically gather data on academic and social functioning; assess the child's social, coping, and problem-solving capacities; review specific symptoms for CD and ODD; explore whether ADHD, depression, anxiety, or other symptom profile may be present; and investigate past attempts to remediate behavior problems.

The social developmental history explores whether any temperamental, medical, behavioral, or developmental milestone issues in early childhood might be relevant to understanding the emergence of DBD symptoms. Family medical and psychiatric history factors are examined, including familial histories of ADHD, disruptive behaviors, and substance abuse. Important historical events including any incidents of divorce, loss, and trauma are identified with an eye toward any link to emergence or intensification of DBD characteristics.

The parent interview begins the process of examining antecedent–behavior–consequence (A-B-C) sequences that typically occur during disruptive behavior displays. The clinician explores multiple examples of problematic parent–child interactions and discipline attempts. Pattern analysis identifies parent skills and resources, environmental constraints, triggering stimuli, and parent and child attempts at exerting control and problem solving. These data will provide focus to both parent behavior-management training and family problem-solving interventions.

Because a DBD may severely affect school performance, comprehensive interviews with teachers are essential. In addition to discipline issues, academic performance and relationships with peers require exploration. Attention to the presence of any learning issues that might trigger behavior episodes is important. A similar pattern analysis of environmental factors, including time of day, class structure, instructional inputs, teacher, and peer factors, creates an interaction pattern profile similar to data collected on home behaviors. A review of behavior management strategies attempted and their relative impact contributes to the eventual development of an FBA and an individualized intervention plan. Children with behavior issues can create rifts or splits between parents and teachers. The exasperation of failed attempts to remediate problems and the longing for a positive adult–child relationship can leave adults susceptible to believing the student's distorted accounts of behavioral incidents and prone to wish that school staff or parents were more effective. Because splitting behaviors are never productive, it is important that the interviewer repeatedly underline the importance of positive parent–teacher collaboration and support as an essential intervention posture.

Child interviews are an essential assessment component. They provide an important opportunity for children to share their views about behavior and discipline issues, family and school stressors, and problematic interaction patterns. This interview is the first opportunity for the therapist to build rapport with a youth who is likely to feel uncomfortable in the spotlight and severely judged. Caution must be exercised in accepting and interpreting information. Youth self-report data may not be consistently reliable for many elementary-age youth (Kamphaus & Frick, 2005), and youth with serious externalizing behaviors tend to have reduced self-awareness and a propensity to project blame for difficulties on authority figures (Barkley, 2013a). On the other hand, as children provide descriptive appraisals of events and attribute motivations to others, their unique social–cognitive perspectives are illustrated (e.g., their perception of threat, meaning, responsibility, expectations). This process may highlight misperceptions and cognitive distortions that may need to be addressed in treatment. Youth who are more distressed by their behaviors and able to take some responsibility for their role in behavioral episodes may provide more accurate information and, in turn, be better prepared to successfully cooperate with interventions.

The Semistructured Clinical Interview for Children and Adolescents (SCICA; McConaughy, 2013; McConaughy & Achenbach, 2001) provides a child-friendly protocol for a comprehensive interview for youth ages 6 through 18 that incorporates behavioral dimensions of the ASEBA rating scales. Related parent and teacher interviews include sections specific to externalizing disorders (McConaughy, 2004a, 2004b). This integrated interview system provides a systematic protocol for gathering multi-informant interview data.

Behavioral Observations and Functional Behavior Assessment

The information garnered through interview and rating scales contributes to the focus of behavioral observations and an FBA. There are a number of structured behavior observation systems for the school setting, including the ASEBA Direct Observation Form (McConaughy & Achenbach, 2009), the BASC–2 Student Observation System (Reynolds & Kamphaus, 2006), and the new phone application version of the Behavioral Observation of Students in Schools (Shapiro, 2013). Naturalistic observation procedures are used to provide descriptive data about behaviors of concerns and to record frequency and intensity. In classroom or group situations, it can be helpful to collect similar data on one or two random peers to compare behavior with typical performance in the same setting. Naturalistic observation can also provide an opportunity to carefully chronicle A-B-C sequences. In the classroom, setting variables such as time of day, subject matter, and type of activity and immediate antecedent events such as an instruction to begin work, verbal reprimand, or peer distraction are delineated. Although the purpose of an observation is to collect data on problematic behavior, it is equally important to note strengths and adaptive behaviors. There are significant advantages to having the therapist conduct the observation; however, if the therapist is known to the student and his or her presence might alter typical behavior, then a colleague can be engaged to collect the observational data. (For extended coverage of observation methods, see Hintze, Volpe, & Shapiro, 2008.)

The FBA process maps A-B-C sequences and attempts to hypothesize the function or goal of the interfering behavior. Goals can be diverse, for example, to get attention, remove the obligation to perform a task, avoid a social situation, calm anxiety, protect oneself against a perceived threat, or have fun. The unstated goal of the behavior is most often either to get something (e.g., attention, control) or to get out of something (e.g., escape from an anxiety-provoking situation or a nonpreferred task). What occurs after the behavior achieves its goal and makes it more likely to be repeated in the future is the *maintaining consequence*. In working with parents and educators, it is important to help them to understand that in this case the word *consequence* is not synonymous with punishment or discipline. The maintaining consequence makes it more likely that the A-B-C sequence will repeat itself in the future and that problematic behavior will continue to occur. The following steps briefly summarize the process of delineating an FBA.

1. *Problem definition.* To accurately collect data and target behavior change, one must define the problem behavior in observable and measurable terms.

2. *Antecedents.* Behavior is influenced by relatively constant environmental and personal factors that set the stage for the triggering impact of proximate antecedents. Because these background factors may also be targets of intervention or affect the character of interventions, it can be helpful to delineate them as well while constructing an FBA. For example, the chronic illness of a single parent may result in erratic structure and limited supervision to support homework completion. This challenge may be further complicated by a neurobehavioral condition such as ADHD, which requires extra supervision and external supports for work completion even when typical support resources are available. If one typical occurrence of the target behavior is a disruptive outburst that occurs when the class reviews homework and the student is told he will miss recess to complete homework (proximate antecedents), it may be necessary to design ways to provide additional supervision and organizational supports at home to reduce the frequency of the triggering antecedents. For example, at the end of the school day, the student and teacher might together e-mail a list of homework assignments to parents to ensure that assignments are known. Parents could set up and enforce a specific homework time and review work to ensure completion. Completion of homework could be immediately reinforced by a motivating reward at home.

The next step is to catalog and examine environmental characteristics. During a behavioral observation, the characteristics of the classroom environment, structure, procedures, interactions, and all elements associated with time and place are catalogued. When considering interventions, it is important to assess these factors' goodness of fit for this student and brainstorm which environmental characteristics can be neutralized, eliminated, or modified.

Then proximate triggering antecedents are assessed. These are events or circumstances that immediately precede a problem behavior (e.g., an academic assignment that is particularly challenging, a teacher request for behavioral compliance, critical feedback, a negative interaction with a peer). Observers zero in on all aspects of potential triggers and strive to identify triggers that might be constant across settings and events, thus, indicating that they are salient antecedents to be addressed in intervention planning. Over time, behavioral responses can become conditioned to the occurrence of certain stimuli and become habitual behavior. Modifying or controlling antecedent stimuli may become a central feature in an ensuing intervention plan.

Not all triggers are clearly evident during observations. *Cognitive factors* play a critical role in A-B-C sequences. Threat appraisals, attributions of the meaning of events, and self-talk can play a mediating role contributing to the occurrence of the problematic behavior. Cognitive factors are sometimes evident from remarks accompanying a behavioral display but may be further delineated or clarified through child interviews. Sometimes student inquiries will reveal that adults have misinterpreted the valence of various antecedent factors or immediate consequences (e.g., a negative comment from a peer may have a greater impact than a teacher reprimand or escaping from performance anxiety may be more central than the presumed goal of attention seeking recognition).

3. *Maintaining consequences.* Changes or reactions in the environment that occur because of the problem behavior and make it more likely to reoccur are maintaining consequences. Often several factors influence or condition behaviors, and assessment must match the complexity of the circumstances. These factors may involve physical, affective, cognitive, behavioral, or social elements (e.g., emotional or physical tension release from a temper outburst, work avoidance, removal from a stressing social setting, reduction in perceived threats, and/or the

security or safety of external control in the face of destructive impulses).

4. *Identification of alternative desired behavior.* To effectively use the assessment data from an FBA, one must define and operationalize the preferred replacement behavior. Observations garnered through the FBA process build an understanding of the setting demands and the social and coping skills that are required to manage the challenges. Integrated with other assessment information, the FBA contributes to an evaluation of whether social and problem-solving deficits are primarily skill deficits (e.g., the student lacks the skill to calm visceral arousal or to appropriately verbally express feelings, needs, and wants); or performance deficits (where the student has the requisite skills but does not use them). Often both are relevant, although in some cases characterized by oppositional behaviors, performance deficits may be central. When considering alternative or replacement behavior, it is essential to delineate the student's strengths, personal resources, and potential environmental supports.

FBAs are designed to directly link to behavior intervention plans. Each element of the FBA may point to possible interventions. Constant environmental and personal factors can be taken into account. For example, knowledge of effective accommodations for ADHD may influence decisions about home-based supports, modifications of the classroom environment and instructional inputs, and the character of reinforcement strategies. Setting and event characteristics might be modified (e.g., the timing, procedure, and location for homework review might be altered or the support for initiating a new assignment changed). Manipulating proximate triggers might involve eliminating some routines or expectations or altering their character (e.g., changing the process for homework review, preteaching expectations paired with reminder prompts regarding potential positive reinforcers, altering the character of reprimands).

To promote an alternative adaptive behavior, it might be necessary for one to teach specific social, coping, and problem-solving skills, which then need to be rehearsed, prompted, and reinforced so that they occur in the natural setting. This process requires integrating the findings of the FBA with the full assessment. From a CBT perspective, students are trained to recognize triggers that prompt behavioral difficulties. Although the initial intervention plan developed from an FBA may begin with adult manipulation of antecedents and consequences, the eventual goal is to enhance student self-awareness to recognize triggers, alter accompanying thoughts and ensuing behaviors, and self-monitor. Reinforcement plans generally need to

nat. reinforcers of performance,
mastery, pos. social recognition

create programmed maintaining consequences such as contingent incentive plans before the natural reinforcers that accompany effective performance, personal mastery, and positive social recognition carry sufficient weight to support alternative desirable behaviors.

The effectiveness of manipulating maintaining consequences demonstrates the direct link from FBA to behavior intervention planning. Whenever possible, the desired behavior should be reinforced by a similar maintaining consequence. For example, if a student has learned that she gets extra attention from her underinvolved parent through misbehavior, then an intervention plan can build in special positive activities with that parent that are earned only through exhibition of the positive adaptive behavior. The power of the maintaining consequence for the problem behavior can provide clues for manipulation of consequences to promote alternatives.

Completion of an FBA is an essential component of a comprehensive assessment of DBDs. Within special education, an FBA and accompanying behavior intervention plan are now required elements of individualized education plans (IEPs) when behavior interferes with learning. (For an expanded treatment of the FBA process and its applications in schools, see Steege & Watson, 2009.) However, delineating A-B-C sequences suggests a linear process that captures only a segment of the complex reciprocal influences and feedback loops that contribute to and sustain both positive and negative behavior patterns. For this reason, it is necessary to incorporate data from the FBA into all sources of information and design interventions that integrate behavioral, cognitive, and systemic approaches.

must do FBA on DBD

Assessment of Aggression and Potential for Violence

Referrals for assessment of DBDs often center on concerns regarding physical aggression and violence. Recent violent episodes in schools have heightened concerns about identification and prevention. The assessment process should delineate the presence and types of any aggressive activities that are manifested. The following distinctions are highlighted in the literature (Connor, 2002). Overt aggression refers to harmful verbal and physical acts toward others, oneself, or property. Covert aggression may include lying, theft, fire setting, sneaky destruction of property, fraud, and defiant rule breaking such as truancy or running away. Relational aggression (more common in females) involves intentional harm to relational status such as withdrawing friendship, spreading untrue malicious rumors, or other activities that impact the social standing or acceptance of a peer. Bullying involves intimidating behaviors toward peers that might be verbal or physical. The character of aggression can be reactive with spontaneous rapid emotional arousal, distorted perception of threat, an intense temper display, and impulsive physical acting

Types of aggression

out. In contrast, _proactive_ aggression may involve planned, purposeful actions that seem more calculated and goal driven, are not necessarily linked to an immediate provocation, and may occur in the apparent absence of physiological and emotional arousal.

These distinctions can be relevant for linking assessment data to selection of intervention approaches. For example, reactive aggression requires interventions that manage hyperarousal, teach skills for emotional regulation, counter cognitive distortions and hostile attributional biases, and highlight alternative problem-solving strategies. Interventions for proactive aggression may require intense contingency management that provides substantial reinforcers that can compete with the perceived benefits of aggression and meaningful response cost to counter the potential benefits that accrue from aggression. Supervision needs to be intensified because proactive aggression may be premeditated. Structured activities that promote empathy and prosocial experiences and attitudes would be provided. Proactive aggression can be reinforced through antisocial peer associations. Strenuous efforts to involve the child in competing supervised activities that foster positive peer associations should be pursued. A complicating factor exists when some youth display both reactive and proactive aggression.

When students have been aggressive at home or school, whether that form of aggression or some more extreme action might take place in the future often becomes a component of the referral question. Although much is known about the general empirical risk factors for aggression, the scientific knowledge enabling accurate predictions of a single individual's risk for violence over a specific time period remains limited. For most school-centered assessments, the important task is to examine the character of prior aggressive episodes, delineate risk factors, assess contextual influences, determine the strength of current stressors, highlight the presence or absence of potential protective resources, and then combine this information with the other elements of a DBD assessment to influence the character, immediacy, and intensity of a multifaceted intervention plan. The goal is development of risk-reduction strategies and implementation of an individualized therapeutic intervention plan.

Initial factors to consider when evaluating potential harm to others include the following: history of past violence and the degree to which it benefitted the child's goals, level of impulsivity, presence or absence of clear triggers for losing emotional and behavioral control, intensity and chronicity of expressed anger, degree of acute and routine environmental stressors, the character and intensity of past interventions, and past responses to intervention (Borum & Verhaagen, 2006; Halikias, 2013).

Early onset of aggressive behaviors increases risks for an escalating aggressive profile. Prior violent behavior remains the best predictor of future

pattern and increased risk of aggression

violence risk (Borum & Verhaagen, 2006). Future risk for violence increases when a more persistent history of episodes occurs. Risk is elevated closer in time to a more immediate past event. Risk assessment has shifted from a search for a violent trait to the consideration of contextual factors (e.g., intensity of approximate stressors and personal vulnerabilities that are dynamic and fluctuate; Borum & Verhaagen, 2006). This is similar to the movement toward dynamic dimensional descriptors of personality that may vary over time on a continuum versus static categorical diagnostic determinations.

Borum (2000) outlined the inquiry into past violent history, considering the following: the context for aggression, whether there was injury to others, involvement of a weapon, perception of lethality of means by aggressor, drug or alcohol impairment, psychotic symptoms, relationship to the victim, purpose of violence, and awareness of cues building up to the aggressive act. It is also important to explore comparable incidents where the youth considered aggression but refrained and to evaluate the youth's perspective on preventing reoccurrence.

Halikias (2013) provided an excellent overview of school-centered risk assessment including sample consent forms, outlines for parent and child interviews, clinical review work sheets, and risk assessment groupings matched to case management strategies. While there is no single instrument for violence risk assessment, the Structured Assessment of Violence Risk in Youth (Borum, Bartel, & Forth, 2006) provides a systematic protocol including an empirically derived checklist of factors that contribute to an overall rating of risk and protective factors. While it contains no specific cutoff scores, this clinical instrument ensures that empirically relevant dimensions are addressed and guide intervention planning.

Despite the horror of the events and the massive publicity associated with them, school shootings are rare; and most perpetrators were not brought to the attention of school officials or referred for an assessment (Halikias, 2013). In addition to the references cited in this section, see FBI threat assessment materials related to school shooters (http://www.fbi.gov/stats-services/publications/school-shooter).

DEVELOPMENTAL CONSIDERATIONS

Prevalence and Developmental Progressions

Although estimates vary, the DSM–5 reports median prevalence estimates for ODD at 3.3% and for CD at 4%. Symptoms for ODD often emerge first, around 6 years of age, with about 25% of children with ODD eventually being diagnosed with CD (Hinshaw & Lee, 2003). Beauchaine, Hinshaw,

[handwritten margin note: when assessing violence/aggression]

and Pang (2010) outlined the typical progression toward delinquent behavior to proceed from severe hyperactive/impulsive behaviors in toddlers to ODD behaviors in preschool to early onset CD in elementary school to substance abuse in adolescence. However, some studies identify distinct but parallel trajectories for ODD and CD (Diamantopoulou, Verhulst, & van der Ende, 2011; Lahey et al., 2009). What is clear is that the long-term course of unresolved CD can lead to impairments that may include substance abuse, other psychological disorders including adult antisocial personality disorder, educational struggles, and occupational problems (Frick, 2012; Moffitt & Caspi, 2001).

Bloomquist and Schnell (2002) summarized the general developmental progression of children with aggression and other conduct problems as follows. In infancy and early toddlerhood (0–2 years), children may exhibit a difficult temperament that is easily frustrated, more irritable, and not easily soothed. In preschool (3–5 years), excessive tantrums may occur, some being aggressive in nature. More defiance and argumentativeness than typical is displayed. In early elementary school (6–8 years), symptoms become more entrenched, and overt and covert aggression emerges. Coercive attempts to control their environment are evident. In later elementary and middle school (9–14 years), overt aggression might decline; however, when it occurs it might be more violent. Covert antisocial behaviors such as lying and stealing may escalate. School and home disruptive behaviors increase. In some cases substance use may begin. In adolescence (15+ years) covert aggression may increase. Although for many, overt aggression continues to decline, but for a subset it might become more violent. Sexual acting out and substance abuse become increasingly prevalent.

Extensive research has focused on the different developmental pathways and symptom manifestation of early childhood onset aggression and conduct problems compared with adolescent onset (Bloomquist & Schnell, 2002; Connor, 2002; Frick, 2012; McMahon & Frick, 2007; Moffitt & Caspi, 2001). Early onset predicts a more severe and persistent course. Adolescent onset appears to be less rooted in troublesome dispositions in early development and thus for many, these problems are less likely to persist into adulthood. Moffitt and Caspi (2001) theorized that late onset is an unhealthy exacerbation of common adolescent rebellion and a consequence of maladaptive struggles to establish a mature independent identity, often complicated by association with antisocial peers. Although for some this is transitory, those who develop legal records, substance issues, or drop out of school are more likely to struggle into adulthood.

Risk factors for childhood onset of DBDs have been identified across multiple domains (Bloomquist & Schnell, 2002). Although there may be some genetic vulnerability to the development of aggression and other conduct problems, it is difficult to separate the impact of negative adult modeling and ineffective parenting. Parental depression and antisocial behavior increase risk and contribute to inconsistent parenting and insufficient supervision. Deficits in emotional regulation and social informational processing complicate peer relationships and can lead to prosocial peer rejection, which then prompts affiliation with antisocial peers. Contextual risk factors include low socioeconomic status, stressful life events, and exposure to violence.

Coercive Family Process

The influential work of Patterson (1982) and his associates at the Oregon Social Learning Center has defined *coercive family process* as central to the development of aggression and antisocial behavior. Through 4 decades of research, this group has refined a social interaction learning model for understanding the development of antisocial behavior (Forgatch & Patterson, 2010; Reid, Patterson, & Snyder, 2002). It is rooted in social learning and behavioral conditioning perspectives for understanding the differential development of behavioral response patterns. In this model, negative reinforcement plays a critical role in the development of problematic behaviors. In negative reinforcement, a behavior is reinforced when it results in an escape from an uncomfortable, aversive, or anxious situation. Negative reinforcement shapes both parent and child behaviors in a reciprocal sequence of interactions. For example, within the coercive process, a child might respond to a parental directive by whining, throwing a tantrum, or other oppositional and aversive behavior. If the parent relents, the child's oppositional behavior is negatively reinforced. If in subsequent attempts, the parent escalates in intensity of command, the child intensifies defiant behaviors until the parent relents again. On the other hand, if the parenting behaviors become more coercive through threatening, yelling, and even physical discipline, and these aggressive attempts are temporarily successful in obtaining compliance, the parental coercion gets reinforced and is more likely to be repeated. The parent is now modeling aggressive behavior as the way to solve problems. This coercive problem-solving cycle becomes entrenched, and the child begins to apply these aggressive strategies for problem solving in school and other environments. Within the peer context, these behaviors can lead to rejection by prosocial peers but may be reinforced by deviant peer groups thus further complicating adjustment.

The Oregon group also delineated the contextual variables that contributed to this unhealthy developmental pathway (Forgatch & Patterson, 2010; Patterson, 1982). As one might expect, adverse social environments add stress to family interactions, expose the child to more frequent aggressive models, and interfere with healthy parent practices. The stresses of poverty, family transitions such as divorce or death, residence in neighborhoods with elevated levels of criminal activity, and medical and mental health issues within the family all have been shown to interfere with adaptive parenting. These factors can foster and exacerbate harmful parenting practices such as inconsistent discipline; inadequate supervision, structure, and monitoring; misapplied contingent reinforcement such as in the coercive process; modeling of aggressive behaviors; chaotic crisis management; inadequate and often seemingly random problem-solving strategies; and inadequate time for nurturing and pleasant parent–child interactions. Patterson and colleagues' research has led to a focus on parent management training and altering family interaction patterns as primary intervention strategies for altering youth aggressive behaviors and antisocial trajectories (Forgatch & Patterson, 2010). Their Oregon parenting training model not only spawned a variety of now empirically supported parent skills training approaches but also contributed to various multisystemic therapies (MSTs) that attempt to simultaneously change family interaction patterns and influence the various contextual factors that complicate antisocial behaviors particularly in adolescence (e.g., Henggeler, Schoenwald, Borduin, Rowland, & Cunningham, 2009).

In addition to the developmental impact of negative reinforcement cycles, aggression can be rewarded through reinforcement mechanisms. When an act of aggression achieves a goal, success increases the likelihood of future aggression as a means to an end. This factor may also be supported by family and social environments that designate "being tough" and physically fighting back as valued traits and preferred problem-solving tools. Although aggressive behavior in school may turn off some prosocial peers, it may garner respect and even social status within antisocial peer groups. Thus, in the end, aggressive children will develop beliefs concerning the use and effectiveness of aggression as a means to achieving their personal goals and protecting social status.

Social–Cognitive Factors

An additional framework contributing to the empirical understanding of the development of aggression is the social–cognitive model (Crick & Dodge, 1994, 1996; J. Larson & Lochman, 2010; Lochman, Powell, Whidby, & FitzGerald, 2012). Adding cognitive elements to the behavioral paradigm, this developmental model established a foundation for cognitive behavior therapy (CBT) protocols for intervention for aggression and antisocial behavior. From this perspective, there is a reciprocal interaction among several key elements of human experience: cognitive appraisal of a situation, physiological arousal, and behavioral response. As will be illustrated later in this chapter from a CBT perspective, interventions may need to address each domain or several in sequence or combination. Difficulties in accurate cognitive appraisal and in solution generation increase development of an aggressive response style (J. Larson & Lochman, 2010). Youth with problems with aggression demonstrate deficiencies in initial encoding of events, recall fewer cues, display selective recall, and attend to hostile rather than neutral cues. This hostile attributional bias leaves them quick to infer that others are out to get them, to overperceive the aggressive intent of others and underperceive their own aggression, and to excessively project blame on others for social dilemmas. These social appraisal difficulties interact with underdeveloped problem-solving skills, where deficiencies in both quantity and quality of solutions are evident. Aggressive youth view and select fewer verbal assertion or negotiated compromise solutions, enact more direct action and physically aggressive responses, and seek more adult intervention supports.

Differences are evident in the social processing styles of different subtypes of aggressive children (Crick & Dodge, 1996; J. Larson & Lochman, 2010). Reactive socially aggressive children tend to display the full range of processing and problem-solving deficits just outlined. These youth are generally viewed as quick tempered and rapidly aroused to angry responses. In contrast, proactive aggression tends to be more purposeful and goal oriented. It appears to be more calculated and less driven by emotional sensitivities and dysregulation. Proactive aggression is positively reinforced when aggressive actions achieve rewarding ends either materially or in social status. Prompted by aggressive modeling, bullying behavior is generally viewed as an example of proactive aggression with rewards that in part derive from an experience of social dominance that purports elevated social status within a peer group or community for feared leaders. However, bullying behavior can also be seen as protection against the vulnerability of being bullied or socially rejected and motivated by fears of inadequacy, in a sense the best defense is a good offense. J. Larson and Lochman (2010) underscored the importance of the reactive and proactive distinction for intervention planning but noted that children can exhibit a blend of these characteristics.

Callous–Unemotional Traits

An emerging focus of aggression research is a more severe subgroup of children who exhibit aggression defined by callous–unemotional traits (Frick & Morris, 2004). The *DSM–5* adds the specifier displaying "limited prosocial emotions" for this subgroup. These youth demonstrate less empathy and remorse, diminished moral reasoning, less fear of punishments, more sensation-seeking behavior, and premeditated aggression. Their instrumental aggressive activity appears to be motivated by anticipation of personal gains rather than by emotional reactivity. The course of their aggression and conduct problems is more severe with some suggestions that it might be a precursor to adult psychopathy (Bloomquist & Schnell, 2002; Frick & Morris, 2004; McMahon & Frick, 2007). Etiology may be more dependent on genetic and neurological factors than on parenting practices and be characterized by less physiological reactivity (Frick & Morris, 2004; Pardini & Fite, 2010). Characterizing early temperament as lacking the fearful inhibitions and sensitive arousal patterns found in emotionally reactive children, Frick and Morris (2004) hypothesized that these characteristics might contribute to an increase in engagement in dangerous behaviors and reduced empathy for the stressful reactions of others. More research is necessary to further confirm and delineate this subgroup profile. Because their aggression incidents do not appear to be driven by physiological and emotional arousal, anger management intervention strategies may not be appropriate. Behavioral contingency management and coordinated multisystemic supervision and supports may have more beneficial impact.

Children displaying repeated harmful aggression and disruptive behaviors can wear out the patience of caregivers who may in exasperation accuse them of a lack of remorse and demand increasingly harsh punishments. Caution is required particularly in the immediate aftermath of a serious aggressive incident. It is necessary to take the time to step back and explore the vulnerabilities of the aggressive youth. My repeated clinical experience has demonstrated that many students who may appear hardened, uncaring, and intransigent may indeed be experiencing significant emotional pain, hiding the impact of past traumatic experiences, and projecting an overlearned protective tough exterior.

Gender Differences

In early development few differences between male and female children are observed in terms of aggressive behavior; however, differences emerge over time in the elementary school years (Crick & Grotpeter, 1995; Moffitt & Caspi, 2001). In general, boys continue to exhibit overt aggression. Girls demonstrate more relational aggression with actions such as withdrawing from a friendship, spreading rumors that harm a peer's social standing, promoting social exclusion of a targeted peer, and manipulating social power in relationships. Girls exhibit more covert forms of conduct problems, such as lying, stealing, running away, and other nonphysical forms of rule breaking and delinquency. Girls are also more likely to develop comorbid depression and anxiety (Bloomquist & Schnell, 2002; Crick & Grotpeter, 1995). Schools are quick to respond to the interference of overt disruptive behaviors. Increasing attention needs to be paid to the negative impact of relational aggression on both victims and perpetrators.

CHILD- AND ADOLESCENT-SPECIFIC INTERVENTION STRATEGIES

As research has identified developmental risk and protective factors that influence the emergence of DBDs, robust attempts have ensued to design and evaluate intervention strategies. The contemporary view underscores the need to target a variety of critical domains: the individual child's behavioral and emotional regulation repertoire; parent and familial interactions; socialization and peer group participation, and critical contextual factors, which can include a complex constellation of community, financial, medical, and school characteristics. Bloomquist and Schnell (2002) proposed a developmental–multisystemic model of intervention. Kazdin (2010) tested models that combine parent and child skills training. Webster-Stratton and Reid's (2010) Incredible Years program evolved to include child, parent, and teacher components. MST designed to address the most severe antisocial behaviors strategically involves a web of community resources in treatment (Henggeler et al., 2009).

As these few examples illustrate, multicomponent intervention strategies are required for effective intervention for DBDs. Empirically supported protocols are drawn from combinations of behavioral, cognitive behavioral, and family therapies. Intervention formats include parent training, individual and group skills training with a focus on generalization, environmental management and supports, and family sessions that may include multiple collaterals. This section will now review sample EBI programs with attention to their contribution to multicomponent frameworks and their synergy with school-centered therapies.

Parent Management Training: Patterson's Oregon Model

Patterson and the Oregon Social Learning Center have designed a series of interventions focused on improving parent management skills and altering the coercive interaction processes that their research defined as central to the emergence of DBD symptoms (Forgatch & Patterson, 2010; Patterson, 1982; Reid, Patterson, & Snyder, 2002). Rooted in social learning theory and behavioral therapy principles involving contingent reinforcement, the Parent Management Training–Oregon Model (PMTO) focuses on teaching parents positive parenting strategies to replace coercive approaches. The program can occur in individual or group formats. Particularly with preadolescent children, the primary focus centers on work with parents, although therapists have the flexibility to include children as appropriate. A deliberate focus on application of skills is maintained through routine home practice assignments and between-session therapist–parent communications.

To shift the focus toward positive parenting practices at the outset of treatment, the initial session spends time helping families identify strengths within the child, parents, and in their relationships. Troubled families tend to overly focus on negative and conflictual interactions, thus minimizing opportunities for positive reinforcement of prosocial behaviors. An early home practice assignment directs families to track observations of strengths and positive behaviors and report on them in the next session. Later, parents will track behaviors that are targets for change and are then coached to develop contingency management systems for shaping and positively reinforcing prosocial behaviors and to use mild punishments for inappropriate disruptive behaviors. The PMTO breaks parenting skills into operationalized components similar to other interpersonal skills training programs. The purpose and characteristics of skills are defined, demonstrated, role played, and practiced at home. For example, parents are taught a sequence for giving effective directions: identify what they want the child to do, calm oneself, approach the child to ensure attention using a neutral tone of voice and posture, state the positive behavior that is desired (not what should not occur) in a brief and concise manner, frame the directive as a request, and then wait 10 seconds before communicating persistent intent. Obviously, this sequence is not magical, but through discussion and role play parents learn how to effectively assert expectations without lapsing into coercive threats or simply giving up.

Limit setting is introduced as a parental teaching tool defined in contrast to the coercive process. Parents and therapists collaborate to design and implement behavior modification contingency management systems with behavior charting and concrete rewards paired with verbal praise and social reinforcement. The goal is to eventually fade out most material reinforcers, but it takes time for entrenched coercive processes to be reversed. The contingency plans are designed not only to change the child's behavior but also the parents'. Because research has shown that inadequate supervision contributes to behavior problems, teaching limit setting also entails training to increase supervision and monitoring of behaviors appropriate to the child's developmental level and behavioral performance. Undersupervised teens are more likely to become involved with antisocial peer groups.

Response cost and enforceable mild punishments are taught as alternatives to coercive threats, which are frequently delivered with negative emotionality and are usually not enforceable (e.g., grounding the child for the semester). Instruction in emotional regulation skills is included to prepare parents to execute positive parenting practices, including limit setting, in a calm and purposeful manner and to improve their modeling of emotional management for their children. For preadolescent children, a time-out procedure is delineated as both a mild punishment and a vehicle for creating momentary distance in what could become heated parent–child exchanges.

Consequences for teens might involve loss of privileges, extra chores, restitution, or other activities that are measured to fit discretions. Role plays guide parents to focus on responding in a pragmatic and measured way to the specific behavior of the child rather than in reaction to their own frustration and emotional arousal. Problem-solving and negotiation skills are taught to parents who are using the same multifaceted training approach with role plays eventually giving way to practice in problematic home situations.

Rather than changing the internal dynamics of the child, the PMTO focuses on changing environmental structures and parental responses, replacing coercive interactions with positive reinforcement, modeling emotional regulation and prosocial behaviors, and establishing effective supervision and limit-setting methods. This approach has received extensive empirical support and has had a profound influence on other approaches to DBDs.

Barkley's Defiant Children and Defiant Teens Parent Training Programs

Although there are significant similarities between Barkley's (2013a) Defiant Children (DC) and Defiant Teens (DT; Barkley & Robin, 2014) parent skills training programs and PMTO, Barkley's incorporation of material related to comorbid ADHD and his focus on managing oppositionality are worth noting. The theoretical foundation of the program is primarily behavioral with an emphasis on operant conditioning principles. Barkley has suggested a training style that mixes didactic presentation of strategies: Socratic questioning to encourage discussion, sharing of experiences, and collaboration in tailoring strategies to individual circumstances; avoidance of unnecessary technical language related to reinforcement technologies; and a focus on home application of strategies. The core concepts of the DC training program illustrate its focus: make consequences immediate, specific, and consistent across settings and between parents; initiate incentive programs for positive behaviors before using punishment for negative behaviors; anticipate problems and have action plans prepared in advance to assist in remaining calm, measured in response, and consistent; and always remember that family interactions are reciprocal to avoid the counterproductive blame game.

Within the DC protocol, Barkley's presentation of the use of time-out procedures (i.e., withdrawal from reinforcement) both at home and in public places is noteworthy for its clarity and practicality. The time-out strategy is paired with instruction in effective commands. Parents are taught how to set up a location that is safe but lacks reinforcement (e.g., no video game gadgets in the child's bedroom). A consistent and persistent protocol is used to give a directive, follow with a brief warning of an impending consequence, wait no more than 15 seconds (no repetitive pleading), follow through with the time-out requirement, and end the time-out not only after the designated time has passed but also after a new directive is followed. Barkley addressed a range of practical counter control strategies for oppositional children (e.g., the child who refuses to leave time-out is told they are not following the new parental directive and thus must serve a new time-out, keeping the interaction on parental terms). See the clinician's manual (Barkley, 2013a) for complete coverage of this advanced parental strategy.

Besides using home practice exercises to promote generalization of skills, the program spends a significant amount of time brainstorming responses to a wide range of potentially challenging scenarios and environments. This emphasis on advance planning or anticipatory guidance prepares parents to identify transitions and activities that are more problematic for their children and to plan ahead with an incentive plan and compliance script, strategies that reduce the risk of parental emotional arousal and reversion to coercive practices. DC and DT include phone consultation and booster sessions for 3 to 6 months after completion of training. Of particular note, Barkley prepares parents for the common trend that persistence in positive strategies is generally harder to maintain for parents than continued application of response cost and punishment strategies.

Multicomponent Programs

Beginning with a focus on environmental engineering and working primarily with parents, DBD intervention programs gradually began to include more involvement of youth within training sessions. This was particularly true in programs focused on parenting adolescents where direct work on problem-solving, negotiation, and conflict resolution skills was a significant focus. This practice has evolved to include integrated programming involving separate groups and occasional conjoint sessions for parents and children, and eventually corollary training for teachers as well. Representative empirically supported programs are referenced next, and their unique strategic contributions noted.

Kazdin's Problem-Solving Skills Training and Parent Management Training Program

As research support began to emerge in support of CBT social, coping, and problem-solving instruction, parallel groups for youth using these curricula were integrated into DBD protocols. Kazdin (2005, 2010) has developed a youth problem-solving program built on the seminal work of Shure and Spivack (1982) and paired it with his parent management training program. The goal of the problem-solving skill training program is to teach and extensively rehearse systematic problem-solving strategies in a game-like format including "supersolver" homework assignments. The emphasis is on generating and evaluating multiple as opposed to impulsive singular responses to real-life challenges, such as responding to provocation, fighting, being urged to participate in antisocial behaviors, and so forth. In the final summary session role-reversal exercise, the child becomes the therapist and teaches the therapist the skills learned in the program.

Kazdin's (2005) corollary parent management training program is rooted in behavior therapy principles similar to the PMTO. The program's format works with individual families and extensively uses role-playing strategies to teach, monitor, and practice parental skills and specific applications to unique family challenges. A key principle for effective intervention in all skills training is active engagement in skills application through role plays and in vivo home situations. Didactic instruction in behavioral management strategies is necessary but insufficient. Kazdin, Siegel, and Bass (1992) reported that combined parent and child training programs had a superior impact to either alone. Adding an element that specifically focused on parental stress management contributed to further gains (Kazdin & Whitley, 2003).

Webster-Stratton's Incredible Years Training Series

The Incredible Years training series (IYT) represents empirically supported comprehensive prevention and intervention programs for DBDs with integrated programs for parents, children, and teachers (Webster-Stratton & Reid, 2010). More than 3 decades of development and research have contributed to this multifaceted training series. Program components target children from early childhood to 12 years of age. This CBT series integrates cognitive social learning theory, including modeling and self-efficacy, Patterson's coercive process delineation, and Piaget's developmental interactive methods. Intervention strategies include core behavior management training with an emphasis on reinforcement and contingency management and cognitive strategies for countering self-defeating angry and depressive self-talk.

The parent training component includes BASIC and ADVANCED curricula appropriate as early intervention and prevention programs and as core components of intervention for DBDs. IYT extends what has been described in the above programs with additional emphasis on training parents to coach their children not only in emotional and social skills but also in persistence and sustained attention. Training promotes increased parental engagement in academic-related activities and increased parent–teacher collaboration. Attempting to counter the isolation of managing a child with a DBD and to enlarge parental support networks, IYT fosters parent networking and emphasizes the importance of parental self-care. Working on the assumption that healthy parental coping skills will benefit parent–child interactions and relieve DBD symptoms, the IYT ADVANCED program teaches CBT anger management and problem-solving skills to parents and then guides their teaching of these same skills to their children.

Recognizing that children exhibiting disruptive and aggressive behaviors present significant challenges to classroom teachers and even at young ages are at risk for exclusion as a primary discipline response, IYT's teacher training program focuses on classroom management strategies, specific responses to aggressive behavior, methods to integrate social-emotional learning into the curriculum, and a framework for parent collaboration.

The IYT child program ("Dinosaur School") applies CBT techniques to teach social and problem-solving skills. This program extensively uses video modeling vignettes (over 180 scenarios) to illustrate skills. Children discuss the feelings and actions of characters then brainstorm and eventually role-play alternative response strategies. IYT tailors interventions to the developmental level of the child incorporating puppet play, cartoons, drawings, and dramatic reenactments of video content.

Video scenarios and models are used with parents and teachers as well. Consistent with social learning theory's emphasis on modeling, Webster-Stratton and Reid (2010) developed an interactive performance training methodology. Videos present scenarios modeling behavior management and problem-solving challenges. A method of contrast is used to highlight the differences between effective and ineffective strategies. Participants then discuss and role play the scenarios, and the therapist tries to build parental self-efficacy by engaging the group in collaborative problem solving. Consistent with sound instructional principles, IYT uses a wide variety of learning activities, is highly interactive, and accommodates visual, auditory, and experiential learning channels.

The effectiveness of the various elements of IYT has been demonstrated in multiple well-designed research studies (e.g., Menting, Orobio de Castro, & Matthys, 2013; Webster-Stratton, Reid, & Hammond, 2004; Webster-Stratton, Rinaldi, & Reid, 2011). The IYT website provides an extensive summary of program goals, components, and materials and training programs for clinicians (http://www.incredibleyears.com).

Cognitive Behavioral Therapy Anger Management Training

As noted above, the social–cognitive model for understanding aggression emphasizes the reciprocal interaction among cognitive appraisal (how a situation is assessed), physiological arousal, and behavioral response. Therapeutic interventions address each one of these domains. Common strategies used in CBT anger management programs include self-awareness training to understand and eventually manipulate the link among bodily reactions, thoughts, feelings, and actions; physical calming techniques to counter visceral arousal that accelerates the aggression cycle; cognitive restructuring therapy to challenge faulty appraisals and cognitive distortions that exaggerate threat assessments; self-talk and self-instruction strategies to prompt rehearsed coping strategies; role playing to practice skills and improve perspective taking; verbal assertion training to state feelings, needs, and wants in an effective and nonaggressive manner; and problem-solving training focused on generating multiple response alternatives to situations that induce angry reactions and using consequential (if this, then that) thinking to evaluate and choose alternatives.

Anger Coping and Think First Curriculums

J. Larson and Lochman's (2010) Anger Coping for elementary age children and Larson's (2005) Think First for high school students are intervention programs that can serve to illustrate the CBT approach. These programs were specifically designed for implementation within the school setting and identify a role for teachers to support and monitor generalization of skills training in the classroom. These interventions target youth who struggle with emotional regulation and display reactive aggression.

Format and Structure. Training is done within a small-group format, preferably with two leaders. Although the roles are not distinct, dual leadership enables one leader to focus on behavior management and the other to guide the lesson plan. The group assembles in a semicircle with no barriers between students so all behaviors can be easily monitored. The atmosphere is part classroom and part group. The group goals are transparent: new ways to solve problems and to control anger. Additionally, students create their own goals, which must be consistent with the purpose of the group, relate to parental and teacher concerns, and be capable of being monitored. Individual goal-monitoring sheets provide weekly teacher and parent feedback on goal progress and provide the data for incentive rewards. This strategy fosters generalization and application of skills and provides routine progress-monitoring data. A token economy behavior management system using points (positive reinforcers) and strikes (response cost) is implemented to motivate students to work toward defined rewards and support behavior management.

Self-Talk and Self-Instruction Training. A review of a sampling of Anger Coping group activities highlights methods and the progression within skills training. The group begins with strength identification, setting the tone that the participants have resources and are more than just someone with a temper problem. To introduce the premise that thinking processes can help to control feelings, the concept of self-talk is demonstrated through a puppet self-control task. After a group discussion defines the concept of self-talk and

[handwritten margin note: strength based? compliance?]

its routine utilization for better or worse in guiding behavior, students brain-storm coping content for self-talk. Using puppets, the group leader models using self-talk to resist negatively engaging with other puppets held by group members who actively taunt the leader. Obviously, this exercise requires firm ground rules (i.e., taunts are directed to the puppets not the person; no sexual language, racial slurs, and so forth) and tight structuring (i.e., clear physical boundaries and marked incentives for appropriate participation), all of which are delineated in detail in the trainer's manual. Although this exercise may initially alarm leaders and create fears that students might lose self-control, Larson and Lochman (2010) emphasized that it is necessary to create in vivo distress to ensure generalization of skills. With proper set-up and execution, the puppet self-control task is an engaging activity that readily demonstrates the power of self-talk to manage stressful situations. Eventually, students are taught how to use self-instruction scripts to use a variety of coping strate-gies for anger-inducing situations. The manual presents a sequence of similar activities that provide opportunities for practicing coping skills when under duress. Repeated practice is necessary for group members to learn the skills and believe in their efficacy.

Perceptual Processes and Perspective Taking. Students also engage in a variety of activities designed to highlight differences in perceptual processes and promote perspective taking. For example, they may privately record and then share interpretations of stimulus pictures portraying emotions and ambiguous problem dilemmas. As members discover that there are multiple perspectives for most events, they explore how a person's viewpoint may lead to certain thoughts and feelings; one person's thought process may stimulate anger and another's may not. Situations can be role played from different points of view to demonstrate that different evaluations of a situation lead to different responses. Role playing different characters in scenes promotes perspective taking which can counter the negative attributional bias that is common to those demonstrating reactive aggression.

Bodily Reactions as Cues for Coping. Training works to identify both the common external triggers and internal physiological arousal signs that are associated with each student's angry reactions. Increased sensitivity to the appearance of these signs enables the child to recognize the onset of an angry reaction. Students are taught how to use bodily reactions as signals that they are beginning to get angry. Once properly recognized, this early warning system can be a cue that prompts them to step back and use self-instruction scripts to prompt coping actions and to monitor their behavioral responses. One self-instruction strand prompts a physical calming action such as taking deep breaths to calm physical tension.

Self-Monitoring: Hassle Logs. Throughout the program, group members maintain "hassle logs" that identify problematic situations that arouse their anger. Similar to cognitive therapy thought records, this self-monitoring tool records the experience of challenging situations and the various aspects of the experience. These scenarios are brought to group sessions and are used in role plays and discussions to practice skills for coping with anger with real life material. Working with real-life material engages members' attention and promotes generalization of skills.

Problem Solving. Problem-solving training emphasizes the need to consider multiple alternatives for responding when anger is aroused and predicts the likely positive or negative consequences of each course of action. Students apply this strategy to events that occurred during the week that are recorded in their hassle log. Attention is focused on what perceptions and self-talk would be associated with each alternative. These exercises underline that slowing down reactions permits recognition of choices that may lead to more positive outcomes (e.g., brainstorming socially acceptable alternatives in the eyes of peers and adults to physical fighting when provoked by a peer). The curriculum's problem-solving model is straightforward: What is the problem? What are my feelings? What are my choices? What will happen (likely consequences for each response)? What will I do?

Video Production Summarizing Strategies. The program's closing activity involves student production of a video illustrating what has been learned about anger management and problem solving. Drawing from challenging scenarios in their own lives, they create a video demonstration that summarizes the adaptive social problem-solving approach taught in the program. This activity serves as a summary and closure activity and further cements learning. The final product can be shown to parents and teachers at a graduation ceremony.

Booster Sessions. Leaders strive to prepare students for overcoming the setbacks that will inevitably occur. In an attempt to avoid all-or-nothing thinking overwhelming students when they have a relapse episode, leaders emphasize that anger can be coped with but not mastered. Booster sessions are scheduled to monitor progress and troubleshoot problems.

Setbacks are inevitable

Adaptation to Adolescents. The Think First program teaches the same strategies with developmental accommodations for teens. Given their more advanced cognitive status, additional cognitive restructuring strategies can be used. A larger repertoire of anger reducers is developed, including physical calming and cognitive distraction techniques. High school students are increasingly vulnerable to misinterpreting social cues. Attribution retraining examines common misreads of others' intentions, such as, "She's staring at me." "They're talking about me." "They'll think I'm weak if I don't fight back."

Trainer Supports. Anger Coping and Think First are both structured manualized programs designed to be applied with clinical flexibility. Manuals suggest developmentally appropriate language for introducing CBT concepts and strategies and anticipate common leadership challenges. Access to demonstration videos can be obtained from the authors (Larson, 2005; Larson & Lochman, 2010).

A. P. Goldstein's Aggression Replacement Training

A. P. Goldstein and his colleagues' "skillstreaming" curriculums have been widely used in schools to teach social and problem-solving skills across all grade levels (e.g., McGinnis, Sprafkin, Gershaw, & Klein, 2011). Aggression replacement training (ART) extends their structured social-learning approach to specifically teach anger management skills (Glick & Gibbs, 2010). They add training in moral reasoning skills to their CBT protocol. The program has received empirical support (see the review in McMahon, Wells, & Kotler, 2006). When schools are already applying the skillstreaming programs, the similar framework and training methods in ART facilitate instruction.

Systemic Therapies

As we have already seen, the field has moved toward multicomponent intervention protocols for intervening with DBDs. The most challenging cases involve complex problems, multiple comorbidities often including substance abuse, inadequate early intervention, progression toward criminal behavior, and chronic school failure. In these situations, adolescent anti-social behavior becomes more dangerous in terms of potential outcomes and more challenging to turn around. The protocols discussed above remain applicable, but additional expanded family therapy and systemic interventions are required. For the most difficult cases, it does seem to "take a village" to respond effectively. Systemic therapies are rooted in family therapy theories and focus on the relational aspects of dysfunctional behaviors while still incorporating the behavioral and cognitive behavioral skills-training strategies already summarized.

EBI systemic therapies for DBDs address not only the family and school systems but also community resources and legal authorities as necessary. Intervention approaches prominently noted in the EBI literature include MST (Henggeler, Cunningham, Rowland, & Schoenwald, 2012; Henggeler et al., 2009), functional family therapy (FFT; Alexander, Waldron, Robbins, & Neeb, 2013), and multidimensional family therapy (MDFT; Liddle, 2009, 2010). There are more similarities than differences across these programs. All of these approaches have a foundation in Minuchin's (1974) structural family therapy framework. This approach targets contextual and relational factors that may foster, exacerbate, or maintain symptoms. Changes in family interaction patterns and supervision and support structures are required to reverse antisocial behaviors. Minuchin's therapeutic approach was refined in work within low SES settings, and it is a strength of systemic approaches that a significant amount of supporting research has included socioeconomically and culturally diverse populations. MST will be reviewed in more detail as a representative example of systemic therapies for DBDs.

Multisystemic Therapy

MST focuses on intensive family interventions with community-based interventions and supports as needed. When adolescents display severe antisocial and delinquent behavior it is necessary not only to change family interaction patterns and individual behaviors but also to address as necessary school failure, legal problems, and involvement with antisocial peer groups. Intervention plans may need to be devised to respond to challenges within each of these systems.

Although MST's foundations are rooted in behavioral and structural family therapies, interventions integrate CBT, motivational interviewing, and other EBI strategies to address specific problem areas. Parents are instructed in contingency management principles to improve discipline practices. Family sessions address repetitive parent–teen conflict cycles. CBT anger management strategies may be taught individually to the adolescent. Motivational interviewing strategies might work with resistance to change, particularly in relation to substance abuse concerns. The intervention plan examines each relevant context in the youth's life that either reduces or exacerbates antisocial behavior risk factors and develops an integrated therapeutic agenda that addresses each domain.

Assisting primary caregivers, generally parents or guardians, is seen as the key to long-term successful outcomes. Even if the caregiver at first appears limited in resources and parenting skills, MST therapists strive to identify and then build on that person's strengths. The therapist's first task is to engage the caregiver by empathizing with their challenges; highlighting that changes in parenting practices will impact their personal happiness as well as improve their child's behavior; offering treatment as necessary for parental depression, substance abuse, or other mental health issues; and identifying potential familial and community supports to assist parenting practices. The focus is on solutions and not blame or fault finding.

Recognizing the negative impact of chaotic, unhealthy, and unsupportive environments, MST strives to increase structure, supervision, and consistency to developmentally appropriate levels. Either authoritarian parenting characterized by high control and low warmth or permissive parenting characterized by high warmth and low control can contribute to disruptive behaviors. Sometimes responses to stresses from extrafamilial systems and challenges can foster negative interaction patterns that become self-sustaining and contribute to antisocial behaviors. For example, if a single parent with a permissive parenting style is working two jobs for economic survival, reduced supervision increases risks for participation in unsupervised delinquent behaviors with antisocial peer groups. Attempting to fit interventions to the real challenges faced by caretakers, an MST therapist works with the caretaker to provide additional monitoring and supervision by reaching out to extended family or other personal resources, facilitate engagement for the teen in prosocial organizations and activities, and brainstorm ways to increase check-ins and monitoring even when not physically present.

Because a wide range of intervention strategies individualized to each situation might be required, MST is not organized around a sequential manualized approach but defined by adherence to nine treatment principles. Henggeler et al. (2009) summarized these principles as follows: (a) *finding the fit*—assessing how the family and other aspects of the child's social environment maintain problems; (b) *strength focused*—build change from current strengths; (c) *increase responsibility*—focus on building responsible behaviors by teen and parents; (d) *present and action oriented*—not blaming past events but taking actions for measurable change; (e) *targeting sequences*—changing patterns of interactions within family and in relation to all relevant systems such as school and community agencies; (f) *developmentally appropriate*—meaningful reinforcement plans and developmentally appropriate monitoring and supervision; (g) *continuous effort*—daily action requirements by all intervention participants; (h) *evaluation and accountability*—monitoring measurable outcomes; and (i) *generalization*—teach, practice, and apply skills that can be used after treatment ends across multiple contexts.

MST strives to engage all participants in present-oriented action planning. This often requires altering patterns of engagement between the teen and parents. Counterproductive negative affect cycles that quickly deteriorate into hurtful blame exchanges are actively interrupted by the therapist. Whenever possible, the therapist reframes messages into more workable and engaging communications (i.e., "When you are yelling at Pete, you really are wanting to tell him how worried you are about him; he means a lot to you and you want what is best for him.").

Parents are trained and coached to increase supervision and monitoring to levels appropriate to age and behavioral history. Many students with DBDs require additional supervision, structure, and accountability. Parents are taught how to effectively issue directives, enforce compliance, and effectively discipline with measured and meaningful consequences. Parents are prepared that inserting discipline and monitoring where it may have been absent before is likely to initially meet significant resistance and require persistent effort and patience to weather angry push back; however, over time it will prove effective. Conflict negotiation and problem-solving skills training become an important focus of family sessions with specific attention to avoiding power struggles.

Contingency contracting is used as a structure to set specific measurable goals, monitor key behaviors, focus on positive achievements, motivate compliance, and ensure appropriately modulated discipline methods. Rewards and incentives must be truly desirable for the youth and readily deliverable. In most cases, some method of response cost, generally losing privileges or loss of points within token system, is necessary to promote positive behaviors. Data may be collected from a variety of sources such as a daily report card from school regarding specific work and behaviors, lab results from urine screens to monitor substance use, compliance with curfew, and other monitored targets.

Whether a parent–child relationship is disengaged or intensely conflictual, MST strives to increase the frequency of positive parent–child interactions to rebuild engagement and establish essential nurturing supports. Just as children with depression may be encouraged to engage in pleasant activities as an anecdote to counterproductive withdrawal, parents and children with DBDs are encouraged to participate in specific enjoyable activities to reengage and repair relationships. Therapeutic goals can often be motivated by creating rewards in contingency contracts that earn a positive parent–child activity (e.g., shopping trip, driving lessons, attending football games).

Multisystemic and other systemic therapies actively engage other social systems and involve key members in sessions. This engagement may mean a communication and planning session with a teacher or other school officials, meeting with a probation officer, a representative from a community agency, or extended family. The goal is to increase support and collaboration and ensure that all critical systems are working in the same direction and not inadvertently maintaining disruptive behaviors. If a student is benefitting from necessary supports at school and is engaged in prosocial activities at the community recreation center, the goals of probation are likely being met as well. FFT recommends completing an FBA that specifically includes antecedent triggers and maintaining consequences that operate across systems (Alexander et al., 2013).

Involvement with antisocial peers complicates efforts at behavior improvement. With limited involvement with prosocial peers or activities, sustaining behavior changes becomes quite challenging. MST guides parents in taking a variety of actions to address negative peer associations. These actions include identifying interests and skills that could be promoted by involvement in prosocial extracurricular activities, increasing contact with peers and their caregivers (includes monitoring what supervision is taking place in other settings), supporting and supervising peer activities at own home, and, for older students, engaging in part-time employment or other structured activities that would enhance responsible behavior and limit time with negative peers. MST emphasizes networking with other parents of prosocial and antisocial peers. School officials and probation officers can often enable access to prosocial community youth organizations. (For an extended treatment of the topic of peer interventions, see Henggeler et al., 2009.)

Substance Abuse

Disruptive behavior disorders and involvement with negative peer groups can also lead to alcohol and other drug abuse. These systemic intervention approaches (MST, FFT, and MDFT) have been identified as EBI interventions for substance abuse (Waldron & Turner, 2008). Substance abuse is viewed as a learned behavior that originates and is maintained by familial, social, and other environmental factors similar to other troubling behaviors. Intervention requires coordinated multisystemic interventions integrated with behavioral and cognitive strategies as individually necessary.

Similar to treatments for antisocial behaviors, adolescents generally do not refer themselves for substance abuse therapy and frequently deny or minimize their use. Lab tests such as urine drops and breath tests for alcohol provide objective measures and can be used within treatment with or without court orders. (For full coverage of drug and alcohol testing protocols, see Henggeler et al., 2012.) Often teens are ordered for treatment, and the initial motivation for participation is to get off of probation or other court restriction or to avoid further school punishments or loss of participation privileges. Even if the only initial shared goal among parents, teen, and therapist may be meeting stipulations to reduce external pressures, this can be a legitimate entry point, cement engagement, and build a foundation toward addressing substance abuse issues more honestly later as therapy progresses. Motivational intervening techniques support engagement and have been used extensively in work with addictions (W. R. Miller & Rollnick, 2012).

In the context of multisystemic work, contingency management protocols for substance abuse intervention have received extensive empirical support (Alexander et al., 2013; Henggeler et al., 2012; Waldron & Turner, 2008). Procedures are similar to other contingency programs with target behaviors beyond abstinence, including alternative positive behaviors such as school performance markers, participation in specific prosocial activities, obtaining a part time job, and so forth. Objective measures are used to assess abstinence. Because contingent rewards must compete with the personal and social reinforcements of using substances, they must be sufficiently powerful and truly valued by the adolescent. Alexander et al. (2013) noted that contingency management systems targeting substance abuse typically must remain in place longer than similar protocols for other behaviors before they are faded.

The functional analysis that is the foundation for contingency management identifies the triggers for substance use, examining setting factors, emotions, the character of triggering events, social affiliations, pressures for performance, and so forth. The intervention plan includes understanding and then manipulating these antecedents, including in some cases eliminating participation in certain activities or social environments.

When substance abuse is triggered by stress or social anxiety, CBT instruction in social and coping skills is applied. Direct instruction in drug refusal skills is taught, rehearsed, and monitored. There is documented support for CBT individual and group interventions (see the summary in Waldron & Turner, 2008). Many practitioners have hesitated to use group methods with teens who abuse substances fearing iatrogenic effects. In their summary review of EBIs for adolescent substance abuse, Waldron and Turner (2008) labeled group CBT interventions as well-established EBI and argued that extensive data supports group methods. For group work in this area and for the full range of DBDs, it is necessary for group programs to be highly structured, have cotherapists when possible, include enforceable behavior management plans, administer specific intervention protocols, and be outcome focused (Simon, 2013). J. Larson and Lochman's (2010) anger management program can serve as a strong model for group intervention work in schools.

INSTRUCTIONAL SUPPORTS, EDUCATIONAL ACCOMMODATIONS, AND CLASSROOM PROTOCOLS

The principles of behavior management outlined in the family interventions described above also directly apply to classroom management, school discipline policies, and individual behavior intervention plans. Comprehensive school programing for DBDs should include school-wide behavior standards, monitoring, and supports; universal social-emotional learning curriculums; multitier intervention strategies, and effective discipline policies.

Students displaying a DBD benefit from well-structured classrooms with clear expectations that are routinely prompted, supported, monitored, and reinforced. The climate of the classroom should be warm and inviting but with sufficient structure to support emotional security and behavioral compliance. Students with a history of DBD are often sensitive to being viewed as "troublemakers" and require extra teacher effort to feel included and valued. Early recognition of strengths and reinforcements for effort toward success and improved behavior are important foundation stones for classroom management. General classroom rules and expectations need to be clearly posted and understood. Rules work best when they are brief; are supported by classroom discussion; have clear rationales; are stated positively in behaviorally specific terms (what to do before what not to do); and are routinely monitored, reviewed, and reinforced.

Effective instruction practices have been well-researched for students with behavior disorders (see J. R. Nelson, Benner, & Mooney, 2008). They include frequent reviews, preteaching goals and expectations, step-by-step instructions, extensive scaffolding, frequent feedback, persistent reinforcement for work production and time on task, multimethod teaching to mastery levels of subskills before introducing new material, guided practice, and periodic reviews to ensure long-term retention. Particularly at the elementary through middle school levels, various "direct instruction" curriculums have been developed and found effective for students with behavioral concerns (Marchand-Martella, Slocum, & Martella, 2004; J. R. Nelson et al., 2008). These programs emphasize carefully delineated skills progressions that are taught to mastery incorporating the instructional elements noted above.

Sometimes behavior problems emerge in subject areas where learning deficits create performance anxiety and elevated levels of frustration. Successfully addressing instructional needs for these students is an important step to reduce classroom behavior problems. A subgroup of students with DBDs also present with ADHD symptoms. The corresponding section on instructional supports in Chapter 4 delineates additional effective instructional practices for students with ADHD. The judicious supplemental use of educational software programs outlined in the ADHD chapter is also applicable to students with DBDs. It can prove particularly effective for students with ODD characteristics, who are prone to power struggles. They are less likely to argue with their laptop than a teacher and may be motivated by appropriate computer time as an incentive for accurate work completion. However, software-based activities tend to be designed for core skill building and should only be one part of any student's curriculum. Rathvon (2008) and J. R. Nelson et al. (2008) are excellent resources for evidence-based instructional practices that support behavioral and academic growth.

Students with DBDs are more likely to struggle in less structured settings and activities. Thus, they require specific supports during transitions; independent activities, including individual seatwork; and in settings like physical education, recess, and the lunchroom where supervision tends to be more limited, expectations are less concrete, and the potential for even inadvertent physical contacts is more likely. If problems emerge in these settings, they can be addressed with specific behavior management plans, which may include additional supervision, setting manipulation, behavioral rehearsal, contingent reinforcement, and, if necessary, response-cost punishments through temporary loss of participation privileges. However, the goal remains teaching and supporting the student in effective participation in less structured settings.

Reinforcement protocols that address whole-class behavior goals and include additional individualized plans for students with DBDs are proven to be more effective than punishment-oriented systems. It is often necessary to use a point or token system for students with behavioral issues, particularly when teachers are responsible for a large classroom. In the context of contingency contracts, response cost procedures can be more readily implemented (i.e., loss of points toward a reward or loss of privileges). Students with IEPs targeting behavioral improvement are required to have an FBA and a corresponding behavior intervention plan. Bloomquist and Schnell (2002) noted that less effective teachers are more likely to emphasize punitive strategies. Less effective teachers use more counterproductive warnings, scoldings, and threats to involve external authorities or remove the student from class. Effective teachers, on the other hand, use more positive reinforcement strategies coupled with mild punishments and work to maintain disruptive students within the classroom environment. When punishments escalate over a period of time, it is necessary to review the intervention protocol and modify its strategies.

Although temporary loss of participation privileges for some activities may be appropriate, exclusionary discipline practices such as out-of-school suspension and expulsion have not proven to be effective (American Psychological Association Zero Tolerance Task Force, 2008; Losen & Skiba, 2010; Sharkey & Fenning, 2012). Instead, these practices may increase risks for behavior problems. Zero tolerance policies that give time off from school for some disciplinary offenses are more likely to leave youth with demonstrated needs for more intensive supervision without sufficient monitoring, may promote increased involvement with truant peers and up risks for participation in delinquency, and further reduce already fragile academic motivation by putting these students further behind or requiring them to complete work without necessary support. Similarly, exclusion from extracurricular activities removes students from prosocial peers and increases involvements with antisocial peers. It can be an appropriate discipline response to exclude a student from the privilege of an event or athletic contest, but continued participation in practices and related activities maintains adult supervision and positive involvement in prosocial activities.

To simultaneously reinforce positive behaviors and reduce power struggles and lengthy arguments surrounding disciplinary events, I suggest use of written *behavioral contracts*. Behavioral contracts are helpful for working with students who exhibit repetitive oppositionality. These contingency contracts clearly define goals, how progress will be measured and rewarded, what constitutes misbehavior, and its consequences. Positively oriented but including response cost and other disciplinary actions, these contracts should be signed by the student, the teacher, and the parents. Adding consistency, clear expectations, and routine to behavior management can reduce arguments. Students with DBDs are prone to blame teachers for being arbitrary. These contracts also assist the teacher in framing student behaviors as choices with anticipated outcomes. With a written contract, a teacher can show a student who is on the verge of a tantrum that he or she is making choices that will lead to already agreed on rewards or punishments; this action fosters consequential thinking and reduces power struggles. Carefully constructing a consequence requires school staff to crystallize intervention plans and include motivating incentives as the primary strategy for shaping positive behaviors.

Research data that define developmental pathways toward DBDs have clearly delineated the importance of early identification and intervention. In the absence of successful early intervention, DBDs deteriorate into increasingly dangerous outcomes and impairments that are more resistant to remediation. School-wide positive behavior support programs provide vehicles for teaching positive behaviors, monitoring progress, and identifying students in need of early intervention (Johns, Patrick, & Rutherford, 2008). Multitiered intervention supports have created support programs for students identified as at risk for serious behavioral, emotional, and social problems. It is important to note that the EBI literature on DBDs recognizes that these behavior disorders are generally chronic conditions that require multifaceted interventions of sufficient intensity for a prolonged period of time. This requires school-centered interventions to be of sufficient scope and intensity at the onset of concern and be implemented for appropriate durations of time. Applying sufficient resources early on can limit the course of behavioral problems and also prove less costly to school districts in the long run. The *least restrictive environment* requirements in special education practice are designed to provide sufficient and appropriate services to students in as typical an instructional setting as possible. Care must be taken to make sure that addressing this requirement does not unduly increase the risk for deterioration, meaning that sufficiently intense interventions and support resources must be applied within standard education interventions. Continuous progress monitoring will indicate whether special education supports and services are necessary to address student behaviors and accompanying academic difficulties. Patience required for allowing interventions to succeed must be repeatedly balanced with risks for chronic impairment that may require more intense services and at times specialized placements.

CRISIS INTERVENTION PROTOCOLS

The goals for crisis intervention for DBDs begin with safety for the acting out students and all others in the environment. Safety is achieved through de-escalation of affect, racing distorted thoughts, and risk for impulsive action. The adult provides realistic reassurance, supports balanced attributions and perspective taking, and engages the student in adaptive short-term action planning.

When necessary, the student should be removed from a peer audience that might reinforce acting out behaviors. Sometimes it is necessary to remove the audience if the only way to move the escalated student is with physical escort. This removal reduces not only the potential danger to others but also the opportunity for showing off to peers. When possible, guide the student to a safe and private setting. Active listening is used to lessen the intensity of the emotional response and provides a nonjudgmental opportunity for the student to tell his or her story—what happened, how he or she was affected, and what actions took place. At the point of emotional escalation, the intervening adult neither agrees with nor disputes the student's rendition of events. Prompts toward physical calming actions can be helpful (i.e., "Take a deep breath; let's take a walk to a private place."). At the moment of a crisis, directives should be assertive but delivered in a calm tone of voice. Singular instructions with a few repetitive words work best. The adult posture is reassuring, determined, and unafraid. An out-of-control student is calmed by a crisis interventionist who is in control but not counteraggressive.

As the student's emotional arousal diminishes, communication can begin to address cognitive distortions that fuel negative behaviors. The crisis interventionist can suggest more realistic attributions, counter all or nothing thoughts, and provide realistic perspective to paranoid thinking. The adult points out the dangers of impulsive actions and connotes realistic hope without promising something that cannot be delivered (e.g., rescue from disciplinary consequences). Student actions are repeatedly framed as choices with consequences and benefits promoting the notion that he or she has the decisive control on the eventual outcome of the situation. This promotes a cause-and-effect framework and teaches consequential thinking.

As emotional arousal recedes, the student is engaged in immediate short-term planning. It is important not to get too far ahead. Planning for reentry into class and reengagement in academic work is the immediate goal. If the student was removed from the classroom, it is optimal to arrange a conference with the teacher to support successful reentry and to problem solve any short-term issues. School staff pledge long-term assistance and doable follow-up. At a later time in a therapeutic debriefing session, it is appropriate to explore whether there are external events or stressors that triggered the vulnerability displayed in this crisis that require direct intervention.

Long, Wood, and Fecser (2001) devised the Life Space Crisis Intervention (LSCI) schema for crisis intervention that has been successfully used in multiple settings. Developed in their work in a residential school program, LSCI has six stages. The three diagnostic stages begin with empathic responding to drain off emotional arousal, guide students to create a timeline of their version of what happened to hear their perspective, and conclude with identification of either the real background source of stress (e.g., just broke up with a boyfriend) or the underlying faulty perception (e.g., "I have to strike back; she was just out to get me."). The three reclaiming stages start with fostering insight into self-defeating response patterns even if only understood in terms of how this behavior is hurting the student (e.g., "Is this getting you where you want to go? What price do you pay for this?"). The next stage identifies coping or conflict resolution skills that will need to be addressed in subsequent therapeutic intervention. Finally, the student plans or rehearses reentry into the classroom and faces the staff member or student who was the counterpart in the conflict situation.

FAMILY AND SYSTEMIC SUPPORTS AND INTERVENTIONS

Because of the central role that family and systemic interventions play in interventions for DBDs, the topic of this section has already been largely covered. However, a few intervention and support tools deserve mention.

Home–School Contingency Contracts

Contingency contracting has been emphasized as a core strategy with this population. The most effective contracts are coordinated home–school interventions. These interventions broaden the range of reinforcers that can be applied to motivate behavioral improvement, decrease the opportunities for the student to manipulate between home and school, and provide mutual support and consistent programming across home and school. Daily report cards can provide data for coordinated contracts and keep parents abreast of school performance. Typically designed as checklists, this tool can be tailored to track specific behaviors and academic progress. Daily report cards can also include homework assignments to direct parental supervision for completion.

Conjoint Behavioral Consultation

Sheridan and Kratochwill (2010) devised conjoint behavioral consultation (CBC) as a structured protocol for positive collaboration between schools and home. CBC is consistent with the intervention principles outlined throughout this chapter. Its strength is its emphasis on collaboration and systematic implementation protocol. It begins with conjoint problem and needs identification across both home and school settings. CBC collects baseline data, designs related progress-monitoring approaches, and operationalizes target behaviors. An FBA is developed that considers both individual and systematic factors in home and school settings. A conjoint intervention plan is designed that includes delineation of specific actions and roles of parents, teachers, and the student. A framework for progress monitoring, ongoing home–school communication, and implementation integrity and sustenance is outlined. The CBC approach is particularly useful when students attempt to split school and home and when behavioral displays are inconsistent across settings. Numerous empirical studies have supported CBC's effectiveness.

Wraparound and Neighborhood Partnerships

The discussion of multisystemic interventions above highlighted the need for building support systems for families that contribute valuable resources to support interventions. Consistent with MST principles, Swenson, Henggeler, Taylor, and Addison (2009) proposed a framework for creating "neighborhood partnerships" that coordinate and support efforts among medical, mental health, law enforcement, youth recreation, and social welfare agencies specifically to reduce adolescent violence and substance abuse. The wraparound initiative is a similar community support structure that has been widely applied in schools (Eber, Breen, Rose, Unizycki, & London, 2008). This program recognizes that a broad array of supports and services might be required to support a troubled youth and his or her family. This support may include services directed at the financial and other support needs of the parent that directly influence the child's behavior and mental health. Parents are equal members of the wraparound team that sets goals and coordinates community resources. This process expands beyond collaboration between community and school mental health workers to include a full range of community resources. These approaches extend the resources that can support students and families within school-centered multitiered systems of support.

CASE EXAMPLE

The following example examines one dimension of a complicated DBD case, specifically illustrating how a home–school contingency contract can address school behaviors and family systemic change simultaneously. Dan, an 11-year-old sixth grader, exhibited repetitive disruptive behaviors in the classroom. The FBA hypothesized that these behaviors were reinforced by attention from peers, the teacher, and eventually parents, and by work avoidance, which relieved performance anxiety. The family assessment revealed that his parents feared his getting in trouble in the community and severely restricted his social activities. Dan spent most of his time under his mother's supervision, but she was not successful in enforcing homework completion or influencing school behaviors. Dan's father was generally underinvolved, except when Dan's mother insisted that he respond to negative school reports. His response tended to involve loud scolding, predictions of future failure, unrealistic threats that he would be sent to live with a relative, and directions for his wife to extend grounding at home. These interchanges were becoming the primary points of contact between Dan and his father.

With considerable outreach activity, the therapist convened a school conference that included Dan's principal, teacher, and both parents. The goal of the conference was clearly delineated as the development of a forward-looking change plan that would require the active involvement of each participant. After considerable discussion and negotiation that required periodic interruption of unproductive blaming and arguing, a contingency contract was developed that addressed specific school behaviors and homework compliance. A daily report card would be used to provide a report of work completion and behavioral performance. Structures to support and monitor both areas were outlined for both school and home. Short- and long-term motivating reinforcers were delineated. The therapist guided the intervention plan to change interaction patterns within the family. A particular emphasis was to increase father's involvement in supervision and to create opportunities for Dan to earn positive activities with his father. At a specified time each night, Dan was required to show his daily report card to his father and display completed homework. Measured positive rewards and disciplinary consequences were clearly specified. Motivating reinforcers identified by Dan included more social time outside of the house, extended curfew and bedtime, enhanced allowance, and special activities with his father (fishing was a shared interest).

The home–school contract was designed to transform the underinvolved and typically negative father–son relationship toward increasingly appropriate supervision and motivating and enjoyable shared activities. Addressing both the individual student and the contexts of his behaviors simultaneously improved school behaviors and altered family interaction patterns in a manner that would set the stage for sustained improvement and more supportive familial relationships. The home–school contract was only one element of a more comprehensive plan that included additional academic supports, similar positively focused school contingencies, coping-skills instruction to manage performance anxiety and his quick temper, and supports for engagement in prosocial recreational programs in the community; but its ability to address systemic change in the family and create a more positive home–school partnership enhanced the success of the total intervention package.

6

PEDIATRIC BIPOLAR DISORDER

Severe mood disorders such as pediatric bipolar disorder (BP) can have a dramatic impact on daily educational functioning. Explosive behavioral episodes negatively impact the school environment, challenge routine discipline systems, and require extensive behavior management and therapeutic support resources. Because a contemporary framework for understanding this disorder is emerging slowly, in this chapter, I examine diagnostic and assessment factors at greater length. This examination sets the stage for exploration of therapeutic and classroom intervention strategies that require differentiation in their application from other externalizing disorders.

http://dx.doi.org/10.1037/14779-007
School-Centered Interventions: Evidence-Based Strategies for Social, Emotional, and Academic Success,
by D. J. Simon

DIAGNOSTIC CHARACTERISTICS
AND ASSESSMENT FRAMEWORKS

Pediatric or early onset BP has only been recognized and differentiated from adult onset over the last 2 decades. Geller and DelBello (2003) and Biederman (2003) and their respective research teams were among the first to delineate an early onset bipolar profile that differed significantly from symptom manifestation in adults. They described a syndrome presenting with severe affective dysregulation, high levels of agitation and aggression, and behavioral dyscontrol. Different from BP in adults, BP in children and young adolescents is characterized by rapid cycling with multiple brief episodes of sadness and mania occurring even within the same day (Geller et al., 2003). Children may experience affective "storms" that move in seemingly without warning, resulting in depressive and angry affect that feeds prolonged temper outbursts. The course of BP in children tends to be more chronic and continuous and less episodic and acute than in adults (Geller & Luby, 1997).

The symptom picture for BP is extensive and can include the following: severe disturbance of mood; rapid cycling between depressive and agitated symptoms; chronic irritability; impulsivity; distractibility; aggression; hypersexuality; physical agitation; depression; sleep disturbance; suicidal thought; grandiosity; increased goal-directed activity; racing thoughts; and accelerated, pressured, or increased amount of speech (Geller & DelBello, 2003).

Differential Diagnosis

The broad symptom list complicates diagnosis and challenges practitioners' attempts to link assessment with intervention. Elements in the BP symptom profile overlap with several other common childhood disorders, compromising assessment, identification, and treatment. Of particular note is the common comorbidity with attention-deficit/hyperactivity disorder (ADHD). Estimates vary greatly, but meta-analyses indicate that as many as 62% of children with BP also meet the criteria for ADHD (Kowatch, Youngstrom, Danielyan, & Findling, 2005). Most children eventually diagnosed with BP were initially treated for ADHD. Because of early manifestations of impulsivity and distractibility, school staff will often report and focus on ADHD symptoms first. However, interventions addressing these characteristics prove to be insufficient for addressing emerging mood and aggression issues. Some children may demonstrate increased aggression and agitation if first placed on stimulant medications. This response may also occur in reaction to some antidepressant medications.

Because the goal of assessment is to guide interventions, it is important to be able to differentiate between ADHD and BP symptoms. ADHD symptoms tend to present as stable and continuous. In contrast, BP symptoms are generally cyclic or episodic with variability in both timing and intensity of their display and some periods where they are not clearly evident. Although children with ADHD and BP both demonstrate hyperactivity, those with the mood disorder may also reveal *grandiosity*, a sense of inflated worth, power, or ability. The impaired judgment evident within a grandiose manic cycle can lead some children to express a sense of entitlement or a misplaced confidence that they can "pull off anything." Eventually this attitude may crash when mood cycles toward depression. Although children with ADHD alone may get angry when thwarted from getting their way or confronted with the boundaries of adult limit setting, children with BP may become enraged without clear provocation. Parents and teachers may report "walking on eggshells" to attempt to avoid actions that might trigger an explosive episode, never quite sure when it may occur or what might set it off. Children with isolated ADHD versus BP display different affect in response to critical feedback or aversive consequences. Youth with BP appear hypersensitive to correction and may escalate rapidly to an explosive emotional outburst or even aggression.

In companion studies, Geller, Zimerman, Williams, DelBello, Bolhofner, et al. (2002) and Geller, Zimerman, Williams, DelBello, Frazier, et al. (2002) researched the key differentiating symptoms between ADHD only and BP in contrast to a normal control group. Irritability, hyperactivity, accelerated speech, and distractibility were common in both ADHD and BP groups but not in controls. Key discriminating criteria present only in the BP group centered on the mania-specific symptoms of inappropriate elation, grandiosity, flight of ideas–racing thoughts, decreased need for sleep, and hypersexuality. To illustrate the character of these key BP symptoms, Geller and colleagues went on to contrast typical healthy psychological presentations and BP manifestations across these discriminating domains.

Regarding displays of elation, healthy children will display excitement appropriate to context, and their enthusiasm will not impair functioning (e.g., anticipation and excitement when preparing for a trip to an amusement park). In contrast, pathological elation is inappropriate to context and impairing (e.g., becoming excited and giggly in a classroom for no apparent reason and struggling to stop). Healthy children will engage in expansive and imaginative play. After school they may create an imaginary classroom, willingly taking turns playing the roles of teacher and students. In contrast, a child exhibiting manic grandiosity may stand up in class and try and tell the teacher how to instruct the class or even demand to the principal that the teacher be fired. Healthy youth generally do not report racing thoughts or flight of ideas, whereas some children with BP may even verbally articulate the need for a "stoplight in my head" or to stop feeling like "the Energizer bunny." Typical children sleep 8 to 10 hours per night and are tired if they sleep less than their usual routine. A child experiencing a manic phase may stay up to 2 a.m. playing feverishly and then at school that morning still show no signs of fatigue or slowing down. Parents and teachers of students with BP often describe the daunting challenge of keeping up with the intensity of their energy levels. Some children with BP display hypersexuality. While a healthy 7-year-old child may play doctor with a same-age friend and a typical 12-year-old child might peek at a pornographic magazine, an unhealthy sexual preoccupation may result in inappropriate sexual actions or expressions such as impulsively touching others in private areas, imitating sexual activity, or repetitive inappropriate drawings of naked people. The five differentiating symptoms just described frequently occur in BP but are not present in typical children nor within a typical ADHD profile in the absence of a mood disorder.

In schools, the challenge for differential diagnosis is often between ADHD with a comorbid oppositional defiant disorder (ODD) and BP with comorbid ADHD. Both combinations occur frequently, but they require different intervention protocols. School service and intervention protocols will be compromised if assessments related to special education identification stop at the point of delineation of significant emotional and behavioral interference with educational progress and fail to pursue further diagnostic clarity. The key differences between these two profiles center on the episodic nature of BP. Children with ODD are consistently hostile and defiant toward authority figures. A propensity toward repeated power struggles reveals excessive control needs. Temper outbursts are clearly related to a specific event such as being thwarted by an authority figure. The temper display may be meant to be intimidating or manipulative to maintain control of the relationship or circumstance. In BP, there is a clearer picture of mood disturbance, including *rapid cycling*, that is, overexcited–manic behaviors followed without warning by explosive anger and episodic depressive symptoms. Grandiosity presents a more intense and unrealistic sense of entitlement, in some cases special powers, than the battle surrounding who is in charge in an ODD power struggle. Temper displays in BP may be triggered by environmental stress but are less predictable and more clearly impacted by internal factors. In this case, parents and teachers may be befuddled about the origins of an angry outburst.

Children diagnosed with posttraumatic stress disorder (PTSD) also experience some symptoms that appear to overlap with BP and complicate differential diagnosis. Both disorders may display irritability and emotional volatility. Posttraumatic stress disorder symptoms of increased arousal may include hypervigilance, exaggerated startle responses, sleep disturbance, and irritable sensitivity. In PTSD, there is a developmental history of exposure to a traumatic event that threatened physical integrity. The anxious avoidance of any stimuli that might remind the child of the trauma is clearly founded in an environmental event and is an acquired coping response. Although BP symptoms may be exacerbated by stress and environmental influences, their origin appears to be neurobehavioral. Hyperaroused episodes often occur without clear evidence of a precipitant. In BP, it is common to have a family history of affective disorders suggesting a genetic factor. Although it is possible that someone with BP might have experienced a traumatic event, in general, ruling out trauma history is important in the differential diagnostic process and will directly affect intervention selection.

DSM–5 Changes

The diagnostic process for BP has been further complicated by new definitions introduced by the DSM–5 (American Psychiatric Association, 2013). This revision of the psychiatric diagnostic manual describes five primary categories of BP and related disorders and introduces a new diagnostic category recommended for use with children with mood dysregulation who do not meet BP specific criteria. For a Bipolar I diagnosis, the DSM–5 requires evidence of at least one manic episode lasting at a minimum of one week and present through most of each day. At least three of the following symptoms must occur to constitute a manic episode: grandiosity, decreased sleep need, excessive or pressured speech, racing thoughts, distractibility, increased goal-directed activity or psychomotor agitation, and engagement in activities with a high potential for painful consequences. The manic episode is severe enough to significantly impair social or occupational functioning. Although not uncommon, hypomanic or depressive episodes are not required to meet criteria for Bipolar I. In contrast, Bipolar II disorder requires episodes of hypomania (lasting at least 4 days) and major depression (lasting at least 2 weeks) without any manic episodes. Symptom presence is of shorter duration and severity than in a full manic episode. Impact on social and occupational functioning is less significant. Cyclothymic disorder involves chronic mood disturbance (at least one year duration for children), but neither the hypomanic nor the depressive symptoms are of sufficient incidence, severity, or duration to meet criteria for Bipolar II.

The DSM–IV–TR also used the category of Bipolar Not-Otherwise-Specified (BP-NOS) to address cases where bipolar symptoms were present but either in character or duration did not fully meet criteria for either Bipolar I or II designation. Because symptoms in children did not always mirror those of adults, diagnosticians often used this category with children and young adolescents who did not yet meet the full Bipolar I criteria. Some have criticized this practice as merely using a "catchall" designation for clearly mood-impaired youth who did not fit adult diagnostic protocols. The DSM–5 eliminated BP-NOS but delineates two nonspecific BP categories to address symptom presentations characteristic of BP, which cause significant distress and functional impairment but do not specifically meet the full criteria of BP or related disorders: (a) Other Specified Bipolar and Related Disorder requires identification of a missing criteria (e.g., short duration or insufficient number of symptoms), whereas (b) Unspecified Bipolar and Related Disorder does not require a specification of what full BP criteria are not met. The latter category is meant to apply when there is insufficient information for more diagnostic specification such as in an emergency room context.

As the field struggled to understand the unique symptom display of mood disorders in youth, concerns were raised in some quarters that BP in children might be becoming overdiagnosed. The *DSM–5* committees responded to this controversy by adding a new diagnostic category, disruptive mood dysregulation disorder (DMDD), which was placed in the manual's section on depressive disorders. This category was designed to separate out children who display chronic irritability but not specifically manic characteristics such as grandiosity, racing thoughts, psychomotor agitation, or other characteristics that define a manic episode. DMDD criteria include temper outbursts occurring at least three times per week that are out of proportion to the situation and inconsistent with developmental levels. A persistent negative mood is observable on a nearly daily basis for a period of at least 12 months. The symptoms are manifested in multiple settings. Age of onset is before age 10 years but not formally diagnosed before age 6. The primary distinction from BP is absence of manic episode. The difference from ODD is the severity and frequency of temper outbursts and the persistent mood impairment between angry displays.

The publication of *DSM–5* has not settled the controversies surrounding diagnosis of BP in youth. Leading psychological researchers Fristad and Youngstrom (2010) and notable psychiatric researchers Axelson et al. (2012) have questioned whether there is sufficient data to support the new DMDD category and have expressed doubt that BP is being significantly overdiagnosed in children. Fristad, Goldberg-Arnold, and Leffler (2011) used the term *bipolar spectrum disorders* to describe a range of mood disorders. Fristad et al. noted that psychological treatments have many essential similarities across the mood disorder spectrum and that treatment for depressive symptoms is often critical for children who exhibit a BP I manic episode as well. Fristad et al. proposed a "psychoeducational protocol" that integrates cognitive behavior and family therapy approaches for the treatment of bipolar spectrum disorders. This state-of-the-art intervention approach is delineated later in this chapter.

International Classification of Diseases, Tenth Revision, Clinical Modification

The *International Classification of Diseases, Tenth Revision, Clinical Modification* (ICD–10–CM) does not include a DMDD category but continues to include a BP unspecified code (F31.9; Goodheart, 2014). Similar to the *Diagnostic and Statistical Manual of Mental Disorders* (fifth ed.; *DSM–5*; American Psychiatric Association, 2013), *ICD* diagnostic codes specify BP subtypes according to symptom severity, type of current or most recent episode (i.e., manic, depressed, or hypomanic), whether psychotic symptoms occur, and active or remission status.

Ongoing Longitudinal Studies

Formal research on mood disorders in children is relatively young. Diagnostic clarity will require the study of the long-term development of children who display these serious symptoms. A major barrier has been the differences in diagnostic parameters used in research studies as the field's emerging understanding of youth mood disorders developed. In an attempt to better understand children diagnosed as BP-NOS, the National Institute of Mental Health funded two large ongoing longitudinal studies: Course and Outcome of Bipolar Youth (Birmaher et al., 2006) and the Longitudinal Assessment of Manic Symptoms (Findling et al., 2010). These investigations use the same set of operationalized criteria for BP-NOS. They studied children with an elated or irritable mood with three or more of the following characteristics: inflated–self-esteem–grandiosity, decreased need for sleep, more talkative–pressured speech, flight of ideas–racing thoughts, distractibility, and increase in goal-directed activity–psychomotor agitation. A demonstrated change in functioning needed to occur with a duration of over 4 hours within a 24-hour period and a frequency of four or more episodes. It is my hope that these studies will clarify the long-term course of children with mood disorders and contribute to our understanding of the relationship between pediatric BP and BP in adults.

Emerging Psychological Assessment Protocols

The challenges and controversies surrounding assessment of pediatric BP require the practitioner to understand the full range of mood disorders, common comorbid conditions, and current assessment procedures. Accurate assessments are critical for the design of appropriate treatment interventions. Youngstrom, Jenkins, Jensen-Doss, and Youngstrom (2012) made substantial contributions to the empirically supported assessment of BP. Youngstrom et al. suggested a 2% incidence in youth and recommended a multistage assessment process. For an initial screening protocol, they identified indicators for specific BP spectrum screening: family history of BP, early onset depression (particularly if treatment resistant), antidepressant coincident mania (manic episode in apparent reaction to antidepressant medication), episodic aggressive behavior, psychotic features in the context of mood disorder, and the maintenance of high energy despite less sleep. Youngstrom et al. recommended beginning with broad measures that include externalizing scales such as behavior rating scales commonly used in school-based assessments (e.g., Achenbach System of Empirically Based Assessment [ASEBA; Achenbach & Rescorla, 2001] or the Behavior Assessment System for Children—Second Edition [BASC–2; C. R. Reynolds & Kamphaus, 2004]). Using the ASEBA Child Behavior Checklist, Mick, Biederman, Pandina, and Faraone (2003) reported clinical elevations (T scores >70) for Aggression, Anxiety/Depression, and Attention scales for their BP sample. Although this pattern of elevated scores was similar to children with ADHD and others with externalizing problems, the score elevations were significantly higher in the BP sample. This finding suggests that the attention difficulties in ADHD comorbid with BP are typically more severe than in ADHD alone. It is important to underline that broad measures are sensitive to the presence of BP symptoms but that elevated scale scores are not necessarily specific to BP. The presence of this pattern confirms the critical need for additional investigation.

In the presence of screening indicators and broad measures identifying externalizing factors as noted, Youngstrom suggested adding a mania scale as a next step (e.g., Child Mania Rating Scale; Pavuluri, Henry, Devineni, Carbray, & Birmaher, 2006) to assess the presence of specifically manic symptoms. Youngstrom underlined the need to use multiple informants in both rating scales and diagnostic interviews, gathering data from the child, parents, and teachers. There is greater diagnostic validity regarding manic symptoms from parent than from youth reports. When there is a convergence of supporting data from multiple sources, there is an increased likelihood of BP and a more severe symptom manifestation. Structured diagnostic interviews can systematically investigate BP markers (e.g., WASH-U-KSADS; Geller, Williams, Zimerman, & Frazier, 1996). As these steps are followed in investigating BP, it is important to simultaneously assess possible comorbidities not just to differentiate diagnoses but because their presence may impact both psychiatric and psychological treatment regimens.

School Personnel Contributions to Diagnosis

The accurate assessment of BP and related mood disorders is essential to guide effective intervention planning. The emerging framework for understanding manifestation in children remains complex and at times controversial. School-centered professionals need to collaborate extensively with prescribing psychiatrists and thus must understand the nuances of *DSM–5*. Their daily observations of children provide critical feedback to physicians regarding both diagnosis and medical management. Concerns about possible

BP symptoms tend to emerge over time. School-based professionals are in a unique position to observe children in their natural setting over an extended period of time in the presence of readily available comparisons to peer behavior and development. This opportunity for early identification can be of enormous benefit for children potentially reducing the length and severity of the disorder's course. Multistage screening and assessment protocols can be used as concerns are identified and behavioral incidents escalate. Multiinformant, multimethod, and multisetting assessment methods are readily available. With proper assessment protocols, mental health practitioners working with and within schools can delineate and initiate interventions that are appropriate for addressing BP and common comorbidities.

DEVELOPMENTAL CONSIDERATIONS

Because of so many potential confounding developmental factors, it is challenging to make definitive diagnosis of a mood disorder during early primary grades. Symptoms can begin to emerge at very young ages, but many developmental factors potentially influence symptom manifestation. These include medical, genetic, familial, and social factors as well as influential environmental and historical events. A comprehensive developmental and family history is required. Key discriminating symptoms such as grandiosity, inappropriate elation, racing thoughts, and hypersexuality will tend to emerge as clearly divergent from same-aged peers in most severe cases even at younger ages. Attempting to rule out competing explanations for the presence of symptoms is an important assessment step (e.g., do symptoms of hypersexuality result from sexual trauma experience?). In the school context, it is also essential to account for the impact that any academic frustrations may contribute to irritability and low frustration tolerance. Early identification and intervention attempts within a response to intervention (RtI) framework can provide information relative to symptom severity, resistance to intervention, and persistence of symptoms that might be attributable to BP after symptoms of other disorders have been addressed (e.g., interventions for ADHD or ODD). Many of the cognitive behavior therapy (CBT)-based therapeutic interventions designed for BP are appropriate for youth demonstrating high degrees of irritability, hyperactivity, and volatility even if a mood disorder diagnosis has not yet fully emerged.

The key developmental difference between early onset BP and late adolescent to early adult onset is the presence of recurrent rapid cycling mood disturbances as opposed to longer unipolar manifestations with relatively nonsymptomatic periods in between mood swings. In their early research into childhood mood disorders, Geller and Luby (1997) summarized developmental

TABLE 6.1
Hypothesized Course by Age of Onset

	Prepubertal and young adolescent	Older adolescent and adult
Initial episode	Major depressive disorder	Mania
Episode type	Rapid cycling, mixed	Discrete with sudden onsets and clear offsets
Duration	Chronic, continuous cycling	Weeks
Interepisode functioning	Nonepisodic	Improved functioning

Note. From "Child and Adolescent Bipolar Disorder: A Review of the Past 10 Years," by B. Geller and J. Luby, 1997, *Journal of the American Academy of Child and Adolescent Psychiatry, 36*, p. 1171. Copyright 1997 by Elsevier. Reprinted with permission.

differences, initial manifestation, type and duration of episode, and interepisode functioning as displayed in Table 6.1.

Geller, Zimerman, Williams, DelBello, Bolhofner, et al. (2002) reported that 87% of children with BP demonstrated concurrent elation and irritability. This characteristic is evident in adult samples as well. The prevalence of mixed cycling episodes exhibiting both manic and depressive symptoms found in children suggests similarities to symptoms in adults with chronic BP mixed cycles who have demonstrated limited responses to treatment. This factor raises concerns about the long-term course of very early onset BP, but more longitudinal study is needed. In contrast to this similarity across age groups, Geller, Zimerman, Williams, DelBello, Bolhofner, et al. (2002) reported that the widespread presence of comorbid ADHD is not found in cases with late adolescent or adult onset.

BP diagnosis is not always clear in younger children. A comprehensive developmental history, attention to potential comorbid conditions and rival diagnostic hypotheses, and careful documentation of a child's response to intervention efforts can combine to provide clarity. Despite substantial progress, a significant need prevails for increased understanding of the developmental nuances in BP presentation and subsequent intervention particularly before adolescence. The relationships between pediatric and adult BP are not clearly established (American Academy of Child and Adolescent Psychiatry, 2007).

CHILD- AND ADOLESCENT-SPECIFIC THERAPEUTIC INTERVENTION STRATEGIES

The intervention protocols described in this section address students with BP and severe mood disorder issues generally coupled with comorbid ADHD symptoms. This is the most common clinical presentation encountered in schools. The intervention strategies are drawn from emerging literature that point to the positive impact of specific CBT and family therapy strategies as well as our own experience with this population at a public therapeutic day school.

Emerging Evidence-Based Interventions for Children and Adolescents

The primary focus of the literature regarding pediatric BP has been on differential diagnosis and medication interventions. It is only relatively recently that studies have begun to explore psychosocial strategies and psychotherapeutic protocols and then only within clinical contexts external to the school setting. Before outlining a school-centered intervention protocol, four psychological intervention programs that have demonstrated some empirical support are highlighted: Fristad's psychoeducational psychotherapy (PEP; Fristad, Goldberg-Arnold, & Leffler, 2011), Pavuluri's child- and family-focused CBT (Pavuluri, 2008), Miklowitz's family-focused treatment (Miklowitz, 2008), and Goldstein's dialectical behavior therapy for adolescents (T. R. Goldstein, Axelson, Birmaher, & Brent, 2007).

Psychoeducational Psychotherapy

Fristad, Goldberg-Arnold, and Gavazzi's (2002) initial intervention research focused on psychoeducational and training support for parents. Their model evolved into treatment protocols that involved working with individual families and children (IF-PEP) or multiple families and children (MF-PEP). PEP targets children ages 8 to 12 and is designed to intervene with students experiencing any mood disorder. Fristad et al.'s treatment protocol integrates psychoeducational training, CBT, and family therapy approaches. Fristad et al. stressed that many cognitive techniques can be adapted for use with younger children if they are presented with sufficient scaffolding. This often involves physical activities ranging from drawing to role plays to rehearsing coping skills. Creating age-appropriate metaphors can often assist young children in applying cognitive strategies. Similar to many CBT protocols, written exercises, workbook activities, and homework assignments are used involving children and parents. IF-PEP occurs across 20 to 25 weekly sessions generally alternating between parent and child sessions, although parents are involved in check-in activities at the beginning and end of a child session.

The overarching principle of PEP emphasizes that children and parents are not to be blamed for symptoms and did not cause the symptoms of this disorder, but together they share the responsibility for managing symptoms. Treatment targets begin with education about the illness and the nature of treatment. The biological foundation of mood disorders is emphasized. A key family intervention target is the reduction of expressed emotion. Responding to the labile moods and disruptive behaviors of a child with BP or other mood disorder can lead to significant parental frustration and significant family tension and conflict, resulting in increasing patterns of critical feedback, hostile exchanges, and counterproductive emotional overinvolvement in the child's illness. Work with parents focuses on identification and recognition of negative interaction cycles and coaching in more adaptive response approaches. Paralleling the CBT coping strategies taught to their children, parents learn how to recognize the links among thoughts, feelings, and actions to support their attempts at altering negative and unproductive response cycles.

The PEP curriculum targets symptom management, problem-solving, and communication skills through an integrative approach. Behavior outbursts and mood episodes are redefined as problems to be solved. Resisting the instinct to take verbal attacks personally, parents are coached to first communicate empathy and look for the likely meaning behind inflammatory comments (e.g., "I hate you" may be an inappropriate way of communicating that "I'm upset that you can't stop my sister from picking on me"). Parents and children are taught relatively parallel schema for problem solving and how to practice it together. The child sequence is illustrated as follows: First, *stop*, take a moment to calm down; second, *think*, define the problem clearly, then brainstorm various possible solutions; third, *plan*, decide on an action to take; fourth, *do*, take action; and fifth, *check* how it turned out and decide whether it worked or another plan of action is needed. This process emphasizes that when moods escalate, it is necessary to pause and slow down to avoid a reactive response that may escalate to a negative behavioral cycle, communication may become distorted and increase conflict, and almost all situations present a variety of response options that can be evaluated as potential action plans. PEP centers on symptom management, coping skills training, and improving family crisis response cycles. Including siblings in a session ensures that the interaction patterns of the entire family system are addressed.

Similar to CBT protocols targeting other symptom profiles, PEP child sessions focus on teaching the child to build a symbolic tool box of coping strategies. Self-calming breathing strategies, helpful actions to take when angry or sad, reminder coping thoughts, and identification of knowledgeable and reliable adult supports are examples of elements to include in a coping repertoire. A core CBT paradigm used in PEP is a thinking, feeling, doing framework. Children are taught to increase their self-awareness of feelings, expand their affective vocabulary, and identify triggering events that escalate their emotional arousal. Work sheets, social stories, and in-session processing of stressful events explore these connections. There is a particular focus on the identification of triggers for mad and sad feelings. The therapeutic approach emphasizes that we may have no choice about how we feel but we can choose how we respond. Consistent with cognitive therapy schema, PEP guides children and parents toward an understanding of the differing impact of hurtful compared with helpful thoughts on both emotions and behaviors. Written exercises juxtapose the different outcomes generated by hurtful versus helpful thoughts. Similar to work with other externalizing disorders, development of consequential thinking is promoted.

Child- and Family-Focused CBT

Pavuluri's (2008) child- and family-focused CBT is intended to serve as an essential adjunct to psychotropic medication treatments. Its roots are in cognitive behavioral, family, and interpersonal therapies. Pavuluri uses the acronym of RAINBOW to organize her team's approach to treatment. The goal is to develop family structure and routines, communication strategies, and coping skills to assist affected children in staying in the middle of the mood spectrum:

R = Routine. Develops stable predictable schedules and structures to reduce stress and potential conflicts.

A = Affect and anger management. Uses mood charts to provide feedback relative to medication effects, modify routines, and prepare for application of learned coping strategies.

I = "I can do it." Highlights the need to maintain a positive attitude and not merely define the child by his or her illness and encourages the development of positive self-statements.

N = "No negative thoughts." Applies CBT cognitive restructuring with training in adaptive thinking strategies for improved problem solving. Similar to the concept of mindfulness, living in the here and now is emphasized.

B = "Be a good friend." Coaches the child in establishing and maintaining positive peer friendships; and B also prompts parents to "live a balanced lifestyle" and recognize that they won't be effective supports for their children if they are overly immersed in their child's illness.

O = Optimal problem solving. Emphasizes collaborative parent–child dialogues that take place after rage subsides, being especially careful to avoid immediate consequences for undesirable behaviors.

W = "Ways to get support" for the child and family members. Involves having children draw a support tree with the names of people they can rely on when stressed or escalating.

Involving multiple resources can also reduce the potential for negative intensity in the parent–child relationship. Similar to Fristad's PEP, this approach alternates child and family therapy sessions.

Family-Focused Treatment

Miklowitz's (2008) family-focused treatment targets BP in adolescents. It is rooted in behavioral family therapy with a target of creating a family environment that supports problem-solving practices that promote mood stability and limit the extremes of conflict and explosive outbursts. Consistent with other approaches, the entire family is educated to understand the biopsychosocial nature of BP, what is controllable and what can be managed, and collaborative problem-solving strategies. Miklowitz employed a multiple-levels-of-analysis approach that focuses on the interactions of individual and familial stressors and vulnerability inherent in BP and examines the risk and protective factors within family functioning. Therapy assists families in identifying triggers and early warning signs for mood episodes. The family is then guided to conduct relapse drills during periods of relatively stable functioning so that crisis responding is characterized both by early recognition and intervention and a calmer, preplanned, less reactive support response. Role plays are used to engage families in direct interpersonal skills training, targeting the expression of positive feelings, using active listening, making positive requests for changes in one another's behaviors, and providing constructive negative feedback. Skills are practiced in and out of session, addressing common areas of disagreement and behavior management challenges. This model pays particular attention to the delicate balance between adolescent needs for individuation and independence and the realistic limitations presented by BP symptoms. After the initial course of treatment, family-focused treatment maintenance sessions are scheduled that may occur for a period of up to 2 years.

Dialectical Behavior Therapy

T. R. Goldstein et al.'s (2007) dialectical behavior therapy approach extends the therapeutic framework initially used for teens with borderline symptoms to the treatment of BP (A. L. Miller et al., 2007). Dialectical behavior therapy's focus on emotional regulation skills, the development of middle-path perspectives, and mindfulness appears applicable to BP. The model's mix of individual and family work and structured social-skills training is similar to elements of the other approaches covered above. Miklowitz and Goldstein (2010) specifically highlighted the similarities between family-focused treatment and dialectical behavior therapy treatments for adolescents with BP.

Common therapeutic themes are apparent in this brief review of the emerging evidence-based intervention (EBI) literature. Systemic interventions are required that involve the child, family, and school. BP is identified as a chronic illness that is no one's fault but needs a team approach to manage symptoms. It is important to separate the child as a whole from the illness even though symptoms often mask his or her positive characteristics. Symptom management involves the implementation of specific strategies to manage the intensity of the child's moods and emotional expression and to reduce negative response cycles within the family. Instruction and practice in CBT coping skill building is a central intervention task for both the child and the family. CBT focuses on understanding and altering the connections between bodily reactions, thoughts, feelings, and actions. Specific instruction and rehearsal in crisis intervention and problem-solving strategies is essential preparation for modulating the intensity of BP episodes.

School-Centered Protocol

Over the last decade, one of the most common referrals to our public therapeutic day school were children and young adolescents either diagnosed with BP or demonstrating significant mood disorder symptoms. The impact of BP symptoms on individual educational functioning and on the school environment can be substantial. In response, we developed an intervention protocol that integrated and applied the emerging EBI literature to the school setting (Simon, 2010, 2011). The protocol addressed individual, family, and classroom issues requiring and benefitting from collaboration among students, teachers, parents, school administrators, school-based therapists, collaborating community-based therapists, and prescribing physicians. As a Tier III intervention, therapeutic day schools serve youth with the most severe interaction of psychological and educational concerns. However, the intervention strategies delineated apply to less structured educational environments as well. Program evaluation research demonstrated significant improvements in behavioral and academic functioning, including a significant decrease in incidents of aggression (Clevenger, 2011).

Principles outlined in this school-centered protocol are also applicable to parents and caregivers. However, it is important for therapists to recognize that schools generally have additional support resources beyond those available to a parent, guardian, or caregiver.

Build Rapport in "Good Times"

It is essential to build positive rapport with a child diagnosed with BP during symptom-free periods. A hyperaroused, potentially explosive student is more likely to permit assistance in de-escalation with someone with whom he or she has a positive history. The assessment and recognition of student strengths and proactive coping-skills instruction are critical initial steps in the intervention process. Time spent by the school therapist before explosive episodes can help limit their occurrence and, when they do happen, position the therapist to be an effective resource for restabilization. A positive rapport builds a foundation that can soften and survive angry conflicts that may require adult limit setting even in the face of aggressive verbal attacks. It is important for the affected child to know that the relationship with the therapist can endure even the most explosive outbursts and meltdowns.

General Stress Reduction

Although stress does not directly cause BP, an elevated general stress level or a negative event can trigger explosive behavior and intensify or prolong a manic or depressive episode. Interventions strive both to teach the child coping skills and to reduce environmental stressors. Learning strategies to manage routine daily stressors lays the foundation for coping with the severe disruption of bipolar cycles. The provision of additional structure and predictable routines throughout all aspects of the child's life can significantly reduce stress. At home this may involve establishment of a relatively consistent schedule for meals, family time, play, homework, and sleeping. At school it may include additional scaffolding for instruction, clearly stated behavioral expectations, measured but predictable disciplinary consequences, and additional supervision or support during less structured times such as physical education, recess, lunch, or passing periods. Advance preparation and preteaching of expectations is necessary before transitions, field trips, or other special events and any major changes in schedules and routines.

Focus on Self-Awareness

Treatment begins with a focus on the development of self-awareness, the foundation for instruction in coping skills that will follow. Youth who experience intense mood episodes often feel like leaves blown by a sudden gust of wind, tossed out of control without notice, and not in charge of their own destiny. Self-awareness training can be organized within the framework of the self-understanding model (SUM) central to the therapist's case conceptualization and delineated in Chapter 3 (Kapp-Simon & Simon, 1991; Simon, 2012). The SUM targets an understanding of the impact of experiences on physical reactions, thoughts, feelings, and behaviors. An advanced awareness of the interdependency and link among these dimensions of personal experience will serve as the foundation for eventual increased self-management of BP symptoms.

Adult observations and feedback focus the child's attention to recognize changes in their sensory, cognitive, and affective arousal, fostering heightened self-awareness. The child, parents, teachers, and therapist become engaged in trying to recognize the earliest signs of cycling behaviors, which requires concentrated focus on changes in the child's appearance, mannerisms, and behaviors. Careful monitoring can reveal certain actions, physical postures, comments, or interactions that might signal escalating tension, arousal, or irritability. These signals will be highly individualized. One student may begin tapping a pencil persistently on his desk while exhibiting an increasingly tense physical posture; another student may begin rocking back and forth in her chair, struggling to stay still and remain focused on academic tasks. Some students may begin to withdraw, whereas others will heighten stimulation with negative comments or actions toward the teacher or classmates. These examples of precursors can signal the potential onset of a BP episode.

A corollary task is the identification of events or circumstances that trigger emotional and behavioral escalation. It may be criticism from a peer, a particularly frustrating or nonpreferred academic task, loss of a game in gym class, or other occurrence that unbalances the child's mood. Systematic observations as part of a functional behavioral assessment can be a helpful process for delineation of common triggering environmental influences. The eventual goal is to teach the student to recognize the first internal signs of rising affect whether it is manic and angry or depressive in nature. Although this identification is an essential task, it can be quite challenging for a child who experiences moods as sudden storms that swoop in and out of his or her experience. The therapist and other school staff can serve as mirrors illuminating subtle patterns of indicators and triggers. In a calm, empathic, nonjudgmental manner, staff share their observations of student behaviors, postures, social interactions, and moods. Adult recognition and communication regarding early warning signs fosters self-awareness; provides an opportunity for teaching the student to associate physical, cognitive, emotional, and behavioral cues within him or herself with rising affect and behavioral risk; and promotes eventual self-monitoring.

Most often, a physical reaction or internal visceral or sensory clue is the first recognizable sign that there is escalating risk for a disruptive mood episode. The therapist combines external observations from teachers and parents with structured processing of significant events to help the child identify instinctual bodily reactions that signal the onset of stress. It is often helpful to practice physical recognition with positive events such as successes and fun activities and then explore the experience of difficult but less intense experiences before processing extreme behavioral incidents or emotional meltdowns. Social stories, bibliotherapy books, and children's literature can provide examples. Homework exercises can ask students to identify an experience with emotional impact and highlight their bodily reactions, thoughts, feelings, and actions. Teaching children physical calming strategies to use at the first sign of rising physical tension is an important coping technique. Recognition of the onset of tension can be coupled with a self-statement such as "I'm feeling tense," "I'm bothered by__," or "I need to take action." The action might involve calming breathing techniques, tightening and relaxing of muscles to release tension, taking an approved time-out walk, or some related strategy. These calming responses serve the purpose of countering rising emotional arousal, delaying immediate reactive behaviors, and becoming positive triggers for initiating preplanned coping strategies. Self-soothing actions that counter escalating hyperarousal serve to balance moods and modulate behavioral responses.

Psychoeducation: Nature of a Mood Disorder

To a child, the experience of BP or other mood disorder symptoms can appear like a foreboding, mysterious, and powerful force. Emotional ups and downs feel like uncontrollable waves. The therapist can remove some of this mystery by labeling and defining the experience, thereby reducing some of the terror associated with the overwhelming thoughts, feelings, and behavioral impulses. Defining a problem is the first step in any problem-solving process. Once a child understands what he or she is up against, the therapist and child can start planning strategies and solutions. The psychoeducational phase of treatment involves teaching the child at a developmentally appropriate level about the existence and nature of the disorder. The therapist prepares the student to view BP as an illness that can be treated rather than as a set of negative characteristics that define him or her as a "bad person."

Analogies to relatively common childhood medical conditions like allergies and juvenile diabetes prove helpful. Children with diabetes did not cause their illness, but with adult support they have a responsibility to manage it through diet, lifestyle, and medications. The more children with diabetes understand the nature of diabetes and its treatments, the better prepared they will be to manage its effects and exert some personal control over its symptoms. This same approach is applicable to BP. The critical catchphrase presented to the child is "I am not responsible for having a bipolar disorder (mood disorder), but I am responsible for managing it." This phrase sets the tone and defines the theme of treatment. The child will not be blamed for having symptoms but will still be responsible for learning how to manage emotions and behaviors. If someone experiences a disability, they strive to understand its impact, learn how to compensate for its limitations, and marshal other strengths to accommodate for challenges encountered.

Communicated to all caregivers, this perspective assists school staff and family members in avoiding blaming the child and instead prompts support toward helping to manage responsibility for behaviors. This empathic framework lessons the risk that caregivers will resort to reactive counteraggression or rejection responses to serious behavior episodes. For both the child and adults, this psychoeducational process attempts to separate the child from the illness. The child has a wealth of strengths or other characteristics that are more than BP. Establishing this framework sets the stage for introduction of the externalizing the symptom coping strategies that will be a key element of treatment.

Externalizing the Symptom

The cognitive strategy of externalizing the symptom originated in M. White and Epston's (1990) work with narrative therapy. A key feature of March and Mulle's (1998) EBI protocol for managing obsessive–compulsive disorder (OCD) used a "naming the enemy" strategy for externalizing OCD urges. Similar to BP, OCD is a neurobehavioral disorder that can leave the child feeling as if thoughts and behaviors are out of control. This approach was applied to the treatment of BP by Fristad, Gavazzi, and Soldano (1999). The goal of this strategy is to view the symptoms as separate entities rather than innate qualities or fixed attributes of the child. This perspective reinforces the critical distinction between being a child experiencing BP symptoms as opposed to a BP child whose personal identity becomes solely defined by the illness. This viewpoint sets the stage for mobilizing self-management strategies.

Naming the enemy can provide a concrete visual image or tool for the child to use in coping strategies to combat the overwhelming aspects of BP. The therapist guides the student in describing the experience of either an extreme manic or depressive episode. Particularly for young children, drawings may be helpful for capturing the impact and personal view of symptoms (Child and Adolescent Bipolar Foundation, 2003). Creating a visual image sets the stage for externalizing the symptom. With either a verbal description or a visual image depicting the emotional tumult of a cycling episode, the student is encouraged to name the "enemy"—the mood disorder illness. Naming the enemy personalizes the illness and provides an identity apart from the child. Children may choose titles like "fire," "storm," "tiger," or another powerful image of the threatening force of their moods. The child can personalize interactions with the enemy by using adaptive covert self-talk strategies, talking within one's head or under one's breath to the enemy (e.g., "I can feel that you're coming, 'storm'; but I know what to do to stay calm. I need to take a deep breath, then__"). In this way naming the enemy provides the initial step toward constructing a self-instruction coping protocol to fight back the symptoms of BP (March & Mulle, 1998; Meichenbaum, 1985).

Fristad et al. (2011) designed additional strategies for naming the enemy and separating the child from his or her symptoms. In two separate columns on paper, children are asked to delineate their positive characteristics and BP symptoms. Then the paper is folded in half to create a visual image of how the symptoms are hiding the child's positive attributes. The symbolic message in this activity is that children are separate from their mood disorders and that treatment strategies will help them put symptoms behind them. The self-talk image the therapist reinforces is, "I am masked by the enemy and need to reveal more of me." This two-column exercise can be repeated with parents to reinforce this perspective. It provides an opportunity for parents to communicate to their child that they recognize their many positive qualities and will work with them to control the symptoms that get in the way of those qualities showing. A similar strategy can be used to juxtapose and compare hurtful versus helpful thoughts and actions, negative versus positive coping thoughts, catastrophic versus realistic thoughts, mood or rage fueling versus calming thoughts and actions. The externalizing the symptom strategy can be integrated into a multistep cognitive behavioral intervention protocol.

Some children may resist or struggle with naming the enemy. This occurs most often when the parent and/or the child struggles to accept and come to terms with the mood disorder diagnosis. In this case, the therapist can continue to model defining and personalizing the enemy as an external force to promote acceptance (e.g., "You are really restless and looking like you want to jump out of your skin." "That stormy mood is coming over you again and you are feeling really angry." "Take a deep breath and blow its tension away." "Let's do something to keep it from taking you over and getting you in trouble."). The therapist's communication is suggestive of the coping self-talk that is a key CBT intervention strategy.

Cognitive Therapy Strategies

A core assumption in CBT intervention models is that cognition can be a mediating variable for behavioral responses. How we attribute meaning to events and what we say to ourselves have implications for our feelings and actions and either enhance or limit our capacity to cope with stress. If a child perceives an external locus of control, consistently attributes causality for despair or an angry outburst to the actions of others, and appraises stressful events as threatening beyond typical rational perspectives then he or she will feel helpless and be unable to control mood cycles. Therapy explores the character of covert assessment of events and the covert self-talk that provides direction to behavior (e.g., "When the teacher corrected my mistake, she was really just saying I was stupid; now I don't care if I get in trouble ripping up the paper and storming out of the room . . . she deserves it.") Counterproductive patterns of negative appraisals and self-defeating thoughts can be examined outside of the crisis of an escalated emotional or behavioral cycle. Then the therapist can provide more realistic alternative frameworks for judging the threat in events and can use external prompts to guide eventual self-instruction coping strategies. The goal of this process is to interrupt the automatic nature of the reflexive angry or hopeless thoughts and assist in slowing down the emergence of either a manic or depressive cycle. Cognitive restructuring, rational analysis, tests of evidence, and other cognitive therapy techniques can prove helpful. Some younger children may struggle with some of these techniques and require a more concrete focus on replacing self-defeating thoughts with self-instructions for coping.

Multistep CBT Intervention Protocol

The individual elements of the school-centered protocol can be integrated into a multistep CBT intervention approach that is consistent with the dimensions of the SUM case conceptualization model and complementary with the highlighted EBI frameworks for treating BP. The first step teaches the student to learn to recognize the earliest physical cue that physical, emotional, or behavioral arousal is occurring. Sensory and physical warning signs will vary greatly from one child to the next. Examples are tension in the stomach, heart pounding, adrenalin rush, tightening muscles, and an overall sense of restlessness. This visceral recognition becomes a signal to prompt initiation of practiced self-instructions to deploy rehearsed coping strategies beginning with a physical calming response. This may take the form of a relaxing breath, a brief tightening then relaxing of the muscles in the hands and arms, or other personalized physical tension release. These calming actions strive to maintain a sense of personal control, slow the onset of arousal, and diminish the risk of damaging reactive behaviors.

After physical calming begins, the child identifies and challenges any immediate self-defeating or counterproductive thoughts that can paralyze thinking and action at the potential onset of a meltdown. Training in developing and applying covert self-instruction scripts works to block out racing and overwhelming thoughts (Meichenbaum, 1985). The therapist has prepared the child to block and replace self-defeating comments (e.g., "It's happening to me again; there is nothing I can do about it; might as well just let it all out") with adaptive self-instructions that can directly address the enemy and moderate its impact (e.g., "I need to control these feelings; I'm not going to let you [the negative mood] control me; I'm going to stay in control by__").

The next self-instruction prompts an action or deployment of a specific rehearsed coping strategy. The therapist and child need to have explored and delineated practical coping behaviors that can foster self-control and reduce the risk of a mood episode. The earlier focus on self-awareness will have identified some actions that make matters worse and some that have proven helpful. The therapist brainstorms achievable options with the child and suggests some additional healthy alternatives. Although the goal is for self-instruction to enable the child to initiate coping actions, the therapist, parent, or teacher may need to prompt their use. Particularly in early stages of treatment, the child may require a time-out or an exit strategy to regain composure and avert a meltdown. A brief removal from the scene of the stressful action may ward off an explosive incident. At home this may take the form of retreating to a specific location apart from family members and engaging in a soothing activity. At school it could be moving to a study carrel on the other side of the classroom or using a preapproved code to take a time-out walk by receiving a hall pass to go to the nurse's office or some other safe location. Learning to take a self-initiated time-out can bolster a child's self-confidence in her or his ability to maintain self-control and avoid conflict escalation; it also avoids the humiliation of being sent out of the classroom at school or to one's room at home because of escalated behavior. Self-initiated time-outs should be brief. Care must be taken that they do not become manipulative attempts to avoid work or used to avoid processing interpersonal challenges. However, they are preferable to intense behavioral episodes in the classroom and may be frequently necessary in early stages of treatment. The long-term goal is to develop a repertoire of actions that can occur during the moment in the setting at hand. Individual child preferences and setting demands will define what is workable, but it is most helpful to actively do something, such as drawing or reading or executing a physical task, to reduce ruminating moods or unimpeded racing thoughts. The goal always remains enhancing self-monitoring and self-control. The final step in the coping sequence is a calm reentry into the prior activity or situation. Although key adults must praise and reinforce the child's attempts at adaptive coping, it is equally important to train the child to build positive self-reinforcement comments directly into the self-instruction coping protocol.

This multistep CBT protocol integrates what the child has learned through an understanding of the nature of BP and related mood disorders and an increased self-awareness of the connections among personal physical reactions, thoughts, feelings, and behaviors in response to mood episodes. Bolstered by training in externalizing the symptom and identification of adaptive coping actions, it provides a proactive sequence for managing the onset of symptoms and modulating emotional and behavioral responses. A summary of the CBT intervention steps follows.

1. Recognize at the earliest stage possible the internal physical signal and/or external trigger that indicates that hyperarousal has begun and that there is elevated risk for the onset of mood cycle.

2. Initiate a self-calming action to quiet increased physical tension.
3. Talk back to the "enemy" to combat the energy of an impending mood episode.
4. Interrupt escalating catastrophizing and self-defeating thoughts and replace them with a rehearsed self-instruction coping script.
5. Take positive coping actions; if necessary, move oneself away from the immediate stressful setting.

This coping sequence is learned and practiced outside of the context of a cycling episode, but the therapist, parents, or school staff can prompt and support its application in a crisis moment.

This intervention protocol is considerably more challenging to implement if the student or parents are in denial about the mood disorder or if the primary teacher is convinced that the student is being manipulative and willfully acting out. The therapist can still prompt and model adaptive self-talk, including casting the onrush of the negative mood as an external agent (e.g., "Take a deep breath; let's go for a walk; you can fight back against this anger and control it"). Patient and consistent scaffolding will be required to teach each element of the coping sequence. Emphasizing consequential thinking to evaluate the implications of competing behaviors may be helpful. Motivational interviewing strategies, which combine empathy with the juxtaposition of choices, may assist the buy-in to use of coping techniques (Naar-King & Suarez, 2011).

Case Anecdote

The implementation of the various strategies in the school-based protocol requires significant individualization. Jack's mood and behaviors at the start of the school day were dependent on the stress level he carried with him into the classroom. A poor start to the school day would lead to explosive episodes, and afterward he would feel like his whole day was ruined, withhold effort, and struggle behaviorally. To assess his mood and provide support to get his day off to a good start, he was scheduled to start each school day with a brief contact with his school therapist (a backup colleague was also designated). The therapist would assess his mood and discuss any stressful events that occurred since the last school day. Consistent with therapeutic work on enhancing self-awareness, the SUM was used to help him process the relationships between his thoughts, feelings, and behaviors in regard to both positive and negative events that occurred at home. Particular attention was paid to how what he said to himself affected his mood and behavior. When the therapist judged that he could smoothly transition to class, she reminded him of immediate expectations as he entered the room and then reviewed his troubleshooting plan in case his mood became depressed or agitated. This plan included how he would signal a need for a time-out to avoid an outburst, where he would go, what self-soothing coping skills he would apply, and what rewards would be earned through his contingency plan for keeping his cool.

Classroom staff were coached to recognize and empathically point out to him the first observable signs his mood was escalating (i.e., stopping work, excessive fidgeting, distracting talk-outs). Their feedback to Jack was designed to help him become aware of mood changes as early as possible and was an important element in increasing his self-awareness to support self-management. If supportive attempts to redirect him failed, staff would encourage him to take a time-out and were prepped with a protocol to assist him in restabilizing his mood and avoiding a major behavioral incident. In case Jack lost self-control, the staff protocol also delineated his personal crisis response plan. These two small components of Jack's intervention plan illustrate how a CBT protocol can be implemented and reinforced throughout the school day.

INSTRUCTIONAL SUPPORTS, EDUCATIONAL ACCOMMODATIONS, AND CLASSROOM PROTOCOLS

There is very little information on educational achievement of children diagnosed with BP. In a small case-based sample, Clevenger (2011) described the school performance of students with BP. Ability level was generally high, but academic performance patterns were erratic undoubtedly influenced by disruptive mood cycles. Cumulative achievement data that emphasized high performance points revealed a child's best potential. A single standardized test or curriculum-based measure is more readily affected by the daily ups and downs of mood cycles and is a less reliable index of performance. Work products shaped by formative feedback and portfolios may provide more accurate work samples to evaluate progress. Children in the Clevenger sample demonstrated an initially high incidence of aggression and disruptive behaviors in the school environment, but there was a rapid decrease in aggression when children were educated in structured classrooms that provided therapeutic supports.

Classroom teachers have an important role in the day-to-day treatment of children with BP. Therefore, teacher education regarding the nature of mood disorder symptoms is essential. Educators require training to understand the intense challenges affected children have with impulse and emotional control, the nature and course of emotional lability, and the importance of not personalizing student aggression that may target staff. Teachers can play an important role in assisting students with BP in recognizing the onset of behavioral and emotional episodes and in prompting their use of prescribed coping strategies.

When teachers understand the triggers for a potential behavioral escalation they can initiate early intervention and, thus, more effective behavioral management. Nonjudgmental teacher reflection to the child regarding the onset of observable signs of emotional arousal can foster self-awareness within the student that can eventually contribute to self-management and enhanced self-control.

Collaborating with the therapist, the teacher must be actively involved in individualized stress management plans and coping protocols. The teacher is coached to discreetly prompt the student to initiate self-calming and self-instruction strategies. Teachers can use a rehearsed nonverbal signal that turmoil appears to be rising (e.g., a hand briefly placed on a corner of the student's desk to call student attention to elevated risk for a mood episode). As the student learns earlier personal recognition of mounting emotional or behavioral arousal, he or she can also communicate with a nonverbal signal (e.g., holding up some designated colored card to indicate the need for a time-out or other prearranged stress management intervention). If necessary, the teacher and therapist can guide the student through a pretaught exit strategy. Explosive students may require a routine, practiced protocol for leaving the situation where they are experiencing escalating risk for an explosive outburst.

These time-out strategies should be coupled with personalized coping protocols that have been developed in therapy. It is far better for a student to temporarily remove him- or herself from a classroom under control than to exhibit an embarrassing behavioral meltdown that requires removal from the classroom and compromises relationships with peers. It is important to note that this exit or time-out strategy is not a punishment. Although it may remove the student from the stimulation of a stressful environment, it is not designed to be a traditional time-out that focuses on altering disruptive behaviors through removal from social reinforcers. The break from class should be as brief as possible and a return to academic on-task behavior an expectation. Astute teachers who are knowledgeable about BP symptom manifestation and their students can monitor these stress management plans to ensure they are not used merely to avoid challenging academic work.

At times, students with BP may be hypersensitive to correction or critical feedback. The administration of frequent legitimate positive feedback builds a foundation for an effective teacher–student relationship and will enhance openness to correction. While avoiding "walking around on eggshells" to avoid behavioral escalation, it remains important to recognize when the student is most capable of receiving critical feedback. This is often one on one and not in front of other students. Academic feedback is received more openly if it is routinely scheduled.

The behavioral episodes and emotional meltdowns of students with mood disorders can be exasperating and overwhelming for teachers. These outbursts disrupt the entire class and may even create physical danger. Teachers are the first staff members on the firing line when a student escalates—and they may feel like they are literally on the firing line if they are being verbally attacked. Therapist support and reassurance is essential to prepare teachers for these intense encounters. As the first responder, the classroom teacher provides reassuring feedback and expresses confidence that the student can stay in control. Prompting deployment of coping strategies, the teacher empathically repeats reassurance that the child can self-soothe, calm emotional arousal, and remain in control of behavioral impulses. When a student with BP is hyperaroused or escalates to an explosive, aggressive, or manic episode, fewer words, frequent empathy statements acknowledging emotional discomfort or pain, and simple directions are preferred communication approaches. It is important to avoid delineation of disciplinary consequences at the moment of escalation, concentrating instead on de-escalation. It is critical that classroom teachers have readily responsive backup support for managing an explosive episode. Particularly if the teacher is the displaced target of student attacks, an additional adult voice and presence is essential. The next section further delineates crisis intervention requirements for these challenging students.

CRISIS INTERVENTION PROTOCOLS

School staff working with children with mood disorders should have in place routine strategies for problem-solving de-escalation, processing, and postcrisis intervention. All staff working with the student should be prepared to implement and support consistent protocols that are designed to establish stress-reducing predictability and structure at every point that requires intervention or support. Detailed replicable response plans are as important for staff as they are for students because explosive incidents can arouse emotional and defensive reactions in educators as well. This preparation reduces the risk of counteraggression by school staff when encountering the intensity presented by aggressive outbursts.

Children with mood disorders require crisis intervention plans that are different from those for students identified with ADHD, ODD, or other externalizing disorders. Serious explosive episodes, aggression, and self-harm frequently occur with students with BP. Risk for harm to self and others can be significant. Crisis intervention protocols require advance planning, differential application given the unique characteristics of the disorder, and collaboration among various staff members. When a student's hyperarousal surpasses his or her tolerance threshold, the focus shifts to managing meltdowns and explosive incidents to ensure safety and limit their intensity and duration. At these times the intervention stance approaches damage control, not new instruction.

The crisis intervention protocol draws from the elements of the coping strategies model just outlined, but a plan must be individualized to address the unique response patterns of each specific student. The crisis interventionist communicates empathic concern coupled with calm, precise, and brief instructions. Voice tone is firm but nonjudgmental, models self-control, and communicates that the situation will be safely managed for everyone's benefit. Particularly if risk for physical acting out is evident, it is important to provide sufficient physical space. The adult does not want to appear intimidated but must avoid being misperceived as counteraggressive or threatening and then become a target. In most scenarios, it is necessary to remove the escalated student from a classroom, school corridor, or other public context. It is best to provide a prearranged safe place that is not associated with school discipline. Staff members guide the student to this de-escalation setting beyond the observation of peers. When possible, it is best to avoid rushing in any way that might escalate a confrontation or intensify a power struggle. Obviously, the impact on others and general school safety must be taken into account. Students with BP do have a responsibility for managing their behaviors, but the crisis point is not the moment to delineate discipline actions or provide critical feedback. This processing must occur later.

The crisis interventionist communicates empathic recognition of the feelings of the student, acknowledging hurt, pain, anger, frustration, or other emotions on display. The staff member expresses confidence that the student can regain self-control, make positive choices, and avoid harmful escalation. Prompts to use practiced self-instructions and coping strategies also reinforce the message that the student can regain control and make healthy choices. Selection of prompts may be guided by information from prior brainstorming with the student regarding what is helpful once a meltdown is already occurring. Prompts may be nonverbal if prearranged signals have been discussed and are easily understood by the student. During the crisis intervention, the supporting staff member reinforces the student for every attempt to use self-calming strategies and to refrain from aggression.

After de-escalation, the student is prepared for reentry into the classroom. Individualized assessments are required to determine the timing of processing the incident. For some students, it is best to process the event and accompanying interactions before returning to class. This is particularly true for many primary grade students. For others, it may be better to merely focus on regaining control and preparing for a successful reentry while processing or debriefing at a later time when the child may be able to acquire increased perspective through a more distant review. In this case, the teacher must be prepared to accept and welcome the student's return knowing that their interaction even if conflictual will be processed at a later time. If the incident included conflict or aggression with a peer, it will be necessary to engage in formal peer problem solving to ensure that unaddressed hostility does not lead immediately to a reoccurrence of conflict. However, it is imperative that the student with BP is coached and supported in problem solving with both adults and peers.

Treatment of BP and related mood disorders requires resilience and patience from all caregivers. Even when progress is substantial, a serious mood episode can occur. The classroom teacher must communicate to the student that although behavior during a meltdown was unacceptable, all is not lost and staff remain committed to helping the student progress in overcoming these issues.

FAMILY AND SYSTEMIC SUPPORTS AND INTERVENTIONS

School-centered therapy can be instrumental in supporting families with a child with this chronic illness over many years and across multiple developmental transitions. Because siblings are likely to attend the same school district, school counselors have the opportunity to support and intervene with the entire family system. Parent and family members require supports and protocols similar to those outlined above for educators. However, it is important to remember that parents face an extra challenge because they do not have the available backup resources that a classroom teacher, school psychologist, or social worker may be able to depend upon during an explosive episode. Our review of empirically supported treatments for BP focused on the integration of CBT and family therapy interventions. Because stress can trigger rapid cycling events, it is important to counsel parents in ways to manage stress in the home environment and use crisis management responses similar to those described above for school staff. Psychoeducation for parents and family members not only helps them understand the nature of BP but also underlines the message that neither children nor parents are to be blamed for symptoms; neither caused the symptoms to appear, but together they share the responsibility for managing them. As parents learn the neurobehavioral nature of the disorder, they become better equipped to help their children understand their overwhelming experiences. For all family members, a shift from guilt and blame to resolute and patient problem solving is the goal. When school staff report explosive incidents at school, parents may initially feel overwhelmed or embarrassed. It is important to establish a collaborative tone, maintain a problem-solving focus, brainstorm how parents and teachers can support one another, and communicate hope for improvement.

Therapists assist parents in devising realistic strategies for managing environmental stress at home and in the community. Family sessions review the character and process of family interactions in response to mood displays. Strategies are introduced to decrease expressed emotion, the intense critical feedback loops and reactive argumentative cycles that arise from the repeated frustration of struggling to manage BP cycles. Parents are introduced to communication strategies similar to what were prescribed above for educators such as empathic responding, prompting and encouraging the use of coping strategies, reassurance, safe and structured limit setting, brief clear directions, and presentation of behavioral choices and their consequences.

Parents become readily attuned to the early warning signs of an emerging mood episode. They can enhance their child's self-awareness at those moments and prompt initiation of the coping skills learned in therapy, including naming the enemy imagery and the full range of cognitive self-instruction strategies. To effectively intervene, parents require coaching in altering their own self-talk and in the development of self-instruction strategies similar to what their child is learning in therapy. Parents must learn to move on from reflexive fatalistic and self-defeating reactions (e.g., "Oh no! Here we go again: There is nothing I can do!") to initiating their own physical calming response and reminding themselves of the communication strategies that modulate their child's escalation (e.g., "Oh no! Stop! Take a deep breath! Don't yell! Remind her").

Burned by the intensity displayed in BP meltdowns, parents can easily fall into the trap of bending over too far backward to avoid an outburst. Management of mood symptoms may require flexibility but is hampered by an absence of limit setting. Reasonable boundaries increase the child's sense of security and safety. Increased structure and predictable daily home routines are beneficial. Healthy eating and sleep patterns and prescribed homework times should be built into daily schedules. In their excellent parent guidebook for raising youth with mood issues, Fristad and Goldberg-Arnold (2004) articulated the middle-ground balancing act required by parents. Keep rules and communication simple and straightforward. Be realistic about what both the child and parent can accomplish. Avoid over- or underregulating approaches to rule making and discipline. Choose battles wisely: Recognize that not every issue can be addressed, and some boundaries and limits are more critical than others.

Maintaining a problem-solving approach to management of BP symptoms is essential. When moods emerge, the focus centers on what may be triggering this escalation and what need the child may be expressing, however inappropriately. This stance shifts the focus from paralyzing blame and guilt to modulated action planning.

Parents can be helped to develop early intervention and crisis response protocols that are similar to those used in school but realistically applicable to the home setting and its available resources and barriers. Cooling off and time-out strategies are devised and can be simulated and rehearsed in family sessions. These strategies may include delineation of a location in the house where a child can or must go to avoid potential physical confrontations. Siblings can be significantly impacted by exposure to BP episodes and can influence their occurrence. Home crisis plans should delineate how sibling needs and roles are addressed during a behavioral outburst. Unlike teachers, parents do not have the benefit of an in-house support community of adults. Delineation of reliable support resources within the extended family, their adult peer group, and community agencies is an essential therapeutic task particularly because of the potential for aggression that can occur during an intense mood episode. Also, because BP carries with it a sharp increase in suicidal risk factors, it is essential to prepare parents to decide when, how, and where to access emergency assessment and support resources. This preparation includes information on what to expect in an emergency room and what key information to share with mental health personnel.

Many children with BP require medication supports. Prescribing psychiatrists need extensive information from the school to inform medical decision making and routine feedback on school functioning to monitor effectiveness, dosage, and side effects. Sometimes medications must be administered through the school nurse. The therapist is an important resource for parents in understanding the supportive role of medication even while emphasizing that medication without psychotherapy will be insufficient to address BP symptoms. Active communication between the psychiatrist and the school-centered therapist is necessary for the coordination of treatment and to support adherence to appropriate medication regimens.

The burden of managing a chronic illness requires that parents must develop the patience and endurance necessary for the long haul. Even with successful therapy, mood issues may reemerge during acute stress or at the point of key developmental transitions. A key advantage of school-centered treatment is the ready access to a therapist who is familiar with the child, the family, and prior effective intervention protocols. Scheduled periodic therapeutic checkups can provide necessary sustaining supports for managing the long-term impacts of a chronic disability. It is also important for parents to be encouraged to continue to lead a balanced life. Overinvolvement with the child with BP will not only compromise other family relationships but also will eventually diminish the parent's capacity for balanced and effective responses to the challenges of helping the child with BP. It is beneficial for the child and parent to identify other members of the extended family and/or adult friends who can be helpful when the parent is not available to respond or the tension between parent and child has become overwhelming. The therapist encourages parents to take care of themselves and extends an invitation for periodic consultation. It is important for school-centered therapists to engage families with community-based supports that can provide assistance when school is not in session.

7

DEPRESSION

Sometimes viewed as a silent or masked disorder, depression affects some children and many adolescents, with negative effects on school performance and social development. As an internalizing disorder, depression is slow to be manifested within the school context, and affected youth are seldom targeted for early intervention. For some youth, untreated depression can result in lifelong struggles with symptoms that can compromise psychological and physical health. For a small group, particularly during adolescence, depressive symptoms can dangerously elevate suicide risk. This chapter examines the indicators for depression in children and adolescents; delineates intervention protocols to improve psychosocial and academic functioning; and proposes a framework for early identification, intervention, and support in schools.

http://dx.doi.org/10.1037/14779-008
School-Centered Interventions: Evidence-Based Strategies for Social, Emotional, and Academic Success,
by D. J. Simon
Copyright © 2016 by the American Psychological Association. All rights reserved.

Diagnostic Criteria

Major depressive disorder (MDD) as defined by the *DSM–5* requires five or more of the following symptoms: persistent depressed mood, significantly diminished interest in pleasurable activities, substantial change in weight (5% increase or decrease), daily difficulties with sleep either insomnia or hypersomnia, observable psychomotor agitation or retardation, chronic fatigue, feelings of worthlessness, trouble concentrating and making decisions, and/or suicidal ideation (American Psychiatric Association, 2013). For children and adolescents, mood may appear to others as irritable. For a diagnosis of MDD, the depressed mood or loss of interest in activities and related symptoms must occur for at least 2 weeks. Similar to *DSM–5*, the *International Classification of Diseases, 10th Revision, Clinical Modification* (*ICD–10–CM*) delineates subtypes of MDD according to episode severity, whether single (F32) or recurrent (F33) episodes, presence of psychotic features, and remission status (Goodheart, 2014).

Persistent depressive disorder or dysthymia is presented by the *DSM–5* as a less intense but chronic depression (*ICD–10–CM*; F34.1). Formal diagnosis requires a depressed or irritable mood that is present most days and persists for a period of over a year with at least two of the core symptoms for MDD. Suicidal ideation is only associated with MDD. (See Chapter 6, this volume, for assessment and intervention for pediatric bipolar disorder and disruptive mood dysregulation disorder.)

Assessment and intervention for youth experiencing depressive symptoms should not be limited to those meeting the specific categorical *DSM–5* criteria. Depression in youth is best viewed on a continuum (Hankin, Fraley, Lahey, & Waldman, 2005). Symptoms that fall short of formal diagnosis contribute to impairment and may interrupt healthy developmental trajectories resulting in difficulties that persist longer than the presence of acute depressive symptoms. Early intervention for subclinical depression may prevent social and academic difficulties and interrupt progression to acute episodes.

Assessment

Unlike externalizing disorders that readily call attention to themselves, internalizing disorders like depression are slower to be recognized by significant adults who might refer children for assessment. School initiatives toward universal screening for mental health concerns hold some promise for improving early identification. Concern for suicide prevention in schools has resulted in the development of brief screening scales (e.g., the 14-item Columbia Health Screen), which are designed to identify students who may require more formal assessment (Husky et al., 2011; Shaffer et al., 2004). Training teachers to recognize signs of concern regarding depression is essential for early identification and referral of youth with depressive indicators. Warning signs that might be observed by parents and teachers include depressed or irritable mood accompanied by negative comments about the self, decline in academic effort and production, social withdrawal, decline in enjoyment and participation in activities, and physical symptoms related to sleep disturbance or motor agitation or lethargy. The three principal assessment strategies related to depression involve familial social-developmental history, behavioral rating scales, and semistructured clinical interviews.

Familial Social-Developmental History

The evidence that depression tends to run in families is extensive (Klein, Dougherty, & Olino, 2005; Rudolph & Lambert, 2007). This association is likely a result of the combination of genetic influences and, in some cases, the impact of child-rearing factors that develop when a parent is depressed, such as modeling, reduced capacity for support, and less resources for managing environmental stressors. A family history can reveal any potentially inheritable psychological traits and delineate significant family events and stressors that could contribute to depressive symptoms. In some cases, knowledge of a significant stressor (e.g., serious illness of a family member) may prompt problem-solving and family structuring interventions that can quickly address emerging symptoms.

Behavior Rating Scales

Broadband and symptom-specific rating scales are appropriate for the assessment of depression. Broadband scales like the Achenbach System of Empirically Based Assessment (ASEBA; Achenbach & Rescorla, 2001) and the Behavior Assessment System for Children—Second Edition (BASC–2; C. R. Reynolds & Kamphaus, 2004) include parent, teacher, and youth self-report versions that address the full range of externalizing and internalizing disorders. This expansive view is important for assessing overall psychosocial functioning, potential comorbidities, and the relative impact of depressive symptoms. The standard ASEBA profile scales include Anxious/Depressed, Withdrawn/Depressed, and Somatic Complaints. The ASEBA DSM–5 profiles include separate scales for Depressive and Anxious Problems. Similarly, the BASC–2 reports scores for anxiety, depression, and somatization. With either instrument it is important to note the relationship between externalizing and internalizing scales. In some cases children's acting out behaviors might be prompted by underlying depression.

When broadband scales confirm the need, depression-specific rating scales should follow. Appropriate measures include the Children's Depression Inventory—2 (Kovacs, 2014), the Reynolds Child Depression Scale—2 (W. M. Reynolds, 2010), the Reynolds Adolescent Depression Scale—2 (W. M. Reynolds, 2002), and the Beck Depression Inventory—II (BDI–II; Beck, Steer, & Brown, 1996). The BDI–II reflects the transition to an increased focus on cognitive factors in depression (Beck, Rush, Shaw, & Emery, 1979). It targets adolescents 13 years of age and older. The original version of the Children's Depression Inventory—2 was an attempt at a downward extension of the first edition of the Beck Depression Inventory. This recent updated version has the advantage of including parent and teacher report forms in addition to youth self-report. It is appropriate for ages 7 to 17. The Reynolds Child Depression Scale—2 targets youth ages 7 to 13; the Reynolds Adolescent Depression Scale—2 is used for 11- to 20-year-olds. The Reynolds instruments are youth self-report measures only. These are all straightforward, time-efficient instruments. The face validity of these self-report measures makes it clear when a child or adolescent is experiencing the pain of depression. However, false negatives (understating symptoms) can readily occur when the youth adopts a socially desirable response bias. For this reason, it is important to integrate all rating-scale findings into the broader data set, which must include an assessment of symptoms apparent to reliable adult reporters and demonstrated impairments in personal and social behaviors, academic performance, and other areas associated with depressive symptoms.

Semistructured Interviews

Clinical interviews investigate the myriad of behavioral, emotional, and cognitive factors contributing to depression from the perspective of different raters. Semistructured interviews provide systematic coverage of key symptoms and impairments with the ability to explore individual nuances in a child's presentation. Although most formal systems include only parent and child versions, it is equally important to interview teachers for symptoms that may be manifested within the classroom. In their independent summary reviews of assessment protocols for youth depression, Klein et al. (2005) and Rudolph and Lambert (2007) recommended the Schedule for Affective Disorders and Schizophrenia for School-Age Children (Kaufman et al., 1997), the Diagnostic Interview for Children and Adolescents (Reich, 2000), and the Child and Adolescent Psychiatric Interview (Angold & Costello, 2000). Each of these protocols has sections focused on *DSM*-identified symptoms of depression in addition to exploring a broader range of potential disorders.

To link assessment to intervention in the context of school-centered therapy, it is important to examine academic performance, paying particular attention to any changes in effort, motivation, and persistence; social approach and withdrawal; and comments related to self-perception, negative attribution biases, pessimism, hopelessness, self-criticism, or cognitive distortions.

Assessing Very Young Children

The occurrence of depression in preschool children is rare and less well-understood. The Preschool Feelings Checklist (Luby, Heffelfinger, Koenig-McNaught, Brown, & Spitznagel, 2004) is a brief parent screening focused on depressive symptoms. The ASEBA parent- and teacher-rating scales have downward extensions for preschool children. When mood concerns emerge for very young children, similar patterns and characteristics may be explored but with a wary eye toward alternative hypotheses. The occurrence of a traumatic event or significant stressor should be explored. The character of the response to interventions for behaviors of concern may determine whether more intense interventions or prolonged monitoring is warranted.

Comorbidities

Most children with significant depression symptoms experience comorbid symptoms (Klein et al., 2005). Common comorbidities include anxiety, conduct disorders, and substance abuse (Angold, Costello, & Erkanli, 1999). The high incidence of co-occurrence of anxiety and depressive symptoms makes it unclear whether there is a unique comingled internalizing disorder or whether the two symptom patterns reciprocally prompt then exacerbate their separate markers. The high overlap of personal distress indicators such as somatic complaints complicates differential diagnosis. Although both conditions respond to cognitive behavioral treatments and target a core set of coping strategies, the specific treatments for various anxiety conditions generally require exposure therapy and symptom-specific interventions that go beyond depression management strategies. Thus, when anxiety and depression are comorbid, it is necessary to establish intervention priorities based primarily on the critical nature of impairments and then target both symptom profiles.

It can be challenging to assess comorbid depression when externalizing symptoms are present. However, many students who demonstrate severe acting out behaviors experience underlying depression. Whether depression fuels externalizing behaviors or is in part a result of the personal and social consequences that occur because of antisocial actions, it can be fruitful to address the sadness and in some cases underlying hopelessness that occurs with conduct problems. In my own clinical experience, empathically responding to comorbid depressive symptoms can play a significant role in crisis de-escalation.

Similarly, depressed teens who self-medicate with alcohol and other drugs must address their mood dysregulation to reduce substance misuse.

Progress Monitoring

Monitoring progress is essential during the application of intervention protocols. Symptom-specific rating scales have demonstrated some sensitivity to recording treatment effects. However, Klein et al. (2005) cautioned that repeated measures can result in an attenuation effect when raters tend to downgrade symptom severity even in the absence of marked improvement. This caution can generally be addressed by also collecting data on behavioral impairments (e.g., school performance, activity participation).

DEVELOPMENTAL CONSIDERATIONS

The incidence of depression in adolescence has been estimated to be 5% but with a cumulative lifetime rate of up to 20% by age 18 (Klein et al., 2005). In elementary-age children, prevalence is estimated in the range of 1% to 3%, and manifestation in 3- to 6-year-olds is rare and often associated with abuse and neglect (Klein et al., 2005; Stark, Schnoebelen, et al., 2006). Keeping in mind that prevalence studies focus on categorical diagnosis, it is clear that mild-to-moderate forms of depression may affect many children and adolescents over time. The most common age of onset falls between the ages of 11 and 15 (Klein et al., 2005; Rudolph & Lambert, 2007). Although the literature has focused on adolescents, clinical experience is indicating a significant rise in childhood occurrence.

Almost twice as many girls as boys experience depression. Hypotheses attempting to explain this phenomenon have suggested that girls carry increased cognitive vulnerability because of tendencies to respond to negative events with rumination and a stronger negative inferential style (Hankin & Abramson, 2001; Stark, Streusand, Krumholz, & Patel, 2010). Because girls demonstrate stronger affiliation needs, the interpersonal consequences of depression may exacerbate their risk (Rudolph & Lambert, 2007).

Although the presentation of depressive symptoms is generally similar across developmental stages, younger children tend to exhibit more irritability, sadness, and shorter mood periods, and mood manifestation is more environmentally specific. Teens may exhibit longer moods, increased cognitive symptoms such as hopelessness and low self-esteem, anhedonia (difficulty in finding pleasure in activities), and more neurovegetative symptoms such as disturbances in sleep and appetite. Although most singular episodes of depression are likely to subside even in the absence of treatment, the course of youth depression is generally recurrent with significant associated impairments. Childhood depression ups the risk for adolescent depression in part because of accompanying difficulties in psychosocial functioning and developmental consequences resulting from impairments. The acquisition of essential healthy social and emotional skills may be compromised. In clinical samples, the median duration of a depressive episode is 7 to 9 months. These periods may involve intense bouts interspersed with periods of improved functioning. Birmaher et al.'s (2004) 5-year longitudinal study reported a 40% recurrence rate. Female gender, increased guilt, prior episodes of depression, and parental psychopathology increased the severity of the course. Adolescent depression is associated with heightened risk for adult depressive experiences (Birmaher, Arbelaez, & Brent, 2002). Childhood onset may be associated with a more severe adult course, but further study is needed to fully understand the developmental progression of early onset depression. Biological factors may influence course and severity as well, but they have not been thoroughly studied in youth.

CHILD- AND ADOLESCENT-SPECIFIC THERAPEUTIC INTERVENTION STRATEGIES

Research supported psychotherapies center on cognitive behavioral and interpersonal therapies, which include family interventions.

Cognitive Behavior Therapy

CBT frameworks begin with assumptions similar to adult protocols for the treatment of depression based on Beck et al.'s (1979) cognitive conceptualization of depression and its treatment. Beck et al.'s cognitive perspective defined depression as rooted in distorted negative perceptions of one's self, life experience, and future: the *negative cognitive triad.* Depressed youth view themselves as skill deficient, unlovable, and guilty or unrealistically responsible for their problems. They view the future with pessimism, expect the worse, and have limited belief in their self-efficacy. This negative sense of self can lead to social withdrawal, which may become a self-fulfilling prophecy for fears of social isolation or loss of interpersonal support. This recursive pattern solidifies the impaired self-concept and intensifies depression. The attempted solution inadvertently exacerbates the problem. From a cognitive therapy perspective, depression is sustained by faulty information processing. Faulty thinking patterns stimulate depressive affect, contribute to physical lethargy and somatic complaints, compromise social problem solving, and prompt social withdrawal. The therapeutic task involves engaging the child in a guided discovery process to understand these connections between thoughts, feelings, and actions with the goal of changing self-defeating thought patterns to more realistic and adaptive healthy perspectives.

CBT intervention protocols begin with psychoeducational strategies that guide children and adolescents to understand the connections among their experiences, somatic sensations, thoughts, feelings, and behaviors. The self-understanding model delineated in Chapter 3 of this volume is applicable. The focus of teaching enhanced self-awareness centers on the impact that thoughts have on feelings, coping actions, and behavioral choices. Thought diaries, debriefing weekly experiences, social stories, cartoons with thought bubbles, and metaphorical games are examples of wide-ranging therapeutic strategies used to examine the impact of reflexive faulty thinking patterns and cognitive distortions on mood and behaviors.

Building awareness of counterproductive thinking patterns begins by identifying self-defeating automatic thoughts and cognitive distortions. Examples include the following:

- Reflexive self-criticism messages that communicate "I can't" or "I'm no good" (e.g., "I'll never be good at math" or "I'll always be the last one picked because I'm not any good").
- All-or-nothing thinking that is rigid and fails to perceive the middle ground in problem solving (e.g., "If I don't get an A, it's not even worth trying"; "If I don't fight him everyone will just think I'm weak"; "If I mess this up, nothing will ever work out, I might as well be dead"; "If I don't go to the prom, I will never be able to have a date or get married").
- Catastrophizing that predicts nothing but worst-case scenarios (e.g., "I'm going to be so nervous giving this presentation that I'll just freeze. Everyone will laugh at me, then I'll get a failing grade, then I won't pass the class, then __").
- Faulty beliefs that make unrealistic assumptions (e.g., "Those teachers will never believe I've changed and give me a second chance" or "Girls can never be good at sports").
- Entrenched faulty beliefs can become limiting self-definitions that impact performance and social engagement (e.g., "My classmates don't like me. I won't ever have friends. It's not even worth trying").

After maladaptive thinking patterns and their connections to feelings and behaviors are identified, CBT protocols begin to challenge faulty belief systems and self-defeating thoughts. It is not enough to just tell the child to think and act differently. Rather, the therapist guides the child on an investigation to discover the thought–feeling–behavior connections that sustain depression. Beck et al. (1979) termed this process *collaborative empiricism*.

It is empirical because it uses multiple miniexperiments to test beliefs and assumptions about personal experiences, the self, and the world. Entrenched assumptions, beliefs, and behavioral patterns are reexamined as hypotheses to be tested. The process is collaborative because the child is engaged in personally discovering alternative ways of thinking and acting. The therapist serves as the coach who guides the child through the investigation.

Adapted to fit the cognitive capacities of children of various ages, cognitive therapy utilizes *Socratic questioning*, essentially thought-testing questions, to invite children to evaluate inferences, judgments, appraisals, and conclusions about themselves and their experiences. The Socratic method is a doubt caster sown amid faulty thinking patterns. The following queries are examples of this approach: "What's the evidence that this is true?" "Is this always the case?" "Is there an alternate explanation?" "What would have happened if instead you __?" Taking this approach into a counseling session, a therapist listens as a child with depression shares that she was walking past a lunch table and assumed that the classmates who were laughing were laughing specifically at her. The therapist challenges this untested reflexive appraisal by engaging her in an exploration of a list of what else the girls could be laughing about as she randomly walked by and then discusses how different she might feel if one of those other alternatives were true. The client is challenged to consider what might be alternative thoughts for this situation and how to apply them.

Older children are more readily capable of engaging in these cognitive investigations. Younger children may require experiential activities, social stores, play illustrations using puppets or dolls including self-talk, video models, or personal behavior experiments with contingent rewards for attempting new behaviors. Age-appropriate analogies and metaphors can also be helpful. For example, to help children understand catching and changing thought patterns, Friedberg and McClure (2002) contrasted "caterpillar" and "butterfly" thoughts and guided children in identifying which of their own thought patterns fall into which category and how caterpillar and butterfly thoughts differentially impact their feelings and actions. (See Friedberg & McClure, 2002, and Friedberg, McClure, & Garcia, 2009, for extended examples of age-appropriate analogies, games, and activities to apply cognitive strategies to interventions with both children and adolescents.)

As children learn to catch their automatic depression-inducing thoughts, they engage in therapeutic exercises to brainstorm alternative counter-thoughts that are realistic and adaptive. Therapists teach positive self-talk scripts and covert self-instruction coping strategies to use when facing situations that commonly trigger depression or social withdrawal. Role plays of troublesome scenarios rehearsing internal dialogues and scripted positive self-instructions can help children apply cognitive coping strategies to daily dilemmas. Younger children in particular might benefit from simple repetitive scripts or mantras to use when stressed and feeling bad about themselves.

Youth who are depressed experience significant deficits in personal and social problem solving (Stark et al., 2010). Training in problem-solving skills is a central feature of CBT intervention programs for depression. The focus is on replacing passive resignation with active engagement, systematically generating then processing alternatives, flexibly countering rigid and often pessimistic assumptions and perspectives, and using appropriate social supports.

Because interpersonal difficulties, particularly social withdrawal, frequently accompany depression, social skills instruction is a standard component of CBT depression intervention protocols (Stark et al., 2010). Interpersonal skills training centers on direct communication skills for expressing legitimate feelings, needs, and wants; social initiation skills; and conflict resolution skills. This training is particularly important for youth whose depression periodically externalizes to aggression or antisocial behavior. These children need opportunities to explore the connection between their depression and their angry outbursts and may be helped by exploring the personal and social consequences they experience from conflictual episodes.

The ACTION Treatment Program

One of the most extensively researched and empirically supported CBT programs, the ACTION treatment program for depressed youth, was specifically designed and evaluated for efficacy in the school setting (Stark, Schnoebelen, et al., 2006; Stark et al., 2007; Stark, Yancy, Simpson, & Molnar, 2006a, 2006b). The original versions of this program date back to the 1980s (Stark, 1990). The program has evolved to integrate the latest findings on CBT approaches for treating depression. The current version is specifically designed for girls ages 9 to 13 years; however, it has been successfully adapted to treat boys and can be modified for a larger age range of youth (Stark, Streusand, Arora, & Patel, 2012). It has also been shown to be effective with girls with diverse cultural backgrounds, including Latina and African American children (Stark et al., 2012). Therapists work closely with teachers to identify appropriate referrals and then solicit their support in reinforcing program strategies within the classroom. Conducting groups within the school setting engages youth who might not attend clinic-based programs, ensures attendance, enhances the opportunities for generalization of depression management skills to the daily environment, increases the ease of monitoring progress in associated social and academic impairments, and assists in engaging parental involvement and support.

Goals and Structure. The ACTION program is a manualized program that systematically teaches skills for coping with depression and social problem solving. The content of group discussions is drawn from the real-life experiences of participants. Thus, like all manualized programs, ACTION requires fidelity to a prescribed intervention protocol but also must be flexibly adapted to address individual needs and concerns. Therapists develop individualized goals and treatment plans for each participant and family in addition to the systematic group protocol.

ACTION is designed for up to six group participants. Smaller groups ensure adequate individual attention and minimize potential behavior management challenges. The standard program involves 20 group and two individual sessions over an 11-week period. In addition, there is a 10-session parent training program with half of these sessions involving the girls and two individual family sessions. Individual therapeutic needs may require additional individual or family intervention sessions. ACTION is an acronym for the core coping skills taught in the program: A—Always find something to do to feel better, C—Catch the positive, T—Think about it as a problem to be solved, I—Identify the emotion, O—Open yourself to the positive, and N—Never get stuck in the negative muck. The program uses a systematic skill-building model that follows a developmental progression with one skill essential for acquisition of the next. Use of real-life material during skills training introduces an experiential learning component that promotes transfer of learning. It also uses workbook activities to be completed outside of group sessions to solidify learning skills and structure in applications to life activities. The goals of the program are to teach a problem-solving approach to life; change how girls perceive themselves, relationships, the world, and their future; and teach a repertoire of coping skills for managing depression that takes into account what can and cannot be controlled.

Affective Education. The program begins with affective education that teaches participants the nature of depression from a CBT perspective, how to monitor moods, and to use increased self-awareness to initiate differentiated coping strategies. Affective education involves investigation of the "three Bs" related to depressive experiences: how the Body is reacting; how the Brain (thoughts) is processing; and how they Behave when depressed. Each participant meets individually with the therapist to collaboratively set three personal goals, which are then shared with the group for support and monitored for progress at the beginning of each session.

Coping Skills Training. Coping skills training directly links mood monitoring to response strategies. When girls share affect-laden experiences, they rate their moods, engage in a coping strategy, and then rerate their mood to assess the effects of the coping strategy. For example, depressed mood often results in social withdrawal and cognitive rumination. As students discuss depressive episodes, they can be asked to identify and rate the intensity of their mood and then engage in a fun and distracting group activity after which they rerate their mood. In this manner, they directly experience the personal impact of a coping strategy and its relevance to their lives. True to the ACTION name of the program, the targeted coping skills involve specific actions that the authors have phrased in simple language: Do something fun and distracting; do something relaxing and soothing; talk to someone; do something that uses a lot of energy; and think positive. Each of these skills is practiced within group, and members brainstorm which skills apply best to which life experiences. During this process, workbook exercises focus students on catching the positive in their lives. Monitoring pleasant events is likely to increase the frequency of engagement in these events and links directly to the action-oriented coping skills learned. Pleasant activity scheduling is a common strategy across all ages for countering the tendency to socially withdraw when depressed.

Problem-Solving Skills Training. Teaching a problem-solving perspective and schema is designed not only to provide an organized strategy for tackling life's problems but also to change the mind-set that everything is out of the students' control. The program's schema includes problem definition, goal setting, solution generation, evaluating the consequences of choices, and self-reinforcement for active coping. It is important that students are taught to use problem-solving strategies when they are faced with something they might be able to change and to use a coping strategy when they face an issue they cannot change. For example, a child probably can work toward solving conflicts around privileges with parents, but if the child is depressed about parental plans for a divorce, he or she cannot change that event and must instead engage in actions that keep the child from ruminating in the pain and worry associated with that stressor.

Cognitive Restructuring. The next stage of ACTION focuses on cognitive restructuring strategies. Activities establish a connection between negative thoughts and depressed moods. The initial focus is to identify negative thoughts in themselves and group members and to identify the situations in which they most often emerge. These are the automatic thoughts that cognitive therapists strive to interrupt and dispute. When students describe negative thinking, they are guided in examining the limited evidence in support of that perspective and encouraged to find another way to look at the problem. Cognitive restructuring involves metacognition skills that may be challenging for some participants. ACTION uses an *externalizing the symptom* strategy to concretize negative thoughts, separate them from the self, and provide a framework for battling back against restrictive negative thinking. The therapist notes that everyone gets "stuck in the muck" of negative thoughts from time to time and needs to extract themselves. The colorful image of the "muck monster" is used to represent their negative thoughts. Children are taught to "talk back to the muck monster." In one engaging exercise, children draw caricatures of the muck monster. The therapist or another group member holds up the image and spews forth the personalized negative statements of the muck monster to a group member, who then is challenged to assertively argue against the unrealistic negativity of those thoughts. Group discussion and workbook exercises reinforce how to catch negative thinking, talk back to it, and then engage in a coping response.

Strength Recognition. Girls also engage in activities designed to identify strengths and build a more positive sense of self. The therapist polls parents, teachers, and group members to identify a list of strengths that are then shared with each student. Girls then create a self-map that highlights their strengths and presents a visual image of an increasingly positive sense of self.

Parental Involvement. The parent and family components of ACTION reflect and reinforce the goals of the youth sessions. Parents learn what skills their daughters are learning in group and are specifically taught empathic listening and problem-solving skills. They are encouraged to increase supportive messages and activities to counter their children's tendencies to focus on the negative. If there are family issues or conflicts that interfere with progress, more extensive family intervention may be necessary to create a home environment that will support and sustain the progress of participants.

Adolescent Coping With Depression Course

Curry and Reinecke (2003) identified the common core components of efficacious treatments for adolescents as mood monitoring, identification and modification of maladaptive cognitions, problem-solving training, social skills instruction, and affect regulation strategies. The Adolescent Coping with Depression Course (CWD-A) is an empirically supported psychoeducational CBT group program for adolescents ages 13 to 18 that incorporates these intervention elements (Clarke, Lewinsohn, & Hops, 1990). The program was designed to be used in day treatment and school settings where a group work format was particularly viable. An individually administered variant of the program is also available, but the authors believe that a group format is optimal for teens (Clarke et al., 2005). This is an intensive and highly structured manualized program designed for 16 two-hour sessions in groups between 6 and 10 adolescents. Adaptation to a typical school context would require a year-long program of a class period per week. A parallel eight-session parent course is available from Lewinsohn, Rohde, Hops, and Clarke (1991).

Consistent with its CBT framework, CWD-A targets similar depression management skills as the ACTION program. The core therapy components include cognitive restructuring to address negative and self-defeating thoughts and beliefs, behavioral therapy to counter social withdrawal and improve interpersonal skills, problem-solving skills training to address peer and family conflicts, relaxation training for stress management, and personal goal setting to increase self-efficacy. Presuming that the etiology and manifestation of depression is multidimensional, Clarke and DeBar (2010) believed that different elements of the program will produce more powerful benefits for individual participants. The therapist assumes an active and directive role, encourages peer to peer feedback and support, uses role playing and experiential learning for skills training, routinely acknowledges individual differences, and manages resistance consistent with all therapeutic work with teens by avoiding power struggles and making training exercises as close to real life as possible.

Routine mood monitoring is designed not only to enhance self-awareness but also to encourage participants to see that various intervention strategies do make a difference. Particular emphasis is placed on increasing involvement in appropriate pleasant activities and on cognitive restructuring exercises. Triggers for depression, familial influences on distorted belief systems, and self-limiting consequences of self-defeating thoughts are explored initially through engaging cartoons and external examples but eventually through group discussion of personal experiences.

Interpersonal Therapy

The other evidence-based approach to adolescent depression emphasizes the social context of depression. Interpersonal psychotherapy for depressed adolescents (IPT-A) is a relatively brief, symptom-relief-focused group or individual treatment for teens (Mufson, Dorta, Moreau, & Weissman, 2004). IPT-A begins with the assumption that adolescents are developmentally focused on the social aspects of their lives and that depressive symptoms must be understood within an interpersonal context. This perspective defines *intervention goals* as connecting symptoms to interpersonal events and difficulties in interpersonal relationships. So the psychological context for intervention involves addressing familial and peer conflicts, improving social competence, and improving effective direct communication of affect and needs.

The etiology of depression is viewed as an interaction of biological vulnerabilities and environmental stressors. However, interpersonal difficulties are viewed as a particularly important and developmentally relevant contributing factor for adolescents (Jacobson & Mufson, 2010). Although CBT targets cognitive distortions, IPT-A focuses on changing relationship patterns. However, both focus on social problem solving, and IPT-A's emphasis on interpersonal skills training mirrors many elements of CBT protocols.

Psychoeducation

IPT-A is designed as a 12- to 15-session intervention protocol to be delivered in either clinical or school settings. The first phase of treatment begins with psychoeducation about the nature of depression. The therapist makes an analogy to physical illness (e.g., pneumonia) to describe the drain on performance and energy caused by depression and to project the hopeful image that as interventions impact this illness more adaptive functioning will slowly emerge. A *limited sick role* is assigned to the teen to assist in reframing expectations and judgments from parents to encourage less criticism and blame about falling short in meeting responsibilities and counter any temptation to define depressive lethargy and withdrawal as merely laziness. To assess the current status of significant interpersonal relationships, IPT-A therapists ask the teen to complete a *closeness* circle to identify key relationships and a *depression* circle to identify key precipitating interpersonal events that influence moods. These tools serve to define the focus of treatment in terms of interpersonal skills and relationships. Additional assessment includes exploration of any significant grief events, parent–child or peer conflicts, and current family or life stressors.

Interpersonal Skills Training

The next phase of the intervention protocol centers on skills training regarding identification and assertive communication of affect, including how to employ "I" messages to directly express feelings, needs, and wants. These skills are applied to specific relationships clarifying expectations, negotiating conflicts, increasing social engagement, and interpersonal problem solving. Therapeutic activities are both directive and exploratory. Role plays and workbook exercises promote social awareness and competence and lead to direct communication in key relationships. Parent–child tensions might be addressed in conjoint sessions with parents. Peer interactions are rehearsed in session with prescribed action plans for meeting with the targeted peer between sessions followed by supportive debriefing the subsequent session.

Confronting interpersonal tensions can be quite challenging, so teens are encouraged to start small, with less threatening content as they build toward skill mastery. Patience and persistence in the face of parent or friend reticence to change is emphasized to negate a quick assertion that the improved skills do not work and that change is futile. In addition to conducting role plays, therapists model skills and engage the adolescent in functional analysis of conflictual or otherwise disappointing interactions. These postmortems include perspective taking regarding the likely feelings and expectations of the other party, assessing the impact of the interaction on depressive symptoms, and exploring what was left unsaid or could have been stated differently.

Closure and Relapse Prevention

The final phase of the IPT-A protocol prepares the teen to identify and respond to warning signs that depressive symptoms may be reoccurring. Skills learned and their specific applications to key relationships are reviewed. The adolescent is asked to summarize skills and treatment gains to parents. Because this is a brief treatment format, it is necessary to evaluate whether other comorbid issues (e.g., substance misuse, a trauma experience) require further targeted intervention.

Long-Term Follow-Up

Particularly when there appears to be a biological vulnerability to depression, a persistently dysfunctional home or social environment, or high risk for substance abuse, depression management might require periodic monitoring or therapeutic booster sessions. Booster sessions should be routinely incorporated into intervention protocols for youth with personal or environmental stressors that are known to escalate the risk for relapse. Although the therapist can work with the youth and family to identify signs that additional therapeutic support is needed, it is also important for similar communication and guidelines to be shared with school counselors and other staff who might have persistent contact with the student.

Dialectical Behavior Therapy

Dialectical behavior therapy (DBT) uses CBT and family therapy strategies but integrates them with an Eastern philosophical view of mindfulness and dialectics. DBT was first developed by Linehan (1993) for the treatment of adult borderline personality disorder (BPD) and chronic suicidal behavior, but A. L. Miller et al. (2007) extended its application to work with adolescents who are suicidal. Many of the youth with severe depression they treated also showed emerging signs of BPD: recurrent suicidal thoughts or self-harm activity, impulsivity, unstable moods, repetitive self-denigrating comments, and intense "hot and cold" relationships, including with therapists. Linehan's biosocial theory views etiology of these symptoms as the interaction of a biological vulnerability to *emotional dysregulation* (heightened emotional sensitivity coupled with difficulty returning to calm baseline) and *environmental instability* characterized by invalidation of the youth, poor attachments, and chaotic problem-solving styles.

DBT views the central problem in depression as difficulty with emotional regulation. These adolescents need to learn how to label and regulate emotional arousal, tolerate distress, and accurately appraise events so that cognitive distortions do not contribute to emotional overreactions and behavioral impulsivity. Self-injurious behavior (e.g., cutting) is described as a maladaptive attempt to regulate emotions. Self-injurious behavior can be a dramatic attempt to elicit help from others, express pain, or release emotional tension (Hollander, 2008; A. L. Miller et al., 2007).

The dialectic in DBT defines its strategy of balancing change and acceptance. This emphasis on balance or the middle path is used throughout treatment. Teens are taught to accept the gray between black-and-white thinking and emotional volatility. Rather than grieving the past or fearing the future, mindfulness is learned as the capacity to focus in the moment while still maintaining the larger life perspective. This practice also means accepting what cannot be changed but remaining open to new solutions and skills. The therapist empathizes with painful developmental experiences and their impact but encourages the teen to shift the focus toward what can be controlled and finding healthier ways of coping, relating, and problem solving.

DBT strategies include (a) a functional assessment of behavior, which helps to define the functional intent and maintaining consequences for self-injurious behavior; (b) CBT strategies for coping skills with an emphasis on learning alternatives to self-harming behaviors and different responses when experiencing depressive moods or suicidal ideation; (c) problem-solving strategies that examine and evaluate an expanded array of alternative courses of action that are marked by the middle path perspective; and (d) interpersonal skills training for establishing healthier relationships, with a particular emphasis on empathy training to more realistically understand others and appraise their intentions and direct communication of feelings and needs. DBT works with parents to establish middle-ground consistency and predictability in supervision and limit setting and in crisis responses to self-harm behaviors. Family sessions apply problem-solving and emotional regulation skills to parent–adolescent conflict resolution, emphasizing negotiation and compromise.

Increasing distress tolerance is an essential antidote for depression and lowers risk for self-harm. In DBT, this tolerance includes coaching in distraction skills to assist in emotional regulation. Similar to pleasant activity scheduling, DBT strategies focus on doing something active and engaging to defocus and distract from a negative mood (e.g., do something active when sad; read or do a puzzle; shift focus to someone else by doing something nice for them; or create alternate physical sensations by running, exercising, or taking a shower). The goal is to build up tolerance for stress with active strategies that are alternatives to being mired in depressive thoughts or tempting to engage in self-harm. Active self-soothing and distracting activities boost self-efficacy and self-confidence.

Because chronic suicidal thoughts and recurrent self-harm behaviors carry significant risk, A. L. Miller et al.'s (2007) intervention protocol is conceived in stages that progress from decreasing life-threatening behaviors to decreasing behaviors that interfere with the quality of life to essential skills for managing stress and social relationships. To support maintenance of gains, booster sessions are offered in groups. Working with suicidal adolescents can be very stressful for therapists. Effective therapeutic work and self-care both benefit from routine collegial consultation and support.

INSTRUCTIONAL SUPPORTS, EDUCATIONAL ACCOMMODATIONS, AND CLASSROOM PROTOCOLS

Educational Impact

Depressed students without comorbid conduct problems are likely to exhibit passive school problems. Academic performance impairments may be displayed as reduced motivation, effort, and attention to assigned tasks. Struggles with self-confidence may influence persistence when frustrated. Initiating work, sustaining effort, and completing assignments may be concerns. Prone to self-criticism, these students may quickly internalize negative feedback from teachers or parents regarding inadequate or declining performance. When work is completed, they may evaluate their own performance harshly. If they fall behind in assignments, catching up may seem daunting and overwhelming and thus reduce effort and intensify academic withdrawal. Social reticence and withdrawal decrease required academic help-seeking behaviors and active participation in class discussions. Social withdrawal may reduce interactions with classmates and limit contributions in group work.

Instructional Supports

Teacher–student relationships must be based on encouragement. The limited sick role perspective that IPT-A proposes can assist teachers in achieving the right balance between support and accountability for work production (Mufson et al., 2004). As with other students experiencing health issues, teachers need to be informed of temporary performance limitations evident when depressive symptoms are elevated. This illness perspective requires a balance between modifying expectations and encouraging work production. Facing an overwhelming mountain of owed assignments may lead to a shutdown of effort and motivation. Punitive confrontations tend to be counterproductive. Instead, increased continuously scheduled positive reinforcement strategies that are frequent, immediate, and salient are more likely to motivate the student. Contingency contracts for completed work that include positive time with a preferred teacher or classmate may enhance effort and result in pleasant social activities that in themselves are countermeasures to depression. It is important to make early success achievable in any contingency-supported work completion program to maintain hope and motivate effort.

Reduced energy and confidence inherent in depression can make it difficult to initiate work. Direct assistance and additional supervision in getting started with assignments can be helpful at school and are likely to be essential to support homework completion. Other academic accommodations might include shortened assignments with a focus on quality over quantity, varied methods of instructions (i.e., oral and visual, which are presented one step at a time), reduction in environmental distractions, and use of high-interest or otherwise stimulating material (when appropriate permitting student selection in topics or sequence of work).

To increase social supports, assignment to cooperative group assignments with positive peers can be supportive and enhance attention and work completion. Extra supervisory and instructional effort may be necessary to encourage participation in social activities during recess, lunch, and physical education classes. Supervision to prevent teasing or bullying is particularly important for affected students, who may already judge themselves as socially unacceptable.

It is important for all school staff to be informed of warning signs related to self-harm and increased symptoms. Teachers should know what content in submitted papers might warrant review by a mental health professional. Some of the most important referrals to psychologists and social workers in schools originate from English and art teachers who recognize disturbingly depressive or even suicidal content in student work products. All staff must know that any reference to harm self or others cannot remain confidential, no matter what the student requests. I have often met with teachers and students together as teachers described their concerns for students whose papers or activities might indicate significant psychological pain or even a cry for help. Uniformly, students felt supported by the recognition and efforts of their teachers, and that support in and of itself reduced risk for self-harm.

CRISIS INTERVENTION PROTOCOLS

Crises for depressed students may take various forms. In general, the principles of the CBT and interpersonal therapy protocols outlined above apply. However, the concern for ensuring physical safety is the first priority in a crisis response to a child or adolescent who is seriously depressed.

Withdrawal

For some students with depression, a crisis is evident in intensified withdrawal from social activities. This may include school refusal particularly when the student feels hopelessly behind academically or is being routinely picked on or bullied. Whatever effort that is required should be activated to resume attendance and reengage in school participation. This may necessitate intensified parental involvement in bringing the student to school, short-term before- and after-school support sessions with a school therapist, home visits, and/or nurturing but firm supports from legal officials who enforce school attendance like school resource and truancy officers. A realistic and achievable plan for making up missed work with the provision of necessary instructional supports must be outlined and initially provided even if the student appears to resist such supports. All of these efforts communicate concern, support, and value to the student who is mired in self-blame and social withdrawal.

Agitated Depression and Externalizing Behaviors

For some students, a crisis emerges when depression becomes agitated or leads to an emotional or behavioral meltdown that may or may not include an angry episode. In the event of the latter, the student should be escorted to a safe more private area to de-escalate and manage overwhelming affect. The therapist uses nonjudgmental active listening, communicates empathic recognition of troubling affect, and provides reassurance of support and expectation that this crisis will pass. Active direction to implement coping skills with an initial emphasis on physical calming strategies (e.g., deep breathing) can be helpful. In some cases, reminders to combat old cognitive distortions or self-defeating comments can assist the youth in regaining perspective. At crisis moments, it is important for a child or adolescent who feels emotionally out of control to experience safe boundaries, supportive limit setting, and reassurance that the adult is competently in charge of ensuring safety for everyone involved in the crisis situation.

Interpersonal Conflicts

If the crisis was precipitated by an interpersonal conflict with either a teacher or peer in school or identified through discussion as a family conflict, an opportunity to express anger and frustration followed by brainstorming initial problem-solving response plans may ease the intensity of depression. Extending the interpersonal therapy perspective of depression, social problem solving or conflict resolution may be a key to lifting suicidal ideation. A significant aspect of suicidal depression can be unexpressed anger and a sense of hopelessness in a significant relationship. In my crisis intervention experience, exploring with whom a student may be angry and processing that conflict may reduce immediate risk for harm more rapidly than other lines of inquiry.

Suicidality

The most alarming risk in crisis intervention with children and adolescents who are depressed relates to suicidality. Although suicide is the third leading cause of teen death, completed suicides are relatively rare compared with the high incidence of suicidal ideation in adolescents (Centers for Disease Control and Prevention [CDC], 2010). In national statistics for 2011, the CDC (2012) reported that 15.8% of students seriously considered suicide during those 12 months. More than twice as many high school students have reported being depressed enough to consider suicide at least one time in their lives. Every instance of suicidal ideation requires assessment and intervention. Addressing concerns openly and directly reduces the risk for self-harm.

Risk factors for suicidality may be proximate or distant ones and can include substance abuse, prior self-harm, impulsivity, expressed hopelessness, severe problem-solving deficits, childhood sexual abuse history, family history of self-harm behaviors, life stress, and lower perceived social support and sense of isolation. Specific warning signs include previous attempt, specific suicide threat or expression of desire to die, sudden changes in behavior, severe depression, increased risk-taking or substance abuse, increased tendency toward isolation, hopeless expression of not fulfilling parental expectations, deteriorating personal appearance, and making final arrangements such as giving away prized possessions and engaging in a symbolic goodbye.

All suicidal talk must be taken seriously. Immediate therapeutic interventions include encouraging the student to talk about it directly; identifying any immediate precipitating events, losses, or stressors; providing extensive talking time before taking action; challenging minimizing or quick denials of risk; and exploring associated feelings, thoughts, and action plans. If the student shares a suicide plan, the character of the plan contributes to the assessment of immediate risk. In general, the more specific and detailed the plan, the more lethal and available the proposed method, and the more distant potential intervening helping resources would indicate the greater risk for immediate harm. For younger children in particular, it is important to note that the child's perception of the lethality of the plan may be more important to evaluate than the actual means.

Given the interpersonal factors involved in adolescent depression, it is important to explore who the teen may be angry with and consider offering to support the student in a direct conflict resolution session. Often parents are the targets of a youth's anger. They will need to be notified of the suicidal ideation, and if there is immediate risk, parents may be required to join the assessment and intervention session. Teens often fear that involving parents will only escalate the situation or lead to retaliation later at home. The therapist's role is to help the student tell his or her story and explain the current psychological pain. Sometimes parents are unaware, and other times they contribute valuable risk-assessment information. If it is judged that there is no immediate need for a referral to consider protective psychiatric hospitalization, the therapist works with the family to devise a support plan, ensure that the teen's fears of re-escalation at home are minimized, specifically out-line short-term follow-up supports, and outline indicators that require an immediate hospital emergency room evaluation.

Most often this evaluation process will reduce immediate risk for self-harm. However, if the risk does not lessen, it is important that the youth not be left alone and arrangements be made for immediate hospital referral. (For a more comprehensive treatment of suicide assessment and intervention, see Berman, Jobes, & Silverman, 2006; Lieberman, Poland, & Cassel, 2008; and D. N. Miller, 2010.)

Prevention

The role of teachers in prevention was noted above. Depressed students may disclose painful depression or thoughts of suicide to peers first. Particularly at the middle and high school levels, it is important for prevention programs to screen for depression and to instruct students in healthy ways to respond when they are concerned about a friend. At one large metropolitan high school, our psychosocial team administered a survey as part of a freshman advisory pro-gram presentation describing our student support services. Alarmingly, nearly 40% of the students noted that a friend had discussed thoughts of self-harm with them. Specific delineation of appropriate steps to take when friends are troubled is an important part of depression and suicide prevention programs. The Columbia Health Screen noted in the assessment section of this chapter is an example of a universal screening tool. The SOS Signs of Suicide® Program (Aseltine & DeMartino, 2004) includes both gatekeeper training for students and a brief screening instrument. As with all other psychological symptoms addressed in this text, depression management should be integrated into a comprehensive school-wide social–emotional learning curriculum.

FAMILY AND SYSTEMIC SUPPORTS AND INTERVENTIONS

The comprehensive therapeutic intervention programs for depression described above all incorporated parent psychoeducation about depression, interpersonal skills training, and direct parent–child conflict resolution into their protocols. Because a family history of depression is known to contribute to the incidence of youth depression, it is always possible that a parent of the referred child may experience clinical levels of depression and require per-sonal treatment support. Because parental depression can impact parenting, referring the parent for treatment could, in turn, benefit the child. Family environmental risk data point to significant risk factors that can contribute to depression and thus might be direct targets of parent skills training or family therapy interventions. These risk factors include lower levels of family cohesion and shared activities, abuse or neglect, fewer expressions of warmth, punitive or critical parenting style, and more frequent parent–child conflicts (Rudolph & Lambert, 2007; Stark, Schnoebelen, et al., 2006). Because the etiology of depression is complex, involving biological factors and multiple contributing pathways, it is necessary to note that there will be exceptions to these influencing factors.

Structural family therapy interventions can address either cohesion or enmeshment concerns and promote increased planning of shared pleasant family activities. Parent training encourages a reduction in negative communications, less critical social interactions, and increased recognition of strengths. Alternative incentive-oriented discipline strategies can be introduced and structured through contingency management plans that increase reinforcement opportunities and rewards for meeting home and school responsibilities. Special parent–child shared activities can target positive reinforcers that also influence changes in family dynamics. Parent–child conflict negotiation and resolution not only reduces a potential contributor to depression but reinforces the interpersonal skills training that is a core element of youth intervention protocols.

It is important to note that parents may need extensive personal support not only for effectively responding to their child's depression but also for managing its effects on their own emotions and self-concept. Parents may face some of the same family stressors and negative events that the child faces (i.e., death of a parent–grandparent). Some parents experience unrealistic guilt related to their child's depressive symptoms. Many complex influences contributing to depressive symptoms are beyond their control. Parents require support in adopting and modeling a problem-solving approach to life's stressors. Coaching parents to model adaptive self-talk and healthy cognitive attributions will, in turn, influence the child's cognitive style in a healthy manner.

Case Anecdote

Holly, a high school sophomore, was referred for therapy and support services at school because of concerns over her depression, which was evidenced by periodic suicidal ideation, social withdrawal, precipitous decline in academic performance, and cutting behavior on her legs and arms. Environmental stressors were significant. Her parents had divorced during her eighth-grade year, and she and her mother moved to a new community. Holly was formerly close to her mother, but their relationship had become conflictual. Holly's anger about these changes intensified when her mother began dating someone new. Now their most consistent communication focused on Mom's disappointment with Holly's declining grades and mixture of worry and anger about her cutting herself. Holly had struggled to make friends in her new school and was feeling isolated.

Consistent with a DBT paradigm, the first goal was to ensure safety and decrease life-threatening and self-injury behaviors. To increase both support and supervision, Holly was enrolled in special education resource periods for the first and last periods of the day. Goals included emotional check-in, establishing a supportive relationship with a consistent teacher, and academic assistance. Holly was ambivalent about giving up cutting, but she agreed to a daily visit to the nurse for a checkup to see if she had engaged in any cutting behaviors. This check-in was private and straightforward; however, the nurse worked at establishing a warm, validating relationship. The assessment before her placement had hypothesized that in part both suicidal ideation and cutting behaviors were distorted forms of communication regarding her stress or her anger. If she had engaged in self-injurious behavior, her therapist met with her later in the day to explore with her what stressful triggers may have contributed to cutting. Frequently, anger or disappointment with her relationship with her mother surfaced as significant factors. The therapist helped Holly articulate what direct verbal communication could honestly replace the self-injurious behavior. Depending on the issue, direct processing with her mother either in a conference phone call or in a routinely scheduled conjoint session would ensue.

Therapeutic dialogue provided examination of Holly's self-talk and distorted personal and social appraisals. A variety of CBT strategies were used to counter her reflexive cycle of stress, distorted self-blame, all-or-nothing thinking, and self-destructive behaviors. These strategies included thought diaries, identification of triggers for her depression, early recognition of escalating stress by monitoring her physiological reactions, replacement stress management and distress tolerance strategies, and cognitive restructuring through Socratic dialogue and tests of evidence. Over time Holly developed a personal plan guided by self-instruction to relax her physical tension, temper her cognitive distortions by reminding herself to take a more balanced view, and decide whether to engage in a positive distracting activity or seek social support. She also participated in a depression management group, which provided skills training and countered her sense of isolation with her depression. When her emotional and behavioral regulation was stabilized, she was encouraged to increase her social engagement with peers. Holly became a peer tutor for the math department, an area of academic strength, and because of her involvement in a drama program in her old community she was introduced to the high school's technical theater director, who invited her to participate in their crew. This multidimensional approach was necessary to address the personal, familial, and peer factors sustaining her depression.

8

ANXIETY AND RELATED DISORDERS

Anxiety is a mood state that at adaptive levels is essential for monitoring personal safety and enhancing performance. It is appropriate to be anxious when faced with a dangerous situation. At manageable levels, anxiety enhances perception and focus, but at debilitating levels it may immobilize our capacity to respond effectively to danger and increase personal risk. Adaptive levels of anxiety are necessary to motivate performance in academic, social, and athletic endeavors and can improve focus and performance. However, overwhelming anxiety can interfere with competent performance. Students facing a major exam take the energy from their anxiety and put in extra preparation time, but out-of-control performance anxiety prevents students from demonstrating their full knowledge of material. Learning to adaptively use and manage anxiety is an important developmental task.

http://dx.doi.org/10.1037/14779-009
School-Centered Interventions: Evidence-Based Strategies for Social, Emotional, and Academic Success,
by D. J. Simon

Anxiety disorders emerge when symptoms interfere with performance and socialization, when the accompanying physical arousal impairs health and adaptive behavioral responses, and when distorted cognitive appraisals of risk and fears impair psychosocial functioning. Anxiety is evident in a wide range of psychological disorders, and there is a great deal of variability in the focus and manifestation of anxiety in the range of specific anxiety disorders. In a departure from the prior editions, the *Diagnostic and Statistical Manual of Mental Disorders* (fifth ed.; *DSM–5*; American Psychiatric Association, 2013) separates out obsessive–compulsive disorder (OCD) and trauma-related disorders from general anxiety disorders while continuing to acknowledge their shared characteristics. *The International Classification of Diseases—Tenth Revision, Clinical Modification* (ICD–10–CM) groups these disorders under a broad category that includes both anxiety and stress-related disorders (Goodheart, 2014). Because anxiety is a core feature across these conditions, I begin this chapter with an overview of common characteristics of anxiety symptoms and later examine intervention strategies for specific disorders.

DIAGNOSTIC CHARACTERISTICS AND ASSESSMENT FRAMEWORKS

Anxiety manifests itself in physiological, emotional, cognitive, and behavioral reactions. Physiological reactions vary from individual to individual but generally begin with heightened physical arousal that may include sweating, nausea, shaking, and/or accelerated heart rate. Emotional arousal involves excessive anxiety, fearfulness, and worry. Cognitive symptoms can include distorted appraisal of risk or personal capacity, unrealistic anticipation of failure or catastrophe, reflexive self-defeating thoughts, and overwhelming self-doubt. Behavioral responses typically involve avoidance, withdrawal, excessive procrastination, or misdirected attempts to control the environment as might be displayed in controlling social actions or interfering compulsive behaviors. The nature and severity of impairments in performance of age-appropriate personal, social, and academic tasks indicate whether anxiety has reached clinical levels and requires therapeutic intervention.

Assessment requires a multimethod and multi-informant approach. Given the subjective nature of anxiety, youth self-report is a central assessment component. Clinical interviews and rating scales collect diagnostic data from the child, parents, and teacher. Behavioral observations systematically assemble data on task and social performance. Familial and developmental data investigate potential genetic, historical, environmental, and interactional patterns that might contribute to excessive levels of anxiety.

Semistructured Interviews

Semistructured interviews increase the reliability of interview data while still providing latitude for the clinician to explore individual features of a specific child's presenting problem. The Anxiety Disorders Interview Schedule for *DSM–IV*: Child and Parent Versions (ADIS–IV: C/P; Silverman & Albano, 1996) is a child-specific interview that both identifies and quantifies symptoms including situational and cognitive factors. The ADIS–IV: C/P has been extensively used in research and reports positive reliability and validity data (Kendall, 2012a; Silverman & Ollendick, 2005; Southam-Gerow & Chorpita, 2007). This interview protocol diagnoses separate anxiety disorders and additionally examines potential comorbid conditions. The parent interview explores relevant familial and developmental history. Widely used in studies assessing the effectiveness of cognitive behavior therapy (CBT) interventions, the ADIS–IV: C/P has demonstrated sensitivity to treatment gains (Silverman & Ollendick, 2005).

Anxiety Rating Scales

Self-report rating scales address the subjective experience of anxiety by obtaining the child's perspective on symptoms and distress. The two most commonly used rating scales that specifically assess anxiety in youth are the Revised Children's Manifest Anxiety Scale: Second Edition (C. R. Reynolds & Richmond, 2008) and the Multidimensional Anxiety Scale for Children, Second Edition (March, 2012). These empirically supported instruments both have relatively recently been updated and revised. The full Revised Children's Manifest Anxiety Scale: Second Edition is normed for youth ages 6 to 19 years, contains 49 yes/no items, and takes only 10 to 15 minutes to complete. The first 10 items constitute a short form applicable for screening purposes. It reports scale scores on physiological anxiety, worry, social anxiety, and defensiveness. It includes an inconsistent responding index that measures response bias. The Multidimensional Anxiety Scale for Children, Second Edition is normed for youth ages 8 to 19 years and includes both self-report and parent rating scales, each containing 50 items. In addition to a total score, subscales reported include Separation Anxiety/Phobias, Generalized Anxiety Disorder Index, Obsessions and Compulsions, Physical Symptoms, Harm Avoidance, and an Inconsistency Index. These instruments have been found to identify children with clinically significant anxiety symptoms and are appropriate for assessment of treatment gains (Kendall, 2012a; Silverman & Ollendick, 2005; Southam-Gerow & Chorpita, 2007). Even with subscales attempting to assess response bias, it remains important to compare all self-report data with other sources of information because some youth may underreport anxiety.

The broadband Achenbach System of Empirically Based Assessment (ASEBA; Achenbach & Rescorla, 2001) parent, child, and teacher rating scales have also been extensively researched in relation to youth anxiety. Internalizing Subscales include Anxious/Depressed, Withdrawn/Depressed, and Somatic Complaints. The DSM Oriented Cross-Informant Scales include an anxiety problems category. The 2007 software scoring update includes Obsessive–Compulsive and Posttraumatic Stress Problems scales. A benefit of these scales is the addition of a teacher rating form. The scales also provide a broad assessment of potential comorbidities including externalizing disorders. However, the ASEBA may not readily distinguish between comingled anxiety and depression symptoms. In their review of evidence-based assessments for anxiety, Silverman and Ollendick (2005) recommended using the Revised Child Anxiety and Depression Scale (Chorpita, Yim, Moffitt, Umemoto, & Francis, 2000) to discriminate between anxiety and depression symptoms.

A few rating scales have been developed for investigating specific syndromes of anxiety. The Child Yale–Brown Obsessive–Compulsive Scale (Scahill et al., 1997) is designed to specifically assess obsessive–compulsive disorder (OCD) symptoms. There is a 10-item clinician-administered version and a 79-item self-administered checklist. The School Refusal Assessment Scale (Kearney, 2002) is a 24-item rating scale that attempts to ascertain the function of school refusal behaviors. Subscales include Avoidance of Fear-Provoking Situations, Escape from Aversive Social Evaluation Situations, Attention-Getting Behavior, and Positive Tangible Reinforcement. This focus readily links assessment to intervention.

Behavioral Observations and Functional Assessment

There have been several structured observation protocols developed to catalog responses during behavioral avoidance tasks in school, playground, or home settings. Kendall (2012a) cautioned that these tools may be neither sufficiently standardized nor verified to add sufficient incremental validity to the diagnostic process. However, behavioral observations in naturalized settings are important not only to observe the frequency, severity, and other observable features related to anxiety but also to analyze the antecedents and consequences that trigger and maintain behavioral avoidance or observable physiological symptoms.

Because avoidance conditioning plays an important role in maintaining avoidant and withdrawal behaviors, a systematic functional behavioral assessment (FBA; Steege & Watson, 2009) should be developed that maps out the influence of familial, peer, and classroom interactional patterns, proximate environmental antecedents, and the immediate maintaining consequences sustaining the avoidant or withdrawal behaviors. For example, for a student experiencing debilitating performance anxiety, an FBA might reveal the following: a history of dependent schoolwork completion with age-inappropriate parental homework assistance and protective reduction in classroom work completion expectations, particularly observable anxiety symptoms during math and science work and shutting down when faced with tests in these subject areas, and frequent passes to the school health office in response to somatic complaints on an exam day resulting in a release from the expectation to complete the examination. Even with these few details, an FBA is able to identify the external antecedent–behavior–consequence (A-B-C) relationships that maintain anxious avoidant behaviors and assess the inadvertent role that adult support behaviors may play in maintaining avoidance. A comprehensive FBA should also assess cognitive and bodily reaction factors. Child interviews can strive to delineate negative self-talk, faulty cognitive appraisals, and catastrophic expectations that might exacerbate anxious feelings and prompt avoidant behaviors. Identifying the bodily reactions that accompany the onset of anxious episodes is equally important.

Integration of Assessment Data to Inform Intervention

Interview data, rating scales, observations, and an FBA can be integrated to understand the child's subjective experience of anxiety in physical, cognitive, affective, and behavioral domains; familial, social, and developmental influences; and immediate internal and external antecedents and consequences that trigger and maintain withdrawal or avoidant behaviors. The resulting intervention plan may target changes in social interaction patterns within the family and school contexts, manipulation of antecedents and consequences to counter avoidant conditioning, cognitive restructuring to address self-defeating thoughts, and self-calming strategies to reduce somatic reactions to stress and anxiety. Skill deficits may also be defined through this integrative process. A socially anxious child may lack some of the interpersonal skills necessary for more independent peer functioning or for social problem solving. As in the performance anxiety example above, a specific academic deficit such as a learning weakness or disability in a particular subject area may need to be addressed simultaneous to intervening with avoidance behaviors.

Primary Anxiety Syndromes

The *DSM–5* delineates several specific anxiety disorders. Although many components of treatment interventions are similar, it is important for school-centered therapists to understand the primary features of the more common anxiety disorders.

Separation Anxiety Disorder

Separation anxiety disorder is characterized by developmentally inappropriate and excessive anxiety regarding separation from parents or other key attachment figures. Unrealistic fears of harm to self or a significant caregiver can result in emotional stress, clinging behaviors, and refusal to be separated from the attachment figure for even brief periods of time. Typical age of onset is near the start of elementary school. The *ICD–10–CM* code is F93.0.

Generalized Anxiety Disorder

Generalized anxiety disorder involves excessive and difficult-to-control worries and fears about multiple situations. The experience of anxiety is pervasive and may involve family, school, performance, and social concerns. Symptoms may include restlessness, fatigue, difficulty concentrating, irritability, muscle tension, and sleep disturbance. At least three of these symptoms are present on most days for a period of at least 6 months. Typical age of onset is middle childhood and the intermediate school grades. The *ICD–10–CM* code is F41.1.

Social Anxiety Disorder or Social Phobia

Social phobia centers on fear of social evaluation not just in relation to adults but also with peers. Fear of embarrassment, humiliation, or rejection may occur when a child faces even routine social situations. In younger children, social demands may be accompanied by emotional meltdowns, freezing, or shutting down. To reach the *DSM* diagnostic threshold, symptoms must persist for at least 6 months and be associated with significant distress. Social phobia onset is most common in early adolescence. The *ICD–10–CM* code is F40.1.

Specific Phobias

Specific phobias are marked by unrealistic and excessive fear or anxiety in relation to a specific stimulus. *DSM–5* cites common examples as fear of heights, animals, receiving an injection, or seeing blood. To reach clinical significance the phobic reaction must demonstrate significant distress; impair an important area of functioning, such as social or school participation; and persist for over 6 months. Age of onset is generally before age 10. *ICD–10–CM* coding (F40.2, etc.) requires specification of each feared stimulus.

Agoraphobia

Agoraphobia may emerge in adolescence. It presents with marked anxiety in public or enclosed places or when alone outside the home. Nearly half of those affected also experience panic attacks. The *DSM–5* notes that if agoraphobia and panic disorder criteria are both met, each diagnosis should be specified. *ICD–10–CM* specifies agoraphobia with (F40.01) and without (F40.02) panic disorder.

Panic Disorder

Panic disorder involves recurrent abrupt panic attacks that quickly escalate for no clear reason. The attacks involve strong physical symptoms such as sweating, fast heart rate, chest pain, nausea, or dizziness. Associated thoughts may include fear of losing control, "going crazy," or even dying. The affected child may then worry about possible future attacks and might change or restrict behaviors to reduce perceived risks. This disorder is seldom observed before adolescence. The *ICD–10–CM* (F41.0) rules out a diagnosis of panic disorder if agoraphobia is present, whereas the *DSM–5* allows for comorbidity.

Selective Mutism

Selective mutism is a rare disorder with onset in early childhood. Diagnostic criteria specify a consistent failure to speak in common social situations, such as in school, although speaking fluently with immediate family members. This impairment is the result of significant social anxiety; selective mutism is not a communication disorder. When manifested in school, it can impair academic progress because of compromised communication with the teacher and classmates. The *ICD–10–CM* (F94.0) places selective mutism under disorders of social functioning.

DEVELOPMENTAL CONSIDERATIONS

Anxiety is a normal part of life and can serve important motivating and protective functions. However, excessive and persistent anxiety greatly interferes with healthy psychological and physical development and contributes to significant impairments in social and academic functioning. Reports of prevalence rates for clinical anxiety disorders vary greatly. Southam-Gerow and Chorpita (2007) summarized prevalence data to fall within the range of 6% to 15%. Because anxiety is a feature associated with many psychological disorders, it is clear that anxiety symptoms are one of the most common clinical concerns for children and adolescents. Anxiety rates reported for females are approximately double those of males; however, cultural stereotypes related to gender roles may influence the number of clinic referrals for males (Kendall, 2012a).

As children mature, many childhood fears gradually recede as more realistic appraisals of risk emerge, increased understanding of expected outcomes of events and social interactions develop, and self-confidence and problem-solving capacity grow. When children struggle with important developmental transitions, risks for specific anxiety issues escalate. A young child who struggles to increase age-appropriate independence may be at risk for separation anxiety. As social awareness and social demands heighten in early adolescence, so may concerns regarding peer acceptance and social evaluation, which can increase risk for social phobias. Thus, anxiety symptoms can be understood as a disruption of developmentally appropriate progress toward independence and individuation and a failure to develop age-appropriate self-efficacy, social and coping skills, and competence in personal and social problem-solving skills.

Impairments that arise from excessive anxiety affect multiple life functions. As anxiety disorders in children negatively impact successful attainment of critical developmental tasks, social and academic consequences can multiply. Early childhood onset predicts adult symptoms, and in the absence of successful intervention, symptoms will worsen over time. Children who experience anxiety disorders are at increased risk for comorbid disorders, particularly depression and substance abuse, and impaired functioning in academic, social, and occupational domains (Kendall, 2012a).

As with other psychological phenomena, multiple factors contribute to the development of anxiety symptoms (Kendall, 2012a). Genetics and temperament likely create a biological predisposition or vulnerability toward excessive anxiety. An inhibited temperamental style may limit risk taking and predispose the child to a more defensive posture in facing new experiences or challenges. If parents model anxious appraisals and anticipation of harm, risk for symptom development multiplies. Recently, attention on the role of cognitive informational-processing deficits in exacerbating anxiety has increased. Anxious youth demonstrate errors in information processing, appraising events as unrealistically negative or threatening. They have limited confidence in their capacity to protect themselves from stressors, fear failure in multiple performance areas, and perceive themselves as lacking control of events and their responses to them. This limited confidence may make them more dependent on key caregivers, and when they perceive parents or teachers as unable to provide sufficient psychological or physical protection, their anxiety escalates further. Possessing a reduced sense of self-efficacy appropriate to their developmental stage, anxious youth are less likely to trust their own problem-solving skills.

Anxious children have heightened vulnerability to physiological arousal and to negative affectivity, demonstrating an increased sensitivity to negative events and potentially threatening objects and experiences. Thus, bodily reactions may quickly signal arousal, affective and cognitive states are prone to overestimate threat, and then instinctual protective flight responses might be activated. If withdrawal or avoidance immediately reduces anxiety, conditioning may begin to entrench a maladaptive response pattern.

Difficulties with emotional regulation also are evident in children with anxiety disorders. Compared with unaffected youth, these children struggle to manage emotional experiences, modulate the intensity of emotions, and appropriately express feelings (Suveg & Zeman, 2004). Their emotional reactions are more labile and contribute to less flexible response patterns.

Parenting factors often play a role in the development of anxiety symptoms. Parents with anxiety and mood disorders are more likely to raise children who exhibit anxiety disorders (Hughes, Hedtke, & Kendall, 2008). Anxious parents model anxious behavior, and if they use overprotective parenting styles, they may inadvertently restrain the child's progression toward healthy individuation and a positive sense of self-efficacy. If parents routinely express their own threat biases and project a stance that life is largely beyond their control, children are more likely to develop avoidant response styles and perceive themselves as having limited control of their environment and social challenges (Kendall, 2012a). These data clearly point to the importance of addressing parenting style within intervention protocols with particular attention to fostering age-appropriate independence, balanced risk appraisals, and proactive and engaging problem-solving strategies.

Traumatic experiences, including loss and grief, medical issues, harmful accidents, and victimization, can impact multiple aspects of healthy development. These interfering circumstances naturally raise at least transitory anxiety, but if they result in sustained overprotective parenting, entrenched familial negative threat appraisals, and consistently pessimistic confidence in personal control, clinical levels of anxiety may develop and in turn alter developmental trajectories for other key steps toward adaptive individuation.

Many factors contribute reciprocal influences on one other to impact the risks for maladaptive anxiety. Kertz and Woodruff-Borden (2011) proposed a developmental model of anxiety that outlined the complex interplay among biological vulnerability, parenting factors, cognitive processing, emotional regulation, and avoidant behavioral response styles. All the relationships are viewed as multidirectional. For example, anxious children can prompt overly protective responses from parents just as parental anxiety or emotional dysregulation can model unhealthy coping strategies. In another instance, a child experiencing a significant medical condition might realistically require extra precautions from parents and be delayed in addressing certain developmental milestones, but if this protective stance persists when no longer necessary, it may contribute to a more entrenched and inflexible anxious coping style in the child. Assessment and intervention targeting symptoms of anxiety must take into account a wide range of developmental considerations.

CHILD- AND ADOLESCENT-SPECIFIC
THERAPEUTIC INTERVENTION STRATEGIES

Core treatments for anxiety involve behavioral, cognitive behavioral, and coping-skills training interventions and family therapy strategies to change parent–child interaction patterns around anxious behaviors.

Specific strategies that can be integrated into a systemic cognitive behavioral approach include psychoeducation about the nature of anxiety; relaxation strategies for calming the somatic discomfort associated with anxiety; cognitive restructuring; modeling of cognitive and behavioral coping strategies; systematic desensitization, including mastery imagery and exposure strategies with response prevention; contingency management to counter avoidance conditioning and support acquisition of new skills; problem-solving training; integrated systematic training in coping strategies that address the interplay among physical, cognitive, emotional, and behavioral elements of anxiety; and structured family therapy interventions.

Psychoeducation

Part of the power anxiety holds over an affected individual involves the mystery of the onset of intense bodily and cognitive stress and the fear of future unknown events and their consequences. These factors combine to leave the child feeling powerless or out of control and prompt extraordinary measures to gain control and attempt to secure physical and psychological safety. Psychoeducation teaches the child and parents about the nature of anxiety and its manifestation. The child is introduced to the various aspects of anxiety and how they impact one other: somatic pains and discomfort, personal feelings associated with anxiety, thoughts and self-talk that assess threat and influence responses, and actions or behaviors that exacerbate or reduce stress and their consequences for resolving or reinforcing anxiety. The goals of psychoeducation are to demystify the experience of anxiety and set the stage for targeting each element of experience that is affected by anxiety and either exacerbates or relieves symptoms and sustains or resolves anxious response patterns.

Physical symptoms associated with anxiety are highly individualized but may include stomachaches, headaches, or a generalized tense bodily arousal. Children and parents learn how to distinguish between physical illness and the onset of anxiety and to understand how intense anxiety can make one feel sick even when otherwise healthy. Children are taught to monitor the onset of somatic discomfort and to note whether the discomfort occurs in relation to an event, such as a particular social challenge or a pending performance evaluation and, thus, is an anxiety reaction, or whether it is not linked to a pending event and, thus, is more likely a medical illness.

Affective Education

For a chronically anxious child, a variety of feelings may merge into an overwhelming experience of anxiety. Affective education teaches children to identify and pair experiences that are associated with specific moods such as anger, excitement, and sadness. This disentangling of experience and emotions can eventually contribute to specific coping responses. For example, if the dominant affect is actually anger at a perceived slight, the child may benefit from an assertion training strategy to directly voice displeasure, stand up for self, or directly communicate a need. The intended movement is from an experience of acute emotional arousal that is solely categorized as anxiety to a differentiated awareness of the broad range of human emotions.

Many children with chronic anxiety falsely believe that they are the only ones who experience emotional hyperarousal and its limiting impact. Teaching them to recognize the emotional experiences of others in a more realistic way can be reassuring and is a step toward improved perspective taking regarding their own and others' dilemmas and challenges. Besides debriefing and disassembling their own affective experiences, a variety of activities can be used to improve recognition of feelings in self and others; develop a broader and more nuanced vocabulary for describing their experiences; learn to differentiate the physical sensations associated with various emotions; and more readily and appropriately communicate their feelings, needs, and wants. Affective education activities can take many forms. Vocabulary can be expanded through the construction of "feeling wheels" that display various related shades of emotion with color shades to emphasize their distinctions and relatedness. *Nervous* might be described as different from *afraid, apprehensive,* or *excited. Angry, resentful, frustrated, furious,* and even *depressed* are related but distinct shades of emotional experience. Other activities might involve role plays of stressful situations and discussions of characters' feelings or reading short stories that reveal the impact of different feelings. Feelings collages and feelings charades can be used to visually demonstrate the nonverbal characteristics of emotional expression and engage children's attention.

Anxiety and depression often occur together in youth and adults. Kendall (2014) offered a useful distinction regarding their differences while highlighting the interaction between thoughts and feelings. Automatic thoughts related to anxiety tend to be lengthy and anticipatory, fearing social judgment, performance failure, or physical danger before an event.

Depressive thoughts are often retrospective and self-blaming, tending to be short, declarative, and judgmental.

Self-Awareness and Self-Monitoring

The concepts and strategies described in the self-understanding model (SUM) delineated in Chapter 3 are appropriate to improve self-awareness and integrate understanding of bodily reactions, thoughts, feelings, and behaviors. Self-monitoring is beneficial in many ways. It enhances self-awareness, sets the stage for developing a more internalized locus of control, and prepares the child for contributing to a measured continuum of exposure tasks for confronting excessive anxiety. Self-awareness training strives to link the various dimensions of an anxious experience (i.e., identifying the earliest physical cue that I'm getting anxious so I can pay attention to my emerging automatic thoughts and how realistic their appraisal of threat might be). Self-monitoring may use structured logs of anxious experiences or debriefing within therapy sessions to delineate the various aspects of anxiety-provoking circumstances. Record keeping may describe the event or stimulus, note bodily reaction, automatic thoughts, associated feelings, and actions taken. Self-monitoring contributes to the delineation of *fear ladders* that quantify the intensity of various aspects of anxious stimuli (Chorpita, 2007; Kendall & Hedtke, 2006). Rating the intensity of reactions to various stimuli defines the agenda for what to address first during training and exposure activities, progressing systematically from less to more anxiety-provoking stimuli. Fear or anxiety ratings can also monitor progress from the perspective of the youth. Encountering the same experience with lower rated anxiety can be rewarding and motivating for the child to maintain therapeutic engagement.

Relaxation and Self-Calming Strategies

Debilitating anxiety is often accompanied by intense physical discomfort, heightened wary alertness and tense arousal, and increased muscular tension. The part of the body that registers anxiety first may vary from child to child. For some, it might be a stomachache or the feeling that their stomach is tied in knots; for others, it might be a racing heartbeat or a combination of symptoms. Through self-awareness training, students identify their physiological responses to stress, fear, and anxiety. They begin to associate these visceral sensations with anxiety rather than medical illness. Eventually they will be coached to use this awareness not as a foreshadowing of an impending overwhelming event but as a cue to initiate planned coping strategies. It is easier to maintain rational perspectives, stick to a coping plan, and engage in problem solving when physical arousal is calmed to manageable levels.

Relaxation training for stress management goes back to Edmond Jacobson's groundbreaking work with adults over 50 years ago. That work has been extensively adapted to work with children (Kendall & Hedtke, 2006; King, Hamilton, & Ollendick, 1988). In this context, relaxation training serves several purposes. After self-awareness training identifies somatic reactions associated with the onset of anxiety, the child explores what relaxation strategies work to calm physical tension. These strategies include taking deep relaxing breaths, squeezing and releasing a stress ball, taking a brisk walk, or whatever else might suit a particular child. The relaxation response can then be paired with recognition of physical tension at the onset of an anxious episode to dampen the physical response. This relaxation response is an active coping strategy that initiates taking control of the anxiety-producing circumstance. The somatic stress recognition becomes a signal to do something self-calming and then to apply additional coping strategies learned in other stages of the intervention protocol. It might be paired with a mantra (e.g., "Stay calm, you can manage this") and prompt self-instructions to use rehearsed coping strategies.

Progressive muscular relaxation involves systematically tightening and then releasing the tension in muscle groups throughout the body, generally starting with extremities and eventually progressing to the body's core. It enhances bodily awareness and recognition of what specific muscle groups tense during anxious episodes and how they can be relaxed. Full-body progressive muscular relaxation is not practical to use at school or in other public settings in the stress of the moment. However, tightening and releasing specific muscle groups can be done and be effective without drawing unnecessary attention to the child.

In the context of therapy sessions, full progressive muscular relaxation has been successfully used as part of a systematic desensitization protocol for childhood fears and phobias (Ollendick & King, 1998). In this application it may be used during imaginal exposure activities as part of a gradual systematic desensitization program that exposes the child in small steps to feared objects or activities, or it can paired with mastering imagery that shows the child successfully managing a fear or phobia. A child can use progressive relaxation with mastery imagery before an anticipated challenging experience. Analogies from the sports world may be useful in persuading youth to try relaxation strategies. For example, before free throws, professional basketball players will often bounce the ball a few times to relieve muscular tension, take a deep breath, visualize the ball going in the basket, and then shoot. Simulating this in the therapy room with a wad of paper and a waste basket can be a fun way of engaging a student in working with the concepts and applications of relaxation strategies.

Cognitive Strategies

Cognition plays a critical role in the exacerbation or management of anxiety symptoms, and cognitive therapy strategies are central to empirically supported protocols (Chorpita, 2007; Kendall, 2012a; Silverman, Pina, & Viswesvaran, 2008). Anxious children and adolescents tend to overly focus and elaborate on negative information. Their initial mind-set expects things to go wrong, influencing a coping stance that is passive, reactionary, and pessimistic and that heightens anxiety stimulating physical arousal. Affected youth are overly sensitive to fearful cues. They are prone to cognitive distortions, perceiving circumstances as unrealistically threatening. They engage in catastrophic thinking expecting the worse to happen. Their self-perception is one of powerlessness embedded in an external locus of control, judging themselves as dominated by external events but having limited influence in coping with the negative aspects of their experiences. Automatic thoughts and repetitive self-talk are dominated by self-defeating messages: "I can't," "I'm powerless," "I'm overwhelmed," "I'll fail," "I'll be done in __," and so forth. Anxious automatic thoughts are anticipatory, most often unrealistically fearing social judgment, personal failure, or physical danger. After an experience of debilitating anxiety, automatic thoughts may become self-blaming and connote hopelessness reflecting damaged self-esteem and fueling depression, thus comingling symptoms of these two internalizing disorders.

Children with interfering anxiety symptoms may experience a flood of negative and self-defeating thoughts that they are reticent to share with others, for fear of embarrassment and additional loss of control. Kendall (2014) emphasized the importance of creating a therapeutic environment where it is safe to talk about thinking. The therapist can introduce the topic through modeling by describing an anxious experience that he or she has faced and the self-talk that accompanied this stressful event. The purpose is to counter the student's misperceived isolation of being the only one who experiences these disturbing thoughts and encourage exploration of self-talk and its influence. Later, when teaching self-instruction strategies, the therapist can model the use of adaptive self-talk.

Cognitive restructuring strategies address the cognitive distortions, faulty thinking patterns, and self-defeating self-talk elements of excessive anxiety (Chorpita, 2007; Friedberg, McClure, & Garcia, 2009; Kendall & Hedtke, 2006). Thought diaries, debriefing of anxiety-laden experiences, and examination of negative self-talk explore the character of reflexive thinking patterns and outline the connections between bodily reactions, thoughts, feelings, and actions. Socratic dialogue, tests of evidence, probability estimation, and rational analysis strategies are used to guide the student in examining the faulty logic in self-defeating cognitions and faulty risk appraisals. The child is guided to question the rationale of negative self-talk and explore more realistic and adaptive alternatives that can guide active coping strategies rather than prompt avoidance and withdrawal. The first goal is to counter misinterpretations of events, and the second is to develop self-talk and self-instruction strategies that prompt deployment of active coping strategies. Adaptive self-talk and cognitive appraisals can be modeled by the therapist and practiced by the student.

Kendall (2012a) noted the importance of reducing negative and anxious self-talk as the key change variable. It is easier to stop a flood of negative cognitions when actively replacing them with other adaptive thoughts. Self-instruction protocols that are initially scripted to provide sequential self-talk to guide coping strategies can serve this purpose.

This approach promotes a proactive and self-efficacious approach toward coping with anxiety. Under therapeutic guidance, the youth constructs a personal repertoire of coping strategies that are then applied to anxious situations beyond the therapy session beginning with less anxiety-provoking situations and gradually progressing to the most overwhelming challenges. A variety of coping strategies are learned and figuratively available in a personalized toolbox to apply to differing anxiety-producing scenarios. Parents are made aware of these strategies and coached in appropriate ways of prompting their application in moments of stress.

Behavioral Strategies

From a behavioral perspective, anxiety becomes a conditioned response to fearful stimuli. This can occur through escape conditioning, in which a response stops a negative condition (e.g., abruptly leaving an uncomfortable social situation), or through avoidance conditioning (e.g., refusing to go to school to avoid academic and social stress), in which a response prevents a negative condition from occurring. The escape or avoidance provides reinforcing relief, thus making it more likely for those counterproductive strategies to be used during the next occurrence of the anxiety-provoking circumstance. Exposure with response prevention strategies, outlined below, strives to counter this conditioning by gradually exposing the student to the anxiety-provoking experience until the anxiety response is lessened and eventually becomes manageable. Progress steps can be reinforced with external contingent rewards but are also reinforced by the internal relief of personal mastery.

Contingent reinforcement protocols based on operant conditioning principles can be developed to shape approach responses and participation in intervention activities as well. Reinforcement of successive approximations to the goal applies. Subgoals are agreed on, and the child is tangibly rewarded for demonstrating progress. For example, a student with a social phobia may initially target just being present in a common peer situation for a specified period of time, but then the bar is gradually raised toward achievement of increasing social interaction. This approach has been particularly beneficial for work with fears like being at heights, in the dark, interacting with pets, and similar challenges. Linking cognitive, behavioral, and self-monitoring strategies, youth are also taught to use self-talk for positive reinforcement. Older children in particular may be responsive to self-directed reinforcers, but in the end the goal is for mastery to provide its own natural contingent reinforcement.

Exposure

Exposure has been identified as the key element in anxiety treatment (Chorpita, Daleiden, & Weisz, 2005). Application of contingent reinforcers to support each step of progress toward tolerating exposure to the feared stimulus enhances treatment effects (Chorpita, 2007). Exposure involves step-by-step repeated presentation or experience with the feared stimulus. This may begin in imagery but eventually must progress to in vivo trials, which means conducting exposures outside of the therapy room either directly with the therapist in the environment where the overwhelming fear emerges or as homework between sessions with parental or teacher support. Exposure provides a corrective learning experience as the child's experience in an exposure trial results in a gradual weakening of the association between the stimulus and a feared outcome. Theoretically, this might be conceptualized as an extinction process or, from a respondent conditioning perspective, a gradual disassociation of the conditioned feared stimulus from the feared outcome.

A careful assessment process is required to effectively guide the student through exposure activities. The therapist works with the client to develop a hierarchy of fears or anxiety-provoking situations. For children, this is often conceptualized as a *fear ladder*, progressing from less anxious to more anxious items as one climbs up the ladder. The child is trained to use a rating scale to assign numerical value to the intensity of anxiety experienced. During an exposure activity, fear ratings are periodically taken to assess whether the child is gradually becoming habituated to the stimulus, moving from a higher to a lesser rating of anxiety as feared reactions do not occur despite prolonged exposure to the feared situation. Ideally, distress ratings are recorded before, at timed intervals during, and then after the exposure. Practice records are maintained to monitor progress and make decisions about readiness for moving up the fear ladder to more challenging exposures. Carefully selected homework assignments calibrated for success are added with specified parental or teacher support. The eventual goal is for the student to become habituated to the fear both during and between exposures.

Treatment for anxiety disorders requires a mixture of support and challenge. Paradoxically, the only way to overcome debilitating anxiety is to experience it and realize that the consequences of feared situations either do not occur or have been substantially overestimated. A useful metaphor to suggest to the student is that the fear or anxiety is a *false alarm* and that the therapeutic task is to conduct controlled experiments to better determine when anxiety reactions are false alarms or real danger and then how to effectively respond within each condition. The cognitive strategy of *tests of evidence* is consistent with this anticipatory set. It is always made clear to the client that the goal is not total absence of anxiety since anxiety can serve a protective function and is simply just a natural part of human experience.

In many cases, significant adults have inadvertently contributed to escape conditioning by rescuing the anxious child from a fearful circumstance. During a therapeutic exposure activity, the therapist merely observes and saves comments and supportive reinforcement for the concluding review. If there is classroom or home practice of an exposure activity, the teacher or parent is coached as to the character and level of support to provide. In some cases, prior to the exposure activity, it can be beneficial for the therapist or a surrogate to model successful participation in the selected exposure activity, including verbalizing coping instructions that might otherwise be covert self-talk.

A partial examination of the blending of separation anxiety and school refusal in a primary grade child can provide an example for creating exposure sequences and hierarchies to gradually prepare for full school participation. The child might be prepared for the start of the school year by experiencing an increasing number of opportunities to be cared for by known caregivers in the absence of the parents. Before the school year begins, there can be practice visits to school, including visiting the classroom and spending some time with the classroom teacher while the parents are out of the room. If school refusal or emotional meltdowns emerge as classes begin, school staff may need to supportively escort the student to school while the parent is encouraged to leave without lingering. Initially the student may need to work under teacher aide supervision within the school but not inside the classroom. However, the student remains for the full school day with typical work expectations. Supervising staff are warm and encouraging but not supportive of work avoidance. Once a child is acclimated to the school, a plan can be enacted to gradually work the student into participation within the classroom and eventual engagement in regular academic and social activities. There might be multiple half steps along the way that are supported by significant contingent rewards. Home contingent rewards might include a special activity with a parent earned only if successful completion of the school day occurs. The initial insistence on full-day attendance coupled with the arrangement of substantial supportive school resources may be described as a *flooding* exposure activity and requires persistence and a united stance on the part of both family and school; however, the longer the child is safely exposed to the school setting, the more likely it is that anxiety will diminish. This example collapses the intervention process into smaller steps than might be necessary for some children. Each circumstance requires an individualized assessment and intervention plan, but this example illustrates how anxiety can be faced with exposure and prevention of avoidant responses reinforced with operant contingency management. Chapter 3 provides an extended illustration of an intervention protocol for socially anxious and school avoidant children. Also, see Chorpita's (2007) description of the art and science of exposure for an extended illustration of the principles of these strategies.

Problem-Solving and Social-Skills Training

The goal of therapeutic intervention across symptom profiles is to teach the child and family effective problem-solving skills for independent application. To develop the proactive self-efficacy necessary to sustain gains in anxiety management, therapists teach systematic problem-solving approaches, including delineation of when and how they should seek consultation and support and when they have the capability and responsibility to independently address challenges. Summarizing the research literature in this area, Kendall (2012a) noted that problem-solving training has been demonstrated to reduce relapses. Common problem-solving sequences include defining the problem, brainstorming a breadth of possible solutions, evaluating the likely outcomes of potential action plans, choosing a solution and acting on it, evaluating the effectiveness of the response, and repeating problem-solving elements as necessary.

Social anxiety disorders might require interpersonal and social problem-solving skills training. In this case, there appears to be a reciprocal relationship because limited social skills may raise anxiety regarding social participation, and in turn limited social participation may delay development of age-appropriate social skills. Anxiety that presents as another anxiety syndrome (e.g., generalized anxiety disorder) might also impair social involvement. It is always necessary to evaluate whether the student needs social-skills training to support social participation even when excessive anxiety symptoms are reduced.

Comprehensive Empirically Supported Protocols: The Coping Cat and The C.A.T. Project

The Coping Cat (Kendall & Hedtke, 2006) program for children ages 7 to 13 and The C.A.T. Project (Kendall, Choudhury, Hudson, & Webb, 2002) for adolescents are well-researched CBT protocols for anxiety management.

Coping Cat provides an example of a manualized program that integrates the intervention principles and strategies outlined above. Although committed to proven treatment strategies, Kendall eschewed robotic cookbook approaches to intervention rather using the approach of "flexibility within fidelity." The program's therapist manual provides a systematic and sequential intervention protocol but also includes "tips from the trenches," practical examples for adapting materials to special circumstances or challenges. The program has been applied in individual and group formats and within clinic and school settings with substantial empirical support.

The first part of Coping Cat presents a psychoeducational overview of anxiety and the coping skills foundation for managing anxiety at an age-appropriate level. The second half of the program focuses on exposure and application activities for generalization of results. Kendall and Hedtke used an acronym, the FEAR plan, to organize their presentation of concepts and interventions.

F Is for Feeling Frightened?

This first stage teaches awareness of physical signs of anxiety and then proceeds to teach relaxation strategies for calming emotional arousal. Workbook exercises help the child to identify the body parts that are particularly tensed when anxious and then through a combination of relaxing breathing and muscle relaxation exercises, the child learns how to reduce the physical tension introduced by anxiety. Once she or he has mastered this skill, the child teaches the parents what has been learned to cement skill acquisition and to prepare parents for prompting use of the skill under pressure in home situations.

E Stands for Expecting Bad Things to Happen?

This portion of the training program explores faulty beliefs, cognitive distortions, and unrealistic expectations. In response, cognitive restructuring strategies are introduced. To assist younger children in exploring thoughts and understanding the concept of self-talk, the therapist uses workbook exercises using cartoon characters with thought bubbles to teach children to see that there can be a variety of thoughts and self-talk messages that might occur in the same situation. The nature of those thoughts can determine whether someone feels anxious and how interfering it might be. Self-statements and automatic thoughts generated by the student in personal anxiety-provoking situations are explored. The therapist models and then the student practices coping self-talk and balanced rational expectations in place of anxiety-stimulating fearful thoughts, catastrophic expectations, and covert self-defeating messages. In this stage, anxiety hierarchies or fear ladders are created and *fear thermometers* are introduced as rating tools for self-monitoring the intensity of anxiety and the benefits of using coping strategies.

A *Stands for* Attitudes and Actions That Might Help

This section focuses on application of problem-solving strategies. Students integrate material already learned to appraise the challenge of anxiety-stimulating situations, being careful to monitor unrealistic thoughts, brainstorm alternative courses of action, and then apply learned coping strategies to navigate the problem's dilemma with reduced anxiety. The same intervention pattern is used: modeling by the therapist, designing specific applications to the child's real experiences, practicing within sessions through role plays and in workbook exercises, and applying strategies in homework assignments to foster generalization and transfer of skills.

R *Stands for* Results and Rewards

This section focuses on self-monitoring and contingent reinforcement. The therapist provides verbal reinforcement for successive approximations of the coping skills learned, striving to counter an all-or-nothing quest for perfection that is common for children with anxiety disorders. The child is coached to realistically self-monitor progress and to generate and use rewards for successful progress. This framework is consistent with the goal of increasing the student's sense of being in charge of self while emphasizing progress and personal strengths that are too easily dismissed by anxiety sufferers, who tend to judge themselves unrealistically harshly.

Applying the Strategies

The second phase of the Coping Cat protocol applies the coping and problem-solving strategies involved in the FEAR plan to increasingly anxiety-provoking exposure tasks. The therapist models exposure activities, and the child rehearses them in session and then implements them in vivo in the setting where anxiety might escalate. Because it takes firm conviction to challenge a reticent child to engage in a feared exposure task, Kendall advocated incorporating humor and playful creativity in designing exposure tasks whenever possible. The review and summary activity for the intervention protocol requires the child to make a commercial that demonstrates what he or she has learned in the program. When video recording is not possible, a booklet or other vehicle for creative expression can be used. The commercial is then shown to parents. This activity is consistent with the dictum that to really cement learning, teach what has been learned. This activity celebrates the progress that the student has made and helps to provide closure to the therapeutic experience.

Web-Based and Computer Assisted Interventions: Camp Cope-A-Lot

Kendall and Khanna (2008) developed a DVD to accompany the Coping Cat program. Kendall (2014) is currently involved in further development of interactive web-based anxiety intervention programs. He views them as enhancing treatment, motivating intervention participation and practice for youth, and extending availability of quality services; however, he does not view technical resources as replacing the need for live therapeutic direction and support. Integrating technology and web resources is being explored for a wide range of treatment protocols. For example, adolescents may be more likely to complete thought records and track mood intensity through a phone app rather than in a paper-and-pencil form. Khanna and Kendall (2010) reported significant positive treatment results for Camp Cope-A-Lot. They found that the computer-assisted intervention demonstrated more therapist treatment fidelity than the comparison approaches. This may indicate that the built-in structure of the DVD fostered improved adherence to the intervention protocol. Novice therapists in particular may benefit from this structure. Integrating interactive web-based programming into CBT protocols may truly be the wave of the future.

Modular CBT

In contrast to manualized programs, Chorpita (2007) outlined a modular approach to the treatment of childhood disorders. He asserted that exposure is the central element in treatment of all anxiety disorders. His core intervention protocol has four stages: (a) development of a hierarchical list of fears; (b) education about the nature of anxiety; (c) exposure practice of feared situations; and (d) preparation for maintenance of coping skills, highlighting the need for ongoing practice of skills and continued exposure to troublesome stimuli. Beyond these essentials, all other intervention modules are selected on an individualized need basis rather than incorporated into a manualized sequence. For example, some children with anxiety might need social initiation skills, whereas others might not. Some parents may require training in active ignoring, contingency management, or effectively managing anxious meltdowns, but this will not be necessary for all parents. Intervention modules are drawn from the empirical literature but only applied as necessary. The modular concept works to link assessment to specific interventions and apply a parsimonious approach to treatment. It adds structure based on empirical data to the therapeutic process but incorporates flexibility and individualization. The child is armed with a toolbox of coping strategies, and the therapist must have a cabinet full of empirically supported intervention strategies.

Obsessive–Compulsive Disorder: Specific Strategies

Although anxiety is a primary feature of OCD, the *DSM–5* for the first time assigned OCD and related disorders into its own diagnostic category. In the *ICD–10–CM*, OCD (F42) falls under a broad category that includes anxiety disorders. The *DSM* change is the result of family, genetic, neuropsychological, and pathophysiological research that point to differences in etiology and neurological involvement compared with other anxiety disorders (Barrett, Farrell, Pina, Peris, & Piacentini, 2008). However, many of the core CBT intervention strategies used for anxiety disorders are incorporated into interventions for OCD, beginning with the emphasis on exposure with response prevention (ERP) and including psychoeducation, self-awareness and self-monitoring, relaxation and self-calming, cognitive restructuring, behavioral strategies including contingency management, problem solving and social-skills training. Thus, in this section we will primarily highlight the OCD-specific intervention for challenging obsessions and compulsions.

The *DSM–5* reports an OCD prevalence of 1.2% and that 25% of cases are identified before age 14. OCD is a neurobehavioral disorder characterized by the presence of *obsessive* thoughts, impulses, or images that are experienced as intrusive and that cause marked distress and anxiety and/or *compulsions* or repetitive behaviors or mental acts that try to suppress obsessive thoughts, reduce anxiety, or prevent a feared negative occurrence despite the reality that no clear rational connection can be made between the ritual and the feared event. Common obsessions include contamination, sexual themes, religiosity, aggression, or violence. Common compulsions include washing, ordering or arranging items, checking, counting, touching, or repetition (Albano, Chorpita, & Barlow, 2003; March, 2007).

The behavioral conception of OCD posits that obsessive and compulsive behaviors are developed over an extended period of time through negative reinforcement sequences (Piacentini, Peris, March, & Franklin, 2012). Obsessions are unwanted thoughts and images that trigger anxiety. Compulsive behaviors including mental actions are attempts to push obsessions away and relieve the anxiety associated with them. If they temporarily relieve the negative thoughts and feelings, the compulsions are likely to be repeated the next time obsessions emerge. Exposure-based CBT protocols are the current standard for treatment of pediatric OCD (Franklin, Freeman, & March, 2010; March, 2007; March & Mulle, 1998; Piacentini et al., 2012).

March and colleagues' (March, 2007; March & Mulle, 1998) intervention protocol can serve as an example. Psychoeducation defines OCD as a neurobehavioral disorder. Going one step further, March used an externalizing the symptom strategy (M. White & Epston, 1990) to guide the child to define OCD as an outside agent or "enemy" to fight against. Children are encouraged to give OCD a funny name, but they can just refer to it as "OCD." Talking back to OCD is then incorporated into self-instruction protocols that are used with exposure tasks and to stave off OCD behaviors when stressed. This youth-friendly approach is designed to help the child see the self as separate from the symptoms, improve a sense of active internal locus of control and self-efficacy, and contribute to reliable and repeatable scripts for resisting obsessions and compulsions. For younger children, the enemy can be concretized through a drawing or symbol that is either shown as defeated or talked back to in practice sessions to develop self-instruction scripts.

The strategy of externalizing the symptom is incorporated into a larger tool kit of cognitive and behavioral strategies the child can draw on to resist OCD actions. A symbolic or tangible tool kit may include thought stopping and redirection techniques, a cheat sheet for remembering rational thoughts or self-instruction scripts, a picture of the OCD enemy being defeated, a list of alternative distracting activities, and a person to call when stressed and anxious. An example of a cognitive script is the concept of *cultivating non-attachment*. The OCD thoughts are reframed as a brain hiccup, annoying but capable of being weathered. For example, as an obsession emerges, the child covertly addresses it, calling it by name, i.e., "Hi (OCD)" to immediately externalize the symptom. This begins a self-instruction script noting that "my brain is hiccupping again (thus, not a rational worry); these hiccups will pass if I go away and do something pleasant or distracting to avoid focusing on them."

The cognitive and behavioral strategies in the tool kit are generally insufficient in and of themselves to successfully manage OCD. The core intervention strategy similar to other conditions characterized by severe anxiety is ERP. The self-instruction protocols and other toolbox strategies are used to support exposure activities and prevent recurrent episodes in natural settings. Before beginning ERP, the factors influencing OCD are mapped. This mapping includes identifying triggers, analyzing family transactions that may support the negative conditioning sequence, and constructing a hierarchy from least to most debilitating obsessions and compulsions. Exposure activities always begin with less anxiety-provoking stimuli and work their way up the ladder of difficulty. Exposure generally begins within the therapy context using imaginal and when possible in vivo exposures. Talking back to OCD and self-instruction protocols are modeled by the therapist and then used by the student during an exposure. During exposures, the child is put in contact with a feared thought, object, or action one small step at a time and encouraged not to respond with a compulsive behavior. Periodic ratings of anxiety are gathered during the exposure activity and then graphed to demonstrate progress and motivate continued therapeutic compliance. The process of habituation begins when the child's anxiety is reduced without using a compulsive action. Parents are then taught how to assist in home practice. The therapist also coaches school staff on how to assist the student in practicing coping strategies to avoid OCD responses.

March and Mulle (1998) applied an additional creative approach to gradual exposure. They encouraged the child to engage in actions that violate the rules governing their OCD. This engagement might mean merely delaying or shortening a ritual or performing it differently or slowly. For example, they may direct a child with hand washing issues to delay washing for an hour, then wash hands in a different manner and sequence, thus altering the rigidity of the compulsion's control.

In exasperation, family and school staff often accommodate OCD behaviors in an attempt to limit the child's experience of anxiety. March's protocol focuses on encouraging the child to take charge of combatting OCD. However, parents must be involved to support their child's efforts, assist with home-based exposure activities, prompt use of the tool kit of coping skills, model addressing OCD as an outside agent, and manage emotional meltdowns that may accompany overwhelming anxiety without reinforcing inappropriate behavior. Parental withdrawal from their roles in maintaining or participating in OCD rituals must be coordinated with the hierarchy of exposure tasks and thus should be planned and gradual with the child's participation and therapist's guidance rather than arbitrary and all at once.

Youth Trauma and Posttraumatic Stress Disorder: Specific Strategies

Two areas related to trauma have been studied within the intervention literature. Response to trauma can affect a large number of youth in a community simultaneously in the event of a natural disaster, a fire or major accident, or a public act of violence (e.g., a school shooting). Response to clinical symptoms of posttraumatic stress disorder (PTSD) can result from unresolved trauma from a major community event, or they can occur because of personal trauma, such as witnessing a homicide, involvement in a life-threatening situation, or being the victim of physical or sexual abuse.

PTSD Symptoms

Although characterized by excessive anxiety and previously included within the Anxiety Disorders category, the *DSM–5* established a separate category for Trauma and Stressor Related Disorders. The *ICD–10–CM* (F43.1) does not make this distinction. Posttraumatic stress disorder results from exposure to a traumatic event involving serious threat to physical integrity. Intrusive symptoms emerge that may include recurrent distressing recollections of the event (sometimes evident in themes during play), recurrent dreams, flashbacks in which it may feel as if the event is recurring, or intense distress or reactivity even when only exposed to cues or symbols that remind the victim of the traumatizing event. Persistent avoidance of activities, places, people, or thoughts that might be associated with the trauma may occur. Negative disturbance in mood and cognitions may develop in which distorted cognitions and negative self-beliefs; intense affect such as fear, anger, or guilt; feelings of detachment; or difficulty expressing positive emotions may persist. Hyperarousal or reactivity may emerge including hypervigilance, startle reactions, and difficulty with concentration.

Response to Community-Wide Experiences of Trauma

Posttraumatic stress symptoms are common after natural disasters such as hurricanes or other traumas that might affect an entire school community. Although for most children symptoms diminish over the course of the year, as many as 30% may experience persistent symptoms indicative of PTSD a year later (La Greca & Silverman, 2012). Although numerous studies have examined the impact of trauma on children, the nature of sudden disasters makes it difficult to establish research protocols to evaluate intervention strategies. Much of the literature operates under the framework of trauma-focused CBT for personal traumas such as sexual or physical abuse. Reviewing this literature, La Greca and Silverman (2012) divided response strategies into three stages: postimpact, short-term recovery, and long-term recovery.

Immediately after an event, the first focus of responders is on safety and security. The psychological support response generally involves some form of empathic debriefing, often conducted within a group context, in which students are encouraged to share their feelings, connect with peers, and receive reassurance regarding both physical safety and the normalcy of their emotional responses. This context also provides the opportunity to dispel rumors and share facts regarding events and to preview predictable steps in response and recovery. The National Child Traumatic Stress Network outlines psychological first aid responses. Recommended crisis interventions encourage children to express their feelings verbally and through drawings. The immediate postimpact response emphasizes clarification regarding facts and procedures, delineates support resources, and screens for those who might require more intense individualized assistance for coping with trauma.

During the short-term recovery phase, children are monitored for lingering effects, and some children judged slow to recover may require specific follow-up. A support group for these higher risk students would combine further processing of the event, specific coping skills instruction, and more intense peer and adult supports. One problem after a community disaster is the challenge of addressing the needs of a large number of children with only limited mental health resources. In response to this dilemma, Wolmer, Laor,

Dedeoglu, Siev, and Yazgan (2005) developed the school activation program as a teacher-mediated, follow-up crisis support program. The school activation program trained classroom teachers to teach CBT coping skills strategies to their students over a 4-week period. They evaluated the impact of implementation 4 to 5 months after a major earthquake in Turkey, and rates of PTSD were significantly reduced, with higher adaptive functioning for participants reported even at 3-year follow-up. The advantages of using school staff, known and trusted by the students, are readily evident. However, school staff in these kinds of situations have experienced the traumatic event themselves and even with advance training in crisis intervention may require extra support to be able to respond appropriately to at-risk students. The long-term recovery phase requires more intense specific individual treatments for post-traumatic stressors.

Therapeutic Intervention for PTSD and Severe Trauma

In their review of evidence-based interventions for youth exposed to trauma, Silverman, Ortiz, et al. (2008) noted the efficacy of trauma-focused CBT (Cohen, Mannarino, & Deblinger, 2006) and two school-based CBT programs, Cognitive Behavioral Intervention for Trauma in Schools (Jaycox, 2004) and its adaptation, the Mental Health for Immigrants Program (Kataoka et al., 2003). Another school-based program with empirical support is the grief and trauma intervention program for children (Salloum, 2008; Salloum & Overstreet, 2008). The grief and trauma intervention program for children was applied extensively in schools in New Orleans following Hurricane Katrina, but the model has also been used for children exposed to homicide and violence. The school-based applications are noteworthy because they have offered trauma intervention services for underserved minority youth in low socioeconomic status communities, where risks for exposure to trauma are heightened.

All of these programs share a similar therapeutic framework: CBT coping skills training and exposure coupled with various forms of narrative therapy. Trauma-focused CBT is primarily an individual treatment with conjoint work with parents, although Rivera (2012) described a school-based application that combines individual and group treatment. The school-based group programs may include some individual sessions particularly centered on development of the personal trauma narrative and then conduct parent and teacher education modules. The central elements of trauma intervention protocols are similar to strategies described above for anxiety disorders, including psychoeducation, relaxation training, emotional expression and modulation, cognitive coping and restructuring, and graduated exposure to fears, in this case related to the trauma experience. With that in mind, this section will focus on the trauma narrative.

Trauma Narratives

Children with PTSD often resist talking about their trauma experience for fear that it will overwhelm them and increase their psychological pain. However, the unresolved emotional impact of the trauma permits its effects to linger and significantly limit their functioning and well-being. Constructing a trauma narrative does not occur until after affective and cognitive coping skills have been addressed. Sometimes in preparation for creating a trauma narrative, the child might be asked to create a narrative of a positive event particularly one in which he or she behaved well or showed courage. This practice introduces the technique and serves as an advance reminder that the child's view of self should not merely be defined by a traumatic experience. Before initiating the trauma the child and parents are prepared for the task, and its therapeutic rationale is shared: Talking through a trauma will gradually overcome its power and permit the child to move toward a happier, healthier, and less limiting lifestyle. Trauma-focused CBT treatment may include a preparatory review of youth stories about trauma (e.g., see Holmes, 2000).

The trauma narrative is conceptualized as a graduated exposure task. Through drawings, writing, and discussion, the child gradually narrates the trauma story in increasing depth. Memories of traumatic events are often fragmented. Through the narrative process, a full coherent understanding emerges, and as it sees the light of day, the power of these events over the child gradually decreases. Cohen et al.'s (2006) trauma narrative sequence illustrates this.

Over several sessions, the student is encouraged to describe details of the event, starting with less threatening information. The therapist prompts the child to describe it as if it were happening now. Many creative forms may be used to create the story: symbolic play, drawings, writings, and narration to the therapist serving as "recording secretary." Each time the story is revisited, elaboration increases and more vulnerable aspects are addressed. The similarity to a fear ladder hierarchy is apparent as the client moves from less painful to more painful and fearful elements of the story. The elaboration of the narrative eventually desensitizes the child to the trauma reminders. During the construction of the narrative, cognitive distortions, faulty attributions, and maladaptive self-blame may emerge. The therapist uses various cognitive restructuring strategies to rebalance perspectives and counter any tendency to blame oneself for being victimized and encourages the student to incorporate these healthier perspectives into the elaborated narrative. Because this process can create emotional dysregulation, the therapist must artfully manage the pace of disclosures and intersperse narrative activities with relaxation exercises or distracting activities as necessary. Whether occurring in the school or clinic, it is necessary to anticipate the closing of sessions and ensure that there is adequate time for closure and a discussion or activity that is defocused from the narrative.

As the final form of the narrative emerges, the child is asked how he or she is different after this exploration and what advice he or she might share with another child who experienced something like this. These tasks encourage the child to summarize a healthier integration of the meaning of the trauma and to articulate coping strategies learned through the process. Sometimes at this stage, it can be helpful for the child to share his or her narrative with a parent if in the therapist's judgment that would further contribute to leaving it behind. However, some parents may have been affected by the same trauma or for other reasons might not be healthy enough to participate in this step. Careful therapeutic assessment is required by the therapist. Narratives regarding a common shared event such as a natural disaster or from a similar trauma such as exposure to gang violence might benefit from sharing in supportive group work. Sexual trauma narratives are generally developed in individual work. However, Deblinger, Behl, and Glickman (2012) reported that involvement of a nonoffending parent in understanding the narrative can enhance treatment outcomes.

After the trauma narrative is fully processed, imaginal and in vivo exposure strategies are used to desensitize the student to any activities, locations, or other symbolic reminders of the trauma. If the trauma reaction includes grief over the loss of a loved one, it might be helpful to spend some time focusing on positive memories of that relationship. Therapy dealing with childhood trauma covers intensely vulnerable ground. Extra attention is necessary to secure adequate emotional closure to the therapeutic relationship.

Summary Data: Effectiveness of CBT Interventions for Anxiety in Schools

A premise asserted throughout this text is that schools are generally the most appropriate setting for therapeutic intervention for children and adolescents. Mychailyszyn, Brodman, Read, and Kendall (2012) reported a comprehensive meta-analysis of outcome studies for school-based CBT interventions for anxiety and depression. Mychailyszyn et al.'s findings supported the efficacy of these interventions and noted that outcomes delivered by school staff were comparable to outcomes achieved in clinical settings by research staff. This analysis supports the transportability of evidence-based intervention approaches to the field setting where anxiety management skills are required by children and adolescents on a daily basis and where unresolved anxiety disorders can result in significant academic and social impairments.

INSTRUCTIONAL SUPPORTS, EDUCATIONAL
ACCOMMODATIONS, AND CLASSROOM PROTOCOLS

Screening

School staff may not be immediately aware of a student's experience with anxiety. Similar to other internalizing symptoms, it is important that each school structure screening-assessment protocols to identify youth who may be quiet sufferers. Universal screening should include not only self-report measures but also structured data collection from teachers. As part of this process, teachers can be provided brief training on observable signs of anxiety, heightening their awareness of these students' needs.

Performance Anxiety and Work Completion

Students prone to excessive anxiety require extra supports in the school setting. Anxiety can interfere with performance, compromise social participation, and defocus attention to task. Since these students are often overly self-critical, it is important that they receive extra appropriate positive reinforcement and encouragement. *Strength bombardment* strategies that provide intermittent but frequent verbal recognition of the student's competencies help to counter a negative self-image. Repeated reassurance that perfection is not required is important but without selling competencies short.

Performance anxiety is common across anxiety conditions. Although schools should routinely teach all students strategies for minimizing performance and test anxiety, a student with debilitating performance anxiety may require additional supports. Adaptive strategies for taking tests and giving presentations can include the use of deep breathing and other physical calming strategies, rehearsed covert self-instruction scripts, and self-reinforcement plans.

Mirroring graded exposure tasks, students may benefit from taking multiple minitests to habituate to performance reviews and increase self-confidence. A shaping protocol can assist those who struggle to verbally respond or give presentations in class (e.g., giving a presentation to a teacher alone, then to the teacher and some supportive peers, and eventually to the entire classroom).

Academic accommodations may be required for students based on individual needs but must be coordinated with the overall intervention protocol. Overarching treatment priorities will guide educators in balancing the need between countering avoidance conditioning and promoting educational progress. Some students may be helped by shortened assignments and tests. The focus would emphasize quality instead of quantity of work. In some cases, the same amount of total work might be required but task completion be promoted through breaking requirements into less overwhelming and achievable segments. Criterion mastery rather than traditional grading may be more appropriate. Anxiety may impact attendance and keeping up with assignment timetables. Falling behind may intensify anxiety and immobilize the student, intensifying a self-defeating cycle. To address this challenge, make-up work can be broken into achievable chunks with realistic but closely monitored deadlines.

For some anxious students, the hardest part of an academic task is getting started. Extra structure and support at the beginning of a project may calm anxiety and provide a platform for successful progress. Support might involve individual attention to promote focusing at the start of an assignment, additional modeling or examples of expectations, periodic check-ins to ensure progress is occurring, and appropriate praise for effort and task persistence. In some situations, the designated availability of a supportive peer may extend the teacher's capacity to provide support. On the other hand, the teacher can look for opportunities for the student with anxiety concerns to assist another student in an academic area of substantial strength. This helper role would counter a tendency to view oneself as dependent and needy in peer relationships.

Social Anxiety

Treatment for student social anxiety begins with careful assignment of understanding and compatible peers for group work, prompting and supporting student attempts at social initiation, pairing classmates during field trips to reduce social isolation, and providing opportunities for the student with anxiety to demonstrate academic tasks in an area of strength. Socially anxious students might dread less structured social situations like lunch and recess. The teacher might need to either provide direct assistance to foster social involvement or instruct adult supervisors in those settings to offer specific interventions tailored to the individual's needs. For example, sitting at a lunch table with suitable peers is preferable to isolation. Socially anxious students use withdrawal and avoidance as coping strategies, but they remain at increased risk for victimization by bullies. Supervisors in all settings must be prepared to intervene if necessary in concert with the school's standard procedures for bullying prevention.

Obsessive–Compulsive Disorder

Supports already noted also apply to students with OCD. It is important for teachers to thoroughly understand the academic strengths and weaknesses of children with OCD and accommodate any areas of academic weakness. If the student presents with reading compulsions, use of books on tape, oral instructions for tasks, or peer or adult readers may prove helpful. If the student has difficulty taking notes or completing written tasks because of compulsions, helpful accommodations may include recording lectures, providing advance copies of presentation materials and outlines of lectures, assistance from a peer note taker, and electronic supports for assignment notebooks such as online assignment lists. The therapist's intervention protocol may directly intervene in these areas, but usually academic accommodations will be required as the hierarchy of obsessions and compulsions are addressed. Although OCD behaviors might sometimes be characterized by task avoidance, most students with OCD want to complete their work, but they require direct support for initiating and sustaining on task performance.

Posttraumatic Stress Disorder

Teachers must be mindful of the vulnerability of students with trauma symptoms. Mood swings, waves of anxiety, and misplaced anger are common. Care with physical proximity is important. Educators must be sensitive to the threat innocent physical contact may present to someone who has been physically abused. Trust may be an issue particularly when trauma symptoms stem from an abuse experience. The student may occasionally unconsciously act in ways to push caretaking adults away. It is important for teachers to avoid personalizing any angry or rejecting behaviors and respond with calm empathy, appropriate boundaries, and reasonable discipline all with a tone that communicates acceptance and permanency of the relationship.

CRISIS INTERVENTION PROTOCOLS

Crisis events for children with anxiety may manifest as momentary panic attacks, intense emotional meltdowns, behavioral shutdowns and withdrawal, or oppositional tantrums. In all cases, responding adults need to assist children in slowing down racing, self-defeating, and catastrophic thoughts by refocusing attention on the present and immediate task, prompting initiation of coping strategies, and stating rational problem perspectives to counter catastrophic and faulty appraisals of threat and inflated anticipation of doom.

If the child has a meltdown, responders not only provide empathy and support but also establish reasonable boundaries and communicate safety by calmly being in charge of the environment. Use of a safety or time-out location may be necessary for regrouping, but calm reentry into the classroom environment should be as rapid as possible. The adult acknowledges the child's vulnerability and communicates empathy and reassurance that everything will be okay while carefully avoiding treating the child as too fragile. It may be necessary to guard against letting controlling temper tantrums lead to prolonged work avoidance or inappropriate control over school authorities or the classroom environment. Experience with the child and teacher–therapist collaboration will foster the correct balance. The therapist works with classroom staff to identify crisis intervention strategies consistent with the student's intervention plan and feasible within the school setting. The teacher should be aware of any self-instruction scripts, physical calming strategies, or other coping skills protocols that the student is learning in treatment so their application can be prompted when the student's anxiety is aroused.

If a student with PTSD symptoms has an explosive incident, it might be important to give space even while giving empathy and reassurance. Close physical proximity might stir memories of a trauma experience and be misinterpreted as aggression or an intrusion. If the student angrily lashes out at an adult, the appropriate response is an acknowledgment that the child is very angry and upset followed by a reminder that he or she is not really angry at the crisis responder but is frustrated with a situation that can be resolved. If the student becomes aggressive, escorting him or her to a safe and private location is appropriate, trying if at all possible to patiently guide the student to that area while still giving physical space. For students prone to episodes, it can be helpful if a routine is established with a predefined and predictable protocol and a consistently designated safe location. If the aggression becomes combative, dangerous, and requires physical management, specially trained staff should intervene, exercising care to avoid any symbolic re-creation of the traumatic event, being particularly alert for potential sexual overtones in acting out behavior of sexual abuse victims.

For all crisis events, time should be allowed for emotional decompression and restabilizing balance and composure before returning to normal activities. Postvention processing includes reassurance of self-worth, communication of forgiveness, support for any use of adaptive coping skills, and expectation of a successful return to the classroom or other activities.

Sometimes crisis events can have a school-wide impact and increase vulnerability for clinical anxiety or traumatic reactions in previously unidentified youth. The National Association of School Psychologists has developed the PREPaRE school crisis prevention and intervention training program (Brock, Nickerson, Reeves, & Jimerson, 2008) The PREPaRE program provides a comprehensive framework for the development of school crisis and safety plans and for effective responses to a range of potential crises that may impact the school community. It addresses both prevention and response plans. PREPaRE's protocols are particularly appropriate for guiding schools in responding to community-wide trauma such as natural disasters and serious school violence. The National Association of School Psychologists uses a trainer-of-trainers model, providing workshops and materials for school psychologists so that they can then assume leadership in crisis prevention and management within their own schools.

FAMILY AND SYSTEMIC SUPPORTS AND INTERVENTIONS

Throughout all of the intervention protocols delineated above, parent participation has been highlighted. Parents receive psychoeducation about the nature and treatment for anxiety and personal support for the challenge of appropriately supporting their children. Parents are trained to be critical collaborators in home-based exposures with particular attention focused on management of their own distress when observing their child's overwhelming anxiety and on strategies for encouraging response prevention as required for compulsive and avoidant behaviors. When parents experience their own difficulties with anxiety, they may require personal intervention support so that they reduce modeling an anxious coping style to their child.

Over time, patterns of responding to anxious behaviors within the family may become entrenched. This can be particularly problematic if family responses inadvertently but continuously reinforce avoidant behaviors. Changing engrained response patterns requires preparation for managing the escalated anxiety that might occur when escape or avoidance behaviors are blocked. Emotional meltdowns or tantrums may result. Consistent with the construction of fear hierarchies, gradual exposures, and successive approximation protocols for shaping coping skills, the therapist and parents together prioritize which interaction patterns to address since it would be overwhelming to simultaneously attempt transaction changes on all fronts. Parents also are involved in contingency reinforcement plans to support their child's efforts at change and attainment of each successive intervention subgoal. Besides targeting behavior change for the child, contingency plans can shape parental behaviors by shifting focus to adaptive functioning. When a contingent reward for successful coping includes a special activity with a parent, the potentially dominant role of anxious behaviors for engaging with parents is also countered.

The child's anxious behaviors and rituals can have a controlling effect on a wide range of family interactions. Siblings of the affected child may resent the attention given to a brother or sister with an anxiety disorder. Family therapy sessions involving all members may be required to address these issues and initiate changes in maladaptive interaction patterns within the family. Just as the child with anxiety receives training in problem-solving skills, it may be necessary to coach the family to engage in more effective problem-solving strategies. Some families may struggle with challenging stressors, such as poverty, medical problems, or caretaking responsibilities for extended family. The anxious child may absorb a significant dose of this stress. Although there is not much that can be done about these intense stressors, adjunctive family sessions can brainstorm stress management approaches for family coping and reducing the burden on the affected child. Consistent with structural family therapy principles of generational boundaries, it might be necessary to compartmentalize adult worries from child concerns. Parent discussions of their own stressors might need to remain within the marital dyad and only be shared in limited amounts with their children.

The child with anxiety symptoms risks a slower transition to age-appropriate independence. Anxiety may be fostered by overprotective parenting that occurs accidentally in response to childhood illness or other circumstances. Parental psychoeducation and, if necessary, individual family sessions may need to define areas where greater independence should be promoted. Step-by-step shaping of independent behaviors may be required, supported by contingency management protocols. It is seldom beneficial for schools to call parents to come to school to actively intervene with their child's anxious behaviors. School staff need to take responsibility for providing necessary supports. Successful tolerance of anxious episodes at school without direct in-person parental involvement fosters independence and self-confidence. Parents can reinforce the adaptive behaviors of managing anxiety independently.

9

AUTISM SPECTRUM DISORDER

Both in psychological research and in the popular media, there has been an expanded focus on autism spectrum disorder (ASD). This neurodevelopmental disorder involves impairments in social interaction and communication and a restricted repertoire of interest and activities. Consequently, ASD has a significant impact on socialization and educational functioning and can have long-term consequences for independent living and employment (Klinger, Dawson, Barnes, & Crisler, 2014).

The *Diagnostic and Statistical Manual of Mental Disorders* (fifth ed.; *DSM–5*; American Psychiatric Association, 2013) introduced a significant change in the categorization of ASD. The separate disorders labeled in the prior edition of the diagnostic manual as Autistic Disorder, Asperger's Disorder, and Pervasive Developmental Disorder, Not-Otherwise-Specified (PDD-NOS) are now all encompassed under the term ASD. This change underscores the common central social and communication impairments represented in prior

http://dx.doi.org/10.1037/14779-010
School-Centered Interventions: Evidence-Based Strategies for Social, Emotional, and Academic Success,
by D. J. Simon

classifications, but it also recognizes that autism is not a singular clearly defined syndrome but rather a complex spectrum of disorders with shared characteristics that vary greatly in their presentation, severity, and lifespan course. Intellectual disabilities occur in about 31% of children with ASD (Klinger et al., 2014), and many of these children experience the most severe language and communication difficulties.

The *DSM–5* also introduced the diagnosis of Social Communication Disorder (SCD), which is characterized by difficulties in pragmatic language that cannot be explained by low cognitive ability. It is differentiated from ASD by the absence of restrictive and repetitive patterns of behavior. Many of these children would have been identified as PDD-NOS in the past. Pragmatic language deficits are addressed through speech and language therapy and social-skills instruction.

In contrast to the *DSM–5, the International Classification of Diseases, Tenth Edition, Clinical Modification (ICD–10–CM)* still maintains ASD subtype distinctions, Asperger's (F84.5) remains a distinct diagnosis, and SCD falls under other developmental disorders of speech and language (F80.89; Goodheart, 2014).

The emphasis in ASD treatments is on early identification and intervention (S. J. Rogers & Vismara, 2008). With the identification of some symptoms evident in the first years of life, early intervention programs have been designed for ages 0 to 3 years and preschool. This book has focused primarily on school-age children and does in this chapter as well. This chapter focuses on the children on the spectrum without intellectual disabilities. Before the *DSM–5*, these students have been described as demonstrating high-functioning autism, Asperger's, or PDD-NOS with normal intellectual functioning. Because within this subgroup language might not be noticeably impaired before age 3, and other symptoms may only be subtly observed, these children might not be identified until elementary school. Yet, they can face significant academic and social challenges within school and other peer settings. This chapter addresses identification, instructional supports, social skills, and behavior management interventions for this subset of students with higher functioning ASD (HF-ASD).

DIAGNOSTIC CHARACTERISTICS, ASSESSMENT FRAMEWORKS, AND DEVELOPMENTAL CONSIDERATIONS

In some quarters, the categorical changes in the *DSM–5* have created controversy. The heterogeneity in severity of manifestation and variability in functioning across the spectrum is clearly understood. Some have feared that those with milder forms of ASD such as Asperger's disorder would now be underidentified and not entitled to essential clinical and educational services. Klinger et al. (2014) noted that clinicians can reliably differentiate the broad ASD designation from other developmental disorders, but that it was not uncommon for individual children to have changes in subcategory diagnoses based on developmental changes over time in communication and social skills. Huerta, Bishop, Duncan, Hus, and Lord (2012) reviewed a large sample of children with *DSM–IV* PDD diagnoses and found 91% of them to be eligible under *DSM–5* criteria. Further study with the new criteria and categorization will be needed to test their reliability, validity, and impact on the trend toward increased identification of autism.

Clinical Versus Educational Diagnosis

The other challenge in the identification of and service provision for ASD relates to the difference between clinical and educational definitions of autism. It is not required to have an external clinical diagnosis of ASD to be found eligible for special education services under the educational disability of autism. Although the symptom patterns are similar in both classification symptoms, an educational diagnosis of autism requires a negative impact on educational functioning. This difference comes under consideration in cases where the student displays average to above-average intelligence and is able to successfully complete grade-level academic work, as is the case with some children who have previously been identified as having Asperger's disorder. This distinction applies to other disorders as well. For example, some children with attention-deficit/hyperactivity disorder (ADHD) are not found eligible for special education services, but they may be eligible for supports and accommodations under Section 504 of the Rehabilitation Act. It is important to note that educational performance should not merely be defined as grades but should include social and communication skills and other adaptive skills that impact daily living. If the adverse impact on education is primarily because of a separate educationally defined emotional disability (e.g., mood disorder), educational autism would not be indicated; however, if the autism symptoms are primary, it is possible to have a secondary eligibility of emotional disability (e.g., primary disability identified as autism with a secondary emotional disability due to depression). It is important to review the specific delineation of criteria in the student's state of residence.

DSM–5 Criteria

The *DSM–5* criteria center on deficits in two domains: (a) social communication and interaction; and (b) restricted, repetitive patterns of behavior, interests, or activities. Social difficulties must be evident across multiple contexts and may include problems in the following areas: social reciprocity (e.g., impaired capacity for social approach, engagement, and social exchanges); nonverbal communication required for social interaction (e.g., limited eye contact, misreading nonverbal cues); establishing and maintaining relationships (e.g., difficulties in making friends and adjusting to various social contexts). Restricted repetitive patterns of behavior and interests may include repetitive motor movements, speech, or use of objects; inflexible adherence to routines and rigid thinking; a fixated and intense special interest; hypo- or hyperactivity to sensory inputs. The *DSM–5* introduced a severity specifier for each of the two primary symptom clusters that designates the level of support required. It should be noted when symptom manifestation fluctuates in severity across settings. Additional specification is required when ASD symptoms are accompanied by intellectual impairment, language, impairment, another medical condition, or behavioral disorder. Although the diagnostic manual specifies that symptoms must be present in an early developmental period (without specifying an age of onset), some characteristics may not be clearly evident until increased social demands are required, particularly as children move into more peer activities and school-like settings. This is often the case for students with normal intelligence with HF-ASD and is the reason they might not be identified until they are school age.

Prevalence and Etiology

The Centers for Disease Control and Prevention (CDC; 2014) estimated that 1 in 68 children age 8 is identified as having ASD. This represents a dramatic increase in reported incidence over the past 2 decades. The cause of this increase has been vigorously debated, and some have expressed concerns about possible overidentification. Klinger et al. (2014) suggested that better awareness and identification accounts for much of this increase while noting that incidence appears to be on the rise for yet unexplained reasons. More males than females, at approximately a 4:1 ratio, have been diagnosed with ASD (CDC, 2014). Within the HF-ASD population, girls and boys display similar symptom profiles, except that boys are viewed as demonstrating more externalizing behaviors and more restricted and repetitive behaviors (Mandy et al., 2013).

The complete picture regarding etiology has not been scientifically delineated. ASD appears to be a heterogeneous spectrum of disorders with multiple etiologies. Biological factors, including genetic influences and structural and functional brain differences, have been documented (Ozonoff, Goodlin-Jones, & Solomon, 2007). There appear to be multiple genetic pathways involved. Earlier psychogenic models that focused on parenting practices have been abandoned, although certainly child rearing can influence the severity of some ASD symptoms. Continued investigation into environmental factors has not clearly identified a viable causal variable (Klinger et al., 2014; Ozonoff et al., 2007).

Developmental Course

Ozonoff et al. (2007) summarized the developmental progression of ASD as follows. Most children begin to display language and social symptoms before age 3. Beginning in the range of 14 to 24 months, a smaller subgroup of children demonstrates a regressive pattern in which a change or loss of previously demonstrated social and communication behaviors occurs generally. However, HF-ASD children with normal intelligence and without early language difficulties are often not identified until elementary school years. Although there may be retrospective reports of social and communication deficits, their manifestation is subtler and less likely to be detected until increasing social and task demands emerge.

Early intervention has been demonstrated to alter the severity of ASD (G. Dawson et al., 2010, 2012). Nevertheless, ASD is considered a chronic condition with some impairment evident throughout the life cycle. In many cases substantial supports are required to achieve postsecondary education, social, and employment engagement. HF-ASD adults are frequently underemployed, and because there are fewer support programs available for them, they are 3 times less likely to be involved in social activities during the day than their counterparts who also had an intellectual disability (Taylor & Seltzer, 2011). The need for increased transitional and vocational supports is clearly evident. More research is needed to understand the long-term behavioral and cognitive outcomes as students with HF-ASD progress through full adulthood.

Assessment Methods

Assessment of ASD requires collection of information from multiple sources across diverse contexts. Environmental demands can significantly influence functioning. For example, some children may appear much more socially adept in a comfortable family environment than they might in a socially demanding school context. A developmental perspective informs assessment. This is necessary to contrast performance against typical developmental standards, but it also recognizes that developmental achievements can be uneven and that earlier impairments can compromise future adaptation and skill development. ASD assessments generally require multidisciplinary inputs, which in addition to a psychologist may include a speech therapist, occupational therapist, pediatrician, psychiatrist, or neurologist and other specialists as necessary to address referral questions.

Developmental History

Assessment begins with a comprehensive developmental history that includes an investigation of parental concerns; early manifestation of any difficulties in communication and social interaction; relevant family history of medical, psychiatric, and extraordinary social difficulties; and presence of any additional behavioral or emotional symptoms.

Interviews and Rating Scales

The Autism Diagnostic Interview—Revised (Rutter, LeCouteur, & Lord, 2003) is a semistructured parent or caregiver interview that addresses core ASD symptoms. It focuses on the developmental period of ages 4 to 5 years so that an adequate behavior sample can be reported. An interview of approximately 90 minutes collects data that contribute to diagnostic algorithms for social difficulties, communication deficits, and repetitive behaviors. Research on the Autism Diagnostic Interview—Revised has revealed that it discriminates well between the presence of ASD, its absence, and other disorders and is generally considered a gold standard assessment tool for ASD (Campbell, Ruble, & Hammond, 2014; Ozonoff et al., 2007). Unfortunately, it is less sensitive to higher functioning ASD during preschool years but demonstrates improving sensitivity as children age (Ozonoff et al., 2007).

The Social Communication Questionnaire (Rutter, Bailey, & Lord, 2003) is a shorter screening questionnaire based on the Autism Diagnostic Interview—Revised. Two versions, lifetime behavior and current functioning, can be used for diagnostic purposes and for monitoring changes. The Social Communication Questionnaire correlates well with the full Autism Diagnostic Interview—Revised and includes a cutoff score designed to discriminate between autistic disorder and higher functioning ASD.

Autism rating scales can supplement other diagnostic data, but experts caution against their use as sole diagnostic instruments (Ozonoff et al., 2007). Three recent instruments appear promising and also are intended to assess high-functioning ASD: the Autism Spectrum Rating Scale (S. Goldstein & Naglieri, 2009), Childhood Autism Rating Scale, Second Edition—High Functioning version (Schopler, Van Bourgondien, Wellman, & Love, 2010), and the Social Responsiveness Scale, Second Edition (Constantino & Gruber, 2012). The Autism Spectrum Rating Scale used large normative and clinical samples in its development and includes validity scales. Covering the age range of 2 to 18 years, it reports T scores similar to other behavior rating scales. A benefit of the Autism Spectrum Rating Scale is the collection of observational data from both parents and teachers. In addition to the 71-item standard form, there is a short form of 15 items that can be used for screening and progress monitoring. The Social Responsiveness Scale–2 and

Childhood Autism Rating Scale—2 High Functioning Version are revisions of older instruments with updated symptom profiles. The Childhood Autism Rating Scale—2, High Functioning Version involves clinician observation and rating of behaviors with additional information from an accompanying parent questionnaire (for a more detailed review of these rating scales, see Campbell et al., 2014).

Diagnostic Observations

The Autism Diagnostic Observation Schedule (ADOS; Lord, Rutter, DiLavore, & Risi, 2002) is a standardized semistructured observational measure of communication, social interaction, play, and repetitive behaviors. The ADOS can be used with an age range from toddlers to adults and be administered in under an hour. It is an interactive measure in which the examiner presents multiple opportunities for social interaction and then rates responses. Scores are entered into an algorithm to determine whether the child meets ASD criteria. Evidence-based assessment reviews often refer to the ADOS as a gold standard in ASD assessment (Ozonoff et al., 2007). The ADOS–2 (Lord, Rutter, DiLavore, Risi, Gotham, & Bishop, 2012) provides updated protocols and scoring algorithms. The ADOS system requires specialized training and certification through a workshop or the publisher's DVD program to qualify for as an evaluator.

Functional Behavior Assessment

A carefully delineated functional behavior assessment (FBA) is an important element of the assessment protocol. Investigating antecedent–behavior–consequence sequences is essential for understanding social interaction and avoidance behaviors, management of anxiety, the function of any disruptive behaviors, the impact of setting demands, and the communication implicit in behavioral responses. Data for FBAs should be collected across multiple settings. For a student with ASD, social functioning in recess, lunchroom, physical education (PE), and classroom settings may vary significantly and should be understood. The principles for conducting a comprehensive FBA delineated in Chapter 5 on disruptive behavior disorders apply to evaluation of students with ASD.

Cognitive and Academic Assessment

The need for additional assessment in the areas of cognitive and academic functioning depends on individualized referral questions and the character of information available from the school's ongoing academic monitoring systems and teacher reports. This chapter's focus on students with higher functioning and at least normal intelligence suggests that cognitive testing may not be necessary. However, if there are concerns about a possible learning disability, suspicions that learning challenges in specific areas contribute to behavioral difficulties, or unexplained weaknesses in particular aspects of academic performance, further assessment in these areas may be warranted. Assessment should maintain a focus on data that contributes to intervention planning. It is helpful to understand the preferred learning style of all students. Assessing whether a student benefits more from visual or verbal inputs and prompts can be particularly useful for some children with ASD.

Ozonoff et al. (2007) noted that difficulties in executive functioning are common in ASD. Problems are often evident in planning, inhibition, cognitive flexibility, organizational skills, shifting from task to task, and executing complex behavioral responses, particularly if they require processing multiple pieces of data. Chapter 4 detailed the assessment of executive functioning for children with ADHD symptoms. Two commonly used neuropsychological instruments are the Delis-Kaplan Executive Function System (Delis, Kaplan, & Kramer, 2001) and the NEPSY–II (Korkman, Kirk, & Kemp, 2007). The Behavior Rating Inventory of Executive Function (Gioia, Isquith, Guy, & Kenworthy, 2000) is a parent and teacher rating scale that assesses the daily interference of executive functioning deficits on home and school behaviors, which can link assessment data to intervention planning. The Behavior Rating Inventory of Executive Function has been used in studies of children with high-functioning autism and Asperger's syndrome (Gilotty, Kenworthy, Sirian, Black, & Wagner, 2002).

Assessment of Comorbid Conditions

In a population-derived sample, Simonoff et al. (2008) found that 71% of children with ASD had at least one other comorbid condition and 41% had two or more. The most common comorbid psychological conditions for ASD, besides intellectual disabilities, are anxiety, depression, and ADHD (Klinger et al., 2014; Ozonoff et al., 2007). The incidence of anxiety and depression symptoms has been reported to be higher for youth with HF-ASD presumably because they are more aware of the differences between themselves and their peers in terms of social development and inclusion (Klinger et al., 2014).

Broadband behavior rating scales such as the Achenbach System of Empirically Based Assessment (ASEBA; Achenbach & Rescorla, 2001) and the Behavior Assessment System for Children—Second Edition (BASC–2; C. R. Reynolds & Kamphaus, 2004) are recommended as a starting point. Because of deficits in self-awareness and communication, students with ASD may not be reliable reporters on self-report measures; however, parent and teacher data can serve to focus investigation on relevant domains. Once areas of additional concern are identified, evidence-based assessments targeting those symptom clusters are initiated. During any direct assessment activity with the child, the examining clinician must be sensitive to how ASD symptoms may affect test performance.

The *DSM–5* now permits a comorbid diagnosis of ADHD. The heterogeneity of the ASD population is evident in the range of attention problems that may be exhibited. Some children with ADHD will present with a classic presentation of hyperactivity–impulsivity and inattention. Others may demonstrate strengths in sustained attention, particularly around an area of special interest, but struggle with maintaining focused or selective attention, at times overfocusing on minor details and missing the larger picture (Doepke, Banks, Mays, Toby, & Landau, 2014; Ozonoff et al., 2007).

Repetitive behavior patterns occurring in ASD complicate differential diagnosis with obsessive–compulsive disorder (OCD). Klinger et al. (2014) summarized studies on OCD and ASD as indicating that children with OCD were more often fixated on a singular compulsion rather than a broader fixed set of routines. Anxiety in ASD is often related to social stress. The differential diagnosis in these areas remains challenging.

CHILD- AND ADOLESCENT-SPECIFIC THERAPEUTIC INTERVENTION STRATEGIES

Early intervention is the focus of much of the research on interventions for ASD. The foundation for this work was Lovaas's (2002) application of applied behavioral analysis. Subsequent work has focused on training within natural environments, enhancement of child motivation to increase socialization, and parent training. Examples are pivotal response training (Koegel, Koegel, Vernon, & Brookman-Frazee, 2010) and the Early Start Denver Model (S. J. Rogers & Dawson, 2010). S. J. Rogers and Vismara (2008) provided a review of empirically supported early intervention treatments. Unfortunately, most children with HF-ASD are not identified until early school participation reveals the extent of their social deficits. Early intervention involves the application of behavioral strategies and emphasizes intervention and generalization in natural settings. Because of their average cognitive potential, students with HF-ASD can benefit from CBT strategies as well. This section focuses on social-skills training (SST) and behavior management approaches for school-age youth with HF-ASD.

Social-Skills Training

Interventions to address social-skill deficits and improve adaptive social involvement are essential components of core educational curriculum for students with HF-ASD. Their long-term mental health, personal happiness, and successful transition to employment and other demands of adulthood are dependent on it. For these students, SST needs to be viewed as core curriculum alongside reading, math, science, and social studies. Instruction in interpersonal skills requires multiple formats, high intensity, persistent focus, and an overriding emphasis on generalization within the natural environment. When questions have been raised about the efficacy of SST, the concern has centered on the challenges of ensuring generalization of skills taught in isolation from natural environments. Because this area of development is so challenging for these students, to be effective, SST interventions must be consistently oriented toward successful application in the classroom and peer settings.

Individualizing Intervention Targets

There is a great deal of heterogeneity within HF-ASD, and, thus, interventions require significant individualization. S. W. White (2011) summarized common areas of social-skills deficits within this target group. These common areas include difficulty in understanding personal emotional reactions; impaired perspective taking, particularly struggling to understand the feelings and intentions of others; either misreading or failing to take into account nonverbal social cues; failure to establish a shared reference point for interactions; difficulty in flexibly understanding and applying social rules and conventions; and reliance on literal understanding of social interactions resulting in missing the meaning of some symbolic, humorous, or ironic communications, and unintentionally intrusive and blunt communications to others.

Cognitive Behavioral Therapy Efficacy

Several studies have reported the efficacy for CBT individual and group social and coping skills training (Bauminger, 2002; Reaven, Blakeley-Smith, Culhane-Shelburne, & Hepburn, 2012; Wood et al., 2009). CBT strategies appear to be a good fit for many youth with HF-ASD, but implementation may require adaptations geared toward the individual student's unique challenges and learning style. Although CBT studies have described adaptations used to address ASD factors, research has not yet clearly delineated the impact of specific strategies. What follows is a summary of many of the points of emphasis and adaptations that have been applied in SST for children with HF-ASD.

Structuring Training

Organizing either individual or group treatment with a high level of predictable structure and routine matches most students' preferred learning style and is likely to reduce therapy-interfering behaviors. S. W. White (2011) underlined the importance of matching skills training to the specific student's areas of difficulty. Some may require rudimentary instruction in core social skills applicable to a large range of social circumstances. Some students exhibit performance deficits where they may know the skill but not when and how to apply it. Fluency deficits must be addressed when the student knows the skill and tries to apply it, but the awkward or scripted character of social behaviors interferes with success. It is often necessary to learn social scripts before they can become more natural and spontaneous. Fluency training may require extensive practice, differentiation of expectations for various settings and social groups, and modeling and practice of age-appropriate lingo and metaphors.

In group work, structure is required to ensure safety, reduce anxiety, and support behavior management. Motivation for effective participation can be supported by reward-based reinforcement programs. Reinforcement should target effort and reward each step for shaping new skills. Knowledge of the FBA of each student guides behavior management. For some students social participation expectations within a group may create anxiety that triggers interfering behaviors. S. W. White (2011) advised using two group leaders whenever possible so that the flow of the group's lesson plan can continue even if an individual member requires a brief behavior support intervention.

Modeling, Role Playing, and Visually Based Strategies

Many children with ASD benefit from visual learning methods. Modeling of social skills can take many different formats. The therapist can model a skill. A method of contrast can be used to assist the student in recognizing the differences between appropriate and inappropriate social behaviors. The therapist and child can role play the skill from both sides of an interaction. Encountering the effective and ineffective social behaviors demonstrated by the therapist assists the student in understanding their differential impact. Practicing the effective skill can be done with supportive coaching by the therapist.

Video modeling has been effectively used to teach complex social sequences (Nikopoulos & Keenan, 2007). This practice can include specifically designed video models of targeted skills-training sequences and observation and discussion of character behaviors in film clips. Modeled skills can be practiced through role plays. These role plays can, in turn, be videotaped and then reviewed and compared with the original social models leading to further coaching and a repeat of the training sequence. The method of contrast can also be used as group members record videos demonstrating effective and ineffective social approaches, for example, showing the contrast between passive, assertive, and aggressive behaviors. Visual scripts, either in brief words or pictures, can be created to prompt utilization and remind the child of steps for skill application. These can sometimes be discreetly displayed on the inside cover of a notebook or taped to a panel inside a school desk.

Howlin, Baron-Cohen, and Hadwin (1999) used photos and pictures in their curriculum to teach *theory of mind skills*. These skills center on perspective taking and empathy to improve social cognition. Visual prompts can be used as affective education tools to understand feelings and predict behavioral reactions.

Social Stories

Gray (1998, 2000) developed the social story technique to illustrate social concepts and teach interpersonal behaviors directly applicable to an individual child's needs. Social stories can be brief and simply illustrate social cues and rudimentary steps for social participation. For example, a story can be constructed to describe observing a conversation for topic clues and then note an appropriate entry into participation into a peer group discussion. Social story illustrations are generally positively oriented; provide descriptive information about social scenarios; describe the perspectives of characters including feelings, needs, thoughts, and motivations as appropriate; include directives that highlight appropriate social responses; and develop control statements that identify personal strategies to use in real-life situations similar to the story. Social stories teach perspective taking and understanding others' points of reference, familiarize students with necessary social cues, teach understanding of common social conventions and rituals and their rationale, and provide a model for social behaviors. Gray (1998) developed the related strategy of *comic strip conversations*. This tool uses cartoons with thought bubbles to provide a pictorial illustration of social interactions that can include the external communication and internal thoughts of characters. The cartoons can illustrate the various simultaneous dimensions involved in communication. In addition to the spoken word and covert thoughts, colors and other symbols can be used to illustrate emotions and physical stress reactions. Gray's techniques were developed in a school context and provide a facile framework for illustrating social principles to fit the individualized challenges of each student.

Social Scripts

For particularly challenging or anxiety-provoking social situations, SST may begin by teaching and then role playing social scripts. This is particularly useful for repetitive short interactions such as asking for assistance, social greetings, joining in a recess activity, and so forth. Scripts can be compiled in a binder, written on cue cards, or kept privately in a desk or pocket to prompt and guide usage. Learning any new skill tends to begin with more programmed or rote execution. Practice leads to increased fluency and expanded flexibility in social applications. A specific social script is preferable to either social isolation or inappropriate intrusiveness. Because children with HF-ASD are often rule-bound and prefer routines, social scripts can provide comfortable and effective starting points for some aspects of social interaction.

Incorporating Special Interests Into SST

Although an obsession with special interests can at times interfere with socialization, it can also motivate involvement in training exercises by providing partial content for skills training social interactions. Special interests can be the content for initial instruction in reciprocal interactions eventually giving way to practice in alternating a focus on personal interests with the expressed interests of others within a social encounter. Special interest content may provide examples and metaphors for understanding affective and social experiences. For example, an intense interest in baseball statistics could be used by a therapist to explore the feelings and nonverbal behavior of a batter after a home run or a strike out. Examining a base runner's behavioral patterns that might predict an attempt at stealing second base engages the youth in assessment of nonverbal communication. Self-awareness of emotions and stress levels can be described in terms of balls and strikes, errors, hits, and so forth. Motivation for participation in extracurricular social activities might begin with the special interest (e.g., keeping statistics or managing the scorebook for a school team). Depending on its nature, a special interest may eventually evolve into an element associated with career planning. Incentives to earn appropriate participation in a special interest can motivate engagement in SST.

Peer Tutors

It takes a special peer who has been carefully screened to serve as a peer social tutor. When using neurotypical peers in SST group work, they should be taught an understanding of ASD with examples of some of the social challenges they may observe or experience. The specifics of their role need to be specified and carried out with a clear understanding of what information is considered confidential. In group work, peers add authenticity to role-playing scenarios, and their feedback and coaching regarding social behaviors may carry extra weight particularly for older students. Their use of language and comments on the school social milieu and practices can be beneficial. Sometimes youth with HF-ASD are in groups that include neurotypical students who are addressing other psychological issues. In the context of a structured SST group, they may provide informal social modeling in their area of strength. When a student with ASD is in an SST group with peers not on the spectrum, adjunctive individual therapy can shape participation by specifically targeting engagement in certain social behaviors during the group. This engagement requires effective collaboration between the group and individual therapists if the same professional is not engaged in both roles. S. W. White (2011) provided an overview of effective peer involvement in SST. S. J. Rogers (2000) provided a review of peer-mediated socialization strategies that include both formal SST and peer-mediated academic supports.

Activity and Game Strategies

Various game-like activities targeting a variety of issues have been incorporated into CBT SST. S. W. White (2011) provided examples of engaging activities that address frequently seen skill deficits for this population. One exercise, the *conversation ball*, targets turn taking, contingent conversation, and attention to nonverbal behaviors. The first person with the ball starts a conversation with a brief statement followed by a related question and then passes the ball to another group member. That person responds to the question, extends the conversation on the same topic, frames another topic-related question, and then passes the ball to another member. The sequence continues. Each group member eventually takes a turn being the conversation starter. Additional social skills can be practiced during the game as well; for example, summarizing the most important parts of the communication sequence at its conclusion would foster attending, conversation tracking, and listening skills. Therapeutic games can be devised to meet the specific needs of the training group. Playing charades or acting out a brief social scene provides content for examining nonverbal communication and teaches perspective taking for exploring feelings and thoughts of others.

Supporting SST in the Classroom

It is essential that SST carry over into the classroom environment. The focus on generalization of skills learned must be intentional. Ideally, each classroom, whether a standard or a special education setting, will engage in social-emotional learning curriculum that includes specific instruction in social, coping, and problem-solving skills. Then the specific target skills of the child identified with HF-ASD can be incorporated more fluently into general psychoeducational skills training. Unfortunately, that is not always the case.

Direct Training. Routine communication between the SST therapist and the classroom teacher keeps the latter informed of current skills training targets. Specific skills practice can be assigned by the therapist in collaboration with the teacher, who prompts, monitors, and records practice activity. For example, if participating in a classroom discussion were a social-skill target, the teacher would inform the therapist of upcoming class discussions, and the therapist could prepare the student in practice in an SST session. Before the class discussion begins, the teacher can privately review the goal and participation strategy with the student. The student can have a social script written in a private binder that he or she refers to before the discussion begins. After the discussion, the teacher provides feedback and reinforcement to the student and then reports back to the therapist on progress. Contingent reinforcement supports participation. Some students may be capable of learning self-monitoring strategies related to specific social participation and record their own behaviors.

A similar guided practice approach can be used for social interactions in less structured settings like the cafeteria and the playground. In these cases the supervising teacher or support staff would be prepared to prompt, monitor, record, and reinforce appropriate social participation. Performance feedback would be provided to the teacher or therapist who would follow up with the student and adjust training in light of the feedback. When social problems develop, the teacher and therapist can collaborate with the student to address the issue. Social stories, social scripts, and behavioral rehearsal can occur in session and then be applied, monitored, and reviewed by the teacher in the natural environment. Ozonoff, Dawson, and McPartland (2002) used the term *implicit didacticism* to recommend therapist or teacher modeling directly in the setting where the skills need to be applied.

Social Engineering and Supports. Teachers can informally foster social opportunities for students in the course of routine class activities. Peers in classroom work groups should be carefully chosen and the division of labor clearly delineated. Children with HF-ASD always present with some significant strengths. The strength might be knowledge in a particular subject area or a certain academic or technical skill. Sometimes, pairing the child with HF-ASD with a student who can benefit from his or her academic strengths while in return being a positive social choice can advance the likelihood of social reciprocity. Some students can benefit from tutoring younger children in an area of strength. It is important that children on the spectrum not view themselves as the one always in need of supports. Every positive social interaction builds a foundation for social-skill development.

Coping Skills Training and Addressing Comorbidities

Comorbid symptom clusters, particularly anxiety and depression, can complicate intervention planning. For example, motivating social approach efforts when the student experiences social anxiety brings extra challenges. It is beneficial to add CBT coping skills training into SST programs for all students, but these skills are a specific element of most empirically supported CBT interventions for the HF-ASD population. As an example, Reaven, Blakeley-Smith, Nichols, and Hepburn (2011) developed and tested the "Facing Your Fears" program to treat anxiety in children and adolescents with a primary HF-ASD diagnosis. Building on the evidence-based intervention strategies of programs like the Coping Cat (Kendall & Hedtke, 2006), they incorporated strategies similar to those outlined above to accommodate the social, emotional, and communication challenges of these students and ensure engagement in the intervention protocol. These included careful pacing, provision of a visual structure and predictable routine, written examples of core concepts, repetitive practice and behavioral rehearsal, video modeling, hands-on activities, and utilization of special interests. A detailed parent curriculum was included. In general, properly adapted CBT protocols for comorbid disorders appear effective. Significant family involvement is required to support therapeutic homework practice and to ensure appropriate social coaching.

INSTRUCTIONAL SUPPORTS, EDUCATIONAL ACCOMMODATIONS, AND BEHAVIOR MANAGEMENT

The extensive treatment of SST above provides the foundation for examining educational supports. The characteristics of HF-ASD define the necessary accommodations. Behavior management is first addressed by accommodating the social disability and taking into account the student's unique learning style and executive functioning capacity. Although common principles apply, it is important to recognize the heterogeneity of HF-ASD profiles.

Instructional Supports and Educational Accommodations

Students with HF-ASD benefit from structured and predicable classrooms that use routine procedures and repetitive organizational structures. Clear teacher expectations with simple rules that are reliably enforced reduce anxiety and encourage compliance. Sufficient attention must be paid to personal space requirements. Having a study carrel or other more private space in the back of the classroom that can be used as a safe place for destressing, a temporary break, or a time-out when overwhelmed or overstimulated from social and academic demands is often helpful.

Visual supports enhance instructional inputs and organizing routines. Depending on the student's preference, visual schedules, reminders, and prompts can be in pictures, words, or both. These supports confirm routines, prepare for transitions, and prompt behavioral and coping skills. The student should know clearly what is expected, and the most important information including targeted prosocial behaviors should be clearly visible right in front of them. As children age, these prompts and reminders can be placed inside a notebook that can be readily accessed. Typical classroom procedures can be shown inside the book cover for that subject.

Some students demonstrate lower frustration tolerance when faced with challenging academic work. Suhrheinrich, Hall, Reed, Stahmer, and Schreibman (2014) highlighted antecedent instructional strategies that support academic engagement and reduce frustration: clear and unambiguous instructional cues, alternating easy and difficult tasks and retreating to mastered tasks when stressed, and providing choices and sharing control when possible.

Many students with HF-ASD experience problems with executive functioning. Organizational and planning supports similar to those outlined in Chapter 4 for students with ADHD apply. Clear work expectations with step-by-step scaffolding are beneficial in areas of academic weakness. Some students may require supports for understanding overarching themes and gestalt concepts. A subgroup of students with HF-ASD may demonstrate advanced decoding and vocabulary skills but struggle with comprehension of literary themes. Others may demonstrate extraordinary facility with math facts but require supports in application and integration of concepts. Identifying the particular needs of each student is essential.

Students should be challenged within their areas of strength and receive accommodations, scaffolding, and supports in their areas of weakness. Teachers must ensure that they have the student's attention before giving instructions (even though that may not necessarily include eye contact), and then verbal directions should be given in small chunks with extra time allowed for verbal processing. Asking the student to repeat back directions can assess understanding. As necessary, assistive technology can be provided to improve areas of weakness. This may mean completing work on a computer rather than handwriting and incorporating electronic assignment notebooks and calendars into routines.

The motivating power inherent in special interests can be tapped to engage students in academic skill building. A student with a concentrated interest in, for example, wolves might be engaged in a science lesson or a term paper with this content when the lesson's objective is on principles of biology or the process of writing a research paper.

Many students struggle with transitions; however, it is particularly important to prepare and support students with HF-ASD in managing transitions from one activity to the next and changes in standard routines. This may mean taking the time to prepare the student for a change in schedule because of an assembly or a field trip and preparing them for the behavioral and sensory challenges presented in those environments. Social stories, social scripts, and other behavioral supports can be employed to prepare for changes and teach appropriate social behaviors for a new circumstance or a different environment.

In large classrooms, a teacher aide may provide assistance to the teacher or the identified student specifically. The aide should be trained in understanding

ASD and the strategies designed to support this particular student. Most often, it is counterproductive to have the aide solely focused on this student. A delicate balance between providing necessary supports and fostering age-typical independence is required. Given the primacy of social concerns, the aide can facilitate involvement with group and cooperative learning tasks in addition to supporting behavioral management and instructional accommodations.

Behavior Management

Appropriate social and coping skills training, instructional methods, and accommodations are cornerstones of behavior management for HF-ASD youth. Nevertheless, the social and academic challenges of the school environment can overwhelm coping skills and contribute to significant behavioral episodes in some children.

FBA–Behavior Intervention Planning

The student's FBA should help to define antecedent and consequence adjustments that can promote positive behaviors. Understanding environmental triggers related to the classroom setting, structure, academic subject, time of day, social demands, and task requirements can prevent behavioral and emotional episodes. Similarly, understanding the functions of behavior (e.g., avoidance, anxiety or sensory management) and the maintaining consequences (e.g., relief from expectations; release of physical tension) can inform behavior intervention planning. Individualized education plans for students with disabilities require an integration of the FBA data into an individualized behavior intervention plan. This not only spells out the antecedent–behavior–consequence chains but also delineates replacement behaviors and necessary supports.

Behavior Motivation Plans

Behavior motivation plans that are incentive based, focused on earning motivating reinforcers, are effective for teaching new behaviors and supporting behavioral management. The teacher and student can jointly create a list of incentives and rewards. The contingency motivation plan should establish reasonable and achievable target goals and follow the general principles of mastery through successive approximation. In general, punishment strategies are less effective for these students. It is better to have a student fall short of earning a privilege than to endure a punishment. It is common for schools to remove and isolate the student from the peer group as a consequence for the general education population. Obviously, this would directly counter the educational goal of trying to increase socialization in students with HF-ASD.

Depending on their social reticence and interests, exclusionary punishers may actually serve as maintaining consequences to encourage repetition of misbehaviors.

Behavior as Communication: Teaching Problem Solving

Difficulties with communication are a defining characteristic of HF-ASD. Affected students often have difficulty appropriately expressing feelings, needs, and wants. When responding to a behavioral episode, whether a withdrawing shutdown or an explosive tantrum, it is necessary to translate the intent of the behavior into verbal communication. This requires an understanding of the triggers prompting the episode and hypothesizing what implicit message is being communicated by the student's behavior. Is the student angry at a peer who just teased him? Is she frustrated with her inability to competently do the academic assignment? When the escalated student has sufficiently pulled together, the adult can use active listening to help the student identify the trigger or stressor. This process may need to be repeated over multiple episodes but gradually helps the child understand his or her reactions. Teaching students to substitute verbal for behavioral communication is an essential educational and therapeutic task.

Klin and Volkmar (2000) identified instruction in problem-solving rubrics as a critical element of behavior management. Comfortable with scripts and routines, students with HF-ASD can be taught step-by-step problem-solving strategies. These steps can be written or pictured on a note card or in an accessible notebook. Problem-solving approaches can be illustrated through social stories and analysis of literature and film scenes. Then they are applied to frequent troublesome scenarios that are particularly problematic for the individual student. Problem solving includes helping the child understand his or her feelings, thoughts, and physical stress reactions in routinely difficult situations. One goal is to increase the student's personal and social awareness of situations that trigger overwhelming affect and to suggest verbal communications that would appropriately communicate distress and solicit support. Debriefing after a behavioral episode includes identifying triggers, examining internal cues that signal the potential for loss of control, striving to understand the perspective of others in the situation, and brainstorming alternative responses. Klin and Volkmar (2000) asserted that one element of all problem-solving rubrics should be the identification of an adult who can be a resource for support and decision making with details regarding how that person can become involved.

Difficulty with understanding the perspectives of others complicates social problem solving and adherence to some rules and social conventions. Through social stories and other related strategies, the student is taught the rationale for rules, routines, and the expectations and reactions of others. This is most effective when rationales include how an alternate approach to a problem or compliance with a social standard is beneficial to the student as well.

Choosing Your Battles

With its extensive social and work demands, the school day presents multiple challenges for many students with HF-ASD. To avoid overwhelming the child, it is necessary to choose what to accommodate and work around and what to target for change. A teacher shared the example of a student who frequently got into trouble because he struggled to walk appropriately in line to activities like the library and PE outside of the classroom. He tended to walk very fast, would clumsily bump into other children, or be berated by them for passing them in line. This not only resulted in peer conflicts but also raised his stress level as he transitioned to a new environment. Already addressing a full plate of critical behavior targets, the teacher began by accommodating the student and sending him to special activities with another responsible student a few minutes ahead of time. Later, when other behavior issues were under better control, she prepared him to resume walking with the class. She explained the rationale for walking in line, drew up a visual reminder of expectations that he could review immediately before lining up for a transition, and rehearsed it with him in the corridor out of sight of classmates. An incentive plan with strong motivators was designed. Aware that he struggled to control the pace of his walking, she began by assigning him to walk in the front of the line, removing the possibility that he would either pass or bump into other students. After a few weeks of successful transition, she repeated the instructional sequence and assigned him to walk between two peers whom she knew to be relatively tolerant of his behaviors. The incentive for appropriate line walking was enhanced. Eventually, he began to transition in typical student lines appropriately, and after several weeks supports were faded. When issues reoccurred, the incident debriefing referred back to the rationale and behavioral expectations, recognized his long-term improvement, and communicated confidence that he would behave appropriately.

In another case, a student who was a huge sports fan was prone to emotional meltdowns whenever his team lost in PE. He would become so overwrought that it would take excessive time for him to recover and refocus in the ensuing academic class. For a brief period of time, he was assigned to an alternative PE experience with a teacher aide. During this time, his therapist and teacher worked with him to learn appropriate behaviors in competitive situations. Many strategies were used, including social stories; problem-solving rubrics; watching video clips of his favorite athletes at the end of games they won and lost; creating video clips in which he demonstrated appropriate and inappropriate sportsmanship; playing brief games, some of which he won and some which were lost with his therapist; practicing physical calming strategies to use at the moment of disappointment; learning CBT self-talk strategies; and preparing a script to follow with specific steps to take on the completion of a competitive game in PE. Eventually, he was reintroduced into PE and actively coached in managing his excitement and frustration and in following his sportsmanship plan. Significant contingent reinforcers were earned at each phase of this intervention sequence. Eventually he learned to successfully participate in competitive games in PE. Attention was also paid to appropriate behavior in informal competitions that occur during recess. These cases illustrate the integration of a broad range of behavior management and SST strategies and the timing and prioritization of behavior change targets.

Sensory Issues and Managing the Physical Signs of Stress

Some students with HF-ASD display hypo- or hyperactivity to sensory stimuli. They may be sensitive to specific noises, lighting patterns, certain kinds of physical contact, or other sensory inputs. Other students engage in repetitive motor activities like chewing on objects or rocking in their seats. An occupational therapist can create a sensory profile when this is a concern. Little is known about evidence-based interventions to address these issues. In some cases, preferred seating or the availability of temporarily working in a study carrel in the back of room may reduce sensory overload and reduce tension. Fidget toys, stress balls, and other unobtrusive devices appear to help some students manage physical tension and improve academic focus. Whenever possible, routine physical breaks and engagement in typical physical activities are the best ways to provide relief. For example, a student who gradually shows increasing rocking or fidgeting and escalating physical tension may benefit from a productive motor movement break. This may mean loading a bookshelf, taking a message to the office, or any activity that includes both a cognitive and sensory break. As students mature, they can be taught to recognize and monitor their sensory needs just as they would typical signs of escalating physical stress and develop effective routines and coping strategies. (See Attwood, 2007, for a practical summary of strategies for managing sensory sensitivities.)

CRISIS INTERVENTION

The principles outlined in therapeutic interventions and classroom behavior management provide the foundation for crisis responses. If a student is crisis prone, then a predictable crisis response and debriefing plan that takes into account the unique needs of someone on the spectrum should be devised. To reduce the need for physical management for students whose behavioral explosions are intense, the teacher or aide can designate in advance a safe place or time-out location outside of the classroom. When the student is escalated, he or she is likely to require sufficient personal space and time to be alone. This means being with the student but initially refraining from significant social interaction. At any point in the crisis, adult directives should be brief and simplified with one-step-at-a-time instructions that wait for compliance before proceeding to the next step. Visual prompts may be helpful to use pretaught coping strategies. Sufficient time to regroup is necessary before debriefing, processing, and applying a problem-solving rubric. When the child is ready to productively interact, interventionist responses should not excuse inappropriate behaviors but initially focus on empathy and reassurance that the student can recover from this intense moment and eventually reengage in normal activities.

It is important that all school personnel who may be called on to intervene in a crisis are aware of the particular needs and differentiated crisis responses required for students with HF-ASD and, as much as possible, for the specific student in crisis. If she or he is not involved in the crisis intervention, the therapist should be notified and provide follow-up support and problem solving.

FAMILY SUPPORTS AND INTERVENTIONS

Because of the vulnerability of the child with HF-ASD, parental involvement is required beyond what is typically expected. Parents must be integrated into therapeutic activities and involved in all aspects of educational planning. All of the strategies for supporting SST that were identified for teacher implementation are required in home and neighborhood activities. The therapist teaches these strategies and helps parents engage in activities that support positive social interaction. Parents learn how to establish predictable routines, teach social scripts, use social stories, model and role play social initiation and reciprocal activities, and problem solve behavioral episodes.

Daily family activities from parent–child games to conversations at family dinners provide opportunities for coaching social skills. For the child with HF-ASD, home often provides a respite from the social challenges and pressures in school and other environments. So the intent is not to turn home into an additional therapy session but to guide parents in using routine parent–child interactions to shape social skills.

Therapists assist parents in preparing to articulate the supports and accommodations that might be needed for their child to participate in community activities like recreational programs, sport clubs, and scouting. Teachers and therapists who routinely work with students on the autism spectrum often know of programs that are more inclusive, empathic, vigilant, and accommodating within their community. Searching for social activities that incorporate the child's special abilities and interests is encouraged. Some activities are better suited than others. For example, a scouting program with strong and sufficient adult leadership may be able to provide a mix of teamwork activities and individual work on merit badges in a relatively noncompetitive atmosphere. However, the potential for supports may vary significantly from one organization to the next. The child's interests, the receptivity of supervising adults to guidance, and character of structure and supervision should all be taken into consideration.

Ozonoff et al.'s (2002) parent guide is an excellent resource on raising children with HF-ASD. It provides guidance on a range of topics across developmental stages from arranging play dates to supporting involvement in extracurricular activities to preparing for college, employment, and independent living. Balancing sufficient support and promoting realistic independence are ongoing challenges for parents through each life stage. In addition to addressing this topic in family sessions and school conferences, schools can offer on-site parent education and create support groups for parents of children with HF-ASD. A large network of community-based support groups has arisen to support families with a child with ASD. As has been evident throughout this chapter, close collaboration among parents, teachers, therapists, and community supports is required to help these children reach their academic and social potential and enjoy independent healthy and enjoyable lifestyles.

AFTERWORD: COMPREHENSIVE MULTITIERED SERVICES IN SCHOOLS

The high incidence of psychological disorders in youth and their impact on educational functioning and quality of life have been clearly documented. Access to mental health services for children and adolescents is woefully inadequate. Service delivery is too often fragmented and fails to address the multiple life domains of youth in an integrated manner. The central premise of this text is that school-centered therapy can be the most effective format for serving the social, emotional, and behavioral issues of children, adolescents, and their families. Evidence-based therapeutic interventions are more likely to be effective when strategies are integrated across individual, family, and school contexts.

Service provision is enhanced through close collaboration between school and community practitioners. To facilitate coordinated service delivery, therapists in community-supported agencies and in local private practice reconceptualize their intervention efforts as *school centered*. They work

http://dx.doi.org/10.1037/14779-011
School-Centered Interventions: Evidence-Based Strategies for Social, Emotional, and Academic Success, by D. J. Simon

closely with school staff, take advantage of the supports for maintenance and generalization of therapeutic gains available in schools, and work from an eco-logical perspective that is consistent with empirically supported multisystemic therapies. In turn, school staff invite these practitioners to participate as part-ners in prevention and early intervention initiatives and support their access to direct involvement with teachers for behavior management planning. This collaboration increases access to services and encourages evidence-based prac-tice. The result is a holistic approach to child education and psychological treatment in a familiar setting.

Provisions of the Affordable Care Act are intended to foster multi-disciplinary collaboration and fund the establishment of school-based health clinics, which include mental health services. This initiative holds consid-erable promise, but it is important that these intervention services are fully integrated into a school-centered therapy framework and not merely house additional isolated services in the same location. Even in the absence of fed-eral funding, some school districts are already collaborating with local medi-cal and mental health agencies to establish school-based clinics. These efforts hold promise for increasing access to services, integrating multidisciplinary interventions, providing early intervention, and reducing costs.

MULTITIERED SCHOOL SERVICES

Academic and therapeutic supports in schools are now being redefined within a multitiered framework consistent with public health models for population-based services (Stoiber, 2014). This approach emphasizes preven-tion and early intervention services that address the needs of all students. All classrooms participate in programs to promote social, emotional, and behav-ioral health. Psychoeducational and therapeutic services are matched to the needs of students requiring additional intervention. Interventions are gener-ally organized in three tiers of supports.

Tier 1: Universal Supports

The first tier provides school-wide psychological education and univer-sal social–emotional learning supports to all students. Many schools use pro-active positive behavior intervention and support programs to clearly define and teach appropriate social behaviors, screen for emerging behavior issues, and reframe school discipline interventions to teach new prosocial behav-iors (Sugai, Horner, & McIntosh, 2008). Teachers are trained to incorporate social–emotional learning into classroom procedures by using common posi-tive reinforcement strategies targeting specific social and problem-solving skills. Teachers might also be instructed to intentionally address social–emotional learning themes across the curriculum, for example, through character examination in literature or history classes.

Systematic social, coping, and problem-solving training is an essential component of psychoeducational and prevention programs. Just as educators would not forgo direct instruction in reading at the elementary school level and presume that foundation skills will be acquired through social studies and other subject matter, these psychological skills require targeted instruction and specific curriculum time. Universal skills training programs are designed to be developmentally sensitive and teach specific foundation skills that foster self-awareness, interpersonal competencies, adaptive stress management, and effective personal and social problem solving. The framework for these curriculums is centered on the same cognitive behavior therapy principles and strategies referenced in therapeutic intervention programs throughout this text (e.g., McGinnis, Sprafkin, Gershaw, & Klein, 2011; Merrell, 2007; Shure, 2007). Although many of these programs are designed to be implemented by classroom teachers, substantial training, coteaching, ongoing consultation, and monitoring for implementation integrity are required by school therapists and could be supported by collaborating community therapists. A distinct advantage of school-wide adoption of specific curriculums in this area is the creation of a common language to define, prompt, and support prosocial and adaptive coping skills throughout the school day. These social–emotional learning curriculums can support therapeutic interventions of children who also require more intense interventions. The common language helps students understand treatment goals and prepares teachers to understand and support interventions to remediate problems.

Tier 1 programming should also include universal screening for mental health issues. This screening must address internalizing as well as externalizing behaviors. Discipline data collection, such as office referrals, readily identify externalizing problems requiring interventions for disruptive behaviors. However, in the absence of universal screening, no systematic vehicle is available for identifying anxiety and depression problems for early intervention. This screening can take various forms and should be multiformat and multisource. Surveys are available for student self-report or teacher ratings. With proper staff training, school-wide procedures can be routinely implemented for teachers to identify children with emerging issues.

Because of continued stigmatization regarding mental health issues, some have raised concerns about the appropriateness of school screening in this area. It is essential to frame this important activity within prevention and educational frameworks. Consistency with early language screening and required school physicals should be emphasized. In a school that truly establishes social–emotional learning as part of the core curriculum, screening in these areas parallels screening for reading and math difficulties. Screening is more effective, with greater participation and less controversy, when its purpose and legitimacy are supported through school board policy. Districts that have such policies typically do not require parental consent for screening but create an option to opt out of the program. This approach has resulted in most children receiving the benefits of universal screening. Identification of at-risk students prompts more specific assessment and may lead to select services at Tier 2.

Peer assistance programming is an additional component of many Tier 1 curriculums. Examples are suicide prevention and bullying intervention programs. These programs combine psychological education with specific instruction in when and how to seek help for a peer.

Tier 2: Early Intervention and Services for At-Risk Students

Through discipline records, universal screening, and referrals from teachers, parents, peers, or children themselves, students are identified who are experiencing social–emotional behavioral concerns. Additionally, students are identified who carry known significant risk factors or are coping with a significant stressful personal experience such as exposure to trauma, recent loss, substance abuse history, or chronic medical illness. Selected students might be referred to multidisciplinary problem-solving teams, which may recommend further assessment or devise an intervention plan. In-house school psychologists and social workers participate on these teams and provide consultation regarding behavior intervention plans and therapeutic supports.

Student support groups are a common therapeutic intervention offered at this level of service. These programs are capable of providing psychosocial support to a large number of students. Groups are generally organized around specific issues. Examples include the following: anxiety management, depression management, anger management, test anxiety, friendship skills, parental divorce, assertion training, substance abuse prevention, and posthospitalization support. Most groups are time limited. Organizing groups around themes carries important advantages. This approach facilitates referrals and enables group therapists to focus on specific goals and use structured curriculum using evidence-based intervention (EBI) programs specifically targeted for the identified symptom cluster. The cognitive behavior therapy group programs identified in Part II of this book are applicable. Thematic groups can readily build in progress monitoring, specific strategies for generalization of skills in the classroom, and the collection of outcome data. Sometimes students participate in open-ended problem-solving groups. This requires the group therapists to design group-specific structures and individualized progress-monitoring plans for each member. For generic groups, attention must be paid to ensure groups are change oriented and outcome focused so that service is meaningful.

The logistics of scheduling groups is fairly straightforward but requires excellent communication. In elementary school settings, Tier 2 intervention groups might be able to be scheduled to meet at the same time each week; but at most grade levels, it is necessary to rotate the class periods that groups meet. This means that a student participant is unlikely to miss the same academic class more than once in a quarter. Rotating schedules requires reminder notices to students and teachers about group meetings. This practice also provides an opportunity for a teacher to note that there might be a curriculum presentation or examination that cannot be missed for that specific period. On the basis of my experience with large-scale group programming in high schools, this organizational system works and is widely supported by classroom teachers.

Some schools have developed student drop-in centers to address the needs of a wide range of at-risk students. Drop-in centers may offer crisis intervention, informal counseling, academic supports, or a comfortable but supervised alternative to hanging out with antisocial peers. Some students may sign in to the drop-in center in place of a large study hall. A psychologist, social worker, or counselor is scheduled to be present across all periods that centers are open.

Crisis intervention services often define the need and character of Tier 2 activities. The nature of the crisis and the coping capacity of affected students will determine the intensity and extent of services. Sometimes external events have a major impact on large segments of the student body (e.g., a devastating storm, a student suicide, a violent peer or gang clash in school). Crisis supports generally include provision of brief individual and group crisis counseling. Some students may be seriously impacted and require longer term interventions.

School-centered interventions outlined in this text provide the framework and evidence-based strategies for Tier 2 services. Assessment defines the need for individual, group, or family therapeutic interventions. Collaboration with teachers enables appropriate instructional supports and classroom management. In this way, Tier 2 services are not merely add-ons but embedded in the total school experience.

The need for Tier 2 services will vary greatly from school to school depending on the presence of significant risk factors for psychological disorders. If 20% of students experience psychological disorders and fewer than 2% are identified for special education services, then a typical high school of 1,500 students should expect to design programs for early intervention and at-risk services for over 200 students at this level.

Participation of community-based therapists in Tier 2 activities can increase resources for meeting student needs. Involvement in these programs connects them to the school and acquaints them with teachers. Another untapped resource in some schools are classroom teachers who have earned counseling degrees but are not currently functioning in that role. Depending on the scheduling of activities, they can be adjunctive leaders within many support programs.

Tier 3: Therapeutic Services for Students With Defined Intense Needs

Students whose psychological intervention needs have not or cannot be sufficiently addressed at earlier levels of support require intense intervention plans. Programming may include direct individual therapy and systemic interventions addressing classroom and home issues. These students generally require comprehensive special education programs. Children with the most intense needs typically require additional structure, a targeted array of EBI therapeutic activities, classroom behavior management and academic assistance plans, and the ready availability of crisis supports. Some of these students may require the multisystemic supports described earlier to coordinate strategies across multiple community resources and agencies. School-centered evidence-based interventions are the foundation for Tier 3 supports.

THE SYSTEMIC PERSPECTIVE: SCHOOLS AS COMMUNITY SUPPORT CENTERS

Parent Involvement and Support

For families with children, schools serve as community centers beyond the classroom day. Delivery of psychological services within the school context serves to increase access and destigmatize participation. Because contemporary EBIs require coordinated strategies for the individual in his or her context, systemic interventions should be delivered after school hours within the school setting.

Parent education and intervention programs can parallel the multitier services within the school day. Universal parent education and support programs provide general information to all parents regarding child development, supporting academic and social–emotional growth, and managing critical transitions. Targeted programs can address specific issues, for example, supporting students with attention-deficit/hyperactivity disorder. Extended intense programs can provide the parent training interventions identified as first line EBI treatments for students with disruptive behavior disorder. Therapeutic parent conferences occur before or after school to facilitate parent participation around work schedules. Work schedules of school therapists can be modified to include some evening hours to facilitate parental access to interventions. Collaborating community-based therapists could contribute to parent training programs and be provided access to the school building to meet with families in the evening enhancing the family's acceptance of mental health services. The implementation of school-centered therapy would be enhanced if youth community mental health services were relocated into school facilities. Shared overhead might even increase funding for additional professional personnel and service provision. Part II of this text summarized evidence-based protocols for parent training and support and family therapy interventions.

Extracurricular Participation

Extracurricular school activities extend a school's reach and can support psychosocial development. Scouting and other recreational programs often conduct their programs within the school setting.

Many students with psychological needs are underrepresented in official extracurricular school activities and community-based youth organizations. Yet for many of the psychological disorders covered within this text, participation in supervised prosocial peer activities was noted as an important component of the intervention protocol. Pelham, Greiner, and Gnagy's (1997) summer treatment program was the most comprehensive example. Students with disruptive behavior disorder require prosocial peer opportunities to replace antisocial peer activities. Social involvement and pleasant activity scheduling are antidotes to depression. Children with anxiety disorders benefit from structured peer activities to generalize benefits of treatments for social aspects of anxiety. Extra social supports sensitive to necessary accommodations for students with autism spectrum disorder are required for participation in after school activities. Although some of these students can benefit from strategies to encourage their participation in the school's current extracurricular activities, others may be unlikely to do so. Therapists can be catalysts to engage each school and community in a needs assessment to determine what structured social activities would be necessary to assist socially vulnerable nonparticipators. Existing community youth service and recreational organizations can be encouraged to develop new programs, which might occur in either their or the school's facilities.

Coordination With the Judicial System

In the chapter on disruptive behavior disorders, we discussed concerns about the ineffectiveness of many traditional exclusionary school discipline practices. The National Association of School Psychologists (2013) argued strenuously for the adoption of policies and programs to alter the school to prison pipeline, which disproportionately impacts minority students. In addition to creating attractive alternatives to antisocial peer group activities, schools can partner with legal authorities to support and contribute to the design of treatment and social service alternatives to school and prison discipline protocols, to facilitate drug testing requirements when necessary, and to engage with youth and probation officers in problem-solving conferences to support parents' and teachers' efforts at providing increased structure and supervision for youth at risk for lifelong delinquency.

COMMITMENT TO EVIDENCE-BASED PRACTICE

Children coping with psychological disorders require a commitment from school and local community therapeutic service providers to implement empirically supported practices. In turn, these therapists require a sufficient commitment of professional development and personnel resources to enable them to institute state-of-the-art therapeutic programs. University-based researchers can support their efforts by conducting efficacy studies directly in community and school environments. Strong models exist for this research activity already in the work of J. Larson and Lochman (2010) and Stark et al. (2007) on anger and depression management. Formal university–school partnerships can facilitate this activity. Community-based feedback in intervention design will help to tailor intervention strategies to real-life intervention contexts. At the same time, there is a recognition that therapeutic activity will always require both science and art. Field-based practitioners adapt EBI strategies to multicultural and diverse contexts; however, they require training and supports for integrating progress monitoring and an outcome focus to track deviations from EBI and innovative practices. The collaborations necessary to meet these goals hold promise for advancing the quality of psychological treatment for children.

The EBI literature underlines the necessary commitments to address significant psychological disorders. The importance of early intervention with sufficient intensity is abundantly clear and in line with universal screening and prevention initiatives in recent multitiered service delivery models in schools. Research also delineates the chronic nature of many conditions requiring long-term intervention protocols. It is clear that service options provided through many managed care insurance programs are not scientifically based. School districts must assess each case realistically in light of what is known about the intensity and duration of services needed for effective treatment and positive long-term outcomes. When considering least restricted environments in individualized education plans, care must be taken to ensure that sufficient services are being offered to support educational and therapeutic progress. Accurate evidence-based assessments as outlined in Part II of this book should drive service and placement decision making. Children may be poorly served if they move too slowly or too quickly into restrictive specialized placements. The key is to match defined needs with sufficient resources in the light of our scientific knowledge of what it takes to help the child or adolescent. Then monitoring of implementation integrity and evaluation of intervention impact guide efforts and modify interventions as necessary.

FINAL THOUGHTS: A COMMITMENT TO SYSTEM CHANGE

Without a bold vision, PL 94-142's authorization of special education services would never have become a reality, and children with disabilities would never have been adequately served. Without scientific study, the complexity of psychological disorders and the intervention requirements to treat them would not be articulated. Without decades-long advocacy for prevention and early intervention services, public health and multitiered service intervention models would not be taking hold in schools across the country. As a society we have committed resources to a relentless search for treatments for cancer and other childhood medical conditions. With 20% of our children experiencing psychological disorders, we cannot merely say that resources to implement scientifically based treatments are unachievable.

Creative models for implementation of EBIs and school-centered therapy are emerging. In central Illinois, the educational cooperative Livingston County Special Services has contributed to the development of a multitiered countywide children's network (Huber, 2014; Meyers, Tobin, Huber, Conway, & Shelvin, in press). Programming includes medical and mental health interventions. A strong emphasis has been placed on coordination of public and private services, school programming, and service provision in natural settings that would reduce barriers to access to treatment. Early outcome data are encouraging: Eighty percent of at-risk children receive individual or group services at school, universal screening measures indicate a decrease in teacher reported social–emotional–behavioral concerns, a significant increase in families and children receiving therapeutic services is documented, and juvenile police reports have decreased. School-based clinics are emerging across the country, and additional programs will undoubtedly be spurred by supports from the Affordable Care Act. A variety of community sensitive designs will emerge. Effective programs will be school centered with close collaboration with community services.

School-centered therapy attempts to advance the implementation of evidence-based therapeutic strategies into the school and community setting. Its implementation can increase access to mental health services for children, adolescents, and their families. School-centered therapy recognizes that interventions must address the individual student and his or her life context. Educational progress and social–emotional–behavioral growth are interdependent. School-centered therapy provides a holistic and ecologically authentic approach to psychological intervention with children and adolescents.

APPENDIX:
CASE CONCEPTUALIZATION FLOW CHART

1. Assessment
    a. Baseline data available through positive behavioral interventions and supports programs and response to intervention problem-solving data collection
    b. Functional behavioral assessment
    c. Assessment of cognitive variables
        i. Self-talk patterns
        ii. Attributional style
        iii. Locus of control
    d. Assessment of dominant mood states
        i. Stress management style
        ii. Capacity for self-awareness
    e. Systemic–ecological–contextual analysis
        i. Family
        ii. Peers
        iii. Culture–diversity
        iv. Socioeconomic status factors
    f. Biological, neurological, medical factors
        i. Learning issues
        ii. Health concerns and medications
        iii. Relevant genetic history
    g. Diagnostic considerations (evidence-based interventions [EBIs] are symptom specific)
        i. Psychological testing (as necessary)
        ii. Comorbidities
2. Intervention planning
    a. Chart current functioning and potential intervention strategies within each SUM domain
        i. Experiences
        ii. Bodily reactions
        iii. Feelings
        iv. Thoughts
        v. Behaviors
    b. Define social, coping, problem-solving skill needs

  c. Delineate systemic–contextual factors
    i. Family
    ii. Peers
    iii. School
  d. Investigate EBI for symptom profile
  e. Prioritize concerns and set initial intervention targets
  f. Design and implement intervention plan
3. Progress monitoring and outcome assessment
  a. Establish behavioral markers consistent with baseline and pre-intervention assessment data
  b. Use progress monitoring data to modify intervention planning
  c. Within special education build into IEP benchmarks

ESSENTIAL DOMAINS FOR COMPREHENSIVE TREATMENT PLANNING

- Symptom–diagnostic profile examined
- Developmental considerations (assessment and treatment)
- Empirically supported therapeutic intervention strategies
- Classroom instructional and behavior management strategies
- Crisis intervention (differentiated)
- Parent–family intervention considerations

REFERENCES

Achenbach, T. M., & Rescorla, L. A. (2001). *Manual for the ASEBA school-age forms and profiles*. Burlington: University of Vermont, Research Center for Children, Youth, and Families.

Ackerman, S. J., Benjamin, L. S., Beutler, L. E., Gelso, C. J., Goldfried, M. R., Hill, C., ... Rainer, J. (2001). Empirically supported therapy relationships: Conclusions and recommendations of the Division 29 Task Force. *Psychotherapy: Theory, Research, Practice, Training, 38,* 495–497. http://dx.doi.org/10.1037/0033-3204.38.4.495

Albano, A. M., Chorpita, B. F., & Barlow, D. H. (2003). Childhood anxiety disorders. In E. J. Mash & R. A. Barkley (Eds.), *Child psychopathology* (2nd ed., pp. 279–329). New York, NY: Guilford Press.

Alexander, J. F., Waldron, H. B., Robbins, M. S., & Neeb, A. A. (2013). *Functional family therapy for adolescent behavior problems*. Washington, DC: American Psychological Association. http://dx.doi.org/10.1037/14139-000

American Academy of Child and Adolescent Psychiatry. (2007). Practice parameters for the assessment and treatment of children and adolescents with bipolar disorder. *Journal of the American Academy of Child & Adolescent Psychiatry, 46,* 107–125.

American Psychiatric Association. (2000). *Diagnostic and statistical manual of mental disorders* (4th ed., text rev.). Washington, DC: Author.

American Psychiatric Association. (2013). *Diagnostic and statistical manual of mental disorders* (5th ed.). Washington, DC: Author.

American Psychological Association Zero Tolerance Task Force. (2008). Are zero tolerance policies effective in the schools? An evidentiary review and recommendations. *American Psychologist, 63,* 852–862. http://dx.doi.org/10.1037/0003-066X.63.9.852

Angold, A., & Costello, E. J. (2000). The Child and Adolescent Psychiatric Assessment (CAPA). *Journal of the American Academy of Child & Adolescent Psychiatry, 39,* 39–48. http://dx.doi.org/10.1097/00004583-200001000-00015

Angold, A., Costello, E. J., & Erkanli, A. (1999). Comorbidity. *Journal of Child Psychology and Psychiatry, 40,* 57–87. http://dx.doi.org/10.1111/1469-7610.00424

Aseltine, R. H., Jr., & DeMartino, R. (2004). An outcome evaluation of the SOS Suicide Prevention Program. *American Journal of Public Health, 94,* 446–451. http://dx.doi.org/10.2105/AJPH.94.3.446

Attwood, T. (2007). *The complete guide to Asperger's syndrome*. London, England: Jessica Kingsley.

Axelson, D., Findling, R. L., Fristad, M. A., Kowatch, R. A., Youngstrom, E. A., Horwitz, S. M., . . . Birmaher, B. (2012). Examining the proposed disruptive mood dysregulation disorder diagnosis in children in the Longitudinal Assessment of Manic Symptoms study. *The Journal of Clinical Psychiatry, 73,* 1342–1350. http://dx.doi.org/10.4088/JCP.12m07674

Barkley, R. A. (2006). *Attention-deficit/hyperactivity disorder: A handbook for diagnosis and treatment* (3rd ed.). New York, NY: Guilford Press.

Barkley, R. A. (2012). *Barkley Deficits in Executive Functioning Scale—Children and Adolescents (BDEFS–CA)*. New York, NY: Guilford Press.

Barkley, R. A. (2013a). *Defiant children: A clinician's manual for assessment and parent training* (3rd ed.). New York, NY: Guilford Press.

Barkley, R. A. (2013b). *Taking charge of ADHD: The complete, authoritative guide for parents* (3rd ed.). New York, NY: Guilford Press.

Barkley, R. A., Anastopoulos, A. D., Guevremont, D. C., & Fletcher, K. E. (1992). Adolescents with attention-deficit/hyperactivity disorder: Mother–adolescent interactions, family beliefs and conflicts, and maternal psychopathology. *Journal of Abnormal Child Psychology, 20*, 263–288. http://dx.doi.org/10.1007/BF00916692

Barkley, R. A., Murphy, K. R., & Fischer, M. (2008). *ADHD in adults: What the science says*. New York, NY: Guilford Press.

Barkley, R. A., & Robin, A. L. (2014). *Defiant teens: A clinician's manual for assessment and family intervention* (2nd ed.). New York, NY: Guilford Press.

Barrett, P. M., Farrell, L., Pina, A. A., Peris, T. S., & Piacentini, J. (2008). Evidence-based psychosocial treatments for child and adolescent obsessive–compulsive disorder. *Journal of Clinical Child and Adolescent Psychology, 37*, 131–155. http://dx.doi.org/10.1080/15374410701817956

Bauminger, N. (2002). The facilitation of social–emotional understanding and social interaction in high-functioning children with autism: Intervention outcomes. *Journal of Autism and Developmental Disorders, 32*, 283–298. http://dx.doi.org/10.1023/A:1016378718278

Baumrind, D. (1967). Child care practices anteceding three patterns of preschool behavior. *Genetic Psychology Monographs, 75*, 43–88.

Beauchaine, T. P., Hinshaw, S. P., & Pang, K. L. (2010). Comorbidity of attention-deficit/hyperactivity disorder and early-onset conduct disorder: Biological, environmental, and developmental mechanisms. *Clinical Psychology: Science and Practice, 17*, 327–336. http://dx.doi.org/10.1111/j.1468-2850.2010.01224.x

Beck, A. T., Rush, A. J., Shaw, B. F., & Emery, G. (1979). *Cognitive therapy of depression*. New York, NY: Guilford Press.

Beck, A. T., Steer, R. A., & Brown, G. K. (1996). *Manual for the Beck Depression Inventory–II*. San Antonio, TX: Psychological Corporation.

Berman, A. L., Jobes, D. A., & Silverman, M. M. (2006). *Adolescent suicide: Assessment and intervention* (2nd ed.). Washington, DC: American Psychological Association. http://dx.doi.org/10.1037/11285-000

Biederman, J. (2003). Pediatric bipolar disorder coming of age. *Biological Psychiatry, 53*, 931–934. http://dx.doi.org/10.1016/S0006-3223(03)00297-X

Biederman, J., Faraone, S. V., Keenan, K., Knee, D., & Tsuang, M. T. (1990). Family–genetic and psychosocial risk factors in *DSM–III* attention-deficit disorder. *Journal of the American Academy of Child & Adolescent Psychiatry, 29*, 526–533. http://dx.doi.org/10.1097/00004583-199007000-00004

Birmaher, B., Arbelaez, C., & Brent, D. (2002). Course and outcome of child and adolescent major depressive disorder. *Child and Adolescent Psychiatric Clinics of North America, 11*, 619–637. http://dx.doi.org/10.1016/S1056-4993(02)00011-1

Birmaher, B., Axelson, D., Strober, M., Gill, M. K., Valeri, S., Chiappetta, L., . . . Keller, M. (2006). Clinical course of children and adolescents with bipolar spectrum disorders. *Archives of General Psychiatry, 63*, 175–183. http://dx.doi.org/10.1001/archpsyc.63.2.175

Birmaher, B., Williamson, D. E., Dahl, R. E., Axelson, D. A., Kaufman, J., Dorn, L. D., & Ryan, N. D. (2004). Clinical presentation and course of depression in youth: Does onset in childhood differ from onset in adolescence? *Journal of the American Academy of Child & Adolescent Psychiatry, 43*, 63–70. http://dx.doi.org/10.1097/00004583-200401000-00015

Bloomquist, M. L., & Schnell, S. V. (2002). *Helping children with aggression and conduct problems: Best practices for intervention.* New York, NY: Guilford Press.

Blotnicky-Gallant, P., Costain, E., & Corkum, P. (2013). Evaluating a demystification program for adolescents with ADHD. *The ADHD Report, 21*, 1–6, 12. http://dx.doi.org/10.1521/adhd.2013.21.8.1

Borum, R. (2000). Assessing violence risk among youth. *Journal of Clinical Psychology, 56*, 1263–1288. http://dx.doi.org/10.1002/1097-4679(200010)56:10<1263::AID-JCLP3>3.0.CO;2-D

Borum, R., Bartel, P., & Forth, A. (2006). *Manual for the Structured Assessment for Violence Risk in Youth (SAVRY).* Lutz, FL: Psychological Assessment Resources.

Borum, R., & Verhaagen, D. (2006). *Assessing and managing violence risk in juveniles.* New York, NY: Guilford Press.

Breunlin, D. C., Schwartz, R. C., & Mac Kune-Karrer, B. (1997). *Metaframeworks: Transcending the models of family therapy.* San Francisco, CA: Jossey-Bass.

Brock, S. E., Nickerson, A. B., Reeves, M. A., & Jimerson, S. R. (2008). Best practices for school psychologists as members of crisis teams: The PREPaRE Model. In A. Thomas & J. Grimes (Eds.), *Best practices in school psychology V* (pp. 1487–1504). Bethesda, MD: National Association of School Psychologists.

Bucy, J. E., Swerdlik, M. E., & Meyers, A. (2002). Full service schools. In A. Thomas & J. Grimes (Eds.), *Best practices in school psychology IV* (pp. 281–292). Bethesda, MD: National Association of School Psychologists.

Campbell, J. M., Ruble, L. A., & Hammond, R. K. (2014). Comprehensive developmental approach assessment model. In L. A. Wilkinson (Ed.), *Autism spectrum disorder in children and adolescents: Evidence-based assessment and intervention in schools* (pp. 51–73). Washington, DC: American Psychological Association. http://dx.doi.org/10.1037/14338-004

Carkhuff, R. R. (1971). Training as a preferred mode of treatment. *Journal of Counseling Psychology, 18*, 123–131. http://dx.doi.org/10.1037/h0030612

Centers for Disease Control and Prevention. (2010). *Web-based inquiry statistics query and reporting system (WISQARS).* Atlanta, GA: Author. Retrieved from http://www.cdc.gov/injury/wisqars/pdf/10LCID_All_Deaths_By_Age_Group_2010-a.pdf

Centers for Disease Control and Prevention. (2012). Youth Risk Behavior Surveillance—United States, 2011. *MMWR, 61*. Retrieved from http://www.cdc.gov/mmwr/pdf/ss/ss6104.pdf

Centers for Disease Control and Prevention. (2014). Prevalence of autism spectrum disorder among children aged 8 years—Autism and Developmental Disabilities Monitoring Network, 11 sites, United States, 2010. *Morbidity and Mortality Weekly Report, 63*(SS-2), 1–22.

Child and Adolescent Bipolar Foundation. (2003). *The storm in my brain: Kids and mood disorders*. Wilmette, IL: Author.

Chorpita, B. F. (2007). *Modular cognitive–behavioral therapy for childhood anxiety disorders*. New York, NY: Guilford Press.

Chorpita, B. F., Daleiden, E. L., & Weisz, J. R. (2005). Identifying and selecting the common elements of evidence based interventions: A distillation and matching model. *Mental Health Services Research, 7*, 5–20. http://dx.doi.org/10.1007/s11020-005-1962-6

Chorpita, B. F., Yim, L., Moffitt, C., Umemoto, L. A., & Francis, S. E. (2000). Assessment of symptoms of *DSM-IV* anxiety and depression in children: A revised child anxiety and depression scale. *Behaviour Research and Therapy, 38*, 835–855. http://dx.doi.org/10.1016/S0005-7967(99)00130-8

Cichetti, D., & Rogosch, F. A. (2002). A developmental psychopathology perspective on adolescence. *Journal of Consulting and Clinical Psychology, 70*, 6–20.

Clarke, G. N., & DeBar, L. L. (2010). Group cognitive–behavioral treatment for adolescent depression. In J. R. Weisz & A. E. Kazdin (Eds.), *Evidence-based psychotherapies for children and adolescents* (2nd ed., pp. 110–125). New York, NY: Guilford Press.

Clarke, G. N., DeBar, L. L., Lynch, F., Powell, J., Gale, J., O'Connor, E., . . . Hertert, S. (2005). A randomized effectiveness trial of brief cognitive–behavioral therapy for depressed adolescents receiving antidepressant medication. *Journal of the American Academy of Child & Adolescent Psychiatry, 44*, 888–898. http://dx.doi.org/10.1016/S0890-8567(09)62194-8

Clarke, G. N., Lewinsohn, P. M., & Hops, H. (1990). *Instructor's manual for the Adolescent Coping with Depression Course*. Portland, OR: Kaiser Permanente Center for Health Research. Retrieved from http://www.kpchr.org/research/public/acwd/acwd.html

Clevenger, W. A. (2011). *A case study exploration of placement in a therapeutic day school as an educational intervention package for children and adolescents with bipolar disorders*. (Doctoral dissertation). Available from ProQuest Dissertations and Theses database. (UMI No. 3439172)

Cohen, J. A., Mannarino, A. P., & Deblinger, E. (2006). *Treating trauma and traumatic grief in children and adolescents*. New York, NY: Guilford Press.

Conners, C. K. (2008). *Conners-3* (3rd ed.). North Tonowanda, NY: Multi-Health Systems.

Conners, C. K. (2014). *Conners Continuous Performance Test–CPT–3*. North Tonowanda, NY: Multi-Health Systems.

Conners, C. K., Epstein, J. N., March, J. S., Angold, A., Wells, K. C., Klaric, J., . . . Wigal, T. (2001). Multimodal treatment of ADHD in the MTA: An alternative outcome analysis. *Journal of the American Academy of Child & Adolescent Psychiatry, 40*, 159–167.

Connor, D. F. (2002). *Aggression and antisocial behavior in children and adolescents: Research and treatment*. New York, NY: Guilford Press.

Constantino, J. N., & Gruber, C. P. (2012). *Social Responsiveness Scale, Second Edition*. Los Angeles, CA: Western Psychological Services.

Crick, N. R. (1996). The role of overt aggression, relational aggression, and prosocial behavior in the prediction of children's future social adjustment. *Child Development, 67*, 2317–2327. http://dx.doi.org/10.2307/1131625

Crick, N. R., & Dodge, K. A. (1994). A review and reformulation of social information-processing mechanisms in children's social adjustment. *Psychological Bulletin, 115*, 74–101. http://dx.doi.org/10.1037/0033-2909.115.1.74

Crick, N. R., & Dodge, K. A. (1996). Social information-processing mechanisms in reactive and proactive aggression. *Child Development, 67*, 993–1002. http://dx.doi.org/10.2307/1131875

Crick, N. R., & Grotpeter, J. K. (1995). Relational aggression, gender, and social–psychological adjustment. *Child Development, 66*, 710–722. http://dx.doi.org/10.2307/1131945

Curry, J. F., & Reinecke, M. A. (2003). Modular therapy for adolescents with major depression. In M. A. Reinecke, F. M. Dattilio, & A. Freeman (Eds.), *Cognitive therapy with children and adolescents: A casebook for clinical practice* (2nd ed., pp. 95–127). New York, NY: Guilford Press.

Dawson, G., Jones, E. J. H., Merkle, K., Venema, K., Lowy, R., Faja, S., . . . Webb, S. J. (2012). Early behavioral intervention is associated with normalized brain activity in young children with autism. *Journal of the American Academy of Child & Adolescent Psychiatry, 51*, 1150–1159. http://dx.doi.org/10.1016/j.jaac.2012.08.018

Dawson, G., Rogers, S., Munson, J., Smith, M., Winter, J., Greenson, J., . . . Varley, J. (2010). Randomized, controlled trial of an intervention for toddlers with autism: The Early Start Denver Model. *Pediatrics, 125*, e17–e23. http://dx.doi.org/10.1542/peds.2009-0958

Dawson, P., & Guare, R. (2009). *Smart but scattered*. New York, NY: Guilford Press.

Deblinger, E., Behl, L. E., & Glickman, A. R. (2012). Trauma-focused cognitive–behavioral therapy for children who experienced sexual abuse. In P. C. Kendall (Ed.), *Child and adolescent therapy: Cognitive–behavioral procedures* (4th ed., pp. 345–375). New York, NY: Guilford Press.

Delis, D. C., Kaplan, E., & Kramer, J. H. (2001). *Delis-Kaplan Executive Function System (D-KEFS)*. San Antonio, TX: Psychological Corporation.

Diamantopoulou, S., Verhulst, F. C., & van der Ende, J. (2011). The parallel development of ODD and CD symptoms from early childhood to adolescence. *European Child & Adolescent Psychiatry, 20,* 301–309. http://dx.doi.org/10.1007/s00787-011-0175-3

Dishion, T. J., & Kavanaugh, K. (2003). *Intervening in adolescent problem behavior: A family-centered approach.* New York, NY: Guilford Press.

Doepke, K. J., Banks, B. M., Mays, J. F., Toby, L. M., & Landau, S. (2014). Co-occurring emotional and behavior problems. In L. E. Wilkinson (Ed.), *Autism spectrum disorder in children and adolescents: Evidence-based assessment and intervention in schools* (pp. 125–148). Washington, DC: American Psychological Association. http://dx.doi.org/10.1037/14338-007

Doll, B., & Cummings, J. A. (2008). *Transforming school mental health services: Population-based approaches to promoting the competency and wellness of children.* Bethesda, MD: National Association of School Psychologists.

Dryfoos, J. G. (1998). *Full service schools: A revolution in health and social services for children, youth, and families.* San Francisco, CA: Jossey-Bass.

DuPaul, G. J., Power, T. J., Anastopoulos, A. D., & Reid, R. (1998). *AD/HD Rating Scale–IV.* New York, NY: Guilford Press.

DuPaul, G. J., & Stoner, G. (2014). *ADHD in the schools. Assessment and intervention strategies* (3rd ed.). New York, NY: Guilford Press.

Eber, L., Breen, K., Rose, J., Unizycki, R. M., & London, T. H. (2008). Wraparound as a tertiary level intervention for students with emotional/behavioral needs. *Teaching Exceptional Children, 40,* 16–22.

Eber, L., Sugai, G., Smith, C., & Scott, T. (2002). Wraparound and positive behavioral interventions and supports in the schools. *Journal of Emotional and Behavioral Disorders, 10,* 171–180. http://dx.doi.org/10.1177/10634266020100030501

Egan, G. (1975). *The skilled helper: A model for systematic helping and interpersonal relating.* Monterey, CA: Brooks/Cole-Thomson.

Ehrereich-May, J., & Chu, B. C. (Eds.). (2014). Overview of transdiagnostic mechanisms and treatments for youth psychopathology. In J. Ehrereich-May & B. C. Chu (Eds.), *Transdiagnostic treatments for children and adolescents: Principles and practice.* New York, NY: Guilford Press.

Elliott, D. S., Huizinga, D., & Ageton, S. A. (1985). *Explaining delinquency and drug use.* Beverly Hills, CA: Sage.

Eyberg, S. M., & Pincus, D. (1999). *The Eyberg Child Behavior Inventory and Sutter-Eyberg Student Behavior Inventory: Professional manual.* Lutz, FL: Psychological Assessment Resources.

Falicov, C. J. (2013). *Latino families in therapy* (2nd ed.). New York, NY: Guilford Press.

Faraone, S. V. (2000). Genetics of childhood disorders: XX. ADHD, Part 4: Is ADHD genetically heterogeneous? *Journal of the American Academy of Child & Adolescent Psychiatry, 39,* 1455–1457.

Fenning, P. A., Pulaski, S., Gomez, M., Morello, M., Maciel, L., Maroney, E., . . . Maltese, R. (2012). Call to action: A critical need for designing alternatives for suspension and expulsion. *Journal of School Violence, 11*, 105–117. http://dx.doi.org/10.1080/15388220.2011.646643

Findling, R. L., Youngstrom, E. A., Fristad, M. A., Birmaher, B., Kowatch, R. A., Arnold, L. E., . . . Horwitz, S. M. (2010). Characteristics of children with elevated symptoms of mania: The Longitudinal Assessment of Manic Symptoms (LAMS) study. *The Journal of Clinical Psychiatry, 71*, 1664–1672. http://dx.doi.org/10.4088/JCP.09m05859yel

Forgatch, M. S., & Patterson, G. R. (2010). Parent Management Training—Oregon Model: An intervention for antisocial behavior in children and adolescents. In J. R. Weisz & A. E. Kazdin (Eds.), *Evidence-based psychotherapies for children and adolescents* (2nd ed., pp. 159–178). New York, NY: Guilford Press.

Forman, S. G., Shapiro, E. S., Codding, R. S., Gonzales, J. E., Reddy, L. A., Rosenfield, S. A., . . . Stoiber, K. C. (2013). Implementation science and school psychology. *School Psychology Quarterly, 28*, 77–100. http://dx.doi.org/10.1037/spq0000019

Forness, S. R., & Kavale, K. A. (2001). ADHD and the return to the medical model of special education. *Education & Treatment of Children, 24*, 224–247.

Franklin, M. E., Freeman, J., & March, J. S. (2010). Treating obsessive–compulsive disorder using exposure-based cognitive–behavioral therapy. In J. R. Weisz & A. E. Kazdin (Eds.), *Evidence-based psychotherapies for children and adolescents* (2nd ed., pp. 80–92). New York, NY: Guilford Press.

Frias, A., Palma, C., & Farriols, N. (2015). Comorbidity in pediatric bipolar disorder: Prevalence, clinical impact, etiology, and treatment. *Journal of Affective Disorders, 174*, 378–389.

Frick, P. J. (2012). Developmental pathways to conduct disorder: Implications for future directions in research, assessment, and treatment. *Journal of Clinical Child & Adolescent Psychology, 41*, 378–389. http://dx.doi.org/10.1080/15374416.2012.664815

Frick, P. J., & Morris, A. S. (2004). Temperament and developmental pathways to conduct problems. *Journal of Clinical Child & Adolescent Psychology, 33*, 54–68. http://dx.doi.org/10.1207/S15374424JCCP3301_6

Friedberg, R. D., & McClure, J. M. (2002). *Clinical practice of cognitive therapy with children and adolescents: The nuts and bolts.* New York, NY: Guilford Press.

Friedberg, R. D., McClure, J. M., & Garcia, J. H. (2009). *Cognitive therapy techniques for children and adolescents: Tools for enhancing practice.* New York, NY: Guilford Press.

Fristad, M. A., Gavazzi, S. M., & Soldano, K. W. (1999). Naming the enemy: Learning to differentiate mood disorder "symptoms" from the "self" that experiences them. *Journal of Family Psychotherapy, 10*, 81–88. http://dx.doi.org/10.1300/J085v10n01_07

Fristad, M. A., & Goldberg-Arnold, J. S. (2004). *How to raise a moody child: How to cope with depression and bipolar disorder.* New York, NY: Guilford Press.

Fristad, M. A., Goldberg-Arnold, J. S., & Gavazzi, S. M. (2002). Multifamily psychoeducation groups (MFPG) for families of children with bipolar disorder. *Bipolar Disorders, 4*, 254–262. http://dx.doi.org/10.1034/j.1399-5618.2002.09073.x

Fristad, M. A., Goldberg-Arnold, J. S., & Leffler, J. M. (2011). *Psychotherapy for children with bipolar and depressive disorders*. New York, NY: Guilford Press.

Fristad, M. A., & Youngstrom, E. A. (2010). Society of Clinical Child and Adolescent Psychology Response to the *DSM–5* Committee. *Inbalance, Society of Clinical Child & Adolescent Psychology Newsletter, 24*(2), 10–11.

Geller, B., Craney, J., Bolhofner, K., DelBello, M. P., Axelson, D., Luby, J., . . . Beringer, L. (2003). Phenomenology and longitudinal course of children with prepubertal and early adolescent bipolar disorder phenotype. In B. Geller & M. P. DelBello (Eds.), *Bipolar disorder in childhood and early adolescence* (pp. 25–50). New York, NY: Guilford Press.

Geller, B., & DelBello, M. P. (Eds.). (2003). *Bipolar disorder in childhood and early adolescence*. New York, NY: Guilford Press.

Geller, B., & Luby, J. (1997). Child and adolescent bipolar disorder: A review of the past 10 years. *Journal of the American Academy of Child & Adolescent Psychiatry, 36*, 1168–1176. http://dx.doi.org/10.1097/00004583-199709000-00008

Geller, B., Williams, M., Zimerman, B., & Frazier, J. (1996). *Washington University in St. Louis Kiddie Schedule for Affective Disorders and Schizophrenia (WASH-U-KSADS)*. St. Louis, MO: Washington University.

Geller, B., Zimerman, B., Williams, M., DelBello, M. P., Bolhofner, K., Craney, J. L., . . . Nickelsburg, M. J. (2002). *DSM-IV* mania symptoms in a prepubertal and early adolescent bipolar disorder phenotype compared to attention-deficit/hyperactive and normal controls. *Journal of Child and Adolescent Psychopharmacology, 12*, 11–25. http://dx.doi.org/10.1089/10445460252943533

Geller, B., Zimerman, B., Williams, M., DelBello, M. P., Frazier, J., & Beringer, L. (2002). Phenomenology of prepubertal and early adolescent bipolar disorder: Examples of elated mood, grandiose behaviors, decreased need for sleep, racing thoughts, and hypersexuality. *Journal of Child and Adolescent Psychopharmacology, 12*, 3–9. http://dx.doi.org/10.1089/10445460252943524

Gilotty, L., Kenworthy, L., Sirian, L., Black, D. O., & Wagner, A. E. (2002). Adaptive skills and executive function in autism spectrum disorders. *Child Neuropsychology, 8*, 241–248. http://dx.doi.org/10.1076/chin.8.4.241.13504

Gioia, G. A., Isquith, P. K., Guy, S. C., & Kenworthy, L. (2000). *Behavior Rating Inventory of Executive Functioning (BRIEF)*. Lutz, FL: Psychological Assessment Resources.

Glick, B., & Gibbs, J. C. (2010). *Aggression replacement training: A comprehensive intervention for aggressive youth* (3rd ed.). Champaign, IL: Research Press.

Goldstein, A. P. (1999). *The prepare curriculum: Teaching prosocial competencies*. Champaign, IL: Research Press.

Goldstein, S., & Naglieri, J. A. (2009). *Autism Spectrum Rating Scale*. North Tonawanda, NY: Multi-Health Systems.

Goldstein, T. R., Axelson, D. A., Birmaher, B., & Brent, D. A. (2007). Dialectical behavior therapy for adolescents with bipolar disorder: A 1-year open trial. *Journal of the American Academy of Child & Adolescent Psychiatry, 46*, 820–830. http://dx.doi.org/10.1097/chi.0b013e31805c1613

Goodheart, C. D. (2014). *A primer for ICD–10–CM users: Psychological and behavioral conditions*. Washington, DC: American Psychological Association. http://dx.doi.org/10.1037/14379-000

Gray, C. (1998). Social stories and comic strip conversations with students with Asperger syndrome and high-functioning autism. In E. Schopler, G. B. Mesibov, & L. J. Kunce (Eds.), *Asperger syndrome or high-functioning autism?* New York, NY: Plenum Press.

Gray, C. (2000). *The new social story book*. Arlington, TX: Future Horizons.

Guare, R., Dawson, P., & Guare, C. (2012). *Smart but scattered teens*. New York, NY: Guilford Press.

Halikias, W. (2013). Assessing youth violence and threats of violence in schools: School-based risk assessment. In S. H. McConaughy (Ed.), *Clinical interviews for children and adolescents: Assessment to intervention* (2nd ed., pp. 228–252). New York, NY: Guilford Press.

Hankin, B. L., & Abramson, L. Y. (2001). Development of gender differences in depression: An elaborated cognitive vulnerability–transactional stress theory. *Psychological Bulletin, 127*, 773–796. http://dx.doi.org/10.1037/0033-2909.127.6.773

Hankin, B. L., Fraley, R. C., Lahey, B. B., & Waldman, I. D. (2005). Is depression best viewed as a continuum or discrete category? A taxometric analysis of childhood and adolescent depression in a population-based sample. *Journal of Abnormal Psychology, 114*, 96–110. http://dx.doi.org/10.1037/0021-843X.114.1.96

Hart, E. L., Lahey, B. B., Loeber, R., Applegate, B., & Frick, P. J. (1995). Developmental change in attention-deficit/hyperactivity disorder in boys: A 4-year longitudinal study. *Journal of Abnormal Child Psychology, 23*, 729–749. http://dx.doi.org/10.1007/BF01447474

Henggeler, S. W., Cunningham, P. B., Rowland, M. D., & Schoenwald, S. K. (2012). *Contingency management for adolescent substance abuse: A practitioner's guide*. New York, NY: Guilford Press.

Henggeler, S. W., Schoenwald, S. K., Borduin, C. M., Rowland, M. D., & Cunningham, P. B. (2009). *Multisystemic therapy for antisocial behavior in children and adolescents* (2nd ed.). New York, NY: Guilford Press.

Hensley, M., Powell, W., Lamke, S., & Hartman, S. (2007). *The well-managed classroom: Strategies to create a productive and cooperative social climate in your learning community* (2nd ed.). Boys Town, NE: Boys Town Press.

Hinshaw, S. P., & Lee, S. S. (2003). Conduct and oppositional defiant disorders. In E. J. Mash & R. A. Barkley (Eds.), *Child psychopathology* (pp. 144–198). New York, NY: Guilford Press.

Hintze, J. M., Volpe, R. J., & Shapiro, E. S. (2008). Best practices in the systematic direct observation of student behavior. In A. Thomas & J. Grimes (Eds.), *Best practices in school psychology V* (pp. 319–336). Bethesda, MD: National Association of School Psychologists.

Hirschfeld, R. M. A. (2001). The comorbidity of major depression and anxiety disorders: Recognition and management in primary care. *The Journal of Clinical Psychiatry, 3*, 244–254. http://dx.doi.org/10.4088/PCC.v03n0609

Hollander, M. (2008). *Helping teens who cut.* New York, NY: Guilford Press.

Holmbeck, G. N., Devine, K. A., & Bruno, E. F. (2010). Developmental issues and considerations in research and practice. In J. R. Weisz & A. E. Kazdin (Eds.), *Evidence-based psychotherapies for children and adolescents* (2nd ed., pp. 28–39). New York, NY: Guilford Press.

Holmes, M. M. (2000). *A terrible thing happened: A story for children who have witnessed violence or trauma.* Washington, DC: Magination Press.

Howlin, P., Baron-Cohen, S., & Hadwin, J. (1999). *Teaching children with autism to mindread: A practical guide.* Chester, England: Wiley.

Huber, B. J. (2014, September). *Mental health services in schools: An interconnected systems approach to a four-tiered public health model.* Keynote presentation at the Sixteenth Annual Illinois Intern Supervision Day, Illinois State University, Normal, IL.

Huerta, M., Bishop, S. L., Duncan, A., Hus, V., & Lord, C. (2012). Application of DSM–5 criteria for autism spectrum disorder to three samples of children with DSM–IV diagnoses of pervasive developmental disorder. *The American Journal of Psychiatry, 169*, 1056–1064. http://dx.doi.org/10.1176/appi.ajp.2012.12020276

Huey, S. J., Jr., & Polo, A. J. (2010). Assessing the effects of evidence-based psychotherapies with ethnic minority youths. In J. R. Weisz & A. E. Kazdin (Eds.), *Evidence-based psychotherapies for children and adolescents* (2nd ed., pp. 451–465). New York, NY: Guilford Press.

Hughes, A. A., Hedtke, K. A., & Kendall, P. C. (2008). Family functioning in families of children with anxiety disorders. *Journal of Family Psychology, 22*, 325–328. http://dx.doi.org/10.1037/0893-3200.22.2.325

Husky, M. M., Kaplan, A., McGuire, L., Flynn, L., Chrostowski, C., & Olfson, M. (2011). Identifying adolescents at risk through voluntary school-based mental health screening. *Journal of Adolescence, 34*, 505–511. http://dx.doi.org/10.1016/j.adolescence.2010.05.018

Jacobson, C. M., & Mufson, L. (2010). Treating adolescent depression using interpersonal psychotherapy. In J. R. Weisz & A. E. Kazdin (Eds.), *Evidence-based psychotherapies for children and adolescents* (2nd ed., pp. 140–155). New York, NY: Guilford Press.

Jaycox, L. (2004). *Cognitive behavioral intervention for trauma in schools (CBITS).* Longmont, CO: Sopris West.

Jensen, P. S., Arnold, L. E., Swanson, J. M., Vitiello, B., Abikoff, H. B., Greenhill, L. L., . . . Hur, K. (2007). Three-year follow-up of the NIMH MTA study. *Journal of the American Academy of Child & Adolescent Psychiatry, 46*, 989–1002. http://dx.doi.org/10.1097/CHI.0b013e3180686d48

Jensen, P. S., Hinshaw, S. P., Swanson, J. M., Greenhill, L. L., Conners, C. K., Arnold, L. E., . . . Wigal, T. (2001). Findings from the NIMH Multimodal Treatment Study of ADHD (MTA): Implications and applications for primary care providers. *Journal of Developmental and Behavioral Pediatrics, 22*, 60–73. http://dx.doi.org/10.1097/00004703-200102000-00008

Johns, S. K., Patrick, J. A., & Rutherford, K. J. (2008). Best practices in district-wide positive behavior support implementation. In A. Thomas & J. Grimes (Eds.), *Best practices in school psychology V* (pp. 721–747). Bethesda, MD: National Association of School Psychologists.

Jungbluth, N. J., & Shirk, S. R. (2009). Therapist strategies for building involvement in cognitive–behavioral therapy for adolescent depression. *Journal of Consulting and Clinical Psychology, 77*, 1179–1184. http://dx.doi.org/10.1037/a0017325

Kadesjö, B., & Gillberg, C. (2001). The comorbidity of ADHD in the general population of Swedish school-age children. *Journal of Child Psychology and Psychiatry, 42*, 487–492. http://dx.doi.org/10.1111/1469-7610.00742

Kamphaus, R. W., & Frick, P. J. (2005). *Clinical assessment of child and adolescent personality and behavior* (2nd ed.). New York, NY: Springer.

Kapp-Simon, K. A., & Simon, D. J. (1991). *Meeting the challenge: Social skills training for adolescents with special needs.* Chicago: University of Illinois Press.

Kataoka, S. H., Stein, B. D., Jaycox, L. H., Wong, M., Escudero, P., Tu, W., . . . Fink, A. (2003). A school-based mental health program for traumatized Latino immigrant children. *Journal of the American Academy of Child & Adolescent Psychiatry, 42*, 311–318. http://dx.doi.org/10.1097/00004583-200303000-00011

Kaufman, J., Birmaher, B., Brent, D., Rao, U., Flynn, C., Moreci, P., . . . Ryan, N. (1997). Schedule for Affective Disorders and Schizophrenia for School-Age Children—Present and Lifetime version (K-SADS-PL): Initial reliability and validity data. *Journal of the American Academy of Child & Adolescent Psychiatry, 36*, 980–988.

Kazdin, A. E. (2005). *Parent management training: Treatment for oppositional, aggressive, and antisocial behavior in children and adolescents.* New York, NY: Oxford University Press.

Kazdin, A. E. (2010). Problem-solving skills training and parent management training for oppositional defiant disorder and conduct disorder. In J. R. Weisz & A. E. Kazdin (Eds.), *Evidence-based psychotherapies for children and adolescents* (2nd ed., pp. 211–226). New York, NY: Guilford Press.

Kazdin, A. E., & Mazurick, J. L. (1994). Dropping out of child psychotherapy: Distinguishing early and late dropouts over the course of treatment. *Journal of*

Consulting and Clinical Psychology, 62, 1069–1074. http://dx.doi.org/10.1037/0022-006X.62.5.1069

Kazdin, A. E., Siegel, T. C., & Bass, D. (1992). Cognitive problem-solving skills training and parent management training in the treatment of antisocial behavior in children. *Journal of Consulting and Clinical Psychology, 60,* 733–747. http://dx.doi.org/10.1037/0022-006X.60.5.733

Kazdin, A. E., & Weisz, J. R. (2010). Introduction: Context, background, and goal. In J. R. Weisz, & A. E. Kazdin (Eds.), *Evidence-based psychotherapies for children and adolescents* (2nd ed., pp. 3–9). New York, NY: Guilford Press.

Kazdin, A. E., & Whitley, M. K. (2003). Treatment of parental stress to enhance therapeutic change among children referred for aggressive and antisocial behavior. *Journal of Consulting and Clinical Psychology, 71,* 504–515. http://dx.doi.org/10.1037/0022-006X.71.3.504

Kearney, C. A. (2002). Identifying the function of school refusal behavior: A revision of the School Refusal Assessment Scale. *Journal of Psychopathology and Behavioral Assessment, 24,* 235–245. http://dx.doi.org/10.1023/A:1020774932043

Kendall, P. C. (2012a). Anxiety disorders in youth. In P. C. Kendall (Ed.), *Child and adolescent therapy: Cognitive–behavioral procedures* (pp. 143–189). New York, NY: Guilford Press.

Kendall, P. C. (Ed.). (2012b). *Child and adolescent therapy: Cognitive–behavioral procedures* (4th ed.). New York, NY: Guilford Press.

Kendall, P. C. (2012c). Guiding theory for therapy with children and adolescents. In P. C. Kendall (Ed.), *Child and adolescent therapy: Cognitive–behavioral procedures* (pp. 3–24). New York, NY: Guilford Press.

Kendall, P. C. (2014, February). *Treating anxiety in youth: Computer-assisted and web-based program.* Workshop at the meeting of National Association of School Psychologists, Washington, DC.

Kendall, P. C., & Beidas, R. (2007). Smoothing the trail for dissemination of evidence-based practices for youth: Flexibility within fidelity. *Professional Psychology: Research and Practice, 38,* 13–20. http://dx.doi.org/10.1037/0735-7028.38.1.13

Kendall, P. C., Choudhury, M. S., Hudson, J. L., & Webb, A. (2002). *The C.A.T. Project.* Ardmore, PA: Workbook.

Kendall, P. C., & Hedtke, K. A. (2006). *Cognitive–behavioral therapy for anxious children: Therapist manual* (3rd ed.). Ardmore, PA: Workbook.

Kendall, P. C., & Khanna, M. (2008). *Camp Cope-A-Lot: The Coping Cat DVD.* Ardmore, PA: Workbook.

Kertz, S. J., & Woodruff-Borden, J. (2011). The developmental psychopathology of worry. *Clinical Child and Family Psychology Review, 14,* 174–197. http://dx.doi.org/10.1007/s10567-011-0086-3

Khanna, M. S., & Kendall, P. C. (2010). Computer-assisted cognitive–behavioral therapy for child anxiety: Results of a randomized clinical trial. *Journal of Consulting and Clinical Psychology, 78,* 737–745.

King, N. J., Hamilton, D. I., & Ollendick, T. H. (1988). *Children's phobias: A behavioral perspective*. London, England: Wiley.

Klein, D. N., Dougherty, L. R., & Olino, T. M. (2005). Toward guidelines for evidence-based assessment of depression in children and adolescents. *Journal of Clinical Child & Adolescent Psychology, 34,* 412–432. http://dx.doi.org/10.1207/s15374424jccp3403_3

Klin, A., & Volkmar, F. R. (2000). Treatment and intervention guidelines for individuals with Asperger syndrome. In A. Klin, F. R. Volmar, & S. S. Sparrow (Eds.), *Asperger syndrome* (pp. 340–366). New York, NY: Guilford Press.

Klinger, L. G., Dawson, G., Barnes, K., & Crisler, M. (2014). Autism spectrum disorder. In E. J. Mash & R. A. Barkley (Eds.), *Child psychopathology* (3rd ed., pp. 531–572). New York, NY: Guilford Press.

Koegel, R. L., Koegel, L. K., Vernon, T. W., & Brookman-Frazee, L. I. (2010). In J. R. Weisz & A. E. Kazdin (Eds.), *Evidence-based psychotherapies for children and adolescents* (2nd ed., pp. 327–344). New York, NY: Guilford Press.

Korkman, M., Kirk, U., & Kemp, S. L. (2007). *NEPSY–II. Clinical and interpretative manual*. San Antonio, TX: Psychological Corporation.

Kovacs, M. (2014). *The Children's Depression Inventory–2*. North Tonawanda, NY: Multi-Health Systems.

Kowatch, R. A., Youngstrom, E. A., Danielyan, A., & Findling, R. L. (2005). Review and meta-analysis of the phenomenology and clinical characteristics of mania in children and adolescents. *Bipolar Disorders, 7,* 483–496. http://dx.doi.org/10.1111/j.1399-5618.2005.00261.x

Kutash, K., Duchnowski, A. J., & Lynn, N. (2006). *School-based mental health: An empirical guide for decision-makers*. Tampa: University of South Florida, The Louis de la Parte Florida Mental Health Institute.

La Greca, A. M., & Silverman, W. K. (2012). Interventions for youth following disasters and acts of terrorism. In P. C. Kendall (Ed.), *Child and adolescent therapy: Cognitive–behavioral procedures* (4th ed., pp. 324–344). New York, NY: Guilford Press.

Lahey, B. B., Van Hulle, C. A., Rathouz, P. J., Rodgers, J. L., D'Onofrio, B. M., & Waldman, I. D. (2009). Are oppositional–defiant and hyperactive–inattentive symptoms developmental precursors to conduct problems in late childhood? Genetic and environmental links. *Journal of Abnormal Child Psychology, 37,* 45–58. http://dx.doi.org/10.1007/s10802-008-9257-1

Larson, J. (2005). *Think first: Addressing aggressive behavior in secondary schools*. New York, NY: Guilford Press.

Larson, J., & Lochman, J. E. (2010). *Helping schoolchildren cope with anger: A cognitive–behavioral intervention* (2nd ed.). New York, NY: Guilford Press.

Larson, K., Russ, S. A., Kahn, R. S., & Halfon, N. (2011). Patterns of comorbidity, functioning, and service use for U.S. children with ADHD, 2007. *Pediatrics, 127,* 462–470. http://dx.doi.org/10.1542/peds.2010-0165

Lazarus, A. A. (1997). *Brief but comprehensive psychotherapy: The multimodal way.* New York, NY: Springer.

Lazarus, A. A. (2008). Multimodal therapy. In R. J. Corsini & D. Wedding (Eds.), *Current psychotherapies* (8th ed., pp. 368–401). Belmont, CA: Thompson.

Lewinsohn, P. M., Rohde, P., Hops, H., & Clarke, G. N. (1991). *The Coping With Depression Course—Adolescent version: Instructor's manual for the parent course.* Unpublished manuscript.

Liddle, H. A. (2009). *Multidimensional Family Therapy for Adolescent Drug Abuse: Clinician's manual.* Center City, MN: Hazelden.

Liddle, H. A. (2010). Treating adolescent substance abuse using multidimensional family therapy. In J. R. Weisz & A. E. Kazdin (Eds.), *Evidence-based psychotherapies for children and adolescents* (2nd ed., pp. 416–432). New York, NY: Guilford Press.

Lieberman, R., Poland, S., & Cassel, R. (2008). Best practices in suicide prevention. In A. Thomas & J. Grimes (Eds.), *Best practices in school psychology V* (pp. 1457–1472). Bethesda, MD: National Association of School Psychologists.

Linehan, M. M. (1993). *Cognitive–behavioral treatment of borderline personality disorder.* New York, NY: Guilford Press.

Lochman, J. E., Powell, N. R., Whidby, J. M., & FitzGerald, D. P. (2012). Aggression in children. In P. C. Kendall (Ed.), *Child and adolescent therapy: Cognitive–behavioral procedures* (pp. 27–60). New York, NY: Guilford Press.

Long, N. J., Wood, M. M., & Fecser, F. A. (2001). *Life space crisis intervention: Talking with students in conflict* (2nd ed.). Austin, TX: Pro-Ed.

Lord, C., Rutter, M., DiLavore, P. C., & Risi, S. (2002). *Autism Diagnostic Observation Schedule manual.* Los Angeles, CA: Western Psychological Services.

Lord, C., Rutter, M., DiLavore, P. C., Risi, S., Gotham, K., & Bishop, S. L. (2012). *Autism Diagnostic Observation Schedule Manual* (2nd ed.). Los Angeles, CA: Western Psychological Services.

Losen, D. J., & Skiba, R. J. (2010). *Suspended education: Urban middle schools in crisis.* Montgomery, AL: Southern Poverty Law Center. Retrieved from http://www.splcenter.org/get-informed/publications/suspended-education

Lovaas, I. O. (2002). *Teaching individuals with developmental delays: Basic intervention techniques.* Austin, TX: Pro-Ed.

Luby, J. L., Heffelfinger, A., Koenig-McNaught, A. L., Brown, K., & Spitznagel, E. (2004). The Preschool Feelings Checklist: A brief and sensitive screening measure for depression in young children. *Journal of the American Academy of Child & Adolescent Psychiatry, 43,* 708–717.

Mandy, W. P., Chilvers, R., Chowdhury, U., Salter, G., Seigal, A., & Skuse, D. (2013). Sex differences in autism spectrum disorder. *Journal of Autism and Developmental Disorders, 42,* 1304–1313.

March, J. S. (2007). *Talking back to OCD.* New York, NY: Guilford Press.

March, J. S. (2012). *Multidimensional Anxiety Scale for Children—2nd Edition (MASC–2)*. North Tonawanda, NY: Multi-Health Systems. http://dx.doi.org/10.1037/t05050-000

March, J. S., & Mulle, K. (1998). *OCD in children and adolescents: A cognitive–behavioral treatment manual*. New York, NY: Guilford Press.

March, J. S., Swanson, J. M., Arnold, L. E., Hoza, B., Conners, C. K., Hinshaw, S. P., . . . Pelham, W. E. (2000). Anxiety as a predictor and outcome variable in the multimodal treatment study of children with ADHD (MTA). *Journal of Abnormal Child Psychology, 28,* 527–541. http://dx.doi.org/10.1023/A:1005179014321

Marchand-Martella, N. E., Slocum, T. A., & Martella, R. (2004). *Introduction to direct instruction*. Boston, MA: Pearson Education.

Mash, E. (2006). Treatment of child and family disturbance. In E. J. Mash & R. A. Barkley (Eds.), *Treatment of childhood disorders* (3rd ed., pp. 3–62). New York, NY: Guilford Press.

Mash, E. J., & Barkley, R. A. (Eds.). (2006). *Treatment of childhood disorders* (3rd ed.). New York, NY: Guilford Press.

McConaughy, S. H. (2004a). *Semistructured Parent Interview*. Burlington: University of Vermont, Research Center for Children, Youth, and Families.

McConaughy, S. H. (2004b). *Semistructured Teacher Interview*. Burlington: University of Vermont, Research Center for Children, Youth, and Families.

McConaughy, S. H. (2013). *Clinical interviews for children and adolescents: Assessment to intervention* (2nd ed.). New York, NY: Guilford Press.

McConaughy, S. H., & Achenbach, T. M. (2001). *Manual for the Semistructured Clinical Interview for Children and Adolescents* (2nd ed.). Burlington: University of Vermont, Center for Children, Youth, & Families.

McConaughy, S. H., & Achenbach, T. M. (2009). *Manual for the Direct Observation Form*. Burlington: University of Vermont, Center for Children, Youth, & Families.

McGinnis, E., Sprafkin, R. P., Gershaw, N. J., & Klein, P. (2011). *Skillstreaming the adolescent: A guide to teaching prosocial skills* (3rd ed.). Champaign, IL: Research Press.

McKay, M. M., & Bannon, W. M. (2004). Engaging families in child mental health services. *Child & Adolescent Psychiatric Clinics of North America, 13,* 905–921. http://dx.doi.org/10.1016/j.chc.2004.04.001

McMahon, R. J., & Frick, P. J. (2005). Evidence-based assessment of conduct problems in children and adolescents. *Journal of Clinical Child & Adolescent Psychology, 34,* 477–505. http://dx.doi.org/10.1207/s15374424jccp3403_6

McMahon, R. J., & Frick, P. J. (2007). Conduct and oppositional disorders. In E. J. Mash & R. A. Barkley (Eds.), *Assessment of childhood disorders* (4th ed., pp. 132–183). New York, NY: Guilford Press.

McMahon, R. J., Wells, K. C., & Kotler, J. S. (2006). Conduct problems. In E. J. Mash & R. A. Barkley (Eds.), *Treatment of childhood disorders* (3rd ed., pp. 137–268). New York, NY: Guilford Press.

Meichenbaum, D. (1977). *Cognitive–behavior modification: An integrative approach.* New York, NY: Plenum Press. http://dx.doi.org/10.1007/978-1-4757-9739-8

Meichenbaum, D. H. (1985). *Stress inoculation training.* Elmsford, NY: Pergamon Press.

Mental Health Parity and Addiction Equity Act of 2008, Pub. L. No. 110-343 (2013).

Menting, A. T., Orobio de Castro, B., & Matthys, W. (2013). Effectiveness of the Incredible Years parent training to modify disruptive and prosocial child behavior: A meta-analytic review. *Clinical Psychology Review, 33,* 901–913. http://dx.doi.org/10.1016/j.cpr.2013.07.006

Merrell, K. W. (2007). *Strong kids: Grades 3–5.* Baltimore, MD: Brookes.

Merrell, K. W. (2008). *Helping students overcome depression and anxiety: A practical guide* (2nd ed.). New York, NY: Guilford Press.

Meyers, A. B., Tobin, R. M., Huber, B. J., Conway, E. E., & Shelvin, K. H. (in press). Interdisciplinary collaboration supporting social–emotional learning in rural school systems. *Journal of Educational & Psychological Consultation.*

Mick, E., Biederman, J., Pandina, G., & Faraone, S. V. (2003). A preliminary meta-analysis of the child behavior checklist in pediatric bipolar disorder. *Biological Psychiatry, 53,* 1021–1027. http://dx.doi.org/10.1016/S0006-3223(03)00234-8

Miklowitz, D. J. (2008). *Bipolar disorder: A family-focused treatment approach* (2nd ed.). New York, NY: Guilford Press.

Miklowitz, D. J., & Goldstein, T. R. (2010). Family-based approaches to treating bipolar disorder in adolescence: Family focused therapy and dialectical behavior therapy. In D. J. Miklowitz & D. Cicchetti (Eds.), *Understanding bipolar disorder: A developmental psychopathology perspective* (pp. 466–493). New York, NY: Guilford Press.

Milich, R., Balentine, A. C., & Lynam, D. R. (2001). ADHD combined type and ADHD predominantly inattentive type are distinct and unrelated disorders. *Clinical Psychology: Science and Practice, 8,* 463–488. http://dx.doi.org/10.1093/clipsy.8.4.463

Miller, A. L., Rathus, J. H., & Linehan, M. M. (2007). *Dialectical behavioral therapy with suicidal adolescents.* New York, NY: Guilford Press.

Miller, D. N. (2010). *Child and adolescent suicidal behavior: School-based prevention, assessment, and intervention.* New York, NY: Guilford Press.

Miller, G. A. (1969). Psychology as a means for promoting human welfare. *American Psychologist, 24,* 1063–1075.

Miller, M., & Hinshaw, S. P. (2012). Attention-deficit/hyperactivity disorder. In P. C. Kendall (Ed.), *Child and adolescent therapy: Cognitive–behavioral procedures* (4th ed., pp. 61–91). New York, NY: Guilford Press.

Miller, W. R., & Rollnick, S. (2012). *Motivational interviewing: Helping people change* (3rd ed.). New York, NY: Guilford Press.

Minuchin, S. (1974). *Families and family therapy.* Cambridge, MA: Harvard University Press.

Moffitt, T. E., & Caspi, A. (2001). Childhood predictors differentiate life-course persistent and adolescence-limited antisocial pathways among males and females. *Development and Psychopathology*, *13*, 355–375. http://dx.doi.org/10.1017/S0954579401002097

Monastra, V. J. (2005). Overcoming the barriers to effective treatment for attention-deficit/hyperactivity disorder: A neuro-educational approach. *International Journal of Psychophysiology*, *58*, 71–80. http://dx.doi.org/10.1016/j.ijpsycho.2005.03.010

MTA Cooperative Group. (1999a). A 14-month randomized clinical trial of treatment strategies for attention-deficit/hyperactivity disorder. *Archives of General Psychiatry*, *56*, 1073–1086. http://dx.doi.org/10.1001/archpsyc.56.12.1073

MTA Cooperative Group. (1999b). Moderators and mediators of treatment response for children with attention-deficit/hyperactivity disorder: The Multimodal Treatment Study of children with attention-deficit/hyperactivity disorder. *Archives of General Psychiatry*, *56*, 1088–1096. http://dx.doi.org/10.1001/archpsyc.56.12.1088

MTA Cooperative Group. (2004). National Institute of Mental Health Multimodal Treatment Study of ADHD follow-up: 24-month outcomes of treatment strategies for attention-deficit/hyperactivity disorder. *Pediatrics*, *113*, 754–761. http://dx.doi.org/10.1542/peds.113.4.754

Mufson, L., Dorta, K. P., Moreau, D., & Weissman, M. M. (2004). *Interpersonal psychotherapy for depressed adolescents* (2nd ed.). New York, NY: Guilford Press.

Murphy, J. J., & Duncan, B. L. (2007). *Brief interventions for school problems: Outcome-informed strategies* (2nd ed.). New York, NY: Guilford Press.

Mychailyszyn, M. P., Brodman, D. M., Read, K. L., & Kendall, P. C. (2012). Cognitive–behavioral school-based interventions for anxious and depressed youth: A meta-analysis of outcomes. *Clinical Psychology: Science and Practice*, *19*, 129–153. http://dx.doi.org/10.1111/j.1468-2850.2012.01279.x

Naar-King, S., & Suarez, M. (2011). *Motivational interviewing with adolescents and young adults*. New York, NY: Guilford Press.

National Association of School Psychologists. (2013). *Effective school discipline policy and practice: Supporting student learning*. Congressional Briefing Position Paper. Retrieved from http://www.nasponline.org/advocacy/School_Discipline_Congressional_Briefing.pdf

National Institute of Mental Health. (2009). *National survey tracks rates of common mental disorders in youth*. Retrieved from http://www.nimh.nih.gov/science-news/2009/national-survey-tracks-rates-of-common-mental-disorders-among-american-youth.shtml

Nelson, J. R., Benner, G. J., & Mooney, P. (2008). *Instructional practices for students with behavioral disorders: Strategies for reading, writing, and math*. New York, NY: Guilford Press.

Nelson, W. M., III, & Finch, A. J. (2008). *Keeping your cool: The anger management workbook* (2nd ed.). Ardmore, PA: Workbook.

Nikopoulos, C. K., & Keenan, M. (2007). Using video modeling to teach complex social sequences to children with autism. *Journal of Autism and Developmental Disabilities, 37,* 678–693. http://dx.doi.org/10.1007/s10803-006-0195-x

Ollendick, T. H., & King, N. J. (1998). Empirically supported treatments for children with phobic and anxiety disorders: Current status. *Journal of Clinical Child Psychology, 27,* 156–167. http://dx.doi.org/10.1207/s15374424jccp2702_3

Ollendick, T. H., & King, N. J. (2012). Evidence-based treatments for children and adolescents: Issues and commentary. In P. C. Kendall (Ed.), *Child and adolescent therapy: Cognitive–behavioral procedures* (pp. 499–519). New York, NY: Guilford Press.

Olweus, D., Limber, S., & Mihalic, S. F. (1999). *Blueprints for violence prevention: Book nine—Bullying prevention program.* Boulder, CO: Center for the Study and Prevention of Violence.

Ormhaug, S. M., Jensen, T. K., Wentzel-Larsen, T., & Shirk, S. R. (2014). The therapeutic alliance in treatment of traumatized youths: Relation to outcome in a randomized clinical trial. *Journal of Consulting and Clinical Psychology, 82,* 52–64. http://dx.doi.org/10.1037/a0033884

Osher, D., Dwyer, K., & Jackson, S. (2004). *Safe, supportive, and successful schools.* Longmont, CO: Sopris West.

Ozonoff, S., Dawson, G., & McPartland, J. (2002). *A parent's guide to Asperger syndrome and high-functioning autism: How to meet the challenges and help your child thrive.* New York, NY: Guilford Press.

Ozonoff, S., Goodlin-Jones, B. L., & Solomon, M. (2007). Autism spectrum disorders. In E. J. Mash & R. A. Barkley (Eds.), *Assessment of childhood disorders* (4th ed., pp. 487–525). New York, NY: Guilford Press.

Pardini, D. A., & Fite, P. J. (2010). Symptoms of conduct disorder, oppositional defiant disorder, attention-deficit/hyperactivity disorder, and callous–unemotional traits as unique predictors of psychosocial maladjustment in boys: Advancing an evidence base for *DSM–5. Journal of the American Academy of Child & Adolescent Psychiatry, 49,* 1134–1144. http://dx.doi.org/10.1016/j.jaac.2010.07.010

Patient Protection and Affordable Care Act, 42 U.S.C. § 18001 *et seq.* (2010).

Patterson, G. R. (1982). *Coercive family process.* Eugene, OR: Castalia.

Patterson, G. R., Reid, J. B., Jones, R. R., & Conger, R. E. (1975). *A social learning theory approach to family intervention: Vol. 1. Families with aggressive children.* Eugene, OR: Castalia.

Pavuluri, M. (2008). *What works for bipolar kids: Help and hope for parents.* New York, NY: Guilford Press.

Pavuluri, M. N., Henry, D. B., Devineni, B., Carbray, J. A., & Birmaher, B. (2006). Child Mania Rating Scale: Development, reliability, and validity. *Journal of the American Academy of Child & Adolescent Psychiatry, 45,* 550–560. http://dx.doi.org/10.1097/01.chi.0000205700.40700.50

Pelham, W. E., Jr., & Fabiano, G. A. (2001). Treatment of attention-deficit/hyperactivity disorder: The impact of comorbidity. *Clinical Psychology & Psychotherapy*, 8, 315–329. http://dx.doi.org/10.1002/cpp.312

Pelham, W. E., Jr., & Fabiano, G. A. (2008). Evidence-based psychosocial treatments for attention-deficit/hyperactivity disorder. *Journal of Clinical Child & Adolescent Psychology*, 37, 184–214. http://dx.doi.org/10.1080/15374410701818681

Pelham, W. E., Jr., Fabiano, G. A., & Massetti, G. M. (2005). Evidence-based assessment of attention-deficit/hyperactivity disorder in children and adolescents. *Journal of Clinical Child & Adolescent Psychology*, 34, 449–476. http://dx.doi.org/10.1207/s15374424jccp3403_5

Pelham, W. E., Jr., Gnagy, E. M., Greiner, A. R., Waschbusch, D. A., Fabiano, G. A., & Burrows-MacLean, L. (2010). Summer treatment programs for attention-deficit/hyperactivity disorder. In J. R. Weisz & A. E. Kazdin (Eds.), *Evidence-based psychotherapies for children and adolescents* (2nd ed., pp. 277–292). New York, NY: Guilford Press.

Pelham, W. E., Jr., Greiner, A. R., & Gnagy, E. M. (1997). *Children's summer treatment program manual.* Buffalo, NY: Comprehensive Treatment for Attention Deficit Disorders.

Pfiffner, L. J., Barkley, R. A., & DuPaul, G. J. (2006). Treatment of ADHD in school settings. In R. A. Barkley (Ed.), *Attention-deficit/hyperactivity disorder* (3rd ed., pp. 547–589). New York, NY: Guilford Press.

Pfiffner, L. J., & McBurnett, K. (1997). Social skills training with parent generalization: Treatment effects for children with attention-deficit disorder. *Journal of Consulting and Clinical Psychology*, 65, 749–757. http://dx.doi.org/10.1037/0022-006X.65.5.749

Piacentini, J. C., Peris, T. S., March, J. S., & Franklin, E. (2012). Obsessive–compulsive disorder. In P. C. Kendall (Ed.), *Child and adolescent therapy: Cognitive–behavioral procedures* (4th ed., pp. 259–282). New York, NY: Guilford Press.

Pliszka, S. R. (2015). Comorbid psychiatric disorders in children with ADHD. In R. A. Barkley (Ed.), *Attention-deficit/hyperactivity disorder: A handbook for diagnosis and treatment* (4th ed., pp. 140–168). New York, NY: Guilford Press.

Quinn, P. O., & Stern, J. J. (2001). *Putting on the brakes: Young people's guide to understanding attention-deficit/hyperactivity disorder.* Washington, DC: Magination Press.

Raine, A., Dodge, K., Loeber, R., Gatzke-Kopp, L., Lynam, D., Reynolds, C., . . . Liu, J. (2006). The Reactive–Proactive Aggression Questionnaire: Differential correlates of reactive and proactive aggression in adolescent boys. *Aggressive Behavior*, 32, 159–171. http://dx.doi.org/10.1002/ab.20115

Rathvon, N. (2008). *Effective school interventions: Evidence-based strategies for improving student outcomes* (2nd ed.). New York, NY: Guilford Press.

Reaven, J., Blakeley-Smith, A., Culhane-Shelburne, K., & Hepburn, S. (2012). Group cognitive behavior therapy for children with high-functioning autism spectrum disorders and anxiety: A randomized trial. *Journal of Child Psychology and Psychiatry*, *53*, 410–419. http://dx.doi.org/10.1111/j.1469-7610.2011.02486.x

Reaven, J., Blakeley-Smith, A., Nichols, S., & Hepburn, S. (2011). *Facing your fears: Group therapy for managing anxiety in children with high-functioning autism spectrum disorders*. Baltimore, MD: Brookes.

Reddy, L. A. (2012). *Group play interventions for children: Strategies for teaching prosocial skills*. Washington, DC: American Psychological Association. http://dx.doi.org/10.1037/13093-000

Reddy, L. A., Spencer, P., Hall, T. M., & Rubel, E. (2001). Use of developmentally appropriate games in child group training program for young children with attention-deficit/hyperactivity disorder. In A. A. Drewes, L. J. Carey, & C. E. Schaefer (Eds.), *School-based play therapy* (pp. 256–274). New York, NY: Wiley.

Reddy, L. A., Springer, C., Files-Hall, T. M., Benisz, E. S., Haunch, Y., Braunstein, D., & Atamanoff, T. (2005). Child ADHD multimodal program: An empirically supported intervention for young children with ADHD. In L. A. Reddy, T. M. Files-Hall, & C. E. Schaefer (Eds.), *Empirically based play interventions for children* (pp. 145–167). Washington, DC: American Psychological Association.

Reich, W. (2000). Diagnostic Interview for Children and Adolescents (DICA). *Journal of the American Academy of Child & Adolescent Psychiatry*, *39*, 59–66.

Reid, J. B., Patterson, G. R., & Snyder, J. (Eds.). (2002). *Antisocial behavior in children and adolescents: A developmental analysis and model for intervention*. Washington, DC: American Psychological Association. http://dx.doi.org/10.1037/10468-000

Reinecke, M. A., Dattilio, F. M., & Freeman, A. (Eds.). (2003). *Cognitive therapy with children and adolescents* (2nd ed.). New York, NY: Guilford Press.

Reynolds, C. R., & Kamphaus, R. W. (2004). *The Behavior Assessment System for Children—Second Edition (BASC–2) manual*. Bloomington, MN: Pearson Assessments.

Reynolds, C. R., & Kamphaus, R. W. (2006). *BASC–2 Student Observation System*. San Antonio, TX: Pearson.

Reynolds, C. R., & Richmond, B. O. (2008). *Revised Children's Manifest Anxiety Scale: Second Edition (RCMAS-2)*. Los Angeles, CA: Western Psychological Services.

Reynolds, W. M. (2002). *Reynolds Adolescent Depression Scale: Professional manual* (2nd ed.). Odessa, FL: Psychological Assessment Resources.

Reynolds, W. M. (2010). *Reynolds Child Depression Scale: Professional manual* (2nd ed.). Odessa, FL: Psychological Assessment Resources.

Rivera, S. (2012). Schools. In J. A. Cohen, A. P. Mannarino, & E. Deblinger (Eds.), *Trauma-focused CBT for children and adolescents: Treatment applications*. New York, NY: Guilford Press.

Robbins, M. S., Horigian, V., Szapocznik, J., & Ucha, J. (2010). Treating Hispanic youth using brief strategic family therapy. In J. R. Weisz & A. E. Kazdin (Eds.),

Evidence-based psychotherapies for children and adolescents (2nd ed., pp. 375–390). New York, NY: Guilford Press.

Roberts, W., Milich, R., & Barkley, R. A. (2015). Primary symptoms, diagnostic criteria, subtyping, and prevalence of ADHD. In R. A. Barkley (Ed.), *Attention-deficit/hyperactivity disorder: A handbook for diagnosis and treatment* (4th ed., pp. 51–80). New York, NY: Guilford Press.

Robin, A. L. (1998). *ADHD in adolescents: Diagnosis and treatment.* New York, NY: Guilford Press.

Robin, A. L. (2006). Training families with adolescents with ADHD. In R. A. Barkley (Ed.), *Attention-deficit/hyperactivity disorder* (3rd ed., pp. 499–546). New York, NY: Guilford Press.

Robin, A. L., & Foster, S. L. (2002). *Negotiating parent–adolescent conflict: A behavioral–family systems approach.* New York, NY: Guilford Press.

Rogers, C. R. (1957). The necessary and sufficient conditions of therapeutic personality change. *Journal of Consulting Psychology, 21,* 95–103. http://dx.doi.org/10.1037/h0045357

Rogers, S. J. (2000). Interventions that facilitate socialization in children with autism. *Journal of Autism and Developmental Disorders, 30,* 399–409.

Rogers, S. J., & Dawson, G. (2010). *Early Start Denver Model for young children with autism.* New York, NY: Guilford Press.

Rogers, S. J., & Vismara, L. A. (2008). Evidence-based comprehensive treatments for early autism. *Journal of Clinical Child & Adolescent Psychology, 37,* 8–38. http://dx.doi.org/10.1080/15374410701817808

Rudolph, K. D., & Lambert, S. F. (2007). Child and adolescent depression. In E. J. Mash & R. A. Barkley (Eds.), *Assessment of childhood disorders* (4th ed., pp. 213–252). New York, NY: Guilford Press.

Rutter, M., Bailey, A., & Lord, C. (2003). *Social Communication Questionnaire (SCQ) manual.* Los Angeles, CA: Western Psychological Services.

Rutter, M., LeCouteur, A., & Lord, C. (2003). *Autism Diagnostic Interview—Revised manual.* Los Angeles, CA: Western Psychological Services.

Salloum, A. (2008). Group therapy for children after homicide and violence: A pilot study. *Research on Social Work Practice, 18,* 198–211. http://dx.doi.org/10.1177/1049731507307808

Salloum, A., & Overstreet, S. (2008). Evaluation of individual and group grief and trauma interventions for children postdisaster. *Journal of Clinical Child & Adolescent Psychology, 37,* 495–507. http://dx.doi.org/10.1080/15374410802148194

Scahill, L., Riddle, M. A., McSwiggin-Hardin, M., Ort, S. I., King, R. A., Goodman, W. K., . . . Leckman, J. F. (1997). Children's Yale-Brown Obsessive–Compulsive Scale: Reliability and validity. *Journal of the American Academy of Child & Adolescent Psychiatry, 36,* 844–852. http://dx.doi.org/10.1097/00004583-199706000-00023

Schopler, E., Van Bourgondien, M. E., Wellman, G. J., & Love, S. R. (2010). *Childhood Autism Rating Scale, Second Edition (CARS–2)*. Los Angeles, CA: Western Psychological Services.

Shaffer, D., Fisher, P., Lucas, C. P., Dulcan, M. K., & Schwab-Stone, M. E. (2000). NIMH Diagnostic Interview Schedule for Children Version IV (NIMH DISC–IV): Description, differences from previous versions, and reliability of some common diagnoses. *Journal of the American Academy of Child & Adolescent Psychiatry, 39,* 28–38. http://dx.doi.org/10.1097/00004583-200001000-00014

Shaffer, D., Scott, M., Wilcox, H., Maslow, C., Hicks, R., Lucas, C. P., . . . Greenwald, S. (2004). The Columbia Suicide Screen: Validity and reliability of a screen for youth suicide and depression. *Journal of the American Academy of Child & Adolescent Psychiatry, 43,* 71–79. http://dx.doi.org/10.1097/00004583-200401000-00016

Shapiro, E. (2013). *Behavioral Observation of Students in Schools*. San Antonio, TX: Pearson.

Sharkey, J. D., & Fenning, P. A. (2012). Rationale for designing school contexts in support of proactive discipline. *Journal of School Violence, 11,* 95–104.

Sheridan, S. M., & Kratochwill, T. R. (2010). *Conjoint behavioral consultation: Promoting family–school connections and interventions* (2nd ed.). New York, NY: Springer.

Shirk, S. R., & Karver, M. (2003). Prediction of treatment outcome from relationship variables in child and adolescent therapy: A meta-analytic review. *Journal of Consulting and Clinical Psychology, 71,* 452–464.

Shirk, S. R., & Karver, M. (2011). Alliance in child and adolescent therapy. In J. C. Norcross (Ed.), *Psychotherapy relationships that work* (2nd ed.). New York, NY: Oxford University Press. http://dx.doi.org/10.1093/acprof:oso/9780199737208.003.0003

Shure, M. B. (2007). *I can problem solve: An interpersonal cognitive problem-solving program*. Champaign, IL: Research Press.

Shure, M. B., & Spivack, G. (1982). Interpersonal problem-solving in young children: A cognitive approach to prevention. *American Journal of Community Psychology, 10,* 341–356. http://dx.doi.org/10.1007/BF00896500

Silverman, W. K., & Albano, A. M. (1996). *Anxiety Disorders Interview Schedule for DSM–IV: Child and Parent Versions*. San Antonio, TX: Psychological Corporation.

Silverman, W. K., & Hinshaw, S. P. (2008). The second special issue on evidence-based psychosocial treatments for children and adolescents: A 10-year update. *Journal of Clinical Child & Adolescent Psychology, 37,* 1–7. http://dx.doi.org/10.1080/15374410701817725

Silverman, W. K., & Ollendick, T. H. (2005). Evidence-based assessment of anxiety and its disorders in children and adolescents. *Journal of Clinical Child & Adolescent Psychology, 34,* 380–411. http://dx.doi.org/10.1207/s15374424jccp3403_2

Silverman, W. K., Ortiz, C. D., Viswesvaran, C., Burns, B. J., Kolko, D. J., Putnam, F. W., & Amaya-Jackson, L. (2008). Evidence-based psychosocial treatments for children and adolescents exposed to traumatic events. *Journal of Clinical Child & Adolescent Psychology, 37*, 156–183. http://dx.doi.org/10.1080/15374410701818293

Silverman, W. K., Pina, A. A., & Viswesvaran, C. (2008). Evidence-based psychosocial treatments for phobic and anxiety disorders in children and adolescents. *Journal of Clinical Child & Adolescent Psychology, 37*, 105–130. http://dx.doi.org/10.1080/15374410701817907

Simon, D. J. (1984). Parent conferences as therapeutic moments. *Personnel and Guidance Journal, 62*, 612–616. http://dx.doi.org/10.1111/j.2164-4918.1984.tb00137.x

Simon, D. J. (2010). Mental health work: An essential role for school psychologists. *School Psychology in Illinois, 31*(4), 15–17.

Simon, D. J. (2011). School-based interventions for children with bipolar disorder. *School Psychology in Illinois, 32*(4), 5–8.

Simon, D. J. (2012). Organizational tools for social emotional learning: Linking self-understanding and problem-solving models. *School Psychology in Illinois, 33*(3), 11–13.

Simon, D. J. (2013). Enhancing school-based groups: Applications of evidence-based treatments. *School Psychology in Illinois, 35*(1), 7–11.

Simonoff, E., Pickles, A., Charman, T., Chandler, S., Loucas, T., & Baird, G. (2008). Psychiatric disorders in children with autism spectrum disorders: Prevalence, comorbidity, and associated factors in a population-derived sample. *Journal of the American Academy of Child & Adolescent Psychiatry, 47*, 921–929. http://dx.doi.org/10.1097/CHI.0b013e318179964f

Smith, B. H., Barkley, R. A., & Shapiro, C. J. (2006). Attention-deficit/hyperactivity disorder. In E. J. Mash & R. A. Barkley (Eds.), *Treatment of childhood disorders* (3rd ed., pp. 65–136). New York, NY: Guilford Press.

Smith, B. H., Barkley, R. A., & Shapiro, C. J. (2007). Attention-deficit/hyperactivity disorder. In E. J. Mash & R. A. Barkley (Eds.), *Assessment of childhood disorders* (4th ed., pp. 53–123). New York, NY: Guilford Press.

Southam-Gerow, M. A., & Chorpita, B. F. (2007). Anxiety in children and adolescents. In E. J. Mash & R. A. Barkley (Eds.), *Assessment of childhood disorders* (4th ed., pp. 347–397). New York, NY: Guilford Press.

Stark, K. D. (1990). *Childhood depression: School-based intervention.* New York, NY: Guilford Press.

Stark, K. D., Schnoebelen, S., Simpson, J., Hargrave, J., Molnar, J., & Glen, R. (2006). *Children's workbook for 'ACTION.'* Ardmore, PA: Workbook.

Stark, K. D., Schnoebelen, S., Simpson, J., Hargrave, J., Molnar, J., & Glen, R. (2007). *Treating depressed youth: Therapist manual for 'ACTION.'* Ardmore, PA: Workbook.

Stark, K. D., Streusand, W., Arora, P., & Patel, P. (2012). Childhood depression: the ACTION treatment program. In P. C. Kendall (Ed.), *Child and adolescent* therapy: Cognitive–behavioral procedures (4th ed., pp. 190–233). New York, NY: Guilford Press.

Stark, K. D., Streusand, W., Krumholz, L. S., & Patel, P. (2010). Cognitive–behavioral therapy for depression: The ACTION Treatment Program for Girls. In J. R. Weisz & A. E. Kazdin (Eds.), *Evidence-based psychotherapies for children and adolescents* (2nd ed., pp. 93–109). New York, NY: Guilford Press.

Stark, K. D., Yancy, M., Simpson, J., & Molnar, J. (2006a). *Parents' workbook for ACTION.* Ardmore, PA: Workbook.

Stark, K. D., Yancy, M., Simpson, J., & Molnar, J. (2006b). *Treating depressed children: Therapist manual for parent component of "ACTION."* Ardmore, PA: Workbook.

Steege, M. W., & Watson, T. S. (2009). *Conducting school-based functional behavioral assessments* (2nd ed.). New York, NY: Guilford Press.

Stoiber, K. C. (2014). A comprehensive framework for multitiered systems of support in school psychology. In A. Thomas & P. Harrison (Eds.), *Best practices in school psychology: Data-based and collaborative decision making* (pp. 41–70). Bethesda, MD: National Association of School Psychologists.

Stricker, G. (2010). *Psychotherapy integration.* Washington, DC: American Psychological Association.

Sugai, G., & Horner, R. H. (2009). Responsiveness-to-intervention and school-wide positive behavior supports: Integration of multitiered approaches. *Exceptionality, 17,* 223–237. http://dx.doi.org/10.1080/09362830903235375

Sugai, G., & Horner, R. H. (2010). School-wide positive behavior support: Establishing a continuum of evidence-based practices. *Journal of Evidence-Based Practices for Schools, 11,* 62–83.

Sugai, G., Horner, R. H., & McIntosh, K. (2008). Best practices in developing a broad-scale system of support for school-wide positive behavior support. In A. Thomas & J. Grimes (Eds.), *Best practices in school psychology V* (pp. 1487–1504). Bethesda, MD: National Association of School Psychologists.

Suhrheinrich, J., Hall, L. J., Reed, S. R., Stahmer, A. C., & Schreibman, L. (2014). Evidence-based intervention in schools. In L. A. Wilkinson (Ed.), *Autism spectrum disorder in children and adolescents: Evidence-based assessment and intervention in schools* (pp. 151–172). Washington, DC: American Psychological Association. http://dx.doi.org/10.1037/14338-008

Suveg, C., & Zeman, J. (2004). Emotion regulation in children with anxiety disorders. *Journal of Clinical Child & Adolescent Psychology, 33,* 750–759. http://dx.doi.org/10.1207/s15374424jccp3304_10

Swanson, J. M., Kraemer, H. C., Hinshaw, S. P., Arnold, L. E., Conners, C. K., Abikoff, H. B., . . . Wu, M. (2001). Clinical relevance of the primary findings of the MTA: Success rates based on severity of ADHD and ODD symptoms at the end of treatment. *Journal of the American Academy of Child & Adolescent Psychiatry, 40,* 168–179. http://dx.doi.org/10.1097/00004583-200102000-00011

Swenson, C. C., Henggeler, S. W., Taylor, I. S., & Addison, O. W. (2009). *Multi-systemic therapy and neighborhood partnerships: Reducing adolescent violence and substance abuse*. New York, NY: Guilford Press.

Taylor, J. L., & Seltzer, M. M. (2011). Employment and post-secondary educational activities for young adults with autism spectrum disorders during the transition to adulthood. *Journal of Autism and Developmental Disorders, 41,* 566–574. http://dx.doi.org/10.1007/s10803-010-1070-3

Tobin, R. M., Schneider, W. J., Reck, S. G., & Landau, S. (2008). Best practices in the assessment of children with attention-deficit/hyperactivity disorder: Linking assessment to response to intervention. In A. Thomas & J. Grimes (Eds.), *Best practices in school psychology V* (pp. 617–632). Bethesda, MD: National Association of School Psychologists.

U.S. Public Health Service. (2010). *Mental health: A report of the surgeon general.* Retrieved from http://www.surgeongeneral.gov/library/mentalhealth/toc.html

Volpe, R. J., & Fabiano, G. A. (2013). *Daily behavior report cards: An evidence-based system of assessment and intervention*. New York, NY: Guilford Press.

Waldron, H. B., & Turner, C. W. (2008). Evidence-based psychosocial treatments for adolescent substance abuse. *Journal of Clinical Child and Adolescent Psychology, 37,* 238–261. http://dx.doi.org/10.1080/15374410701820133

Webster-Stratton, C., Hollinsworth, T., & Kolpacoff, M. (1989). The long-term effectiveness and clinical significance of three cost-effective training programs for families with conduct-problem children. *Journal of Consulting and Clinical Psychology, 57,* 550–553. http://dx.doi.org/10.1037/0022-006X.57.4.550

Webster-Stratton, C., & Reid, M. J. (2010). The Incredible Years parents, teachers, and children training series: A multifaceted approach for young children with conduct disorders. In J. R. Weisz & A. E. Kazdin (Eds.), *Evidence-based psychotherapies for children and adolescents* (2nd ed., pp. 194–210). New York, NY: Guilford Press.

Webster-Stratton, C., Reid, M. J., & Hammond, M. (2004). Treating children with early-onset conduct problems: Intervention outcomes for parent, child, and teacher training. *Journal of Clinical Child & Adolescent Psychology, 33,* 105–124. http://dx.doi.org/10.1207/S15374424JCCP3301_11

Webster-Stratton, C., Rinaldi, J., & Reid, J. M. (2011). Long-term outcomes of Incredible Years Parenting Program: Predictors of adolescent adjustment. *Child and Adolescent Mental Health, 16,* 38–46. http://dx.doi.org/10.1111/j.1475-3588.2010.00576.x

Weisz, J. R., & Kazdin, A. E. (Eds.). (2010). *Evidence-based psychotherapies for children and adolescents* (2nd ed.). New York, NY: Guilford Press.

White, M., & Epston, D. (1990). *Narrative means to therapeutic ends*. New York, NY: Norton.

White, S. W. (2011). *Social skills training for children with Asperger syndrome and high-functioning autism*. New York, NY: Guilford Press.

Wolmer, L., Laor, N., Dedeoglu, C., Siev, J., & Yazgan, Y. (2005). Teacher-mediated intervention after disaster: A controlled 3-year follow-up of children's functioning. *Journal of Child Psychology and Psychiatry, 46*, 1161–1168. http://dx.doi.org/10.1111/j.1469-7610.2005.00416.x

Wood, J. J., Drahota, A., Sze, K., Har, K., Chiu, A., & Langer, D. A. (2009). Cognitive behavioral therapy for anxiety in children with autism spectrum disorders: A randomized, controlled trial. *Journal of Child Psychology and Psychiatry, 50*, 224–234. http://dx.doi.org/10.1111/j.1469-7610.2008.01948.x

Youngstrom, E. A., Jenkins, M. M., Jensen-Doss, A., & Youngstrom, J. K. (2012). Evidence-based assessment strategies for pediatric bipolar disorder. *The Israel Journal of Psychiatry and Related Sciences, 49*, 15–27.

Zalecki, C. A., & Hinshaw, S. P. (2004). Overt and relational aggression in girls with attention-deficit/hyperactivity disorder. *Journal of Clinical Child & Adolescent Psychology, 33*, 125–137. http://dx.doi.org/10.1207/S15374424JCCP3301_12

INDEX

Change-oriented collaborative problem-solving interventions, 20–21
Charades, 246
Child ADHD Multimodal Program, 90, 91
Child and Adolescent Psychiatric Interview, 178
Child- and family-focused CBT, 157–158
Childhood Autism Rating Scale, Second Edition—High Functioning version, 238, 239
Child interviews, 110–111
Children. *See also* Psychological interventions for children and adolescents; *specific groups, e.g.*: Elementary school children
  ADHD symptoms for, 80
  aggression and DBDs in, 118–119
  anxiety management interventions for, 216–218
  confidentiality rights of, 34
  depression in, 178, 180–181
  group work with, 42
  incidence of mental disorders in, 18
  setting therapy goals with, 34
  "teaching the whole child," 19–20
Children's Depression Inventory—2, 178
Child Yale–Brown Obsessive–Compulsive Scale, 202
Chorpita, B. F., 9, 10, 66, 205, 216, 219
Chronic illness perspective, 24–25, 99–100, 162–163
Chu, B. C., 54
Cichetti, D., 38
Clarke, G. N., 187, 188
Classroom environment, social-skills training in, 246–247
Classroom instruction, 64–65
Classroom management, 94–97, 137–139
Classroom observations, 76
Classroom supports and protocols
  for students with ADHD, 94–98
  for students with anxiety and related disorders, 227–229
  for students with autism spectrum disorders, 248–253
  for students with bipolar disorder, 168–170
  for students with depression, 192–193

for students with disruptive behavior disorders, 137–140
for students with OCD, 228–229
for students with PTSD, 229
Clevenger, W. A., 168
Client-centered treatment, 48
Clinical diagnosis of autism spectrum disorder, 235
Clinical mental health services, 21–23
Closeness circle, 189
Closure, in IPT-A, 189–190
Coercive family process, 119–120
Cognitive approach
  to treating depression, 30, 181–182
  to understanding human experience, 48–49
Cognitive assessments, for autism spectrum disorder, 239–240
Cognitive-behavioral-emotional-developmental-familial therapy, 49
Cognitive behavioral systemic model, 31, 39–44
  assumptions with, 40–41
  cultural and diversity competency with, 43–44
  goals of, 43
  in group formats, 42
  psychoeducation in, 41–42
  therapist skills in, 43
Cognitive-behavioral systems, 49
Cognitive behavior therapy (CBT)
  adaptation of adult, 30
  for aggression, 120–121
  in anger management training, 128–132
  for anxiety and related disorders, 216–219, 225
  assumptions with, 40
  for attention-deficit/hyperactivity disorder, 87–90
  for autism spectrum disorder, 242
  child- and family-focused, 157–158
  for depression, 181–187
  for disruptive behavior disorders, 120–121, 128–133
  and functional behavior assessments, 114
  and integrative/multidimensional therapy, 49–50

Consequential thinking skills, 86
Contextual factors
    in antisocial behavior, 119–120
    in SUM model, 59–60
    in systemic treatment, 40
Contingency contracts
    family–school, 20–21
    home–school, 84–87, 96, 142
    for students with ADHD, 84–87, 96
    for students with DBDs, 135, 139–140,
        142
    for students with depression, 192
Contingency management
    for ADHD, 76, 83–87, 91, 100
    for DBDs, 124, 133
    parent training on, 100
    for substance abuse, 136–137
Contingency motivation plans, 250–251
Contingent reinforcement, 213–215,
    218, 231
Continuous effort, for multisystemic
    therapy, 134
Contracts, contingency. *See* Contingency
    contracts
Conversation ball, 246
Coping, cues for, 130
Coping Cat, 9, 42, 216–218
Coping skills training, 52
    in ACTION treatment program,
        185–186
    in cognitive behavioral systemic
        intervention model, 41–42
    in multitiered support systems, 259
    by parents, 101
    for students with ADHD, 87–89,
        96–97, 101
    for students with autism spectrum
        disorder, 247–248
    for students with PTSD, 224
    for students with substance abuse
        problems, 137
Coping strategies
    linking SUM model to, 56–58
    in psychoeducational psychotherapy,
        156–157
    for students with bipolar disorder,
        165–166, 169
Course and Outcome of Bipolar Youth
    study, 151

Covert aggression, 115
CPTs (computer-administered continuous
    performance tests), 78–79
Crisis intervention protocols
    after trauma, 223
    for students with ADHD, 98–99
    for students with anxiety and related
        disorders, 229–231
    for students with autism spectrum
        disorders, 253–254
    for students with depression, 193–196
    for students with disruptive behavior
        disorders, 141–142
    for students with pediatric bipolar
        disorder, 170–174
Crisis intervention services, 261
Cultural competency, 43–44
Cultural factors
    and developmental expectations, 37
    in integrated approach to human
        experience, 50–51
    in interventions with children and
        adolescents, 52
Culture-responsive treatments, 44
Curry, J. F., 187
CU (callous–unemotional) traits,
    121–122
CWDA. *See* Adolescent Coping with
    Depression Course
Cyclothymic disorder, 149

Daily report cards, 85, 142
Daleiden, E. L., 9
Data-based decision making, 22–23, 66
Dawson, G., 247
Dawson, P., 100
DBDs. *See* Disruptive behavior disorders
DBT. *See* Dialectical behavior therapy
DC (Defiant Children) parent skills
    training program, 125–126
DeBar, L. L., 188
Deblinger, E., 226
Debriefing, after crises, 99, 141
Decision making, data-based, 22–23, 66
Dedeoglu, C., 223–224
De-escalation, in crisis interventions,
    141, 171, 194, 254
Defiant Children (DC) parent skills
    training program, 125–126

Physical domain of experience
    and cognitive behavior therapy, 58–59
    and multidimensional interventions, 61
    in SUM model, 54–58
Physical movement, staff-directed, 97
Physical signs of stress, 253
Physiological arousal, 206–207
Physiological symptoms of anxiety, 200, 208–210
Piaget, J., 127
Pivotal response training, 241
PL 94-142 (Public Law 94-142), 26, 265
Planning supports, 249
PMTO (Parent Management Training—Oregon Model), 120, 123–125
Point of performance, interventions at, 83, 87–89
Polo, A. J., 44
Postimpact strategies, in response to trauma, 223
Posttraumatic stress disorder (PTSD)
    classroom supports and protocols for students with, 229
    and community-wide experiences of trauma, 223–224
    crisis intervention protocols for students with, 230
    intervention strategies for students with, 224–226
    and pediatric bipolar disorder, 148–149
    symptoms of, 222–223
Postvention processing, 230
PREPaRE program, 230–231
Preschool-age children
    ADHD symptoms in, 80
    depression in, 179
Preschool Feelings Checklist, 179
Present oriented action planning, in multisystemic therapy, 134
Prioritization, of intervention targets, 252–253
Proactive aggression, 116, 121
Problem behaviors, 58–59, 112
Problem solving
    in anger management training, 131
    and behavior management, 251–252

change-oriented collaborative, 20–21
    in child- and family-focused CBT, 157
    in crisis response to depression, 194
    developmental influences on, 42
    as focus of interventions, 52
    and therapeutic alliance, 33
Problem-solving skills training, 132
    in ACTION treatment program, 186
    in cognitive behavioral systemic intervention model, 41–42
    in multitiered support systems, 259
    with parent management training, 126–127
    in psychoeducational psychotherapy, 156
    for students with ADHD, 87–89, 96–97, 101
    for students with anxiety and related disorders, 215, 218
    for students with depression, 184, 186
    for students with disruptive behavior disorders, 126–127
Progressive muscular relaxation, 211
Progress monitoring, 66, 180, 268
Psychoanalysis, 48
Psychoeducation
    about ADHD, 92–93
    about anxiety and related disorders, 208–209, 217, 232
    about bipolar disorder, 162–163
    about depression, 182, 188–189
    about obsessive–compulsive disorder, 220
    in cognitive behavioral systemic models, 41–42
    in IPT-A, 188–189
    in multitiered support systems, 258–259
Psychoeducational psychotherapy (PEP), 155–157
Psychological education, 19–20
Psychological interventions (in general)
    destigmatization of, 20–21
    evidence-based. See Evidence-based interventions (EBIs)

ABOUT THE AUTHOR

Dennis J. Simon, PhD, is a licensed clinical and school psychologist with over 3 decades of experience within elementary and secondary schools. For 14 years, he was director of NSSEO Timber Ridge Therapeutic Day School, a zero-reject public program serving the Chicago area. His career has centered on program development and psychological interventions for children and adolescents experiencing social, emotional, and behavioral disorders. Currently, he teaches courses at Loyola University of Chicago on therapeutic interventions, clinical supervision, and consultation for systems change. Dr. Simon is the lead author of the developmental/ecological/problem-solving model of clinical supervision that supports training in evidence-based intervention practices.